TROPICAL RAINFOREST

TROPICAL RAINFOREST

A world survey of our most valuable and endangered habitat
with a blueprint for its survival

ARNOLD NEWMAN

Foreword by Mildred E. Mathias
Professor Emeritus of Botany, UCLA

Facts On File
New York • Oxford

I dedicate this book to my wife, Arlene Ruth, my lifetime companion, without whose assistance this work would not have been possible.

Captions to the photographs throughout the prelims are on page 256

Facts On File, Inc.
460 Park Avenue South, New York NY 10016, USA

Facts On File Limited
Collins Street, Oxford OX4 1XJ, United Kingdom

Library of Congress Cataloging-in-Publication Data

Newman, Arnold, 1941–
    Tropical rainforest/Arnold Newman.
       p.   cm.
    Includes bibliographical references and index.
    ISBN 0–8160–1944–4
    1. Rain forest ecology.   2. Rain forests   I. Title.
QH541.5.R27N49 1990
574.5′2642′0913—dc20   90-3484
                                                        CIP

A British CIP catalogue record for this book is available from the British Library.

Facts On File books are available at special discounts when purchased in bulk quantities for businesses, associations, institutions or sales promotions. Please call our Special Sales Department in New York at 212/683-2244 (dial 800/322-8755 except in NY, AK or HI) or in Oxford at 0865/728399.

10 9 8 7 6 5 4 3 2 1

This book is printed on acid-free paper.

AN EDDISON · SADD EDITION
Edited and designed by Eddison Sadd Editions
St Chad's Court
146B King's Cross Road
London WC1X 9DH

Phototypeset by Bookworm Typesetting,
Manchester, England
Origination by Columbia Offset, Singapore
Printing and binding by Mandarin Offset, Hong Kong

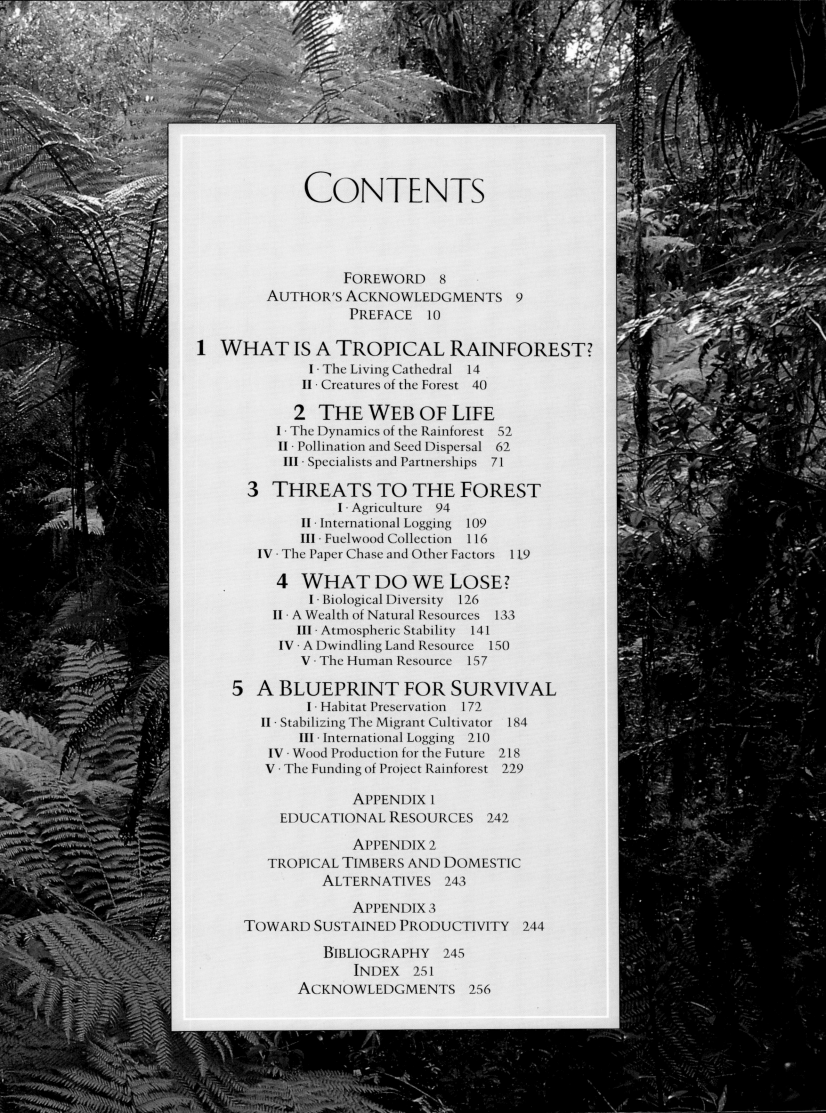

CONTENTS

FOREWORD

David Fairchild once said, "Never to have seen anything but the temperate zone is to have lived on the fringe of the world." Arnold Newman, the author of this volume, has not spent his life on the "fringe" but has had extensive experience in exploration of the tropics on all the continents. He has lived in the rainforest in Central America and traveled far off the tourist track in both tropical Africa and Malaysia. With a series of vignettes based on personal experiences he introduces the reader to some of the excitement of the tropical forests and the great diversity displayed there. His personal observations have led him to join the ever-increasing number of scientists and others to plead for a rational use of the tropics. He views the tropical forest as an integrated "organism" that is vital for the maintenance and functioning of the earth, and emphasizes that man must remember to consider himself as a species, a part of this "organism," in any plan for the future of this "endangered habitat."

MILDRED E. MATHIAS
Professor Emeritus of Botany, UCLA

Author's Acknowledgments

A book of global scope, encompassing many disciplines, evolves only through the assistance of a great many people, equally concerned with the issues addressed here.

Although it is impossible to note them all, my special thanks go to Mildred Mathias, Department of Botany, University of California, Los Angeles, the very matriarch of the tropical forests; the remarkable tropical entomologist Charles Hogue, of the Los Angeles County Museum of Natural History; Andrew Starrett, Department of Botany, University of California, Northridge, and Robert Bailey, Department of Anthropology, University of California, Los Angeles, for their invaluable contributions in editing and expertise; to Joan Larimore, a fine educator, for her undaunting service to the manuscript; and to William Daniels, for meticulous proof reading.

My appreciation goes to my wife, Arlene Ruth, for years of service toward this project's completion, and to our children, Gandhi and Shanti, for their assistance in the field in the tropical forests on many occasions; to the National Geographic Society for their support for me in the African and Asian forests; to the many governments who have facilitated my work and travel in the tropics; to Edward Asner, Roxanne Kremer, and advisors of the International Society for the Preservation of the Tropical Rainforest for their help at home and in the field on many remote expeditions; to Gigi Coyle and James Hickman who, through their belief in this work, while with the Soviet American Exchange, assisted in cementing the environmental cooperation between the two nations; to the countless indigenous and aboriginal people of the tropical forests who unselfishly assisted me, instructed me in their ways and the rhythms of the deep forest, and enabled me to see this awesome spectacle through their eyes.

This book is written in the memory of my mother Johanna Helen and my father Joseph, who raised me to see all nature as a celebration of life.

PREFACE

We are hopeful that in the future the 1990s will be referred to as the decade of scientific and environmental enlightenment; an age characterized by an aware public with the time, inclination, and curiosity to demand a deeper understanding of themselves and their place in the universe. Today, few lands remain unexplored. Yet we still know surprisingly little about the terra incognita of the vast equatorial rainforests, which broodingly retain their secrets.

The exuberant pantheon of the tropical rainforest contains fully four-fifths of earth's terrestrial vegetation. It is the largest terrestrial biomass, and contains, inch for inch, more life than the productive oceanic kelp beds, coral reefs, or African savannas. Given that the tropical forests cover only 6 percent of earth's land surface, yet shelter up to an estimated 30 million species – as much as 90 percent of our planet's total – we shall see how our lives are immensely enriched by this habitat. There is a significant irony in the fact that we can measure the distance from the earth to the moon to within 0.2 inches (0.5 cm) but have identified perhaps less than 6 percent of our species!

Yet even as we are discovering the mystique and lure of this most exotic habitat, the "jungle," as this biome is also known, is dying. Instead of viewing the tropical forest as a sustainable font of products and information, and a source of wonder, the insatiable and escalating demands of the industrialized nations for raw materials, compounded by grossly wasteful agricultural practices in developing tropical countries, are resulting in the cutting of 57 acres (23 ha) of tropical moist forest globally every minute of every day. Outsized machines and armies of chain saws remove 46,500 square miles (120,425 sq km) of forest annually – an area the size of the kingdom of Nepal. It may be easier to comprehend this tragic reality if it is expressed in another way: in tropical forests globally, some 19 million trees are felled daily! Over 40 percent of the tropical forests have disappeared in the five decades since 1940. With the projected increase in the rate of exploitation, and destruction now proceeding at a faster rate than in any other habitat, the tropical rainforest will be virtually extinct soon into the next century! While activities such as slash-and-burn, fuelwood collecting, timber extraction, and cattle raising are not intrinsically wrong, their cumulative effects are proving catastrophic.

The implications of tropical deforestation are so manifold and provocative that the global scientific and environmental community has variously described this as "the sleeper issue of the twentieth century," "the greatest natural calamity since the Ice Age," "the greatest biological disaster ever perpetuated by man," and "a threat to civilization second only to thermonuclear war." At present, an estimated five plant or animal species fall to extinction every day in the tropical forests. With 20/20 hindsight vision, and extrapolating for increased pressure on this tropical resource, we find that within a few years this figure will rise to one species an hour. With on-course escalation, by the turn of the century it is expected that over one million species, the very fabric of life, and the last of the primeval tribes, will disappear forever from the face of the earth. It is during this crucial era that a new-found respect for life and our planet must be cultivated. It will be our actions – or inactions – within this time period that will dictate success or failure. It is speculated that soon beyond that, the future in these diverse issues will have been determined irrevocably.

As we await such well-deserved appreciation for the "Temple of Flora" to germinate and come to bloom, tropical deforestation and the burning of fossil fuels have already contributed to an alarming increase in atmospheric carbon dioxide and carbon monoxide, resulting in a "greenhouse effect" and rising global temperatures. This phenomenon, already an atmospheric reality, may already have been a catalyst to desertification and is a serious concern in many scientific camps. Increasing global warming is speculated to be presently responsible for drought trends and falling agricultural production, as well as a measurable melting of the polar ice caps. Current scenarios forecast a devastating impact on densely populated low-lying coastal areas throughout the world. United Nations Environmental Programme's executive director, Mostafa K. Tolba, has labeled global warming "one of the most serious issues the world is facing." UNEP meteorologist Peter Usher is critically concerned that "virtually no actions are underway to prevent, delay or mitigate the projected (climatic) change."

No issue was ever a more global concern and responsibility, yet it is one seemingly so remote that it has defied political response. As we come to learn that ours is not a disposable planet, and that our resources have quantifiable limits, a new global conservation ethic will be born. It is time, even long overdue, that the vital issues of tropical deforestation be addressed with a sense of urgency.

This book, however, is not a doomsday oracle, but a blueprint of significant hope and opportunity. Viable solutions at our disposal, many evolving out of the cutting edge of recent research and current attention to the dire need to address sustainable development, are coalesced in this volume. A broad public response to the issues and their solutions will insure that the appropriate technologies and mitigating factors are flown into the tropical Third World on the wings of sufficient global budgeting. While many question how we can afford the high ticket price of stabilizing the tropical forest biome while ushering in an age of sustained agriculture and timber extraction, the author asks, "How can we afford not to?" This book is addressed to that outcome by clearly demonstrating that the potentially bleak and unacceptable consequences of our current actions may yet be avoided.

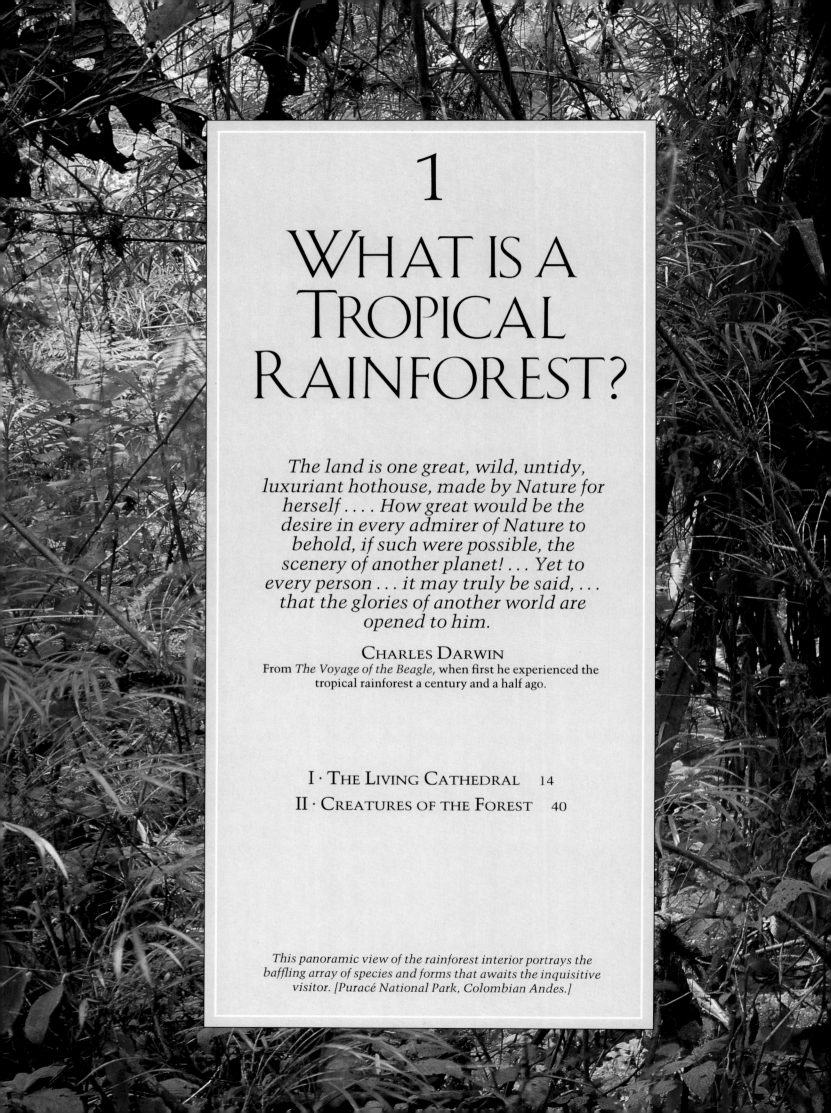

1
WHAT IS A TROPICAL RAINFOREST?

The land is one great, wild, untidy, luxuriant hothouse, made by Nature for herself.... How great would be the desire in every admirer of Nature to behold, if such were possible, the scenery of another planet! ... Yet to every person ... it may truly be said, ... that the glories of another world are opened to him.

CHARLES DARWIN
From *The Voyage of the Beagle,* when first he experienced the tropical rainforest a century and a half ago.

This panoramic view of the rainforest interior portrays the baffling array of species and forms that awaits the inquisitive visitor. [Puracé National Park, Colombian Andes.]

I · THE LIVING CATHEDRAL

The most beautiful thing we can experience is the mysterious . . . the source of all true art and science.

ALBERT EINSTEIN

On 28 October 1492, Christopher Columbus gave the first known written description of a tropical rainforest when he reported to King Ferdinand and Queen Isabella, "Never [have I] beheld so fair a thing; trees beautiful and green, and different from ours, with flowers and fruits each according to their kind; many birds, and little birds which sing very sweetly." When he realized he had not found the Indies, the great navigator decided he must have discovered the Garden of Eden.

We commonly refer to tropical rainforest as "jungle," a name derived from the Sanskrit word *jangala*, which actually means "desert." This confusion has its history, in turn, in colonial India and Persia, where dry, impenetrable scrub brush and low trees were by this time called *djanghael*. British sportsmen of that era found the word jungle easier to pronounce, and more to their liking, and carried it over to include the tall tropical wet forest, which we will see is not a difficult tangle of vegetation at all. But the word jungle, with Rudyard Kipling's help, struck the imagination and stayed with us.

Scientific literature has generally preferred the more accurately defined term tropical rainforest, which derives from the German *tropischer Regenwald*, after A.F.W. Schimper's early classical work *Plant Geography* (1898, 1903). Scientists of the day also used the word *Urwald*, meaning "original" or "primitive" forest, and this was the genesis of the graphic term "primeval rainforest." The heartthrob of the botanical kingdom is also variously referred to as "equatorial rainforest" and "tropical wet broad-leaved evergreen forest."

As you approach the forest from a road cut or riverbank, you face an impenetrable solid mass of towering vegetation. This outside barrier, known as the "wall effect," is approximately 20 feet (6.1 m) thick and is compacted with a tangle of light-hungry vines and climbers. Faced by this intimidating fortification, most people would assume that the interior is just as dense and would require the use of a chain saw to move in any direction. But the edge effect is deceptive. To pierce directly through this armor would require hours of machete work, but the initiated can usually find an animal trail or stream to follow, and thus slip through the "curtain." We may now penetrate the interior of the "terrestrial sea," the very heart of darkness, and explore a realm of natural prehistory.

Enter the interior

Quite suddenly, you find yourself inside a majestic basilica, the height of a seventeen-story building. You are immediately dwarfed (perhaps relegated to proper size) by the sheer immensity of the biomass. Your senses are assailed by the thick, pungent scent of life, and its partner, decay. The aromas of this forest are so vibrant they seem audible – not malodorous but somehow intoxicating.

Your eyes take a few moments to adjust to this world of perpetual twilight. Most everything is a somber shade of green, whose tranquilizing effect lasts for some time even after leaving the forest. Against this background flash such brilliant phenomena as the huge *Morpho* butterfly, flapping its electric-blue wings in a mesmerizing strobe effect, and pendulous scarlet *Heliconia* flower-chains 8 feet (2.4 m) long, ignited in a twilight world by swordlike shafts of light.

The tallest trees tower to a height of perhaps 200 feet (60 m), averaging around 120 feet (37 m), and below these giants are as many as five tiers of straight-trunked trees that refrain from branching until their umbrella heads finally find their own available space in the strata.

The upper layer, often difficult to see from the forest floor, consists of the scattered giant monoliths called emergent trees, that tower over the canopy. In Sarawak, an outstanding specimen of tualang (*Koompassia excelsa*) has been recorded at a height of 276 feet (84 m). It is not uncommon for the expansive umbrella crown of a massive emergent tree to spread over an entire acre (0.4 ha).

The bases of the medium- and larger-size trees very often send out immense flying, snake, or plank buttresses from a height of 20 to 30 feet (6.1–9.1 m) up the trunk. These sinuous, winglike flanges of high-tensile-strength wood help stabilize the top-heavy trees during the frequent gale-force winds and occasional hurricanes and tornadoes that lash the canopy. The characteristics of this extraordinary "tension wood" are not lost on certain indigenous forest

Continued on page 19

▽ *A formidable wall of light-loving photophytic vegetation almost seals the more spacious forest interior from view. This formation, typical of the lowland rainforest edge, fits the common idea of "jungle" and creates the intimidating illusion that the entire forest is of similar density. [Tortuguero, Costa Rica.]*

AFRICAN FOREST STRATA

In the layered world of the forest, individual species find sustenance, safety, in some cases dominance, in their own specialized niches. Plants and animals often occupy specific strata, each with its own climate, while others are generalists, feeding wherever opportunities present themselves.

African gray parrot
Psittacus erithacus

Yellow-casqued hornbill
Ceratogymna elata

Collared sunbird
Anthreptes collaris

African giant swallowtail
Papilio antimachus

Blue fairy flycatcher
Erannornis longicauda

Golden cat
Felis aurata

Golden potto
Arctocebus calabarensis

Four-striped squirrel
Funisciurus lemniscatus

Chimpanzee
Pan troglodytes

Leopard
Panthera pardus

Chequered elephant-shrew
Rhynchocyon cirnei

Giant snail
Achatina sp.

Goliath frog
Rana goliath

Okapi
Okapia johnstoni

African crowned eagle
Stephanoaetus coronatus

The emergents

From its hunting perch, the crowned eagle spots a colobus monkey scratching at a mite. Soundlessly the hunter launches into high soaring flight, then into a power dive. The monkey sees a moving shadow, barks a warning call, and leaps outward, parachuting down to an adjoining tree.

Western black-and-white colobus monkey
Colobus polykomos

The canopy layer

With abundant light, rain, and warmth, the canopy is teeming with life. Alarm sounders like the hornbill alert others to the presence of the leopard, who sees the entire forest as his domain. Yet even he may be deterred by the mandrill's formidable fangs. Boughs laden with orchids carry far-ranging networks of cleared paths.

Mandrill
Papio sphinx

The mid strata

Understory residents are often very mobile. Chimpanzees forage in the canopy; gorillas in lower levels, spending much time on the ground with little to fear but human hunters. Few creatures will provoke the highly venomous mamba, the world's fastest snake, capable of moving at up to 7 mph (over 11 kmph).

Mantid
Mantidae

Jameson's mamba
Dendroaspis jamesoni

The forest floor

The verdant green twilight world beneath the trees has a character all its own, with termite castles lending an air of fantasy to the scene. Here, okapis and antelopes, both full-sized and dwarf, take the place of the varied rodents that are common in the rainforests of Central and South America.

Common chameleon
Chamaeleo dilepis

Congo peafowl
Afropavo congensis

peoples who press their bodies against a buttress wing then hit it with their fists or with a wooden club. The resulting percussions resonate through the body. On my Cathedral Rain Forest Science Preserve in Costa Rica there is one *arbole de ajo* (*Caryocar costaricense*) whose enormous base requires five minutes to walk around without climbing or stepping over the buttresses or surface features. No matter how many times I come across these monolithic wonders I am always taken aback. Face-to-face with a wall of magnificently sculpted wood, I invariably have the impression that these behemoth buttresses are extraterrestrial exotics.

The heads of the trees are bound together by woody vines known as lianas, some approaching 800 feet (244 m) long, and this further serves to stabilize them in the high winds that sweep over the crowns. (Some species of vine coil to the left in the Northern Hemisphere and to the right in the Southern, to make best use of the sun's rays.)

Below the canopy, visibility is usually good for 50 feet (15 m), and often much more. Due to the dim light, which averages less than 1 percent of that falling on the canopy above, vegetation is relatively sparse at ground level. Conceivably, you could ride a bicycle through the forest, although this is not a recommended mode of travel. In the interior of the rainforest, a machete is unnecessary for movement — but very useful for marking your trail. This is highly recommended as the forest interior is so bewitching that it can easily disorient even the most experienced forest explorer.

The land of the giant life-forms

The forest interior is a magical and mercurial place — an enchanted realm where anything is possible. Wandering an unknown planet full of strange life-forms could not be more stimulating; indeed such an image is an apt metaphor for the tropical rainforest experience. Everything appears to grow out of proportion. Families and other taxa that in other habitats are small, grow here as if they were outsized mutants. Woodiness, a predominant feature of the vegetation, allows for part, but not all, of this gigantism. The parade of species reads like a catalog of the inconceivable. Grass in the form of bamboo grows 100 feet (30 m) high, at the rate of 36 inches (91 cm) in twenty-four hours. That's 0.00002 mph (0.00003 kmph)! There are "roses" with 145-foot (44-m) trunks; daisies and violets as big as apple trees; 60-foot (18-m) tree ferns with some of the hardest wood to be found; 37.5-foot (11.4-m) constricting snakes, and lily pads over 5 feet (1.5 m) in diameter which can support a child's weight. The parasite *Rafflesia* boasts the world's largest flower — 38 inches (97 cm) across, weighing 38 pounds (17.2 kg), and holding several gallons of liquid in its nectaries. Here too are basilisk lizards that actually run on the surface of water; bats with 5.5-foot (1.7-m) wingspans; vining rattan palms with 785-foot (240-m) trunks; 18-foot (5.5-m) cobras; moths with 12-inch (30-cm) wingspans; frogs so big they eat rats, and rodents themselves weighing over 100 pounds (45 kg).

The rainforest is our planet's most astounding expression of life, the very womb of creation. Here, a single hectare (2.47 acres) may contain 42,000 different species of insect, up to 750 types of tree, and 1,500 species of higher plant. Try to imagine, if you can, that a typical square yard (0.8 sq m) of tropical forest can contain 800 individual ants of 50 different species. The forest's climate is the key to all this.

Continued on page 22

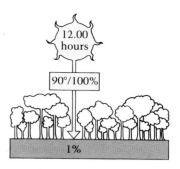
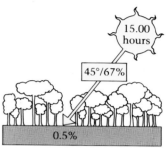
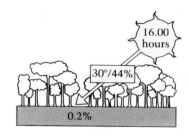

△ The multi-tiered closed canopy absorbs light with astonishing effectiveness. Using noon as a 100% value for light intensity above the canopy, by 4 P.M. on a cloudless day only 0.2% of the light will reach the forest floor. The light of a full moon is not even perceived here. Stepping from the interior into full sunlight can be a dazzling experience.

◁ A tranquil, clear-running stream meanders through a palmy Costa Rican lowland rainforest, indicating the presence of a healthy, intact, forested watershed.

◁ *Like the carnivores after which they are named, wolf spiders like this 4-in (10-cm) leg-span species from Costa Rica run down their prey instead of spinning a web – so keen eyesight is an essential asset. Their nemesis, the hunting wasp, will pursue a spider, then paralyze it, and lay its eggs on the helpless animal leaving them to hatch into larvae which will eat the spider alive.*

◁ *Shanti handles a massive rococo toad (*Bufo paracnemis*), protected from predators by toxins secreted by glands at the base of its head, and by its ability to inflate its body by gulping air. [Argentina.]*

◁▽ *Gandhi has no fear of this mass of frangipani sphinx moth caterpillars (*Pseudosphinx tetrio*) but their colors and platoon behavior signal danger to potential predators. [Petén Forest, Guatemala.]*

▽ *Typifying gigantism, and dwarfing Shanti, the Amazon Basin's royal water lily (*Victoria amazonica*) spreads 7-ft (2-m) leaves on air-filled ribs that produce enough buoyancy to support a child's weight. Red spiny edges deter most herbivores. These quiet "Igarapés," oxbow lakes on the Amazon, are a favored habitat of piranhas (*Serrasalmus* spp.) whose predatory habits may provide a further measure of protection to this elegant African species.*

▷ *The dramatic buttresses of rainforest trees serve as supports – stabilizing the tall, shallow-rooted trees when tropical gales lash the canopy. [Osa Peninsula, Costa Rica.]*

▽ *Author and son examine a thick woody vine rising from the forest floor on Peucang Is, Udjung Kulon National Park, Indonesia.*

Defining a tropical rainforest

It may seem difficult to assign specific parameters to so unrestrained a habitat as tropical rainforest, especially since one forest type often merges gradually into another. Yet such a definition has evolved out of botanical consensus. Schimper's definition, largely unchallenged to this day, states that the lowland rainforest formation is "evergreen, hygrophilous in character [flourishing in perhumid dampness], at least 98 feet (30 m) high, but usually much taller, rich in thick-stemmed lianes [vines] and in woody as well as herbaceous epiphytes." (I would add to this the dominant characteristic of tree buttressing, which we will examine later.)

Lowland tropical rainforest is further characterized by its precipitation. Here, rainfall will never be less than 80 inches (203 cm) and may even exceed 300 inches (762 cm). Totals of 24 to 27 *feet* (732 to 823 cm) have been recorded in the Choco of Colombia. The worldwide annual average for tropical rainforests is roughly 92 inches (234 cm). These forests are incredibly wet, but

△▷ *The strangler fig (*Ficus sp.*) is a huge predatory hemiepiphyte which often begins life when a seed is deposited in a bird's droppings on the branch of a host tree. Germinating there, it drops numerous air roots until they make contact with the ground. Access to an abundant supply of water and nutrients then enables the fig to grow into a full-sized tree, which eventually consumes its host and sometimes neighboring trees as well. [Yala National Park, Sri Lanka.]*

just as important, their rainfall is relatively constant throughout the year. So another criterion for a tropical rainforest is that it must receive at least 4 inches (10 cm) of rain each drought month for two out of three years.

Tropical rainforest requires a mean annual temperature of at least 75°F (24°C) and must be essentially frost free. Conditions are so constant inside the forest that it has been compared to a laboratory culture-growth room.

Where are the tropical forests?

In historical times, tropical forests, including moist evergreen and seasonal forests, clothed some 9,460,000 square miles (24,500,000 sq km) of the humid equatorial belt lying between the Tropic of Cancer and the Tropic of Capricorn (23.5 degrees north and south of the equator). Since 1900 the forests have been reduced by one-half, and the destruction has accelerated greatly since World War II, reducing the forests by 59 percent. Today, approximately 3,865,000 square miles (10 million sq km) remain, and tropical forest still covers somewhat more than 6 percent of the earth's land, in three major areas of the Americas, Africa, and Asia.

The largest of these areas is the American or neotropical forest. It begins in eastern Mexico and forms a broken mosaic running through northern Central America and then down the flank of eastern Central America. Portions remain along the Pacific side of Central America, notably in the Osa Peninsula in southern Costa Rica, and in the Darien region of Panama. The southern Central American forests continue into western coastal South America through Colombia (the Choco) and into Ecuador. Several tropical rainforests survive in the Caribbean, the largest in Puerto Rico and Trinidad and what remains of the Cuban forest.

On the eastern side of the northern Andes begins the earth's largest tropical forest mass, the Amazon Hylaea. (Hylaea, an antiquated Greek term meaning forest, was used by early explorer Alexander von Humboldt, and now refers specifically to this great, expansive forest.) Amazonia is bordered by the geological formation called the pre-Cambrian Shield, consisting of the Guiana Shield to the north and the Brazilian Shield to the south. In this botanical "heartland" of our planet, a man could descend the Andes foothills, enter the Amazon forest, and walk for 2,000 miles (3,218 km) before again seeing the sun directly as he reaches the Atlantic. This is a still largely unexplored wilderness, through which runs the most voluminous river in the world, for which the forest was named. Its arteries drain large parts of the combined forests of the six nations with significant territories in the basin – Bolivia, Brazil (with over half of Amazonia), Colombia, Ecuador, Peru, and Venezuela – as well as the adjacent territories of Guyana, Surinam, and French Guiana. To the north, the Orinoco River Basin drains great expanses through Colombia, French Guiana, Guyana, Surinam, and Venezuela. In some areas, these forests are quite abruptly and intermittently broken by expansive parklike savannas, known locally as llanos. Lastly, a belt of tropical forest survives precariously along much of Brazil's east coast. Altogether 1,369 million acres (554 million ha) remain of these American tropical forests.

The second most extensive block is that comprising the rapidly disappearing Indo-Malayan Pacific forests, a mass of dissected areas extending through the Malay Archipelago, from Sumatra in the west to New Guinea in the east, and into mainland Asia in the north to include the forests of Thailand, Burma,

Continued on page 26

DEFINING A TROPICAL RAINFOREST

The luxuriant and species-rich lowland equatorial rainforests are a product of
unvarying warmth and moisture. Here, foliage is lush and often leathery,
lianas and other typically herbaceous plants are commonly woody, and
epiphytes abound in a truly magnificent "temple of flora."

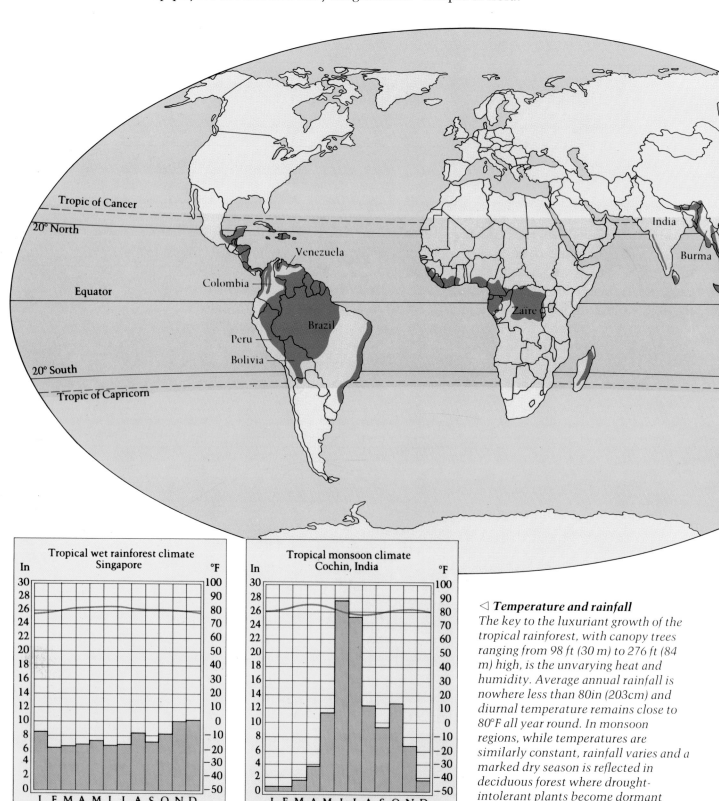

**Tropical wet rainforest climate
Singapore**

**Tropical monsoon climate
Cochin, India**

◁ **Temperature and rainfall**
*The key to the luxuriant growth of the
tropical rainforest, with canopy trees
ranging from 98 ft (30 m) to 276 ft (84
m) high, is the unvarying heat and
humidity. Average annual rainfall is
nowhere less than 80in (203cm) and
diurnal temperature remains close to
80°F all year round. In monsoon
regions, while temperatures are
similarly constant, rainfall varies and a
marked dry season is reflected in
deciduous forest where drought-
intolerant plants become dormant
until the rainy season begins.*

Country	National area		Undisturbed forest		Total forest area		% world
	Sq mi	Sq km	Sq mi	Sq km	Sq mi	Sq km	total
Brazil	3,286,727	8,511,965	1,114,488	2,886,300	1,375,705	3,562,800	30.68
Indonesia	735,057	1,903,650	150,263	389,150	438,547	1,135,750	9.78
Zaïre	905,633	2,345,409	307,900	797,400	407,947	1,056,500	9.09
Peru	496,260	1,285,215	144,104	373,200	267,627	693,100	5.97
Colombia	439,769	1,138,914	149,046	386,000	179,164	464,000	3.99
India	1,222,808	3,166,828	18,862	48,850	177,790	460,440	3.96
Bolivia	424,195	1,098,580	68,577	177,600	169,936	440,100	3.79
Papua New Guinea	183,528	475,300	53,344	138,150	130,164	337,100	2.90
Venezuela	352,170	912,050	29,346	76,000	123,060	318,700	2.74
Burma	261,808	678,030	54,471	141,070	120,446	311,930	2.68
Total for the ten principal regions			2,090,401	5,413,720	3,390,386	8,780,420	75.62
Minor regions in 63 other countries			490,551	1,270,430	1,092,490	2,829,330	24.39
World total			2,580,952	6,684,150	4,482,876	11,609,750	**100.00**

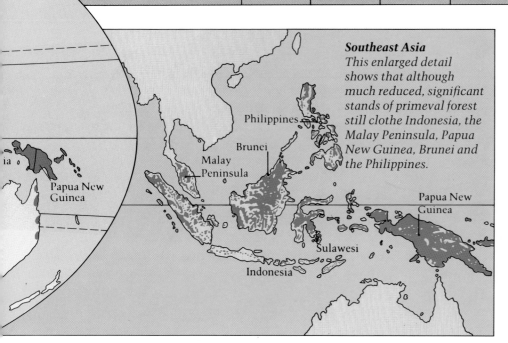

Southeast Asia
This enlarged detail shows that although much reduced, significant stands of primeval forest still clothe Indonesia, the Malay Peninsula, Papua New Guinea, Brunei and the Philippines.

◁△ **The principal tropical rainforest regions of the world**
But for the very specific climatic conditions required for its growth, and the effects of deforestation by man, a dense band of tropical forest would completely encircle the earth's equatorial zone. Primeval forests now clothe some 7% of the land surface – over 3.86 million square miles (10 million sq km), of which the largest blocks are the 2.3 million-sq-mi (6 million-sq-km) Amazonian hylaea, the Ituri Forest in Zaïre, and the now-rapidly disappearing forests of the Malay archipelago. The chart above shows the ten countries within whose borders lie three-quarters of the world's remaining tropical forests.

▷ **Global annual rainfall**
The average yearly precipitation for the whole globe is an estimated 39in (100cm). Over land, where continental air masses tend to be less humid, the average is about 26 in (66 cm), while over the oceans it is 44 in (112 cm). However, such averages conceal huge variations. While many parts of the world receive less than 5in (13 cm) of precipitation a year, there are some that receive over 400 in (1,016 cm). The record is held by Cherrapunji in India, with 1,042 in (2,647 cm).

Mean annual rainfall

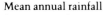

0	1	3.9	7.8	15.7	29.5	59	196.8 In

0	25	100	200	400	750	1500	5000 Mm

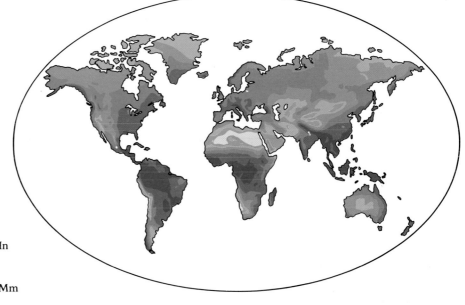

Laos, Assam, Bhutan, and Nepal. Included here are western peninsular India, Sri Lanka, eastern Vietnam, Kampuchea (Cambodia), western Thailand, southern China, Hainan, Java, Borneo, other Indonesian Islands, the Philippines, New Hebrides, New Caledonia, Solomon Islands, Fiji and Samoa, and subtropical outliers south into Queensland and northern New South Wales in Australia. All told, these Asian forests total 610 million acres (247 million ha).

In Africa, we have the least extensive of the world's tropical moist forests. The largest block clothes the Zaïre (Congo) River Basin: it includes the Ituri Forest, and next to the Amazon is the world's largest contiguous tropical moist forest. Large forest areas also exist in Gabon, the Republic of the Congo, and the Central African Republic. Other tropical forests still remain in broken patterns in coastal West Africa from Angola (Cabinda Province) north to Guinea. The cloud forests of the Virunga volcano range bordering Zaïre, Rwanda, and Uganda remain highly threatened. Limited areas of cloud forest and moist forest are also found in Tanzania and Kenya. Altogether the extant tropical moist forests in Africa total 464 million acres (188 million ha).

Outside these three large geographical areas, tropical moist forests can also be found on the islands of Mauritius, Reunion, Rodriguez, and the Seychelles in the Indian Ocean, and in the eastern portion of the Malagasy Republic (Madagascar), though here the forests are rapidly being depleted.

Due to unique protective climatic conditions, formations referred to as subtropical rainforests extend narrowly south of the Tropic of Capricorn in eastern Australia, the borders of Argentina, Brazil, and Paraguay, southeastern coastal Brazil, and southeastern Madagascar. From the Tropic of Cancer, they extend marginally north into China, Burma, and Taiwan.

The womb of the earth

These prolific wombs of life hold the largest biomass of any terrestrial habitat. By far earth's richest environment, they have remained basically unchanged since prehistoric times. We can move through them with awe and know what it was like to walk the earth's lush wilderness of 70 million years ago. They have served as the planet's major gene pool, constantly evolving new microorganisms, insects, fish, birds, and mammals to fill gaps in an ever-changing world. It was here, only 120 million years ago during the early Cretaceous period, that the flowering plants evolved and spread over the surface of our planet. One of earth's most ancient ecosystems, the tropical rainforest has been our Garden of Eden – a veritable cornucopia of life. Far from stagnant in its creativity, one aspect of the forest's history has been constant, and that is its capacity for change.

The forest mass contracts and expands in response to glaciation, tectonic plate movements, and other long-term dynamic phenomena that we are only now beginning to understand. New species have evolved in response to changing conditions, phasing out less adaptive life-forms. Yet the tropical rainforests around the world conform so closely in their structure, and in their parallel evolution of species, that if a lay person were blindfolded and parachuted into one of the tropical rainforests of the world he would find it very difficult to determine on which continent he had landed. Even serious nature students might take time ferreting out clues to their location. General similarities include giant smooth-barked buttressed trees with similar laurel-like leaves, complete with drip-tips; a profusion of palms, spiny and unarmed, with climbing, vining species on several continents, such as *Rattan*

150 million years ago

105 million years ago

35 million years ago

△ *Plate tectonics, the movement of huge "rafts" of the earth's crust by convection currents in the molten rock below, led to the break up of the vast ancient supercontinent of Pangaea; the process is still at work today.*

in the Old World and *Desmoncus* in the New. *Philodendron* exists in tropical America and the perplexingly similar, though unrelated, *Epipremnum* in eastern hemisphere tropical forests. In the New World, boas (Boidae) rule; in the Old World, it is the pythons (Pythonidae). Jaguars (*Onca panthera*) are king in the New World forests; while leopards (*Pardus panthera*) rule in the Old World. Tapirs occur in both hemispheres, and vipers of different species are distributed throughout. These convergences and coevolutionary adaptations penetrate so deeply into the biological fabric that although rattlesnakes occur only in the Americas, in both Old and New worlds other snakes – both harmless and venomous – rapidly vibrate their tails in dry leaves to produce exactly the same alarming sound: similar spaces filled by similar yet unrelated fauna and flora – a recurring theme in the natural world.

Ultimately, the botanist could determine his location, at least to the proper continent. He might recognize bromeliads as basically neotropical, with the unsettling exception of one West African species (*Pitcairnia feliciana*), or staghorn ferns as Old World, despite a similar problem with an inexplicable Peruvian species (*Platycerium andinum*). The zoologist might know the gavial (*Gavialis gangeticus*) as an Indian crocodilian, provided he could distinguish it from its look-alike, the false gavial (*Tomistoma schlegeli*) of Borneo. He might also know the hornbills (Bucerotidae) of Asia and Africa from the toucans (Ramphastidae) of South and Central America.

Although many regions, now separated, were once connected and thus exposed to exchanges of species, it is a matter of great fascination to science that similar niches on different continents have been filled by species quite unrelated yet with much in common. On the other hand, scientists explore and study the tropical rainforest with such zeal precisely because of the staggering differentiation that exists in this laboratory of infinite creativity.

The unique climate of the tropical forests

When people in the humid tropics refer to summer and winter, they talk of the dry and rainy seasons. Summer and winter are marked not so much by temperature, which is only somewhat cooler in the rainy season due to cloud cover, but by the amount of rain. Average temperature for the dry season is 82.2°F (27.9°C) and for the wet season 78.5°F (25.8°C) in the Amazon Basin.

It is clear that temperatures in temperate zone forests and other habitats may soar much higher and, of course, drop much lower than in rainforest areas. Under the forest canopy you are generally comfortable unless performing physical labors, at which time you may become oppressed by the humidity. Summers in New York and Florida, by contrast, are far hotter – and for the most part more uncomfortable.

As time periods are rarely punctuated by extended droughts, a neophyte visiting a tropical rainforest during the height of the dry season might swear he had experienced the rainy season. The dry season is not truly dry but sees rain intermittently, with dry spells perhaps lasting only two or three weeks. Torrential rain is to the rainforest what unmitigated scorching sun is to the desert: enjoyed or just accepted; a fact of life. The rain is the major factor responsible for the unsurpassed biomass, and it takes approximately 40 gallons (152 l) of water to produce each pound of leaves.

Some areas of the tropics are remarkable for the amounts of water cycled. In a record year, between 1 August 1860 and 31 July 1861, Cherrapunji, in what was then called Meghalaya, in India, reached an all-time high of 1,042 inches

Present

△ *We now have proof that continents that today are widely separated were joined in the geological past. Remains of the freshwater aquatic reptile* Mesosaurus brasiliensis *have been found in identical 250-million-year-old rocks (●) where southeast Brazil joined southwest Africa in the Pennsylvanian Period.*

(2,647 cm) or over 86 feet! Perhaps not surprisingly, some parts of India are busy in the rainy season with Arab tourists, who come from their desert homelands where years frequently pass without an inch of rain, to see the grand spectacle of the monsoon.

In Cherri we have an example of one forest type – seasonal deciduous forest, also known as monsoon forest. In such areas, although voluminous rain falls during the monsoon, the year is punctuated clearly with a dry season which may last for four months or more, during which time rain is infrequent and light. During the drought, many monsoon forest trees drop their leaves so as to conserve water by preventing transpiration. Delicate leaves such as those of ferns and some orchids desiccate and wait for the rains to arrive. The canopy here is more open, and trees do not attain the height of forests in areas of more constant rainfall. Adding further to drying conditions in many seasonal forests are hard-driving wilting winds, such as the harmathan, blowing off the Sahara in Africa, which affects forests as far away as Asia.

In the tropical rainforest proper, almost every afternoon during the rainy season there are torrential downpours lasting several hours, after which the sun usually shines, although it is not uncommon for rain to continue for several days and nights without stopping. These rains are an experience on their own, with all the leaves dripping and gleaming. It is true you must "see the jungle when it's wet with rain."

In these forests, humidity is permanently high, oscilating between 88 percent in the rainy season and 77 percent in the dry season (Amazon Basin figures). Unlike the deciduous forests, the tropical rainforest never "dies back," even during its short droughts. To remain evergreen and support feathery vegetation like delicate ferns which would otherwise become desiccated, the tropical rainforest functions like a thermostatically controlled

▽ *Sierra palms (*Prestoea montana*) and heliconias (*Heliconia caribaea*) delight the eye on El Yunque Mountain in the Caribbean National Forest in Puerto Rico – one of the very few tropical rainforests on United States territory.*

greenhouse. Summer or winter, wind seldom pierces this dense mass of vegetation. It is rare for a breeze to be felt on the ground, even, remarkably, as a tropical gale rages overhead. On the floor of the forest, far beneath the canopy, you are insulated from the occurrences of the outside world. Even during cataclysmic rain squalls you are not aware that it is raining until five minutes after the rain commences because of the adequacy of your living roof. These are truly "green mansions." The main canopy under the giant emergent trees appears to roll on forever – the lush green carpet of the "closed forest."

△ *Fully 80% of the forest's food is produced in the canopy – home to two-thirds of the biome's animals and plants. While tropical forests represent no more than one-third of the earth's total forest area, they contain four-fifths of its terrestrial vegetation. Teeming with life, it is here that the majority of new species will be discovered. [Chiapas, Mexico.]*

The rainforest canopy

The hub of life is a three-dimensional jigsaw puzzle, with every plant from the smallest fungus to the giant emergent trees and everything in between filling its own selected (and hard won) niche to perfection. An apt description might be "order out of chaos."

With innovative climbing equipment, pioneering canopy-exploring biologist Donald Perry discovered that wind in the rainforest roof generates a sawing action, pitting large limbs of neighboring trees against each other in a macabre "battle of the trees." Usually the softer wood is worn through first and the contest ends, sending Goliath limbs, together with their burden of clinging epiphytes and lianas, crashing to the ground. Such falls can be heard sporadically throughout the day and night – an eerie and unnerving sound.

The sunlight-bathed canopy is rich in flowering trees, vines, orchids, bromeliads, and other photophytic plants. During the blooming season it is

△ *When many individuals of a canopy tree such as the flaming coral (*Erythrina *sp.) bloom simultaneously in "big bang" fashion, the visual effect is stunning. This habitat, perhaps above all others, has been at the focal point of the evolution of life on earth. [Brazilian Amazon.]*

abuzz with bees, flies, bats, hummingbirds, and countless other pollinators. It is likened to an elevated flower field, and some of the insect residents never go to ground. To our surprise Perry has found some typical ground-dwellers up in the great height of the living roof. They include mice, centipedes, scorpions, cockroaches, and even earthworms burrowing in the build-up of humus in the forks of tree trunks.

Canopy trees are crowned by the jewels of the plant world, the epiphytes. Unlike parasites, which extract sustenance from the plants to which they attach themselves, epiphytes use trees, vines, other plants, and even rocks solely for support, and do not take nourishment from their hosts. Included in this uniquely adapted group of plants are orchids, ferns, bromeliads, and, surprisingly, even cacti among many other less familiar families. When you look up and see a cactus cascading from a tree, with a rainbow-colored flower the size of a man's head, you know you're in a very special place. There are epiphytes in 33 different families of flowering plants in the neotropical forests alone. A single tree has been found to contain 300 orchids and over 2,000 epiphytic plants.

The combined weight of the epiphytic mass is often equal to one-third of the total weight of the tree, and contains approximately 45 percent of the nutrient total of the canopy. Limbs become so overburdened with the weight of epiphytes that they often break and come crashing down. As a result many tropical moist forest trees have evolved smooth bark, or even shed their bark, to discourage overcolonization by epiphytes. Some rough-barked trees, however, contain toxins that may discourage epiphytes, which also harbor insects. Typical of these is the garlic tree, known in Costa Rica as arbole de ajo (*Caryocar costaricense*), whose cut bark precisely mimics the aroma of garlic.

In this competitive world, there are even epiphytes that grow on epiphytes, and on the leaves of other plants. Known as epiphylls, these include the mosses, algae, liverworts, and lichens. These primitive plants will also flourish on rocks and on any other surface they can pirate, including animals. Many a crocodile and mossy-backed turtle is adorned by these growths, which symbiotically offer the protection of camouflage. Algae even grow in grooves in the hair of the sloth, whose pelt is also inhabited by a moth whose larva feeds on the sloth's dung. These relationships can go on open-endedly. Lichen itself is a mutualistic relationship between an alga and a fungus. The alga produces sugar through photosynthesis, and the fungus provides nutrients captured from the environment. Together they form a more effective front from which to ply the available resources.

Plants may be categorized by the method they use to take up nutrients. Carnivorous plants trap and consume small animals; saprophytic plants such as most fungi digest decaying organic matter; parasitic plants tap nutrients directly from living plants, while autotrophytes are the plants we are most familiar with. They take nutrients directly from the soil and manufacture food from carbon dioxide and water using the energy of sunlight to drive the process. Epiphytes, growing far out of reach of the soil, trap falling litter and nutrients in rainwater for nourishment.

In this prolific laboratory we call the tropical rainforest, there has developed yet another, recently discovered, category, an auto-epiphyte ... a plant that is epiphytic upon itself! A few varieties of trees rooted in the ground have rosettes of litter-trapping leaves which collect debris. Into this debris grow roots to absorb the nutrients. Such profound thrift and efficiency typifies the biological processes of the tropical forest.

△ Nature's opportunism at its best. A seed from an upper-canopy tree, probably deposited in the droppings of a passing animal, has taken root and grown into a natural bonsai version of its species, perched on the broken bough of its host.

Microhabitats and aerial highways

In their search for light, the epiphytes have left the ground, but in the bargain they have also had to leave the soil behind. How some of these have adapted to their divorce from the earth is interesting. Ants make their home in the supporting root masses of some epiphytes, and in their constant foraging they bring back much leaf debris, fruit, and other vegetable and animal matter that is shared by the "air plants."

Found almost exclusively in the New World forests, many bromeliads have a water reservoir formed by closely fitting and overlapping leaf rosettes. Great amounts of nourishing leaf debris, as well as water, collect here, sustaining the plant during drought periods. Virtual arboreal marshes, these tanks – which may hold as much as 30 gallons (114 l) of water in the case of *Glomeropitcairnia* sp. – are the home of many and varied creatures, some of which never come to the ground. Microorganisms and insects feed on the algae that grow in the water. Tree frogs, tree snakes, and lizards make these bromeliads their permanent homes or temporary camps. There is even a crab that lives only in the tanks of bromeliads. Birds and monkeys that rarely visit the ground, drink from these benevolent fountains.

Other bromeliads of the genus *Tillandsia* are even more truly "air plants," in that many do not have a tank structure for food and water collection but instead their leaves contain hairlike scales known as trichome cells. These absorb airborne dust, nutrients, and humidity from the air and enable the plant to withstand long periods of drought. A species of *Tillandsia* familiar to many people is Spanish moss (*Tillandsia usneoides*). Not a moss at all, this

epiphyte has a wider range than any other plant in the world. Its fronds are seen gracefully cascading from tree branches and telephone lines, where seeds have been deposited in birds' droppings, all the way from Virginia to Argentina. Birds also propagate it when they use live cuttings to construct their nests.

Monkeys also benefit trees by ripping off epiphytes in their search for grubs and other edible insects or animals. The upper canopy, which contains most of the forest's wildlife, is laden with epiphytes but a clean network of paths exists along the center of certain main limbs and branches. This is a treetop game trail kept clear by constant use. It has been speculated that before the recent cutting of the Transamazon Highway, a monkey could have traveled all the way from Colombia to Argentina without ever touching the ground, crossing even the Amazon River in the trees of floating islands that have broken away from the river's banks.

Under the closed canopy

In the understory below, where you stand, is the grandest spectacle yet. Because of the constants of moisture and warmth at this level, the soft, delicate, and graceful plants make this their home. In most such forests, palms set the mood, and no single plant more typifies the experience. Their diversity is staggering, with over 1,147 species in 81 genera for the New World alone. The arching grace these treelets lend to the floral mosaic might be a definition of splendor; but be warned, their trunks are often viciously armed with whorls of stiletto-shaped spines – often coated with a defensive toxin. (Should one slip on the wet clay forest soil, these barbs invariably offer the nearest handhold.) Here also are many of the shade-tolerant species we have adopted as houseplants; they include ferns and aeroids, such as the philodendrons which climb up tree trunks in a spiral, dropping a cascade of air roots to the ground. You will recognize fleshy friends such as dieffenbachia or dumb cane; intricately veined and red-hued anthuriums with their familiar jack-in-the-pulpit spike and shield; sensuous dracaenas bending into vacant arenas, and many more.

Huge flowering lianas, some thicker than a man's torso, weave along the ground and loop and spiral into the air to knit together the canopy above. Some vines, (*Bauhinia* spp.) called monkey ladders, have see-through windows and zigzag forms resembling staircases; others are perfectly square in cross-section. Gorgeous flowers fall from these vines and trees, often carpeting large areas of the forest floor. Cycads, cone-bearers that resemble the palms and are one of earth's more archaic plants, here before the dinosaurs, are still competing successfully for the limited light. A plethora of diverse species, so many still undescribed, and all forming a superbly artful conglomerate, await introduction into biomedicine, agriculture, industry, and horticulture.

Life in the understory, however, has its hazards. Research indicates that on average, one tree with a diameter greater than 8 inches (20 cm) falls per acre (0.4 ha) per year, a common and mortal danger to seedlings, saplings, and pole trees, which may be flattened to the ground by such objects. Implausibly, it has been recently discovered that when knocked down, a species of palm, *Socratea exorrhiza*, actually forms new stilt roots, picks itself up on stilt legs over a period of time, and "walks out" from under fallen trees, limbs, and other obstructions and back into light and space.

Continued on page 36

◁ △ *Lianas are typified by the woody structure of their stems. Some, like these "monkey ladders"* (Bauhinia spp.) *in Costa Rica, are pierced with natural footholds, and grow to venerable stature.*

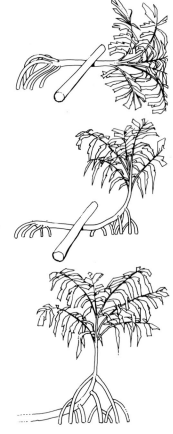

△ *Botanists working in Latin America have found that the palm* Socratea exorrhiza *can literally "walk out" on stilt roots from beneath a fallen tree that would have flattened and killed most species.*

UNDER THE SOUTH AMERICAN CANOPY

The dense canopy of the equatorial rainforest is an all-enveloping umbrella which hides and protects a dimly lit world pungent with the scents of life and death. The visitor's first impressions are of the rapid recycling of living matter and the artful adaptation of each organism to its niche.

The lower canopy

The booming call of a troop-leading howler monkey shatters the still silence of the understory. Then, in an escalating call-and-response chorus, the harsh cries of a macaw join in, building to a crescendo of noise that will draw the attention of a jaguar, who will finally home in on the troop's location by listening for the steady "plop" of discarded fruit cores. Intent on their own business, the understory animals fail to notice the silent Yanomamö hunter as he aims his poisoned arrows.

Three-toed sloth
Bradypus tridactylus

Kinkajou
Potos flavus

Sulfur-breasted toucan
Rhamphastos sulfuratus

Scarlet macaw
Ara macao

Tamandua
Tamandua tetradactyla

Iguana
Iguana iguana

The understory and forest-floor domain

Setting the scene for the understory theater, the morpho butterfly's strobe-effect wingbeats send a blaze of electric-blue impulses direct to the observer's brain – a dazzling phenomenon that typifies the New World rainforest experience. A lone tapir or armadillo may bolt as you approach, sending a hidden ocelot streaking upward into the mid canopy above. Close inspection of logs at your feet reveals a host of beetles, many of them magnificent in size and iridescent color, but beware of testy bands of peccaries – more likely to charge than to flee like the tapir. The aquatic scene is no less dramatic, with pig-sized capybaras swimming unscathed among piranhas and arapaimas.

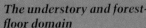

Ring-tailed coati
Nasua nasua

Capybara
Hydrochoerus hydrochaeris

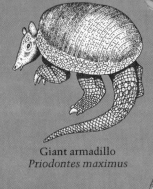

Giant armadillo
Priodontes maximus

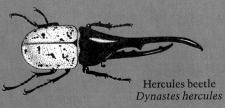

Hercules beetle
Dynastes hercules

Morpho butterfly
Morpho sp.

Spider monkey
Ateles sp.

Howler monkey
Alouatta sp.

Prehensile-tailed
porcupine
Coendou prehensilis

Emerald tree boa
Corallus canina

Arrow
poison frog
Dendrobates sp.

Ocelot
Felis pardalis

Piranha
Serrasalmus notatus

Yanomamö
Homo sapiens

Arapaima
Arapaima gigas

Cloud forests and elfin woodlands

From the lowland rainforest, as elevation increases up mountain ranges and upland valleys, environmental conditions begin to change, and this gradually affects the stature, structure, and composition of the forest. Although the soils are different, the main regulator appears to be temperature. For every 1,000 feet (305 m) increase in elevation, average daily temperature drops by 3.6°F (2°C). This effect, known as the lapse rate, varies from place to place, and also with the time of day, the season, the size and positioning of mountains, and the water vapor content of the air. Biological reactions are retarded as temperature declines, and we find this translated into diminished tree height, reduction in animal and plant diversity, and a transition from the luxuriant five layers of trees to only a few or perhaps just one. Due to the reduction in canopy cover, we find more light reaching the ground and supporting a more profuse shrub growth.

As New Guinea has several peaks in excess of 13,000 feet (4,000 m), it can serve us here as a dynamic example, but because of the factors cited above, these altitudinal demarcations cannot be applied across the board to other areas. Zonations, generally gradual and ill-defined at any particular altitude, can also be abrupt due to, say, prevailing cloud level or sudden accumulations of *Sphagnum* moss. This ecotone or zone of change between lowland forest and lower montane forest occurs at about 4,900 feet (1,500 m). The canopy may still reach 98 to 118 feet (30–36 m) tall here, and the ferns, mosses, and herbaceous flowering plants are abundant.

Above 9,800 feet (3,000 m), upper montane forest takes over. This is divided into two rather distinct formations; the cloud forest between 9,800 and 10,800 feet (3,000–3,300 m) and the lower subalpine forest at 10,800 to 11,650 feet (3,300–3,550 m). As we know, clouds love to congregate and loiter over mountains. This drastically reduces the amount of sunlight available to plants

▽ *Towering tree ferns of the genus* Dicksonia *are a prominent feature of the rapidly diminishing Atlantic rainforest of southeastern Brazil. These forests, quite distinct from the Amazon Basin biome, once covered more than 400,000 sq mi (1,036,000 sq km): today they cover barely 20,000 sq mi (52,000 sq km).*

below for photosynthesis. At this elevation, the arrow-straight giant tree boles of the lowlands, which reach toward the heavens, become more twisted and animated in forms reminiscent of oaks (*Quercus* spp.) Indeed, the higher elevated forests contain more and more temperate species, which include the oaks, and canopy height may reach 60 feet (18 m). Their limbs, however, are overloaded with a profusion of mosses and liverworts due to the high humidity. While species diversity becomes more narrow, the components of the cloud forest are quite artfully assembled.

Here you walk through a forest in the clouds as in an ethereal dream, where the sun rarely shines. There are abundant flowers in the herb layer, countless epiphytes at eye level, and benevolent, wise old trees, twisted into frozen positions, standing silently all around. Sometimes as the clouds waft through this forest, you are almost sure you saw a venerable tree in movement.

Even if it is not raining here, the trees are always dripping. In a process called "cloud stripping," the leaves cause condensation of the moisture from the clouds, and water constantly drips off them. It is interesting that you can generally tell what climate a given plant is from by its manner of directing water, either shedding water away from itself, as in rainforest drip-tip leaves or the feather palm frond structure, or funneling water toward the roots as in agave, cactus, or certain fan palm structures typical of more arid lands.

On higher ranges, between 11,650 and 12,800 feet (3,550–3,900 m), the dwarfed 15-foot (4.5-m) tall and even more diminutive upper subalpine forest can be defined as a rare-air habitat of grotesquely twisted, wind-tortured bonsai specimens, often on exposed ridges. This forest is appropriately known also as elfin woodland.

Above this tree line is a complex mosaic of dwarf shrub heath, short grassland, moss tundra, and fern meadow, classified as alpine vegetation. This gives way to a sparse lichen growth a little higher up. Above 13,120 feet (4,000 m) precipitation falls as snow, which collects permanently at slightly above 14,760 feet (4,500 m). There are even signs of glaciation on New Guinea's Mt. Wilhelm, which reaches 14,793 feet (4,510 m). Life is very sparse here. It seems strange indeed to encounter what amounts to a permanent ice age and glaciers right there on the equator.

Curious "wind forests" are created in areas frequently subjected to the ravages of cyclones or hurricanes. In these formations, trees are mowed down or beaten down in height, and "cyclone scrubs" (so-called in the Queensland rainforests) become abundant in the sunlight-infused gaps in the forests. In these, and at times in other forest formations, dense and impenetrable tangles of vines grow over the treetops to form impressive "climber-towers." These climbers include the Asian rattan palms (*Calamus* spp.) and other closely related genera that have long whips, appropriately called flagella, hanging from their fronds. These are often viciously armed with spines, which serve to anchor the plant to its supports.

It seems rather incongruous to find one mountain supporting lush vegetation on one side and desert scrub and cacti on the other, but this is a common feature and is due to a rain-shadow effect in which most of the precipitation is being dumped on the lush upwind side. Diverse habitats in the Hawaiian Islands are a good case in point. There, rainfall on the windward slopes can average over 400 inches (1,016 cm) annually while the leeward slopes are deserts averaging 15 inches (38 cm) at most.

△ *Cloud forests produce many bizarre tree forms which, seen through the drifting mist, often seem to be in lurching, near-human motion. [Monte Verde, Costa Rica.]*

Continued on page 40

LIFE ZONES OF THE MOUNTAINS

While lowland wet conditions and homogeneous soils produce more consistent
forest formations, a surprising range of variation exists in forests at higher altitudes,
as shown by the Costa Rican cloud forest pictured below. A key factor is decreased
biological production due to lower temperatures.

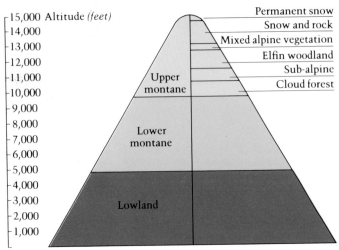

Altitude *(feet)*
15,000 — Permanent snow
14,000 — Snow and rock
13,000 — Mixed alpine vegetation
12,000 — Elfin woodland
11,000 — Sub-alpine
10,000 — Cloud forest
Upper montane
9,000
8,000
Lower montane
7,000
6,000
5,000
4,000
Lowland
3,000
2,000
1,000

◁△ ***Cloud forests and elfin
woodlands***
*The warm, protected
conditions in lowland wet
rainforests produce floral
empires of great luxuriance.
But with increasing
elevation the biomass is
gradually exposed to more
rigorous and demanding
conditions, and these are
directly reflected in the form
and composition of the
forest. As temperature falls,
the cloud forest is blanketed
in almost permanent mist,*
*producing a thick layer of
moss on nearly every
surface. Higher still, in the
elfin woodland (exemplified
here by New Guinea's high
montane forests), trees take
on a stunted and twisted
form, while the forest itself
is poor in species compared
with the rich species
diversity of the lowland
rainforests. Above the elfin
woodland, a narrow band of
mixed alpine vegetation
quickly gives way to bare
rock and snow.*

▷ **Equatorial highlands**
Flanking the Great Rift Valley, Mt Kilimanjaro 19,340 ft (5,595 m), Mt Kenya 17,058 ft (5,200 m), and the fabled Mountains of the Moon – the Ruwenzori Range – 16,794 ft (5,117 m), all share very similar vegetational successions. With increasing altitude the visitor climbs through plant communities that are quite distinctive, in some cases almost alien.

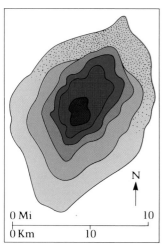

△ **Zonation on Mt Kenya**
A plan view of vegetation zones on Mt Kenya shows a marked asymmetry between the scrub (stippled) of the relatively dry north-facing slopes and the more typical montane forest zones of the wetter southern slopes.

The nival zone
This montane zone is a nightmarish world of tall arborescent (tree-like) plants. It is the upper limit for animals, and one of the few animal sounds heard here is the ethereal scream of the hyrax (Dendrohyrax spp.).

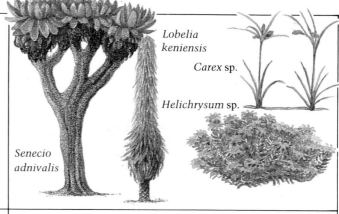

Lobelia keniensis
Carex sp.
Helichrysum sp.
Senecio adnivalis

Moorland/heath zone
Tree heaths dominate the moorland belt while spongy bogs of Carex runssoroensis occupy the wetter valley floors. Wild dogs roam here, and leopards hunt small mammals such as duiker (Sylvicapra).

Erica arborea
Philippia sp.

The bamboo zone
The upper limit of this zone is marked by virtually solid stands of bamboo, which provide a home for the mountain gorilla (Gorilla gorilla beringei), elephant (Loxodonta africana), buffalo (Syncerus caffer), and the giant forest hog (Hylochoerus meinertzhageni).

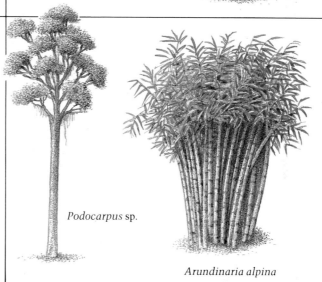

Podocarpus sp.
Arundinaria alpina

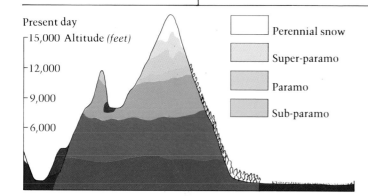

Present day
15,000 Altitude *(feet)*
12,000
9,000
6,000

Perennial snow
Super-paramo
Paramo
Sub-paramo

△ **The Andes today**
The upper zones are higher and broader than they were during the Ice Age. The lowland forests were less drastically affected and so have remained largely intact.

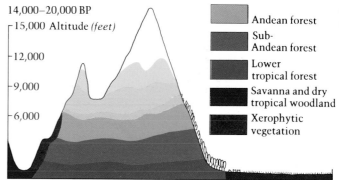

14,000–20,000 BP
15,000 Altitude *(feet)*
12,000
9,000
6,000

Andean forest
Sub-Andean forest
Lower tropical forest
Savanna and dry tropical woodland
Xerophytic vegetation

△ **The effect of the Ice Age**
The vegetation zones became compressed, in some cases by several thousand feet. The lower zones were less affected and became vital refuges for many species.

II · CREATURES OF THE FOREST

The domain of the insect

Quickly apparent to the visitor who has breached the rainforest wall is that this is the domain of the insect; not necessarily bothersome, but myriad in form, color, size, and shape.

Their athletic prowess dwarfs the efforts of the world's Olympic champions. The commonest of fleas can jump 150 times its own length (the equivalent of a man jumping six city blocks from a standing start), go months without feeding, and after a year of being frozen solid, be revived. An ant can lift 50 times its own weight and carry it in its jaws proportionately farther than an average man can walk empty-handed, while to match a bee's strength, a man would have to pull a load equal to a 30-ton trailer truck.

Insects vary in size from 0.008-inch (0.02-cm) long hairwing beetles (Ptiliidae) to the 12-inch (30-cm) wingspan of the atlas moth (*Attacus atlas*) and the 13-inch (33-cm) body length of the Borneo walking stick (*Palophus titan*). The Polyphemus moth larva in its first two days of existence eats 86,000 times its own birth weight in food. And so the catalog runs on.

In this damp, warm habitat, glorious beetles are everywhere, competing for center stage, clothed in brilliant colors, patterns, shapes, and blinding metallic iridescence. British biologist J.B.S. Haldane (1892–1964) was once asked what organic evolution had revealed about God's design. Because there are so many spectacular varieties, his answer was, "An inordinate fondness for beetles."

A species called the bombardier beetle (*Brachinus* sp.) has recently undergone extensive investigation. Results show that hydrogen peroxide and chemicals called hydroquinones are stored in the beetle's glands. At will, the insect mixes these chemicals in a "reaction chamber" containing enzymes, resulting in the formation of benzoquinones and gaseous oxygen as a propellant. It was also found that the chemical reaction causes the mixture to boil in this species, adding scalding heat to an already unique and devastating defense mechanism. These creatures apparently have no need to bite or sting.

The invasion of the giant penlights

Certain beetles assume preposterous proportions and powers. My wife Arlene and I, while investigating a lowland rainforest in the Vera Cruz state of Mexico, had camped, finished dinner, and were sitting around our campfire. Through the trees in the distance we noticed the flashing of fireflies. Being used to the splendid little three-quarter-inch (2-cm) fellows (Lampyridae) of northern latitudes, we watched in the black forest night as they wove in and out of the trees, growing larger and larger as they approached us. This presented no problem at all as fireflies are completely harmless, and this in any case was quite a spectacle. However, *these* "fireflies" continued to grow as they got closer. Without saying a word, we looked at each other and then back at the advancing lights, which were now as big and prominent as a horde of penlights. I then recalled a story told during the building of the Panama Canal, in which surgeons successfully used a jar of luminescent click beetles (*Pyrophorus* sp.) to illuminate a patient for surgery during a power blackout.

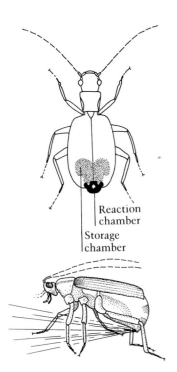

Reaction chamber
Storage chamber

△ *With an explosive "pop" the bombardier beetle* (Brachinus sp.) *blasts its attacker with a scalding jet of irritant chemicals. Tiny though it may be, this 0.8-in (2-cm) creature will deter adversaries as large and varied as mice, praying mantids, wolf spiders, and frogs – for as long as its ammunition supply lasts!*

The penlights kept coming, and finally reached us. What happened next staggered the imagination. They were 3 inches (7.6 cm) long; their green glowing abdomens fully 1.5 inches (3.8 cm) long. Blinded by our fire, these ponderous creatures bounced off trees, careened into our faces, and got caught in our hair, but still they kept coming. What a show. We had to smother the fire (the point of attraction) because some of them were landing in it. Then we were plunged into the pitch black of night, with scores of satellite full moons dispersing through the forest. Back home, identification proved them to be the same giant *Pyrophorus* click beetles that had illuminated the old Panama Canal operating room.

What are the dangers in the tropical forest?

While such episodes as the giant click beetles are far more typical of the tropical forest experience, many visitors anticipate their travel there will abound with violent encounters with dangerous animals. Be assured that such a myth represents one of the world's great misconceptions. As plant defenses against animal depredation are so effective, the undisturbed forest is simply not overburgeoning with animals, and where animals are present they are not apt to be highly visible. One study estimates the animal biomass at 18 pounds (8.2 kg) per hectare (2.47 acres) for ground-dwelling mammals and 21 pounds per hectare (9.5 kg/ha) for arboreal mammals, the equivalent of approximately five domestic cats in weight.

△ *On Komodo Is., Indonesia, I was treed and repeatedly attacked by a 12-ft (3.7-m) Komodo dragon which pressed home its attack despite all attempts to drive it away. It was a rare glimpse into the pre-historic past to be pursued as food by a ruling reptile more than three times my own weight.*

Further, save for mosquitoes and odd parasites, most of the rest of the fauna, with rare exceptions, is shy and retiring and has no specific business with humans. Given that travel in the forest is never silent, most creatures are either in hiding or have vacated the area long before your arrival. Should you be fortunate enough to view one of the animals that enjoy a high public profile, there is still no reason why the incident should become perilous so long as certain basic rules are not violated. These include refraining from handling venomous snakes, and avoiding surprising a potentially dangerous animal by stalking it or by suddenly appearing and blocking its flight path or moving into its attack range.

But perhaps the abundance and complexity of tropical forest beauty cannot be fully appreciated without at least some measure of its antithesis for contrast. In an attempt to set the record straight, we will investigate some of the charismatic creatures of infamy that a traveler in Amazonia, for instance, might possibly, but not probably, encounter.

Piranhas and other dangerous aquatics

Most everyone is familiar with the piranha (*Serrasalmus* spp.), which early explorers called the scourge of the Amazon. Yet although I have seen a school activated into a feeding frenzy by the smell of blood strip a 100-pound (45-kg) animal carcass to bones in a minute or so, it is also true that a person can swim in the Amazon and other waters they inhabit, unmolested, as long as blood is not present and swimming is regular and not panicked. To avoid cannibal fish, it is best to be cautious in the sluggish backwaters of oxbow lakes. Also be aware that more danger exists during low-water periods when the piranha schools are more concentrated. At these times competition for available food is at a peak, and humans are then more likely to become targets. Menstruating women should keep any essential swimming or bathing to faster-moving waters or clear streams at any time of the year.

△ *The teeth of the piranha* (Serrasalmus notatus) *are so formidably sharp that the jaws are used by many tribal people as a tool. By spinning the tip of a poisoned blow-gun dart between the teeth, the tip is almost severed. The result is that should a monkey shot with the dart attempt to pull it out, the deadly tip will break off in the wound, bringing certain death.*

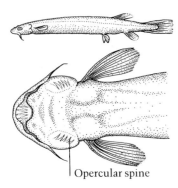

Opercular spine

△ *The dreaded candiru, or carnero (*Vandellia cirrhosa*), inhabits Brazilian rivers. It is a parasite, normally living in the gill cavities of other fish, but will also penetrate the urethra of a human bather unless precautions are taken.*

A catfish, the giant piraiba (*Brachyplatystoma filamentosum*), has an ignoble reputation for purportedly eating small children. This is certainly not its natural diet, and records would indicate that this behavior is extremely rare – if indeed it occurs at all. More deserving of infamy is the candiru, whose unique life cycle has resulted in its being viewed as rather diabolical. These spiny fish, of the family Vandelliinae, may reach 2 inches (5 cm) in length, are attracted to urine and are small enough to enter the human urethra via the genitals and lodge there or in the bladder, which may necessitate surgical removal to save the victim. The tightly woven fabrics of some underwear and bathing suits are a hindrance to this fish, and their use is strongly recommended! (The men of many Amazonian tribes customarily tie off the foreskin over the urethral opening, but it is not yet known whether this is a purely social custom or whether it has originated as a protection against the candiru.)

The electric eel (*Electrophorus electricus*) is one of about forty species that can knock a person senseless and in rare cases cause drowning, but a negative encounter is unusual without having first molested the eel. Similarly, the freshwater stingray (*Potamotrygon hystrix*), if stepped on, can incapacitate you for days, but can also be avoided by refraining from wading in sandy or muddy river shallows. Where such travel is necessary, shuffling, rather than stepping along, will generally encourage the ray to move out of the way without a painful confrontation.

The Amazon and its tributaries are home to the American crocodile (*Crocodylus acutus*) and several species of caiman (*Caiman* spp.) Unprovoked attacks are quite rare in these species, although certain Old World crocodiles, especially rogue individuals, pose a much more real threat.

Your chances of experiencing an attack by the last of the ruling reptiles increase in this species order: the aptly named mugger crocodile (*Crocodylus palustris*) from India, the nilotic crocodile (*Crocodylus niloticus*) from Africa, and the salt water crocodile (*Crocodylus porosus*) of India, the East Indies, and Pacific regions. The salt water croc, which has been measured at 20.5 feet (6.25 m), is possibly the most aggressive animal on earth. Most are retiring, but individuals have been known to attack native canoes 100 miles (160 km) out to sea and even to have devoured the occupants. Crocodilians evolved during the Triassic period, some 200 million years ago, and are grouped with the dinosaurs and pterosaurs in the subclass Archosauria. Fifty million years after the crocodilians appeared on the scene, the archosaurs also produced the birds. It is quite interesting, therefore, to note that crocodilians are actually more closely related to birds than they are to snakes, turtles, or even lizards. Despite this, be certain that they are the last of the ruling reptiles, and although they can outrun a horse for short distances, I have never been attacked by any but captive specimens – a harrowing and indelible experience in itself, nevertheless.

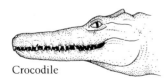

Crocodile

Alligator

Gavial (gharial)

△ *Crocodiles (worldwide) are distinguished from alligators (southern US and China) and caimans (Latin America) by the arrangement of their teeth. In the crocodile, the large fourth tooth in the lower jaw is visible when the mouth is closed; in the other reptiles it fits into a pit and is not visible. The slender-jawed Indian gavial is a specialized fish catcher.*

Our last interesting inhabitant is the anaconda (*Eunectes marinus*). Also called the water boa, it is the largest snake in the world, with a record length of 37.5 feet (11.4 m) and estimated to weigh over 500 pounds (227 kg). Although over the years this giant constrictor may have devoured an unfortunate here or there, you may count such incidents on one hand. To put this into perspective, an average of 51 people die every decade in the United States alone due to honeybee (*Apis mellifera*) stings. We now move to terra firma Amazonia.

Snakes – the most misunderstood of the forest inhabitants

Naturalist Henry Beston (1888–1968) remarked that "animals move finished and complete, gifted with extensions of the senses we have lost or never attained, living by voices we shall never hear."

As snakes are so prominent in many people's minds, and so closely associated with the tropical rainforest, we shall investigate what snakes are and what they are not. It will surprise most readers to know that you may walk for perhaps three days or more in the tropical rainforest without ever seeing a snake, although on another day you may observe several. In no way are snakes abundant, and if you take care when moving through the forest you have very little to concern yourself with. Nevertheless, travelers should always be conscious of snake safety.

Animals and plants that have dangerous or lethal defenses usually have a universal method of warning prey species, or incidental adversaries, of their potential prowess. Hornets are flighty, contrastingly colored, and have a paralyzing hum; the rhinoceros has one or more long horns, and snorts intimidatingly; red seeds or fruits display a general warning of toxicity, as do the orange, red, and black markings of many insects.

The snake is no exception. To protect themselves from being trampled by American mastodons (*Mammut americanum*) and other large animals, rattlesnakes (*Crotalus* and *Sistrurus* spp.) evolved rattles, while others have adopted different fearsome gestures and appearances to avoid having to close with their enemies. Many snakes, as we will see, do not live up to all this posturing; when pressed, others do!

Poisonous snakes inject venom, which kills the prey and also helps to predigest its tissues. Other snakes are constrictors, suffocating their prey by prohibiting the rib cage's ability to expand, and so preventing the victim from inhaling. All must swallow their food whole, so they never attack animals too large for them to eat. Although there are a handful of recorded instances of human beings being killed and a few actually consumed by large constrictor snakes, no snake seeks humans as food.

Constrictors include not only large and small varieties of boas and pythons, but also several more typically diminutive species. A truly large snake, after consuming a heavy meal such as an antelope, can go for as long as two years, if necessary, without feeding. Unless molested, even these giant snakes are of no particular concern to people.

Most people are relieved to know that the snake's flickering tongue is a sensory organ used to pick up scent particles from the air and transfer them to sense organs in the roof of the mouth. It cannot inflict injury. Snakes, in short, are not malignant creatures spoiling for a fight, but superbly adapted (and beautiful) animals that fill a vital niche and are of much benefit to humankind. Their main prey are rodents, and by consuming enormous quantities of these, significantly more food is left for us in the world's fields and granaries. As such, snakes should never be summarily killed when they are encountered. As well as being needlessly destructive, such an action presents a splendid opportunity to be bitten.

As virgin tropical rainforest floors are dimly lit and support moderately scant vegetation, you can easily see where you are walking. In thicker secondary growth, however, more caution is necessary. In any habitat, travelers should always be aware of snake safety. Step on, not over logs or other suitable snake microniches, and always look where you put your feet

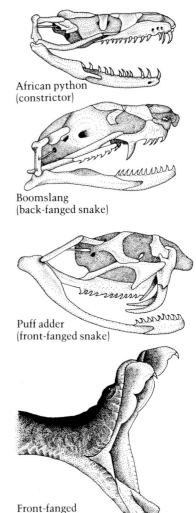

African python
(constrictor)

Boomslang
(back-fanged snake)

Puff adder
(front-fanged snake)

Front-fanged
snake striking

△ *Nonfanged snakes are not venomous. Back-fanged snakes must use a chewing action to deliver their venom, but the front-fanged snakes inject the toxic dose through hypodermic-like erectile fangs.*

△ *A rare sight, witnessed on the Rio Claro, Costa Rica. Here, a 6 ft (1.8 m) cannibal indigo snake (Drymarchon corais) is swallowing – whole – another indigo snake 8 ft (2.4 m) long.*

◁ *The ornate flying snake of southern Asia* (Chrysolopea ornata) *can launch itself from the canopy, holding its body rigid and with the underside concave, glide down to the lower levels quite unharmed.*

▽ *The venomous back-fanged mangrove snake* (Boiga dendrophila) *adopts such an effective aggression pose that it often repels its adversary without having to bite. This snake inhabits mangrove swamps in Asia.*

△△ *A 15-ft (4.5-m) Burmese python* (Python molurus bivittatus) *tracks its prey through giant bamboo.*

△ *The blood python* (P. curtus) *of Malaysia and Sumatra blends with the leaf litter of the forest floor.*

and hands. Following these rules, bites are an extreme improbability. Be assured, snakes do not drop from trees. In a quarter-century of work in tropical forests around the world, neither I nor anyone in my party has ever come close to being bitten. Further, I have encountered in that time only one victim of venomous snake bite (excluding herpetologists bitten while handling specimens). In that one isolated case, in a remote village in Zaïre, a pregnant Bantu woman was bitten by a black mamba (*Dendroaspis polylepis*) while working in tall grass outside the forest. Fortunately our expedition carried antivenin, and in my absence, my son Gandhi, then twelve years old, administered the injection that saved both woman and unborn child.

Very simply, wilderness areas do not abound with snakes. This is especially true in tropical rainforests. There is no abundance of perennially seeding plants at ground level, and thus few rodents. Consequently the snake population is quite low. Many snakes are sedentary, patient, beautifully patterned, and a marvel to behold.

In the Amazon, what then of the much feared and "lethal" fer-de-lance (*Bothrops atrox*), alias barba amarilla (yellow beard) or terciopelo (velvety-one)? It is illuminating to note that although this species causes 80–85 percent of the snake bites reported in its Latin American range, only 2–3 percent of the bites are fatal. These stunningly beautiful snakes will not attack unprovoked. For the great majority of tropical forest travelers, their rare encounters with snakes are nothing more than an exotic memory to embrace. But what of other Amazonian zoologicals of sinister reputation?

△ The emerald tree boa (Corallus canina) has unusually long teeth which enable it to seize and hold the birds on which it preys. Thermoreceptors located in shallow pits on the snake's lips can detect temperature gradients of as little as 0.2°C and are the main sense by which the snake finds its prey and directs its strike.

Ant soldiers and armies

Significantly, we have two ant groups on our list. The first, the giant tocandiras (*Dinoponera* and *Paraponera* spp.) are well respected by all who know them. Not all ants sting; these sting, and bite – and are terribly good at both! A nervous, aggressive, solitary hunter, the giant tocandiras flits about like a wasp on the forest floor, on trees, or on epiphytes, and while its sting is quite painful, at 1 inch (2.5 cm) long it is fortunately quite easy to see, so avoiding confrontation is simple (though I have been assaulted by them on two occasions while inspecting bromeliad interiors).

The second is the army ant (Dorylinae) and its Old World counterpart the driver ant (*Dorylus* spp.) A single ant will weigh not more than 0.000165345 of a pound, which means that a 200-pound (91-kg) man will weigh as much as 1,209,921 ants. It is surprising that creatures this small can be such a major concern for human beings.

Conquering hordes of army ants ride rampant over everything in their path and the sight is extremely impressive. Although a tethered donkey and a caged gorilla are recorded among the ants' unfortunate victims, most mammals this size, in good health, are able to flee in advance of the army as the ants can be heard approaching through the forest-floor debris. Opportunist ant-following birds pick off escaping victims, but the army of the ant marches patiently onward.

On a long trek in the Ituri Forest, Mbuti Pygmies who accompanied our expedition, but who were perhaps more accustomed to quieter travel, inadvertently led us into a swarm of driver ants. Our party was both stung (perhaps one-quarter bee-sting power) and bitten ruthlessly until we could make our way clear of the area under siege.

Even small rivulets are forded, by chains of army ants forming living bridges across the water. So dedicated are they in this effort that many who form these bridges drown. Clearly, the individual is expendable.

Drawing analogies between these ants and human armies is unavoidable: their nest is even called a bivouac. It is to this base camp that the army returns each day during half the month, pressing on in its "pillage-and-looting" march during the other half. Indian villages are usually abandoned in advance of an approaching ant army, and after the horde has passed through, the residents happily return to a village completely cleared of insects, rodents, and snakes.

△ *Individual army ants often sacrifice themselves to the good of the colony. Many perish by drowning when they instinctively form living bridges over water obstructions. The author observed this army ant "tunnel" as the insects emerged from a forest into sunlight. The behavior may reduce the army's vulnerability by concealing its movements.* (Neivamyrmex *sp., South America.*)

No-see-ums

The subject of insects would not be complete without mention of the most infamous of all, the biting midges, alias piums and red pepper gnats (*Culicoides* spp.). Encountered most commonly on sandy river beaches, they can be relentless tormentors. So small they are difficult to see with the naked eye, they easily go through screening and any mosquito net coarser than cheesecloth. Female no-see-ums deliver a nasty little nip, suck blood, and may on occasion transmit filarial worms that infect humans, but the measure of audacity in this pestiferous fly is that one species will drain from a mosquito the blood that the mosquito has just withdrawn from a man. To be rid of them, use extra-fine netting, wait for a good breeze, or break camp on the run.

Vampires

Vampire bats (*Desmodus rotundus*, and two other species, each in its own genus) either concern or intrigue people as they have the dubious distinction of being the only true mammalian parasites.

The bat's first approach at night is to flutter in front of its host's face, and some believe in the myth that it releases a soporific or tranquilizing scent. It then lands on the ground and scuttles forward to pounce. With a downward stroke of the head it pierces the skin with razor-sharp triangular front teeth, either puncturing a neat hole or slicing off a tiny sliver of skin. The host, usually a cow, pig, goat, or similar-size animal, is unaware of the cut on its ear, nose, or foot since the bat's saliva contains an effective local anesthetic. But the adaptation is even more perfect. The saliva also contains an effective anticoagulant which keeps the blood flowing freely while the bat feeds on this its sole form of food.

Amerindian folklore claims that the vampire was responsible for the disappearance of the original American horse, a weak but interesting theory. It is true, however, that vampires are responsible for depletion of cattle throughout their range from Argentina to the southern border of the United States. There is some concern that with the progressive warming trend (due in part to tropical deforestation), vampires will move northward. They would have no problem in preying on humans as well as their more usual hosts, and can transmit rabies, murrina, and other lethal infections which they can incubate in their bodies for long periods without mortality. In vampire country you do well to sleep under the adequate protection of a mosquito net, with toes and nose safely inside.

The great cats

The jaguar, alias *el tigre* (*Panthera onca*) figures in most people's anxiety on entering the South American rainforest. The third largest of the great cats, following lions (*Panthera leo*) and tigers (*Panthera tigris*), the jaguar is less aggressive than either, and unprovoked attacks are rare in the extreme. Count yourself as one of the truly blessed if you even manage to glimpse one in its natural setting.

A reclusive, solitary cat of the deep forest, the jaguar places its privacy in high regard. One resides within the borders of my own Cathedral Rain Forest Science Preserve in Costa Rica, and more than once I have interrupted it on a peccary kill. On two occasions it retired seconds before my arrival. When pressed though, a jaguar proves a fierce and persistent adversary.

Public enemy #1

The mosquito has rightfully earned the position of public enemy number one, being a far greater menace than rats and lice combined. In tropical forests the mosquito can be *the* real hazard. "Wigglers" and "tumblers" (larvae and pupae) require water to complete their development, and depending on species preference, most any water can qualify – salt, fresh, stagnant or clear, down at ground level, or caught in the tanks of epiphytic bromeliads high in the treetops.

It is the female that parasitizes (except for plant feeders and one species that drains out the contents of an ant's stomach) and she needs a blood meal before laying her eggs. Only a tuppence of blood (0.1 ml) is removed through the insect's hypodermic-like proboscis. However, it injects its saliva, containing anticoagulants and anesthetic, so as to assist in making the deed go unnoticed, to avoid being expunged by a swat. It is this saliva that causes the allergic reaction of itching and swelling which is of no more than transient consequence. Unfortunately, however, pathogens too are often introduced via the saliva. As biological vectors, mosquitoes directly transmit the micro-organisms that cause malaria, dengue fever, yellow fever, and encephalitis, as well as many worm parasites (filariasis). The last category includes those that cause elephantiasis, a condition that can swell a man's leg to gargantuan proportions and his testicles to grotesque size.

As well as the notorious *Anopheles* mosquito, the main carrier of malaria, and other members of the Culicinae family that carry dengue or breakbone fever, there are yet more species which enjoy a lower public profile but nevertheless cause untold human misery. To appreciate the scale of the damage they can do, consider that a single outbreak of yellow fever in southwest Ethiopia in the late 1950s killed 15,000 souls – almost 10 percent of the population. Of all transmissible diseases, however, malaria is still the world's number one killer. It accounts for some four million deaths every year, including roughly a million, mostly children, in Africa alone. In the Pacific campaign of World War II, malaria was responsible for five times as many casualties as were inflicted by the enemy.

There are, of course, a host of other diseases that must not be taken too lightly, although the chance of one becoming infected while visiting a tropical forest area for a short time is rather remote provided proper health precautions are taken. Research carried out by the various United Nations agencies (UNESCO, UNEP, and FAO) shows that within the African tropical forest zone there is a significantly lower incidence of disease, especially of malaria, in the deep forest tribes compared to the peoples living in progressively more disturbed forest habitats. Cities, towns, and villages in the tropics are far more likely places in which to become infected, and we will see in a later chapter that many tropical diseases are largely the product of deforestation.

Many tropical forest areas are actually fairly free of disease and mosquitoes for that matter. The basic rules are simple: travelers should always check the conditions of the area they plan to visit and, if necessary, take the appropriate prophylactic to prevent disease. Using common sense and a good mosquito net, most will enjoy what can be the most rewarding of life experiences.

The Amazon: South America's green museum

Amazonia is the greatest, oldest, richest, and largest of the world's great forests; almost 2.7 million square miles (7 million sq km) of mystery – almost 90 percent of the area of the contiguous United States. Through its heart runs the world's greatest river. One-sixth of all the fresh water that flows on earth moves through its vast drainage system, and its flow is greater than the world's next eight largest rivers combined.

At its mouth the Amazon is over 200 miles (320 km) wide. Marajo, a single island in its mouth, is as large as Denmark. Even 1,000 miles (1,600 km) inland it is often impossible to see from one bank to the other. Averaging 100 feet (30 m) deep over much of its course, it is so enormous that an oceangoing vessel may navigate 2,300 miles (3,700 km) of its 4,007-mile (6,450-km) length. This would be like entering Chesapeake Bay and sailing all the way to Denver, Colorado. There are over 1,000 tributaries, 17 of them over 1,000 miles (1,600 km) long, and the average flow of this mightiest of rivers is 170 billion gallons (644 billion l) of water an hour: more than 4 trillion gallons (15.4 trillion l) a day pour into the Atlantic Ocean – enough to satisfy New York City's water needs for 12 years! So powerful is the Amazon's impact on the Atlantic Ocean, that adjacent to its mouth you can lean over the side of a boat 100 miles (160 km) out to sea and fill a glass with fresh water.

The Amazon is so immense and wild that it naturally inspired legend and myth. In 1542, Francisco de Orellana became the first European to travel the

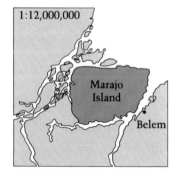

△ *The sheer enormity of the Amazon River can be truly appreciated only by drawing comparisons. In these maps, Marajo Island, located in the mouth of the river is shown at the same scale as the New England coastal states and Switzerland.*

length of the "green tunnel." The river was named after a tribe of giant warrior women his expedition reportedly encountered there. Although such people have never been found, "Amazon" now seems more fluidly to refer to the river and to the region's almost incomprehensible immensity. Amazonia is the size of the United States east of the Rockies, and by itself would be the ninth largest country in the world. Recently, vast mountain ranges have been found far from where they were thought to be, and several large rivers have become known only in the last few years due to satellite scanning.

So scant is our present state of exploration and knowledge here that since Bates first scratched the surface of scientific investigation of the Amazon in the 1850s, when he collected over 8,000 new insects, it was not until the beginning of the 1970s that another large-scale effort was made to discover new fauna and flora in this vast biological frontier. On a recent collecting trip in the Amazon Basin, Oliver Flint of the Smithsonian Institution in Washington, D.C. gathered 55 caddisflies belonging to several different families: 53 of them were species completely new to science, offering a hint at the magnitude of future potential discoveries. The bird life of the great forest is no less rich. On one expedition, 76 different species were counted near the mouth of the river – in the branches of a single tree.

There are almost as many species of fish (around 5,000) in the drainage basin of the Amazon River as there are in the entire Atlantic Ocean. Many of these creatures resemble marine species: electric eels, sting rays, shark-related sawfish, whales in the form of pink dolphins, and manatees – the origin of the mermaid myth. It is estimated that 40 percent of the Amazon Basin's fish species are yet to be discovered.

The Amazon comprises well over one-half of the earth's tropical rainforests, and already roughly 15 percent of it has been removed. As we shall see, the global implications of this are enormous.

△ *Thousands of miles away from the Atlantic Ocean, the Napo is already a vast and impressive river as it sweeps through the wooded Andean foothills of Peru and Ecuador. Yet this is just one of more than 1,000 major tributaries of the Amazon.*

2
THE WEB OF LIFE

Like Aldo Leopold's tinker, who attempts to repair a watch he does not fully understand, we keep all the pieces of our biological fabric to insure us the full spectrum of possibilities for our future.

NEWMAN

A scarlet macaw (Ara macao) in Costa Rica symbolizes the beauty, complexity, and fragility of the rainforest environment.

I · THE DYNAMICS OF THE RAINFOREST

Tropical rainforests differ from the forests of temperate regions in many crucial ways. We have seen the critical range of temperature and rainfall required to support the rainforest and other tropical forest formations, and how those essentially nonseasonal characteristics have conspired to produce such rich and varied plant and animal communities. Because abundant supplies of nutrients are not available to the tropical forest as reserves held in the soil, as is classically the case in the temperate forest, the rainforest depends for its nutrients on a constant recycling of its own enormous biomass.

A myth debunked

△ A fallen canopy tree reveals the shallow root mass and absence of a tap-root so common in rain-forest trees. The basic instability of such root systems is mitigated by buttressing and by the lianas which bind the tree crowns together.

Temperate forests are nurtured by a rich topsoil which may be 7 feet (2.1 m) deep and more, while the leaf mulch itself may exceed a foot (31 cm) in thickness. It was long assumed that the massive and lush tropical forests stood on rich, deep soils as well. It was surprising, therefore, to find that tropical rainforest soils were, in fact, exceedingly thin and fragile. Leaf litter averages a scant 1 inch (2.5 cm) in depth or less, and topsoil will be a mere 2 inches (5 cm) on slopes and often not much more in level areas. Typically, below this soil horizon lies a red lateritic clay. Due to their composition, and given the high rainfall, most of these soils are poor retainers of nutrients. To a large extent, the forest makes a perpetual reservoir for these substances in the biomass itself. In certain areas of the Amazon Basin and Borneo, great forests are, surprisingly, even supported on almost pure white sand. In fact the tropical rainforest has been aptly described as trees growing in a desert.

Dynamics of the rainforest engine

If we can use an engine as analogous to the forest, its fuel is the nitrogen made available to the living plants by the fuel pump, decomposition. The multitude of soil fauna responsible for that ongoing year-round process are rife in the thin topsoil and humus, and as temperatures are so constant, release of nutrients proceeds continuously. We can now visualize how efficiently the biological powerhouse operates – and also how vulnerable it is to disturbance. Inside the forest, temperatures are constant at the optimum level for the teeming soil fauna. Temperatures outside the forest are generally 13–18°F (7–10°C) higher. As long as the forest remains intact, the fuel pump can operate, but exposing the bare earth to the sun leads to baking of the thin fragile topsoil and destruction of the essential soil fauna – halting, or at least drastically curtailing, the flow of nutrients.

To lubricate this engine, rainfall must be high – never less than 80 inches (203 cm) per year – and humidity must also remain high at around 95 percent so that evaporation does not exceed precipitation. Under these conditions the heat of the canopy engine catapults into the atmosphere some 200 gallons (760 l) of water per canopy tree – roughly 20,000 gallons (76,000 l) per acre – and as it is carried upward it condenses into clouds, which eventually release the water again as rain and so complete the cycle. So efficient is the rainforest's water budget that up to 75 percent of its evapotranspiration is returned to it.

The abundance of rainfall in the tropical rainforest, and its constant recycling, laden with nutrients, is the key to this biome's astonishing ability to support the earth's richest vegetation cover on some of the poorest soils imaginable. While the cycle remains unbroken, the forest flourishes; but if the forest is removed, or the water cycle is disrupted, the entire system collapses, the engine stalls.

Recycling the nutrient stock

As we shall see, even though rainfall is recycled back onto the forest that produced it, it is essential that the nutrients and scarce minerals carried in that water should also be harvested back by the forest. This is done, improbably, with hardly any loss to the system. Carbon, now recognized as a pivotal factor in atmospheric stability, is just one of the crucial elements cycled and stored by the forest.

In virgin forests, enormous quantities of nutrients circulate freely between vegetation and soil, and very little is lost to the ecosystem through drainage water. In one study near Manaus, Brazil, the litter raining down to the floor of a forest plot contained 41 pounds (18.6 kg) of calcium. When the area's stream water was analyzed, no calcium was detected. What little is lost is replaced by weathering of rock.

Aside from what weathers out of bedrock, the minerals and nutrients in the moist and wet tropical forest are, in significant part, locked up in the vegetation in an all but leakproof, closed system. Due to the uninterrupted warmth and humidity, falling leaves and other debris decompose at a very rapid pace. (When searching for firewood in the forest, for instance, generally the only material you will locate not already in an advanced state of decomposition will be branches that have been prevented by undergrowth from hitting the ground.) Leaves are most often partially decomposed by insects and fungi even before they fall from the tree. The nutrient budget here may be large, but it is in a constant state of motion; a mass equivalent to that of the entire forest biomass dies and is renewed every forty to one hundred years. This forest quite literally feeds on itself.

The tropical rainforest soil is alive and teeming with fungi and decomposing organisms which very quickly release the nutrients from vegetation debris, animal excretions, and corpses. Most of the giant trees do not have taproots but, along with much of the balance of the vegetation, are very shallow rooted. In fact, aside from support, one of the main functions of their spreading buttresses is to increase the tree's absorptive area. Around 50 percent of the tree's fibrous rootlets, which are the most active in nutrient intake, are found directly under the leaf litter and just below the soil surface. These do not desiccate in the constantly moist conditions and so they can rapidly absorb nutrients released back into the system.

The busy decomposers

A common feature of the forest understory is decomposition: all about you seems to decay and crumble. The facilitators in this endeavor are heat and moisture; the perpetrators – fungi. Once wet, articles never dry out again unless constant efforts are taken to move them into the elusive sun. Leather, especially, soon becomes covered with fuzzy green mildew. Attempts to keep yourself above the fungal morass, in a sense, become a way of life.

Continued on page 57

△ *Only the phenomenal rate of decomposition and the very rapid recycling of nutrients can account for the rainforest's ability to support such a vast biomass on such poor soil. [Petén Forest Guatemala.]*

DYNAMICS OF THE RAINFOREST

While temperate forests rely on a bank of resources and deep rooting structures to
sustain their growth, tropical forests must combat extreme climatic pressures,
nutrient-poor soils, and shallow rooting systems with strategies of remarkable thrift.
They can truly be likened to forests growing in a desert.

Nutrient cycle of the temperate forest

Nutrient cycle of the tropical rainforest

△▷ **Nutrient storage**
*Tropical soils are so thin
that nutrient stocks must be
held in the biomass; in
temperate forests a much
higher proportion of the
stock is held in the soil.*

 Temperate forest

 Tropical rainforest

 Percentage in biomass

 Percentage in soil

   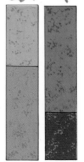  

Nitrogen　　Phosphorus　　Potassium　　Calcium　　Magnesium　　Carbon

◁ **Forest comparisons**
Temperate and tropical
forests process their
resources very differently –
this accounts for the
vulnerability of the
rainforest when its cycle is
broken or disturbed.

◁◁ **The temperate cycle**
Here the primary nutrient
reservoir is in the soil. Not
exposed to intense leaching,
it contains a high proportion
of organic matter which in
turn holds nutrients.
Additional minerals are also
available from weathered
rocks accessible to deep
roots. Recycling is slower
than in warmer climes but
there is always a reserve,
and good farming practices
can maintain the balance.

◁ **The tropical cycle**
In marked contrast, the
tropical forest nutrient
reservoir is in the plants
themselves. A fine network
of surface roots retrieves the
nutrients released from
plant and animal remains
by termites, fungi, and other
decomposers.
    Felling and farming these
forests without careful
conservation measures
quickly results in loss of
nutrients – and the topsoil
itself – stripped away and
lost in surface water runoff.

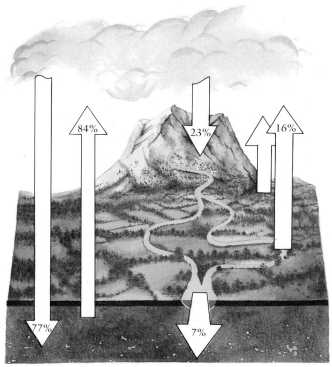

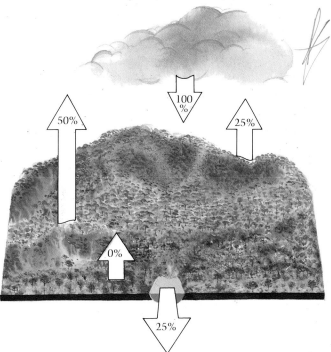

◁ **The global water cycle**
Water is the lifeblood of our
planet. It is an essential
compound in its own right;
it transports dissolved
nutrients, and it cleanses
and refreshes the land by
flushing away wastes.
    The whole cycle is driven
by the sun. Of the water
entering the atmosphere,
84% evaporates from the
ocean surface, the rest from
soil and inland waters and
from evapotranspiration by
plants. Of this water, 23%
falls on land as rain and
about 7% finds its way to
the sea – balancing the
roughly 7% carried inland
on prevailing winds.

◁ **The Amazon Basin cycle**
Up to 75% of the water
falling on the Amazon Basin
as rain will be recycled into
the atmosphere by the
forest vegetation – 50%
by evapotranspiration and
another 25% by direct
evaporation of rainwater
intercepted by the leaves. It
is a virtually closed cycle
quite unlike that of any
other biome on earth. There
is now compelling evidence
that a deforested Amazon
would reduce precipitation
by 26%, evaporation by
30%, and lower outside
moisture entering the basin
by 18%, a total of 74%
reduction. Under those
conditions, the forest would
not return.

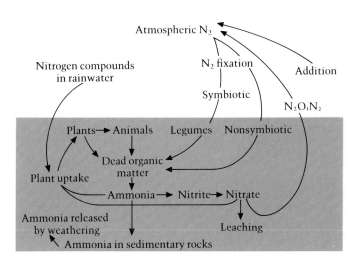

◁▷ **The nitrogen cycle**
The diagram here shows the
broad global cycling of
nitrogen – one of the key
nutrients. In tropical forests
this nutrient is scarce and
some plants have resolved
the problem by utilizing the
nitrogen held in animal
tissues. The carnivorous
pitcher plants of Southeast
Asia (Nepenthes spp.) for
example, digest insects lured
into their pitfall traps by
sweet nectar bait.

◁ Fungi prosper on the physical law that states: "Matter is not created or destroyed, it is simply converted." These wood-decomposing bracket fungi (polypores) reveal only their reproductive parts; the mycelia, or vegetative parts, penetrate deep into the wood, breaking it down into more easily recycled components. [Venezuela.]

▽ The otherworldly earth-star (Geastrum sp.) is a resident of the forest floor in northern Sumatra. The fungus is actually a puffball which, when the papery center is struck by a raindrop or falling twig, discharges a cloud of spores into the air.

△ Carlyle said, "Nature alone is antique, and the oldest art a mushroom." Were it not for fungi like this Lentinus species from the forests of Sumatra, the earth would long since have been buried beneath piles of organic debris.

When I had a field research station and house constructed on the Cathedral Rain Forest Science Preserve in Costa Rica, I remarked to José, the builder and caretaker, that the structure was splendid – but how long would it last? José enthused that it was a *casa fantastica* and that it would last for *mucho tiempo*. I pressed José, saying, *bueno, pero cuantos años exactamente?* José proudly replied, *siete* (seven). In fact, the house lasted only five years, and then had to be completely rebuilt. Termites, dry rot, and wet rot had completely gutted the entire facility.

Other than powdery, troublesome fungi, other strange and elaborately hued species are commonly encountered. There are cup-shaped fungi so deeply orange as to startle the observer. Bracket fungi, some far larger than dinner plates, jut out in tiers on dead trees. Mystical puff balls, some 2 feet (0.6 m) in diameter emit huge clouds of spores at the prompting of a raindrop.

Encounters with some fungal forms can be an altogether otherworldly experience. At dusk in a Papua New Guinea lowland forest, I noticed an eerie green glow emanating from scattered pieces of rotten wood forming a perfect circle on the forest floor some 25 feet (7.6 m) in diameter. When total darkness enveloped the forest, this chartreuse gloaming became as prominent as the rings of Saturn must be as viewed from that planet. This is a variety of fungus that forms "fairy rings." Legend has it that in the night, elves dance around in a circle, their footprints leaving glowing traces. Actually, their "footprints" are luminescent fungi. Beginning as a spore, each consecutive "fruiting" forms ever-widening rings of this strange fungal colony, sometimes expanding for several hundred meters.

Colonies of such luminescent fungi are maintained in the astronauts' living compartments on NASA space missions. Supersensitive to any escape of fuel, chlorine, or other noxious fumes, the fungi cease to luminesce when exposed to only 0.02 parts per million. When all lights are turned off for a routine

▽ *In the darkest parts of the forest, brilliantly colored fungi, such as this damp-loving* Pyrrhoglossum *species of Venezuela, thrive in positions that are unfavorable to other plants. So prolific are they that one millimeter of gill surface can produce 130,000 spores.*

check, and the fungi are not glowing their eerie green, there is an immediate investigation as to what turned them off, rather like the death of the deep miner's canary serving as an indicator of lack of oxygen or presence of dangerous gases underground. Representatives of several aerospace industries were eager to obtain samples of fungi that I had collected on my travels, and I found it pleasantly surprising and sobering to know that modern space science still relies on such primitive yet reliable technology.

Transitional fungal-animal organism

In Costa Rica, I was fortunate to observe a unique example of the potential for species diversity in tropical forests where even distinctions between plants and animals become veiled and finally disappear. A shimmering, simpering, gray translucent jellolike mass of mucus the size of a football, it was one of the most inexplicable life-forms I have ever seen. Stateside, I found that it was a fungus related to the odd and rare type that received so much media attention when it showed up on someone's lawn in Texas, and then climbed a telephone pole! It appeared transitional between plant and animal; indeed, current scientific thinking places it separate from both kingdoms. From the fungal group Myxomycetes (whose derivation means "fungus-animal"), this blob is actually a traveling mass of protoplasm. Somehow it seems a fungus like this would make an appealing pet.

Fungi are saprophytes, like bacteria. Simple nonflowering plants, they have no roots, seeds, leaves, or chlorophyll so they must use food produced by other plants and animals. They can be roughly divided into three ecological categories: decomposers, parasites, and mycorrhizal fungi. The unheralded decomposers, of course, consume and digest dead plant and animal matter and create humus for other vegetation to utilize. Were it not for these, and their cohorts the bacteria and insects, our world would be buried beneath vast accumulations of organic debris.

Parasitic fungi attack living plants and animals, and can be very destructive. Spores of these organisms are sometimes eaten by insects such as wasps and springtails. When the fungus matures, it kills the wasp and from its body emerges a macabre but delicate mushroom. Such corpses are frequently observed in the forest, frozen in their last activities as though their health was sustained until the terminal moment.

The third group, the mycorrhizal fungi, form an extremely beneficial relationship with many forest trees. They surround or penetrate the tree's roots with the threadlike mycelia which form the body of the fungus as distinguished from the aboveground mushroom which is only the temporary "fruit" responsible for producing spores to propagate the fungus. Through these microscopic threads they transfer nutrients directly to the tree.

Practical nitrogen fixers

Plants, we know, rely on nitrogen for their survival and growth. This commodity is rarely overabundant in soil, and most plants must acquire it from the sparse amounts released in soluble nitrate form by microbial decomposition of dead organisms and animal waste products. In the case of legume-producing plants (the bean and pea family, Leguminosae), a marvelous symbiosis exists between the plant's roots and *Rhizobium*, a soil bacterium. Nitrogen makes up 78 percent of our atmosphere, and *Rhizobium* has the rare talent of being able to trap this nitrogen from the air and use it to manufacture ammonium nitrates. In trade for sugar and safe housing in the root nodules of most of the Leguminosae, it passes these nitrates on directly for the plants' use in the production of protein.

The amount of nitrogen acquired ("fixed") by leguminous plants such as alfalfa, peas, and soybeans is so high that it is profitable to plow in these crops when market price is low or after the harvest has been gathered in. This, of course, releases the nitrates for use by another crop. Current research continues to establish this beneficial relationship of *Rhizobium* with other agricultural crops.

Investigation has revealed another similar mutualistic dependency. It has long been noted that certain soils including rainforest soils are alive with fungi, and it was suspected that they served some specific function. The discovery was made that at least some mycorrhizal fungi integrate with the roots of certain tropical forest trees. In some classes of this association, in exchange for sugars, they super-inject nitrogen they have gleaned from the soil directly into the trees' roots. In certain types of this association, insolubles such as phosphorous and zinc are also transferred to the trees. This is believed in part to account for the very rapid uptake of nutrients and certain minerals by tropical rainforest plants. The nutrients are delivered "door-to-door."

Pine trees did very poorly in Australia and Puerto Rico until mycorrhizal fungi from the pines' original territory was introduced into the soil, after which growth was swift. These discoveries are expected to have an even broader agricultural application for it appears that not only all lowland forest trees but almost all nongrain crops can develop this mutualistic relationship between fungi and their roots.

The scramble for light

The constant drama of the survival of the fittest is always quite overt in the rainforest. Not only animals, but plants too compete for their share of light. A small tree sapling, the diameter of a finger, will remain dormant for many years, not growing at all until a large limb or tree falls, creating a gap in the canopy overhead. Some vines are known to use this "dormant" time to grow an energy-storing tuber underground in preparation for the moment of opportunity. When this happens, just as a starter's pistol begins a race, there is a mad scramble of growth among the plants to reach the light and spread their crowns, thus closing the door to unsuccessful competitors. Natural disturbances are very much a part of the forest cycle, and the forest biomass is always prepared to heal the wounds of violent weather, landslides, or simply the termination of senile canopy trees.

△ *A nurse log sprouts what will one day develop into a puzzling arrow-straight line of mature trees. The demise of the parent tree has created a small patch of light – sufficient only for the most competitive species. The plant's red leaves may signal danger to herbivorous insects, so giving the plant just the extra competitive edge it needs. [Osa Peninsula, Costa·Rica.]*

Contrasting with the complex equilibrium and order of the climax forest, the secondary vegetation which replaces it is a riotous community in intense competition, striving for dominance from the very instant light becomes available. The pioneer trees, shrubs, herbs, and climbers differ from the climax species they replace by being light-demanding and shade-intolerant so that they are not only suppressed by shade-tolerant species of the virgin forest but often will not germinate in their own shade. This ensures that their life span on the site is but one generation, so that they quickly yield to climax species after performing their function – which is protection of the soil from erosion.

This they accomplish with remarkable abilities. Recent research unravels some of the mystery of secondary-forest succession. Artificial clearings of 1,000, 2,000, and 3,000 square meters have been made in climax tropical moist

△ A visual reminder of the constant battle for light that typifies life in the rainforest. Once they are established in the lower canopy, some trees become semi-dormant until a tree fall creates a light gap for them to exploit. [Henri Pittier National Park, Venezuela.]

forest, and whereas light gaps of up to 1,000 square meters were soon filled by regenerating climax species, the larger gaps became swamped by the aggressive pioneer (secondary) species. But from where, all at once, does this secondary species seed come, especially as these plants do not occur primarily as adults in mature forest in any numbers?

Trees grow in three ways: from shoots issuing out of roots, stumps, or fallen trunks; from established seedlings; or from seeds. You will not often find light-loving secondary species as seedlings in the dark climax forest. Climax species' seeds generally have a short germination period "window" after which they are no longer viable. It is found, however, that seeds of secondary species, opportunists that they are, can still germinate after many years. They arrive as a gradual but constant "seed rain," by both wind and animal transport. They accumulate steadily through the years and may become buried 8 inches (20 cm) below the soil surface – ready and waiting to sprout when light and temperature dictate. Such specialist species' talents hold a fascination for students of the forest, giving an order to life as we come to know it more intimately.

Further, in their function as forest healers, the pioneer species are quick to provide a protective cover over exposed soil. A wound is covered in only a few weeks' time, and in three years the trees may have attained a growth of some 40 feet (12 m). Such fast growth lends a soft and light quality to the wood, and balsa (*Ochroma* spp.), a typical secondary species of the neotropics, is

well-recognized by model enthusiasts as one of the lightest woods known. Quite commonly a secondary-forest stand is dominated by a single species, in high contrast to the diverse composition of the climax forest.

The study of forest succession is still too young to give hard figures to the time span allotted for forest disturbance, from light-gap colonization by pioneer species, through infusion of climax species and their inevitable eventual dominance over senile pioneer species, to the final return of climax forest. Certain hard facts are known, however, that lead us to believe that that period may be a lengthy one.

As the water content is too high to allow tropical wet or moist forests to burn, under natural conditions, areas of disturbance are generally restricted to sizes that allow the surrounding climax-forest species' seed to infiltrate. (We will see in the following chapter that that is not the case with vast man-made clearings.) Although the precise ages of mature climax trees are not known, due to the absence of tree rings (seasonal fluctuations being largely absent in the wet tropics), it is speculated that some at least reach 200 years and more, though certain species are thought to be far more ancient. Add to that the time period necessary for the full-climax community to out-compete secondary species and mature fully, and today a trained observer may walk through forests originally cleared by Mayans up to two thousand years ago and still distinguish them from virgin formations. It is with this enormous time scale in mind that we must plan for future development in tropical forest areas.

△ *Climbers like this present a curious paradox. It was recently found that as seedlings on the forest floor they initially seek out the heaviest shade. By adopting this unusual strategy they increase their chances of reaching a tree trunk – which will provide them a route to the higher, better-lit levels of the upper forest canopy.*

II · POLLINATION AND SEED DISPERSAL

Shelley wrote, "The forest is the perpetual work of Thy creation; finished, yet renewed forever."

As most rainforest trees are dependent on the services of animals for pollination or seed dispersal, especially the large-seeded species, the interrelationships between members of the plant and animal communities have evolved to such a finely tuned state that the functioning of the forest as an integrated and resilient system has evolved, in turn, a dependence on those very liaisons. By dissecting them we may put our finger on the pulse of the biome itself and better perceive its fragility.

The marvel of the pollination arrangement

Many plant and animal interactions and mutual dependencies are bewildering in their implications for evolution. If we investigate pollination, for example, we find that flowers exhibit very definite constructions, shapes, colors, and scents, which in various cases are linked directly to specific animal pollinators. These well-devised and time-tested plans are referred to as flowering strategies.

Bat-pollinated flowers open at dusk, when the bats are active, and have a sour odor not unlike the smell of the bat itself. The nectar is sticky, and the flower color is usually pale to improve its visibility at night. Flowers are often pendulous and are held away from the foliage by long twigs. These features facilitate bat visitation while discouraging other animals. In their search for nectar the bats pick up pollen on the fur of the head and chest, and subsequently distribute it to other flowers, thus consummating fertilization. Bird-pollinated flowers, such as hibiscus (*Hibiscus* spp.) on the other hand, are scentless, display bright colors, and have a watery nectar.

▷ *Predation ensures that species remain at peak efficiency, be they hunter or hunted. Here in a Trinidad forest, ants of the* Ectatoma *genus lie in wait to ambush the fungus gnats that will come to feed and lay their eggs on the fungi's fruiting body. This is natural selection at work.*

PLANT POLLINATION STRATEGIES

Because the survival of many plant species depends on their success in attracting efficient animal pollinators, numerous complex and intriguing strategies have evolved. In many cases, the plant and its pollinator have evolved together in a close, often exclusive, mutually beneficial partnership. So intricate and specific are these arrangements that they are among the wonders of biological science.

◁ *Hummingbird partners*
The boundless energy of the hummingbird requires a staggering intake of high-calorie nectar. The same daily activity rate would require an average man to consume 155,000 calories – the equivalent of 370 lbs (168 kg) of potatoes or 130 loaves of bread. The swordbilled hummingbird is able to refuel in flight from the long tubular flowers of the Passiflora *plant, and just as the swordbill's hugely elongated bill is matched to the shape of its food-flower, so is that of the white-tipped sicklebill to the flowers of the* Heliconia *plant.*

Swordbill (*Ensifera ensifera*) and *Passiflora*

Sicklebill (*Eutoxeres aquila*) and *Heliconia*

▽ *Darwin's moth*
Seven decades passed before the discovery of the Madagascan hawk moth, with its 8-inch (20-cm) tongue, proved the accuracy of Darwin's prediction that only such an animal could pollinate the Angraecum *orchid.*

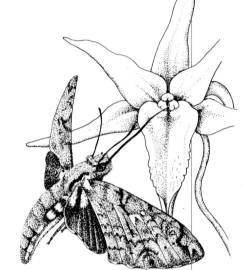

Darwin's moth (*Xanthopan morgani praedicta*) and *Angraecum sesquipedale*

▽▷ *Flies and bats*
Inquisitive observers have been known to faint from the overpowering stench of the giant arum lily, which is pollinated by carrion flies. Long-tongued night-flying bats perform the same function for the pendulous blooms of the Datura *tree.*

Gongora maculata and its euglossine bee helper

Giant arum lily *Amorphophallus titanum*

◁ *The drunken bee*
Intoxicating substances produced by the upper lip of the Gongora *orchid entice bees into the flower. Once inside, they become drunkenly unstable and fall into the lower lip, where pollen they are carrying is deposited on the plant's stigma.*

Bucket orchid (*Coryanthes* sp.) and euglossine bee

Datura sp. in flower

◁▷ *Sweet entrapment*
Both the giant Amazon water lily and the bucket orchid trap their insect pollinators. The lily opens after 24 hours to release its beetle helper, but the bee that assists the orchid must force its way out through the side door while completing its pollination task.

Giant water lily *Victoria amazonica*

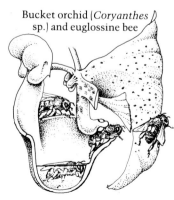

Amorous wasps and bewildered beetles

Males of certain wasp species attempt copulation with specific species of orchids, whose flowers are near-perfect mimics of female wasps of the same species. Covered with pollen after an abysmal disappointment, the male wasp moves on to another flower for another amorous encounter and, incidentally, effects pollination.

If life is full of frustrations, nature balances her cruel deceptions, in this case with a more pleasurable bout between an orchid (*Gongora maculata*) from South America and its bee pollinator. This orchid produces an intoxicating substance on the upper lip of its flower. The bee, attracted by this chemical, must crawl into the flower upside down where he becomes, frankly, quite drunk. In his stupor, he stumbles and falls bodily through the air. He is quite handily caught by the lower flower parts where he deposits the pollen he brought with him and picks up more before continuing on to his next double-martini encounter with life. Fortunately for our bee's "liver," temperance returns with the close of the orchid's flowering season. Another bee, the euglossine, has, marvelously, developed just the precise frequency in its flight-muscle vibrations to trigger the release of a burst of pollen from a flowering plant of the Melastomataceae family.

Closely related plant species even flower at different times as a precautionary adaptation against hybridization. There is much wonder and speculation about the intricacies of these arrangements.

In many of our food crops we depend on quite specific pollinators. It was once thought more profitable to grow plantations of Brazil-nut trees (*Bertholletia excelsa*) instead of harvesting the nuts from scattered trees in the forest. The planted trees grew well enough, but yielded no nuts. It was subsequently found that the insect that pollinated the Brazil nut lived in other types of trees in the natural forest.

It becomes easy to see how a great many of these species obtain exhalted positions as "keystone mutualists," integral and necessary links in the survival of species, both to those they serve directly and to those up and down the food chain as well.

On backwaters of the Amazon River grows the giant royal water lily (*Victoria amazonica*), with leaves big enough, at 5 feet (1.5 m) across, to support the weight of a human child. The lily actually imprisons its scarab-beetle pollinator (*Cyclocephala hardyi*) by closing its enormous flower after the 1-inch (2.5-cm) long beetle has moved in to feed on the flower parts. The reasons for what then takes place are not presently understood, but during the night, the flower raises its temperature an incredible 20°F (11°C) higher than the ambient air temperature. A delicious fragrance similar to a mixture of butterscotch and pineapple fills areas of this river at night. The nocturnal jungle music mixed with this overpowering aroma is truly a memorable experience . . . Exactly twenty-four hours later, the flower opens to release its captive, now covered with pollen, to seek a new flower to fertilize.

The world's largest flower

A journey through the tropical rainforest is clearly an intensely olfactory experience. The aromas, however, are not always the most pleasant: some will be the violent fragrance of decomposition itself.

In the deep tropical forests of Indonesia grows the rafflesia (*Rafflesia* spp.), the world's largest flower. It spans 38 inches (97 cm) across and, holding a special fascination for me as a carrion flower, it both resembles a rotting carcass and smells exactly like one. Not surprisingly, its pollinators are carrion flies (*Calliphora*), always the first scavengers to arrive at the scene of death. Think about the relationship . . . quite overtly this improbable species of exotica has had programmed into its genetic makeup a most bizarre characteristic, solely to ensure its existence – however precariously.

While on an expedition in 1983 to locate the rare *Rafflesia arnoldii*, my then thirteen-year-old son Gandhi and I penetrated a remote upland forest in Gunung Leuser, northern Sumatra, that had been only lightly studied by botanists in the past. The reason for such light scientific scrutiny, we soon found, was this particular forest's extremely heavy infestation with land leeches (Hirudinea). With each hour's travel within the leech forest, we acquired up to twenty-five of these parasites, some several inches in length.

The rafflesia flower we were searching for has a bud the size of a basketball, opens with the hiss of a cobra, and may take as long as two years to develop. The bud then opens to its 36-pound (16.3-kg) full-flower size, which varies within the species. In some, the central cup will hold 1.5 gallons (6 l) of water. The flower remains open for only three days, after which it quickly decomposes. Imagine our delight when we found one – among the very rarest of plants – and one of truly enormous size. To add to its natural scarcity, most of its habitats are heavily deforested. Upon returning home, it was also with considerable gratification that we discovered that this was not *R. arnoldii*

▽ *The links between plants and their pollinators and seed dispersal agents are perfectly illustrated by the parasitic rafflesia of Southeast Asia. The seed of this plant must be carried on the hoof of a large forest animal – one heavy enough to press it into the soil where it can come into contact with the vine roots or stem on which it is parasitic. The eastern limit of rafflesia coincides exactly with that of the larger West Malaysian forest mammals at the demarcation line known as Wallace's Line.*

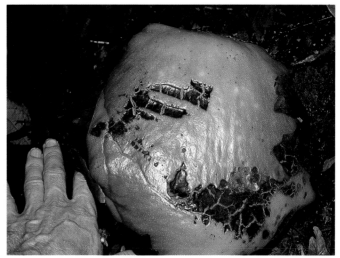

◁ △ *My son and I were awestruck by the size and scent of the new rafflesia species (*R. microbilora*) we discovered in northern Sumatra. The flower was more than 38 in (97 cm) across, and its basketball-sized bud opened with the hiss of a cobra. This perfect mimic reproduces both the pungent odor and the color of rotting meat – an irresistible enticement to the carrion flies that are its pollinators.*

after all, but a new species, and given its close approximation to the maximum size for the genus it is probably the largest of all flowers. Since named *R. microbilora*, the existence of this species had been suspected only from some inadequate fragments of petal material collected in 1911.

The flower's odor was putrid, but still utterly alluring, and it was abuzz with carrion flies. So rare is any species of *Rafflesia* that few who search for it will find it, and yet it manages its precarious pollination strategy on the apparently outrageous assumption that the same fly will seek out yet another flower, in such infrequent bloom, in the vastness of the forest.

To add to its macabre profile, the rafflesia is noted also as being one of the most complete parasites known. The entire plant lives within the root tissues of only a few specific jungle vines (*Cissus* spp.), existing entirely at the expense of the host. Only the flower shows itself to the world as this bizarre and exotic blossom thrusts itself briefly above the ground or from the stem of its host. From its center, an inexplicable incandescent fire seems to glow. We felt fortunate in finding this extraordinary flower and reflected that it was tragic that, though just discovered, it was already endangered. It was, I must say, the most extraordinary and compelling vision I have ever seen.

Darwin's orchid

So as not to be outdone by exotic pollination schemes, the Darwin orchid (*Angraecum sesquipedale*) rests its case on the unimaginable. The legendary Charles Darwin, on his travels to Madagascar, noted that the flower of this orchid was so constructed that its nectary was at the end of an extremely long tubular spur. He concluded that the only plausible pollinator would be a moth with a tongue 8 inches (20 cm) long. At that time, no such moth was known to exist. The scientific establishment guffawed at his deduction. Sixty-five years later, the Madagascan sphinx moth (*Xanthopan morgani praedicta*), which possesses just such a tongue, was discovered. There are many examples of such coevolved adaptations by flower and pollinator. They ensure that flowers are available only to certain animals, who visit these flowers, sometimes dispersed over great distances, and so ensure their pollination.

How did this plant exist before the specific pollinator developed? In mutual dependencies, did both plant and animal rely on the incredible odds of a simultaneous coevolution? Although this is doubtful, the remarkable degree of adaptation expressed by both species begs inquiry. If the explanation of a tropical rainforest is the sum of its functions, these are predominantly orchestrated under biological controls where temperate forests fall under physical control. Where far fewer trees, for example, make up the latter forest structure, wind will be an effective pollinator or seed disperser. In the tropical forest, the enormous diversity of plant life demands the attentions of species'-specific facilitators.

The forest in bloom

△ *Many rainforest plants exhibit cauliflory. Their flowers and fruits sprout direct from the stem where they are openly exposed to the animals that will pollinate and disperse them. This species,* Urera elata, *is from Costa Rica.*

For virtually every situation, we find a solution in unique adaptation. Where rarely a breeze penetrates into the rainforest understory, progeneration has been answered in some plants by a strategy called cauliflory. Instead of flowers and fruits being borne on terminating parts of branches, as we are used to in temperate climate trees, many tropical understory trees carry them right on the trunk, near the ground. This makes a strange and startling display for the jungle traveler, whether human or other animal, and this is precisely its

purpose. This strategy ensures that flowers and fruits are boldly advertised, and so prove tempting to passing animal pollinators and seed distributors. They are much too easily missed if hidden among the leaves. Many forest tree-dwelling animals are specially equipped with prehensile tails, suction cups, or digits of great dexterity so that they may ply this fruit source.

As an alternative, many upper-canopy trees shed their leaves when flowering, and so offer a magnificent bouquet that is hard to ignore. As most trees of the same species are synchronized, the spectacle from a hilltop or from an aircraft, of purple, pink, yellow, or red eruptions of color scattered over the canopy is magnificent.

To add to the already miraculous story of coadaptations, certain pollinating bees have their life cycles timed to coincide with this massive "Big Bang" type of flowering, and set out from their underground or otherwise secluded catacombs after a dormant stage just before the trees explode into bloom.

While this spectacular flowering is taking place, usually during the dry season, some plants such as certain species of lianas, whose flowers contain no nectar, solve the problem of pollination in a cleverly devised deception. They have been blessed with flowers that mimic the nectar-filled blossoms of "Big Bang" and cornucopia-style flowering trees, and they time their flowering to begin at the waning of these trees' display. By doing so, their smaller displays are pounced on eagerly by the pollinators of tree bouquets, who realize too late that the liana's flower gives no nectar reward. Yet another of life's little disappointments, but one which is more than amply balanced by the advantage to another life-form.

△ *Canopy trees in full flower provide a breath-taking sight in the highly endangered Atlantic forest of southeastern Brazil. This eye-catching display is no accident: it is a compelling invitation to the trees' pollinators.*

Continued on page 70

◁ The heliconias or "wild plantains" (Heliconia spp.) are the New World representatives of the Old World banana family. Water collects in the upturned bracts of this perennial herb, providing a watering place for birds and a breeding pool for a myriad tiny freshwater organisms. [Isla de Cano, Costa Rica.]

▽ The heliconias are among the most stunning of the rainforest flowers. This specimen, H. mutisiana from Colombia, is adorned with a newly hatched boa. It is an upland plant, which evolution has equipped with a dense hair coat to insulate it against the cool night air.

◁ Many orchids, like this Cattleya forbesii, a member of the genus from which the corsage orchid was hybridized, are epiphytes. To ensure its survival without contact with the soil, the plant possesses a pseudobulb which stores reserves of food to nourish it through periods of nutrient shortage. [Atlantic rainforest, southeastern Brazil.]

▷ In the fierce competition for space and light, few forest niches remain unoccupied. These epiphytic bromeliads (Vriesea heterostachys), and several unnamed ferns, growing on the moss-covered trunk of a tree, are nourished by the swirling mist and the organic debris raining down from above. [Atlantic rainforest, southeastern Brazil.]

An infinite talent for seed dispersal

Plant species must be sure to distribute themselves over wide areas of their range in order to ensure themselves against extinction. Growing only in localized clusters, individual species would easily fall victim to plagues of insects or other blights. Of course, many plants with featherweight seeds or gliding apparatus very adequately travel by air if they have access to regular breezes, such as occur high in the canopy. Indeed, certain fern sporangia explode when ripe, and high-level winds may carry their spores completely around the world. But what solution is built-in for the many plants with large and often ponderous seeds and seed pods? The plant's good friend and courier – the animal. Many seeds with spurs will hitch a ride on an animal's coat. Birds and bats, of course, eat fruits and later, often at great distances, disperse the seeds in their droppings.

Some plants such as the beke tree (*Irvingia* spp.) of Africa rely not on birds but on the African elephant (*Loxodonta africana*) to eat their seeds and digest away the durable outer shell to effect germination. Horses (*Equus caballos*) and, we can assume, other wild Equidae are also found to retain certain large, tough seeds in their digestive system for almost a year before passing the still viable seed. During the critical beginning then, the seed has a most nutritious and protective medium in which to grow . . . a large, moist, and warm pile of animal dung.

Many fruit-eating carnivores are attracted by a rich odor rather than color, since many of these prowlers are nocturnal. Even though basically a meat eater, the tiger (*Panthera tigris*) has a passion for durian fruit that is legendary.

Of course, fruit is tasty in order to encourage animals to consume it, the seed subsequently to be softened in the animals' digestive tract to facilitate germination, and then dispersed. There are seeds which actually require animals' digestive enzymes in order to germinate. Many such dependencies are acute, and are dramatized by noting that the ranges of some of these animal-dependent plants are abruptly marked by rivers – which also form impassible barriers for their animal partners. Such is the case for the eastern lowland gorilla (*Gorilla gorilla graueri*) and certain plants that make up its diet.

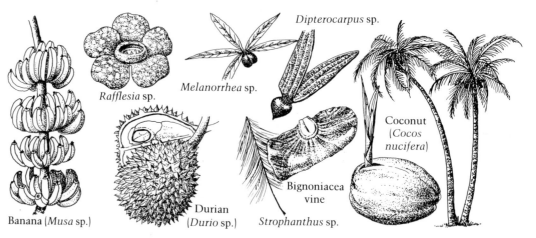

Dipterocarpus sp.

Melanorrhea sp.

Rafflesia sp.

Coconut (*Cocos nucifera*)

Banana (*Musa* sp.)

Durian (*Durio* sp.)

Strophanthus sp.

Bignoniacea vine

△ **Animal dispersal**
To encourage animals to spread their seeds, many plants have attractive fruits, or burrs which cling to the feathers or fur of passing birds and mammals.

△ **Wind dispersal**
In the high, wind-exposed canopy, a prime dispersal strategy of trees is to produce winged seeds that will be carried well clear of the parent tree's shadow.

△ **Water dispersal**
The coconut, rare in its ability to tolerate long exposure to salt water, avoids mass germination in one place by drifting far on ocean currents.

III · SPECIALISTS AND PARTNERSHIPS

The tropical rainforest, even more so than other tropical forest formations, is a surprising synthesis of harmony and competition; an overt rhythm radiating out from the sun itself, the source of the very energy that drives the biome's dynamo. Plants, the primary producers, are the basis for the food chain as they alone are able to capture the sun's energy and incorporate it into their tissues. We have seen how the faunal community is directly and craftfully enlisted by the plants as pollinators, seed dispersers, propagators, decomposers of litter, feeders, and even defenders. That the creatures who perform these services most often benefit themselves, only makes the arrangements so much more ingenious and flawless – the foundation of evolutionary adaptation.

Higher animal food-chain dynamics

By examining the behavioral patterns, methods of locomotion, and food gathering of the higher animals, we will see how their abilities are finely tuned as primary consumers in their quest for plant material, and as secondary consumers as they prey on the plant-eating species.

Animals are not allowed the dubious luxury of senility. If the law of the jungle is the survival of the fittest, the carnivore is the ruling enforcer. Just as soon as the flying lemur or colugo (*Cynocephalus variegatus*) becomes

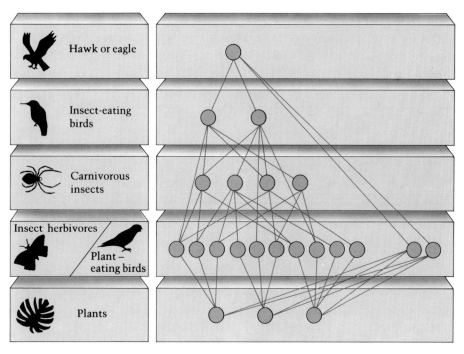

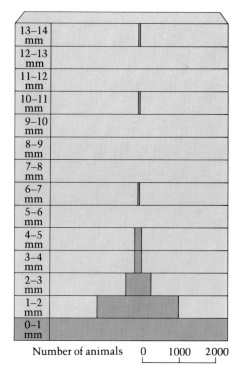

△ **The rainforest food web**
This simplified hypothetical food web pictures a habitat with three plant species, ten plant-eating insects and two seed-eating birds, four predatory insects, two insect-eating birds, and one top predator (which has no enemy but man).

It becomes abundantly clear that overall species diversity is dependent on the basic plant resource, and on the great variety of animals at the first feeding level. There can be no clearer proof of the vital role of tropical vegetation in maintaining our planet's species diversity.

Number of animals   0   1000   2000

△ **The pyramid of numbers**
In this sample of leaf-litter life, the most numerous animals are mites and springtails, all herbivores and scavengers. Carnivorous beetles and spiders are far less abundant.

enfeebled enough to drop its guard in scanning the sky as it forages in the treetops, it will be carried away by the Philippine eagle (*Pithecophaga jefferyi*), its particular nemesis. In South America the harpy eagle (*Harpia harpyja*) will similarly pursue, at 50 mph (80 kmph) through the trees, a capuchin monkey (*Cebus* spp.) caught up in a noisy squabble with his mates.

The ruling mammals at the top of the food chain are the canopy cats of medium size, such as the ocelot (*Felis pardalis*) of Latin America, the golden cat (*F. aurata*) of West Africa, and the clouded leopard (*Neofelis nebulosa*) of Southeast Asia, as well as the leopard (*Panthera pardus*) itself, which ranges across several continents. All have adapted a spotted coat to imitate the broken pattern of the sun-dappled forest background. As secondary consumers they ambush or pursue their chosen prey species, culling infirm individuals by the most natural selection, and thus serving to keep the animal population at optimum level and in good condition, a much tidier method than the alternatives, which are famine and its lethal silent partner – disease.

While many of the predators at the top of the food chain have no apparent natural enemies, they are themselves controlled in part by injuries sustained while dispatching prey, by intersexual aggression, and by territorial competition within their own species. As anyone knows who has acquired an injury in the moist tropical forest, wounds fester quickly and soon become flyblown. The predator is then exposed to the patient pathogens of bacteria, viruses, fungi, and other parasites that await us all. It is sometimes the case that incapacitated large cats, unable to run down their customary prey, will finally resort to killing and eating relatively defenseless humans.

Selective adaptation

Many prey species have themselves evolved intriguing defensive adaptations, thus ensuring that they are not merely so much hapless meat in the treetops – as indeed humankind would be without the benefit of our most highly developed attribute – intelligence. Instead, the flying lemur (*Cynocephalus variegatus*), flying dragon (*Draco volans*), flying squirrels (*Petaurista*, and others), flying or paradise tree snake (*Chrysopelea pelias*), and Wallace's flying

▽ *The fulguroid's fierce appearance convinces many in its Latin American range that it has a bite to match. Such is not the case. The species on the left (*Fulgora servillei*) flashes its eye markings to deter predators. The one on the right (*F. fanternaria*) shows the savage, toothed, but quite empty false head that earns it the name "lantern," "peanut," or "alligator" bug.*

◁ *Protective adaptation is so perfected in this "walking stick" (Pseudophasmatidae) that unless it moves it remains quite invisible against the decayed palm frond that is one of its most common habitats. [Venezuelan rainforest.]*

frog (*Rhacophorus nigropalmatus*), to name but a few, have taken to quite efficient gliding, if not true flight, by the development of expandable membranes on feet, flanks, and tails. The snake can cover 160 feet (50 m), and the lemur's flight has been measured at 443 feet (135 m) with an altitude loss of only 40 feet (12 m). Bats (Chiroptera) we know have taken this option to full fruition as the only mammal to consummate full flight. The giant fruit bat or flying fox (*Pteropus giganteus*), whose wingspan can reach 69 inches (1.75 m), can cover 155 miles (250 km) in a single evening's flight, feeding and dispersing fruit seed as it goes.

The males of many forest birds, such as the birds of paradise (Paradisaeidae), resplendent quetzal (*Pharomachrus mocinno*), cock-of-the-rock (*Rupicola rupicola*), and peacock pheasant (*Polyplectron emphanum*) display incomparably stunning plumage in their bizarre courtship rituals. While these would appear initially to have negative implications for survival value by attracting predators, such bright colors and aggressive movements often serve to signal danger and may even momentarily stun a potential attacker. (It is equally significant that the females of most species have inconspicuous brown, olive-drab, or mottled plumage. What use would bright colors be to a hen bird, tied to the nest, static and vulnerable, while incubating her eggs?)

The cassowaries (*Casuarius* spp.), standing as tall as 6 feet (1.8 m), have evolved such formidable size that most adversaries, including New Guinea tribal people, treat them with great respect, acknowledging that this giant ground bird could gut them with a flash of its massively clawed foot. The aye-aye (*Daubentonia madagascariensis*) from the island whose name it bears (and where profound evolutionary adaptations seem almost the rule) has developed an enormously long third digit on its front paw, which far from being a defensive weapon is used instead as a tool to extract grubs from decaying wood, which it listens for with its exaggeratedly large ears. A great many nocturnal animals, including the bush babies (Galagidae) and tarsiers (*Tarsius* spp.), have faces dominated by colossal eyes, quite circular in outline, which enhance their night vision immensely.

△△ *The casque-headed mantis (Choeradodis rhombicollis) is a perfect mimic of the forest orchid Epidendrum ciliare. Its camouflage is complete, even to the false fungus holes on the casque.*

Continued on page 76

◁▽ *Toucans such as Costa Rica's Swainson's toucan* (Ramphastos swainsonii) *are New World counterparts of the Old World hornbills such as the rhinoceros hornbill* (Buceros rhinoceros) *of the Sumatran forest. Both are known for their personality and inquisitiveness, often checking up on travelers in the forest.*

△ *Spectacular adult male cotingas like this Guianan cock-of-the-rock* (Rupicola rupicola) *often gather in large numbers in forest clearings to perform their elaborate courtship displays in front of audiences of drably colored females.*

▷ *Runaway evolution has given the birds of paradise the most elegant plumage in the avian world. Because the rate of predation in New Guinea is low, the dangers of sporting such extravagant plumes are minimized.* [Lesser bird of paradise (Paradisaea minor).

▷ Complex adaptations are woven into the nesting habits of caciques like the Amazonian yellow-rumped cacique (Cacicus cela). To deter nest parasites their pendulous nests are hung from slender twigs, often in trees infested with wasps. Nevertheless, they are often parasitized by the giant cowbird (Psomocolax oryzivorus), whose eggs they sometimes eject.

▽ Blue and gold macaws (Ara ararauna) are large, powerful birds whose loud and raucous screeches are a frequently heard alarm call in the forest. They range from Panama south to Argentina.

Canopy and mid-strata residents

Looking more closely at the forest's residents we see how they are adapted to their own specific strata in the forest, and then to specific niches in those strata. Through these traits we can see an infinitely efficient design in what appears at first to be reckless chaos. Even more so than the chimpanzee (*Pan troglodytes*) which will move readily from arboreal to terrestrial activities, the appearance of the Asian gibbon (*Hylobates* spp.) reveals it at once as a canopy specialist and premier seed disperser. Its gangly arms are twice as long as those of a human, compared to body length, almost reaching the ground when the animal stands upright. These long limbs and long, strong-fingered hands, facilitate the flowing, rowing, brachiating movement by which the gibbon moves through the trees, sometimes leaping 20 feet (6 m) from one tree to the next. The elegantly plumed tail of the African colobus monkey (*Colobus polykomos*) serves as a rudder and even as a parachute to control (or recoup from) its extended leaps.

In the New World forests, many primates, typified by the woolly monkeys (*Lagothrix* spp.) and spider monkeys (*Ateles* spp.) have answered the need for canopy-top stability by evolving the prehensile tail. This fifth limb also identifies the tamandua (*Tamandua tetradactyla*), kinkajou or honey bear (*Potos flavus*), and tree porcupine (*Coendou* spp.) as arboreal. Through these examples we can clearly recognize convergent evolution at work.

As large size is a limiting factor in the trees, some of these occupants, such as the dwarf anteater (*Cyclopes didactylus*) and the mouse opossums (*Marmosa* spp.), are diminutive in the extreme. The favorite nesting place of one species of the latter is in hollowed-out cocoa pods (*Theobroma cacao*).

▷ *Life in the canopy is full of dangers – rotten branches, frequent gale-force winds, and the ever-present threat of eagles, cats, and other predators. The requirements of travel include leaping from branch to branch, high above the ground, and in the New World, monkeys such as this Brazilian mariqui* (Brachyteles arachnoides) *have the benefit of a fifth limb – a prehensile tail.*

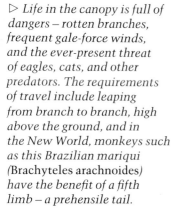

△ *The tamandua or lesser anteater (*Tamandua tetradactyla) *has a prehensile tail to aid its foraging high in the tree canopy. This one is clawing at a termite-filled branch.*

▷ *No one who has visited the Latin American rainforest could ever forget the booming calls of the howler* (Alouatta fusca) *proclaiming his territorial rights.*

Middle-canopy specialists, such as civets (Viverridae), martens (Mustelidae), and marmosets (Callithricidae), are commonly typified by sharp claws to facilitate constant vertical climbing. This stratum is not without its own drama. Of these residents, none is more otherworldly than the tree hyrax (*Dendrohyrax*). Not much larger than a rabbit, this most fiesty mammal is obtusely one of the elephant's closest relatives. Its call is a bone-chilling agonized screeching sound, mimicking hysterical human lamentations. In the Virunga Mountain range in Rwanda, at 10,000 feet (3,050 m) in the middle of the night, we were, to our horror, unable to distinguish it from the latter.

The food resources in mid level are of a particular general makeup consisting of chicks, eggs, the young and tender liana shoots and leaves, and a heavy palm flora whose buds, seeds, and fruits are particularly rich nutritionally. As one would expect, the maneuverable owls (Strigidae) and hawks (Accipitridae) patrol the mid canopy by night and day respectively.

In no way are all forest creatures rigidly relegated to a distinct strata. It is estimated that in order to match the high intensity and energy output of hummingbirds (Trochilidae), and their Old World counterparts the sun birds (Nectariniidae), in their flitting from forest floor to canopy tops in search of flowers, the average-size man would require a daily caloric intake of 155,000 calories – the equivalent of 370 pounds (168 kg) of potatoes or 130 loaves of bread. The margay (*Felis tigrina*) and the coatimundi (*Nasua* spp.), or zorro as it is known in Latin America due to its face-mask markings, ply the full range of forest levels. As a generalist, the zorro's elongated rubbery nose is particularly suited to probing into holes in search of small mammals, bird's

▽ *All forest animals live by the law of the jungle – and this animal is the enforcer. The jaguar* (Panthera onca) *rules from forest floor to canopy, and even the tribal people of the rainforest acknowledge his supreme position at the top of the food chain. [Brazilian Pantanal.]*

eggs, and the like. With a stretch of its traditional definition as a forest-floor dweller, as well as a stretch of its elongated neck and hind legs, the okapi (*Okapia johnstoni*), a deep-forest dweller and only other member of the giraffe family (Giraffinae), predominantly browses on the leaves of sapling and pole-size trees which extend into the mid-canopy levels.

Forest-floor specialists

Ground faunas fill a surprising latitude of form and function. As the soil and litter seldom desiccate in tropical rainforest proper, many life-forms in contact with this microhabitat are rarely seen elsewhere outside of strictly aquatic or cave habitats. Polychaete worms and the centipedelike *Peripatus* owe their paleontological antiquity, in part, to the extreme, steady state of forest-floor conditions.

In illuminating how no resource goes unexploited, we note that in certain forests that are inundated periodically, making them unsuitable for terrestrial termites and ants, the niche of litter disposer is filled instead by a variety of often colorful land crabs (Decapoda), whose constant scuttling is a common sight. Where insects dominate the forest floor, specialist insectivores as well as generally larger mammals, such as the giant pangolin of Africa (*Manis gigantea*), ply the resource. The pangolin's long sticky tongue is tailor-made to consume enormous amounts of ants and such (while intriguingly excluding soil and litter). Its New World counterpart is the giant armadillo (*Priodontes giganteus*). Both are heroically armored and clawed.

As one might expect, many forest-floor species are both large – the Asiatic and African elephants (Elephantidae), pygmy hippopotamus (*Choeropis liberiensis*), tapir (*Tapirus* spp.), and Javan one-horned rhino (*Rhinceros sondaicus*) being prime examples – but also adapted for amphibious life or at least aquatic performance when necessary. The key to these animals' ease in water is the trunks or semi-trunks of elephants and tapir and the nostril arrangements of the rhino and hippo. Full aquatic adaptation by mammals is seen in both the freshwater river dolphin, typified by the pink boto (*Inia geoffrensis*) of the Amazon and Orinoco basins, and the manatee (*Trichechus senegalensis*) of Africa. (The latter is another relative of the elephant, offering possible clues to its liking for aquatic habitats. On this, however, we might be cautioned by H. L. Mencken's retort that "for every complex problem there is a solution that is precise, simple, clear, and wrong.")

Many of the smaller rodents and insectivores, such as bamboo rats (Rodentia) and the foul-smelling moon rats (*Echinosorex gymnurus*), forage in the litter for edibles and new shoots and in turn provide an excellent food resource for the snakes. It is interesting that while New World forest floors are populated with large rodents, such as pacas (*Agouti paca*) and agoutis (*Dasyprocta* spp.), that niche is largely filled in the Old World by miniature ungulates typified by chevrotains (Tragulines), royal antelopes (*neotragus pygmaeus*), and barking deer or muntjac (*Muntiacus muntjak*), the last of which is equipped with prominently exposed canine teeth, probably of importance as a secondary sexual characteristic.

These, together with ground birds such as the ground hornbill (*Bucorvus leadbeateri*) and tinamous (*Tinamus* spp.), ply the forest floor to feed on the constant rain of fruits, flowers, seeds, and leaves that cascades from the canopy. More general forest-floor feeders include the Malay sun bear (*Helarctos malayanus*), Asian sloth bear (*Melursus ursinus*), and the South

△ *The bright red color of this wasp moth (*Dinia subapicalis*) proclaims an aggressiveness and a matching armory that this cunning mimic does not possess. [Mexico.]*

△ *The female ichneumon wasp lays her eggs in a host insect. Later, the larvae consume the nonvital parts first, so prolonging the life of the host. [Venezuela.]*

△ *The offspring of this large wolf spider (Lycosidae) cling to their mother's body for several weeks as they continue to feed on their yolk sacs. [High Andes of Peru].*

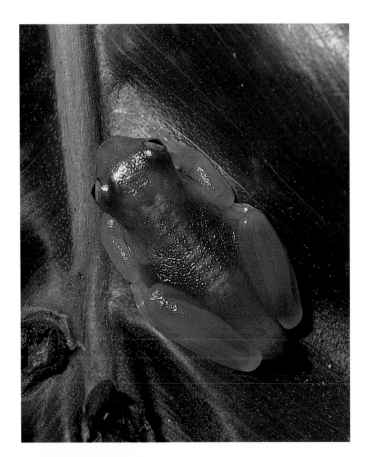

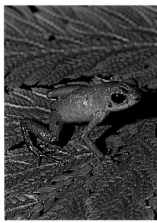

◁ *The skin of the arrow-poison frog (*Dendrobates pumilio*) contains a powerful toxin, used by forest hunters to tip their arrows and blowgun darts. [Costa Rica.]*

▽ *The rudely pugnacious Bell's frog (*Ceratophrys ornata*) is capable of taking prey as large as young rats in its damp rainforest-floor domain. [Argentina.]*

◁ *Delicately transparent green skin camouflages this Costa Rican glass frog (*Centrolenella *sp.) against the leafy backdrop of the canopy.*

▽ *Internal organs are clearly visible through the thin translucent skin of this red-eyed tree frog (*Agalychnis callidryas*).*

American spectacled bear (*Tremarctos ornatus*) – all are omnivorous opportunists not adverse to taking insects and reptiles, eggs and young, and small
mammals as they appear.

Certain mangrove-swamp specialists, typified by the scarlet ibis (*Eudoci-
mus ruber*) and the boat-billed heron (*Cochlearius cochlearius*) have bills with
obvious adaptations to the food resource of their muddy habitat. No such
understanding yet exists for the strangely exaggerated tubular nose of the
mangrove-dwelling proboscis monkey (*Nasalis larvalus*), which in the male
may exceed 3 inches (7.6 cm) in length.

People as forest animals

How then do humans (*Homo sapiens*) fit into this intricately balanced collage
of species? There is no reason to assume that archaic human cultures,
especially nomadic hunter-gatherers such as still exist to some extent in the
tropical forest biome, should be considered a disturbance of the natural order.
Even when primal cultures extend their activities to cultivation, which has
quite widely been the case at least in the past 10,000 years, natural and
regenerative rhythms appear to have dominated those processes – tribes
moving on when the return on hunting efforts fell below acceptable limits;
fauna and flora repopulating the area during healthy fallow periods. Inherently
low population numbers in the past, of course, now contrast with the current
invasion of swidden (migrant) agriculturists. Moreover, the original indigenous population produced almost exclusively for their own sustenance (save
for limited trade with other in-forest, as well as out-of-forest tribes). This, too,
is in marked contrast to modern cultivators, and to the increasing concentration of cash and export crops which have stressed the land beyond anything
resembling healthful capacities.

△ *Heliconius melpomene*
caterpillars absorb the
toxins in passion flower
*leaves (*Passiflora spp.*) and*
retain them even after
transformation into butter-
flies. This makes them highly
distasteful to predators.
Other Latin American
butterflies, many of them
nontoxic, mimic the
Heliconius *coloration and*
patterning and share in its
deterrent effect. The except-
ionally long (nine-month)
life-span of the insect is due
to feeding on pollen rich in
amino acids, and high-
protein food from members
of the melon family.

The forest offers the hunter-gatherer everything he needs. Local materials provide his blow gun, spear, and bow and arrows, while native plants such as *Strychnos* are used in preparing curare for hunting, and timbo vine (*Lonchocarpus* spp.) provides the source of rotenone, widely used for stunning fish. The forest provides building and roofing materials, serviceable string, wild cotton (*Gossypium* spp.) with which to weave clothing, pharmaceuticals, cosmetics, and more. In fact, *all* needs are met from the forest cornucopia. As food in the forest is generally scarce, the resources are never abused. In fact, one of the principle responsibilities of village headmen in Latin American forest tribes is the imposition of seasonal restrictions on such resources as *Dioscorea* for birth control, or *Euterpe* palm for its growing leaf buds, the hearts of which are eaten as a vegetable, thus culturally guaranteeing the regeneration of these natural crops.

Humans, in fact, can be seen in exactly the same context as other forest creatures as efficient dispersers of seed over the most extensive ranges. This is borne out by the fact that today's botanists have no way of identifying the source habitat of many useful cultivated species, such as betel nut palm (*Areca cathecu*) and peach palm (*Bactris gasipaes*) or even the original continent of the coconut palm (*Cocos nucifera*), which was always carried by migrating tribes, even from ancient times, and has been replanted wherever they settled.

Human physical adaptations to the hot, perhumid environment have included relatively small size (perhaps as a result of lower protein intake), and lower basal metabolic rate (BMR), both of which serve to produce less heat and to enhance the body's ability to lose heat faster. In addition, under conditions of 95 percent humidity, evaporation of moisture is impaired. As such, sweating is not an efficient means of cooling, and so human forest residents sweat less, this being immediately apparent to any wringing-wet, outside-forest person following an undaunted, comfortably dry, in-forest person on a trek. Also noticeable is an almost uniform sparcity of body hair which would provide insulation.

In addition, medical investigations have revealed that certain tribes have a degree of immunity to malaria due to high concentrations of gamma globulin (Pygmies), and sickle cells (Congo tribespeople) in the blood. The advantages of the latter far outweigh the disadvantage of the anemia it produces, at least in the forest. Once removed from the forest, however, we can only see sickle-cell anemia as problematical. This is evidenced in West African descendants, now residents of temperate countries, who still carry the anemia, even many generations removed from the forest.

Over the years I have noted, and speculated about, both the remarkably wide, splayed feet of certain Papua New Guinean tribespeople and the Amazonian deep-forest Yanomamo, and the concurrent astounding tree-climbing ability of these forest people. Without the advantage of the ankle wraps used by certain other primal tribes, these indigenes literally run up heavy-trunked vertical emergent trees to the top, then explore the limbs, quite effortlessly and fearlessly. Such plantigrade feet also have advantages in traversing the muddy forest floors typical of the rainforest habitat.

The specializations we have reviewed in forest species variously include genetic dispositions such as aversion to light, extreme heat, and low humidity; strict adherence to routine as dictated by forest rhythms; often very narrow diet options; and a psychological need for pack, herd, flock, or tribal security. In the case of forest people we might add a marked vulnerability to alcohol, and a well-developed religion centering on the forest and its components. Such prerequisites will work to enhance survival in forest conditions: ironically they also prove the undoing of the majority of species if they are removed from the insulation of the forest womb.

The partnership of honeyguide and Pygmy

Mutualistic relations exist between forest people and a number of other species. The Pygmies' caloric intake is highly dependent on their success in foraging for honey, and in that pursuit the Pygmy relies almost exclusively on the greater honeyguide (*Indicator indicator*) to direct him to a hive. Although not a manifestation of rational behavior on the part of the bird, it is even more difficult to comprehend it for what it is – instinctive habit.

UCLA anthropologist Robert Bailey, a leading authority on the Pygmy culture, followed the forest people to 72 beehives over a one-and-a-half year period. On all but three of these episodes, the honeyguide led them to the hives with its rasping, churring chatter, its white outer tail feathers flagging the men to the proper tree. This guiding will often end in success within a half hour, though it can last through a 5-mile (8-km) meander.

It was found only a few decades ago that the bird's insatiable hunger for beeswax derives from its all but unique ability to digest the substance, due to the presence of a hitherto unknown organism (*Micrococcus cerolyticus*) in its stomach. (A sixteenth-century Dominican missionary in Mozambique reported little birds entering his church and pilfering wax from altar candles.)

Once the bird leads the Pygmy to the nest, he climbs the tree with a bundle of smoking leaves to sedate the bees, and then hacks his way into the tree to emerge with baskets full of honey. The waxy remains of the hive are left for the birds as a reward. The honey badger or ratel (*Mellivora capensis*), which is assumed to be the prehuman benefactor of the honeyguide's behavior, would invariably offer the bird this same service.

It is known that the bird, with its short, ineffective beak, could not ply this resource without the aid of its willing helpers. The bird's assistance is rewarded additionally by the deep-seated protection afforded it by tribal groups. In some regions, anyone found killing a honeyguide might have their ears removed as a punishment.

The poison eaters

One riverine plant, *Dysoxylum angustifolium*, from the forests of the Far East, depends on fish, which love its fruit, to ensure its distribution. As an added reward, the seeds taint the flesh of the fish, rendering it poisonous and thus afford the fish some possible protection against predators. Of course, the fish depend on this and other fruits for their daily sustenance, closing again the cycle of interdependency.

We do know that certain plants contain obnoxious odors and tastes due to alkaloids and other substances. Certain fortunate insects, such as the bird-winged butterflies (*Troides* spp., *Ornithoptera*, and others), have overcome this repulsion and feed on the plant. They then taste and even smell like the plant, giving them protection from predators, while the plant benefits from the insect's pollination services.

In some cases, plants contain powerful poisons in the form of cyanide compounds. The foliage of the passion flower (*Passiflora* spp.) is such an

△ So unlikely is the relationship between the Pygmy and the greater honeyguide (Indicator indicator) that for many years naturalists refused to credit it. Here, a Pygmy climbs a tree to reach a wild bees' nest, having been led to it by the flitting flight and chattering calls of this remarkable bird. Smoke from a bundle of smouldering leaves will tranquilize the bees and allow him to remove the honey.

example. Nevertheless, various caterpillars and butterflies are able to eat, metabolize, and retain these poisons, thus making themselves poisonous to predators. Most of these butterflies are very vividly colored and marked. Their protective coloration is, in turn, mimicked by certain other butterflies and moths that do not carry the protective poisons.

The mimosa girdler

Essayist and medical educator Lewis Thomas is filled with awe at the teachings nature will undoubtedly reveal to us in time. He reminds us that the dimensions of human knowledge are dwarfed by the dimensions of human ignorance.

Thomas used mimosa girdler beetles (*Oncideres* spp.) as an example of pre-planned "forethought" in a creature that lacks much of a central nervous system. An amazing scenario unfolds in the life history of this simple-looking beetle. First, the female likes only *Mimosa* trees and won't bother with any other. She will climb a tree, go out on a limb, and there make a longitudinal slit in the bark using her mandibles. She then lays her eggs in the cut, which almost immediately heals over to become invisible. Now, the eggs will not hatch in live wood so she intricately sets about girdling the limb – cutting through the bark right around the limb, so causing it to die. Baby girdlers then hatch out and sally forth across the land to girdle again.

Perhaps more than coincidental is the fact that many mimosa trees are short-lived, reaching only 20 to 25 years of age. They are, however, *very* responsive to pruning, and the activities of the mimosa girdler can extend the life of this tree by 100 percent. The relationship here is symbiotic: both tree and beetle accrue profound benefits from each other, without cost to either. If only we could emulate such clean thrift in our human relations with the environment!

Having broken the girdler-mimosa code, we should now ponder *how* evolution achieved these separate acts of behavior. The tree must produce an attractant scent to lure the girdler, having somehow "perceived" or at least responded to the fact that the beetle can help it. The girdler wants only a mimosa for her offspring, who cannot survive in live wood, and the neatest way to kill the wood (but not the whole tree) is by girdling the chosen branch.

Not all trees, however, appreciate girdling and other predation by insects, and many plants have defenses to avoid this. All of us are well aware of the commercial and recreational value of rubber, but few probably realize that latex, in this case tapped from the rubber tree (*Hevea brasiliensis*), is an adaptive defense. Most insects, after boring into the bark of the tree, find a snoot-full of the sticky liquid (enriched with a natural insecticide) a repugnant, odious experience. There are no "free lunches." This goes for the rubber tree as well, which produces latex at considerable cost. When tapped commercially, the tree's growth slows considerably and it produces fewer seeds, suggesting that latex production has a high ticket price.

Vital and varied roles of the insects

Insects evolved at least 350 million years ago, and survival over this period makes them an infinitely successful group. Outweighing the population of humankind by a factor of twelve, their numbers are estimated at 10,000,000,000,000,000,000 (ten quintillion) and relatively stable due to crucially intricate natural controls.

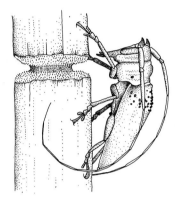
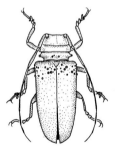

△ *A superb example of specialization: a mimosa girdler (*Oncideres sp.*) rings the bark of a small side branch, simultaneously extending the life of the tree while providing a supply of dead wood for her larvae.*

Current research reveals that the management of the tropical forest is largely the responsibility of insects and lower life-forms, as they serve as food sources or provide pollination for fruit which in turn feeds animals further up the food chain. Perhaps if we come to better appreciate the insect, we can begin to gain a perspective on the full spectrum of creation in the biome.

Dr. Donald R. Davis, chairman of the Department of Entomology at the Smithsonian Institution, states, "Within the next 25 years we may witness the extinction of more than one-half of the world's insect species, about three million, even before they have been made known to science. The vast majority represent essential keys to future pest management programs, crop pollination, soil production, and in brief, healthy ecosystems..."

Consider that although we offhandedly effect mass extinctions of many species, paradoxically humans have never, despite their best endeavors, brought about the extinction of a single agricultural pest insect or other target insect species. The insect develops resistance to our most formidable pesticides in only a minimal number of generations, and because of this the gene pool of the tropical forests performs a critically valuable service to humankind. We can imagine that a prime reason for the insects' success has been their extreme resilience in adapting to ever-changing environmental conditions.

Leaf cutters and cultivators

Leaf-cutter or parasol ants (*Atta* spp.) are fascinating creatures, frequently seen in the neotropical forests. They climb certain trees and cut out dime-sized pieces of leaves and flowers with their sharp mandibles. They then carry these fragments, some fifty times their own body weight, incredible distances to their subterranean nests, often 15 to 20 feet (4.6–6.1 m) below the surface.

To avoid stripping entire trees in their gathering, these consummate conservationists travel hundreds of meters while foraging. Travelers to American tropical cities and towns often wonder why most of the tree trunks in streets, parks, and gardens are painted with white lime. The reason, quite simply, is to deter the leaf-cutter ant.

◁ *Enter the real Tarzan. In what is probably the greatest weight-lifting feat ever recorded on film, this parasol ant (*Atta cephalotes*) carries his incredible burden with apparent ease through the forest of the Brazilian Amazon. Were a man to have the relative strength of an ant he would be able to carry 50 times his body weight – in his teeth. The ant's feat is possible because the hard plates of the exoskeleton store muscle energy like a taut bow, while the insect itself has more muscle per unit of body weight than any human.*

△▷ In a dizzying column of moving leaf fragments a colony of leaf-cutter ants (Atta sp.) carries its bounty along forest routes kept meticulously clear of debris. In their underground nests they cultivate a specific fungus as their sole food source – and will ignore other fungi such as the Caripia montagnei visible in the photograph above right. [Costa Rica.]

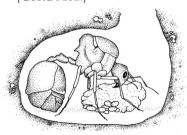

△ Having completed her nuptial flight, the new queen places a small piece of the food-source fungus in an underground chamber and manures it with fecal material. She then lays her eggs, the start of a new leaf-cutter colony.

In the forest, neat and orderly highways are constructed on the ground, cleared of leaves, litter, twigs, and other debris. These highways are alive with moving leaf fragments and the visual effect is mesmerizing.

These ants were one of the first life-forms on earth to engage in a form of agriculture. They do not eat the special leaves they have collected, but take them underground, add saliva to them by chewing, and dab the leaves with an anal secretion. This organic mulch is used to nurture the growth of certain mycelial fungi, which the ants cultivate and eat as their sole diet. They also weed their gardens of any other invasive fungi and use their body secretions to suppress bacterial growth. This is true cultivation in every sense: planting, fertilizing, weeding, pest control, and harvesting. In this mutualism, both the ant and the fungi are solely responsible for each other's survival. Oddly, the fungi appear to have lost (or perhaps never had) the ability to produce reproductive spores. They are found only under the ant's cultivation, and the *Atta* nest is their sole habitat on earth. The growth of the fungus is never left to chance. When a new queen, who reigns for some twenty years, migrates to establish a new colony, she takes with her a small pellet of fungus with which to propagate a new garden.

The web of symbiosis is yet still more intricately woven. Networks of plant and tree roots pervade the leaf-cutters' labyrinth and lend structural support to their extensive catacombs. Recent research on the fungus grown by the ants shows that it exhibits biological activity against certain plant pathogens, thus protecting the supporting trees. This discovery, needless to say, could have enormous practical application in agriculture.

As if all this were not enough, the complex plot continues to thicken. It was recently found that the leaf cutters' most serious threat comes from a small fly (*Apocephalus* spp.) related to the coffin fly. These flies hover above the laboring leaf cutters and try to lay their eggs on the backs of the ants' necks. If successful, when the larvae hatch, they eat away the ants' brains. The ants, not surprisingly, have evolved a response. A scientist working in the tropical forest of Trinidad has discovered that smaller worker ants called "minima" act as bodyguards. They hitch a ride on many of the larger "media" workers' leaf fragments. Riding upside down with their formidable pincers pointed skyward, they snipe at the treacherous flies, preventing them from parasitizing their fellow workers, who are otherwise defenseless while carrying their cumbersome burdens. (Certain aphids parasitized by wasps are now known to commit suicide by jumping to their death. Such "host suicide behavior" is attributed not to psychosis, but to the aphid's instinctive knowledge that such a sacrifice will kill the wasp's eggs as well as reducing the chance of further affliction to other aphids.)

Curious partnerships of ants and plants

Plants that share a symbiotic relationship with ants are called myrme-cophytes, from the Greek word *myrmex* which means ant. In the Indo-Malaysian rainforest, there exist certain curious epiphytes called myrmecodia (*Myrmecodia tuberosa*). They look very much like potatoes that have attached themselves to trees, but unlike most other epiphytes, they have no debris-catching facility by which to feed themselves. However, cutting one open reveals a catacomb of chambers housing ants (*Iridomyrmex myrmeco-diae*). In the center of the interior are roots on which the ants "kindly" deposit the damp humus of their feces. Without this liquid and nutrient material, the myrmecodia would certainly perish. More amazing still, it is found that these very helpful ants gather ripe seeds from the host myrmecodia tree and plant them in detritus-filled areas around the roots. If the mother myrmecodia dies or is dislodged, it may be replaced by offspring sowed by the ants – future security for both plant and ant.

The cecropia (*Cecropia* spp.) or trumpet tree of the New World tropical forests has fruits and leaves that are sought after by many and varying creatures. This quite successful species, however, has an army of protectors – the aggressive Aztec ants (*Azteca coeruleipennis, A. alfari* and others). The cecropia's hollow-noded trunk and branches, similar in structure to bamboo, serve as a fortification for the Aztec ant colonies, who bore into these chambers to establish nests and living quarters.

This tree is a gracious host, providing not only shelter, but food as well. At the base of each leaf petiole are glandular nodules called Mullerian bodies which the Aztecs feed on. Made of 50 percent glycogen, these energy-rich capsules are a drain on the plants' energy resource. In fact, the Aztec ant is a predator species and requires food of animal origin. Wonder of wonders, glycogen is generally a product of animal metabolism; the cecropia is the only plant known to produce it! The ant repays this generosity by viciously attacking anything that touches the tree. Tapping on the trunk will cause legions of ants to boil out from the interior and cover the intruder in moments. Even a vine tip blown against the tree by the wind is chewed to shreds. Other encroaching vegetation is trimmed back also, thus ensuring the cecropia's competitive advantage. The ants are so determined in their attacks that they will actually leap from trunk or leaf onto any unfortunate standing on the ground below. Their bites are treacherous. Only the sloth (Bradypodi-dae), protected by an extremely coarse hair coat, may safely climb the tree to dine on one of its favorite foods, the cecropia leaves.

It is astutely observed that where cecropias grow on Caribbean islands above 6,560 feet (2,000 m), altitudes where Aztec ants are not in attendance, the cecropias produce no Mullerian bodies. One can't help but acquire a more profound respect for the mysterious adaptive aptitudes of the lesser life-forms of plant and insect.

These remarkable ants are also expert herders of livestock, and it is the habit of the Aztec to keep mealybugs (Pseudococcinae) inside the cecropian chambers. We are all familiar with the house and garden pest that sucks the

ANT-PLANT RELATIONSHIPS

Plant evolution has produced a remarkable array of structures apparently designed for the benefit of ants. The relationship is usually mutually beneficial: the plants offer the ants food and safe lodgings, and in return the ants provide protection and nutrient-rich detritus.

△ ▷ The cecropia tree
So beneficial are Azteca *ants, here feeding on the cecropia tree's food-rich Mullerian bodies, that considerably higher than normal levels of calcium, nitrogen, and phosphorus are found in trees inhabited by these insects.*

▷ Cordia nodosa
Azteca *ants also make and defend their homes inside the swollen, soft, pithy stem tips of this common Amazonian forest bush.*

▷ Anthurium gracile
Colonies of the ant Pachycondyla goeldii *often thrive in the hollow root balls of this South American epiphyte. The ants carry detritus into galleries among the roots, so providing the plant with nutrients.*

Cecropia sp.

Acacia sp.

Cordia nodosa

Anthurium gracile

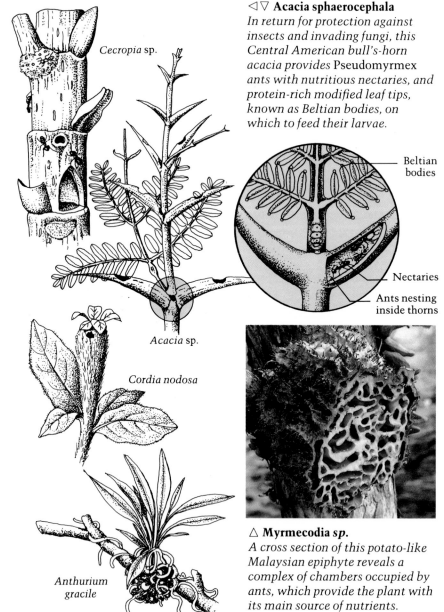

◁ ▽ Acacia sphaerocephala
In return for protection against insects and invading fungi, this Central American bull's-horn acacia provides Pseudomyrmex *ants with nutritious nectaries, and protein-rich modified leaf tips, known as Beltian bodies, on which to feed their larvae.*

Beltian bodies

Nectaries

Ants nesting inside thorns

△ Myrmecodia *sp.*
A cross section of this potato-like Malaysian epiphyte reveals a complex of chambers occupied by ants, which provide the plant with its main source of nutrients.

life-juices from our plants. The mealybugs produce a sugary nectar from this extract that is literally milked from them by the ants. In return, the otherwise vulnerable and defenseless mealy is given shelter and undying allegiance.

The soldier Aztecs will give their lives in defending the mealybug from attack. Where aphids (Aphididae) are tended in the same manner, they are referred to as "ant cows." It is evident that man was not the first to herd and tend livestock.

Other trees, such as *Barteria, Tachygalia, Triplaris,* and certain species of *Acacia* also harbor protecting ants in their hollow interiors. Each of these tree species, distributed globally, has a different and specific type of ant that services it, yet all behave alike to ensure that their hosts survive. Investigations have shown that if some of these trees are sprayed with insecticide and expunged of ants, the trees fail to flourish.

In Asia, shrewd agricultural tribes have enlisted the services of a predatory ant to protect their crops from insect damage. A network of bamboo-strip bridges connects the crops for the ants' convenience. The industrious ants patrol the entire crop and feast on the many injurious insect pests that are attracted to the succulent vegetables. No need for dangerous and costly chemicals here.

Just take the examples above involving insects, and on close inspection we will find the tropical forest's support system is actually an interwoven network of ecologically dependent relationships; plants and animals, including human beings, coexisting in a web of mutual interdependence.

Each to a place of its own

Light intensity plays a dynamic part in the life of the tropical forest, as each strata dances to its own biological rhythms according to conditions at its particular level. Fungi and other shade-demanding forms permanently occupy the dark forest floor, while the sunlit canopy is alive with flowers and light-loving species. When an orchid plant in the sun-loving category is cast to the ground by wind or monkey, its fate is sealed, and I have seen filmy ferns of the dark forest floor shrivel and die in minutes when taken outside the forest's protective shade.

The very specific niches some creatures fill give some further insight into the intricacies of the web of life. Just recently identified by scientists of the American Museum of Natural History is a new species of mosquito, *Anopheles dirus*, from Thailand. Its sole known reproductive habitat is the rain-filled footprints of the Asian elephant (*Elephas maximus*) pressed in to the soft forest floor.

Certain species become so successful in the forest that migration becomes unnecessary. It is common for the ranges of insects as well as other animals and plants to be extremely restricted. Often, a small valley or a single mountaintop holds the entire world population of a species. In 1973 the Po'o-uli (*Melamprosops phaeosoma*), a type of honeycreeper hitherto unknown to science, was discovered in the inaccessible forest clothing the north-eastern flanks of Haleakala volcano on the Hawaiian island of Maui. The bird's entire range covers less than a square mile. More recently, 50 new species of plant were discovered on a mountaintop on the Panama-Colombia border. Forests of this size can be felled in an hour with the mega-equipment in use today, making the situation grave, with a far-reaching web of implications.

Though we often build preservation campaigns around, and become quite emotional over, the possible extinction of a higher, aesthetic vertebrate such as the gorilla, it is often the disappearance of insects and animals on the lower levels of the food chain that may be responsible for the demise of several dozen dependent plant, fish, bird, and mammal species. Unlike our northern and temperate forests, made up of one or only several, very rarely up to even several dozen tree species, a representative 2.47 acres (a single hectare) of tropical rainforest near Manaus in the Brazilian Amazon, contains 235 different tree species. These and countless other plants are directly dependent on the quiet labors of insects for their survival.

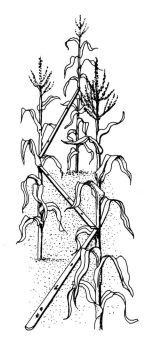

△ *Capitalizing on the predatory habits of many native ant species, certain Asian tribes link their growing maize stems with split bamboo runways to encourage the ants to help rid their crops of destructive insect pests.*

3

THREATS TO THE FOREST

*The forest is a peculiar organism of
unlimited kindness and benevolence
that makes no demands for its
sustenance and extends generously the
products of its life activity; it affords
protection to all beings, offering shade
even to the axeman who destroys it.*

BUDDHA

*From a new road development in Madagascar, a nation already
suffering severe forest loss, workmen look out across vast tracts
of land deforested to make way for agriculture.*

THE WORLD'S
DISAPPEARING FORESTS

Each minute more than 57 acres (23 hectares) of tropical forest are cut globally. Every year 46,500 square miles (120,425 square kilometers), an area the size of the kingdom of Nepal, are removed. Soon into the next century the tropical rainforest will be virtually extinct.

NEWMAN

The anomaly of the tropical rainforest has gained a life of its own. Perceived as belligerent in its levels of biological energy, and supporting an intimidating biomass, its soils, given the ample rain and heat of the clime, will – it is assumed – give forth a bounty to humans in any way they direct.

Such a fantasy is easily supported by simply observing the astonishing regrowth of secondary species that materializes in the space of two weeks if the forest is opened up by a canopy-tree windfall. After a month one needs a machete just to turn around.

So why not remove the hardwoods? Why not plant corn?

One of the major disappointments of the tropics, and the unpalatable answer to those questions, is that the forest has an Achilles' heel. The closed cycle which perpetuates its productivity is quite easily broken, and this outflow of energy cannot be harnessed sustainably by methods currently in use. (We will see later that, fortunately, technologies are available that will allow us to successfully manipulate or even mimic the primary forest without irrevocably breaking the closed cycle.)

But the myth lives on, especially so in tropical governments encouraging wholesale colonization of their "great green realms," despite the fact that their landless peasantry have virtually no access to methods of sustainable development. But we should not be too quick to criticize. It should be acknowledged here that I, and most readers of this page, would without hesitation cut standing forest and move on, repeating the process every two years, if this were the only means we had of feeding our families.

An inherent danger exists that these same areas seem to offer a font of unlimited natural resources in the form of standing wood. That this material and agricultural potential (the first of which is nonrenewable under current methods; the second of which has proved disappointingly illusionary) present highly visible exploitive temptations, may be the forest's undoing. What is the present condition of this habitat, and what are its prospects for the future?

Global Environmental Monitoring (GEM)

The United Nations Food and Agriculture Organization (FAO) in conjunction with the United Nations Environment Programme (UNEP) has completed an ambitious project involving the survey of 76 tropical countries wherein tropical forests lie. Using advanced techniques of satellite imagery and aerial photography, and an extensive network of field observations, their 1982 Tropical Forests Resources Assessment Project at last gave us a more authoritative database to replace the earlier "best-guess" figures. Yet even today, remote-sensing technology is flawed, as is data interpretation, so that even these figures may be subject to gross inaccuracies.

Globally, 2,446 million acres (almost 990 million ha) of undisturbed closed broad-leaved tropical forest remain within the boundaries of these nations – the custodians, if you will, of the earth's tropical rainforest heritage. More than half, 57 percent, lies within the boundaries of tropical America, 25 percent in tropical Asia and 18 percent in Africa. We are cautioned that given

the heroically complex task of cataloging forest losses globally, FAO's figures are not expected to be precise. For example, remote-sensing data recently revealed that India's loss is currently averaging 3.2 million acres (1.3 million ha) annually – a rate *nine times higher* than previously estimated. Brazil's 1987 deforestation of 32,000 square miles (82,874 sq km) was some *four times* FAO's projection for that time period. More alarming still, current World Bank estimates indicate that in Brazil alone almost 373,000 square miles (965,995 sq km) of Amazonian forest (an area the size of France) has already been removed – and 80 percent of this deforestation has occurred since 1980! If we include Colombia, Peru, and Ecuador, the total may well be over 50,000 square miles (129,500 sq km) *annually*, or 3.6 percent of the total region. At that rate all of Amazonia may be deforested within 28 years.

Each day no less than 82,000 acres (almost 33,200 ha) are cut worldwide; an area twice the size of Delaware vanishes monthly. This figure is used here for the sake of extreme conservatism. Working together, Compton Tucker, of NASA's Goddard Space Flight Center, and Albert Setzer, of the Brazilian Institute of Space Research, were stunned to find in 1989 that the rate of deforestation in Brazil alone – 20 million acres (8 million ha) – approached the accepted figures for rainforest lost annually around the world: 29.4 million acres (11.9 million ha). Their enlightened opinion was that this common standard is a "gross underestimate."

We recognize that four factors stand out as causes of tropical deforestation. They are international logging, migrant cultivation (these two are the prominent causes and, as we shall see, are betrothed to each other), conversion of virgin forest to cattle pasture (especially in Latin America), and the fuelwood demand (critical in the drier forest formations).

△ *The bare, ravaged landscape of Haiti provides a stark contrast to the dense forest cover of neighboring Dominican Republic. With her soil fertility washed away, Haiti – now down to bedrock in many areas – is one of the world's poorest countries and is reliant on imports for much of its food.*

I · AGRICULTURE

Regardless of the form it takes – migrant peasant cultivation, large-scale corporate farming, clandestine narcotics production, or animal husbandry related to cattle – agricultural practice in the moist and wet tropics has traditionally followed a destructive course.

As international industrial logging activities proceed they create enormous inroads into virgin forests, and further on we will investigate this impact. Aside from the direct effects of timber extraction, the wounds made in gaining access are quickly invaded by migrant agriculturists and livestock operations. The key to recognizing the cause of escalating deforestation in the moist tropics is the realization that soils and rainfall differ markedly from other regions, such as the American Midwest for example, where agriculture is easily stabilized over long periods.

The impact of "slash-and-burn"

▽ In the long-standing tra-dition of "slash-and-burn," this Cameroon woman burns the felled forest prior to planting. The infusion of nutrients will yield crops for only a few years; the soil will then be exhausted, and the family forced to move on and start again.

Typically, the entire biomass of a future farm plot in the moist tropics is felled and burned to prepare for planting. Some nutrient matter in the ash remains on the surface, and in this enriched soil the farmer sows his seeds. Torrents of rain continue to fall, but the constant rain of leaves and other nutritious debris has suddenly stopped. Without the protective layers of tree cover, the tropical downpours pelt the bare soil, and existing nutrients are flushed away into

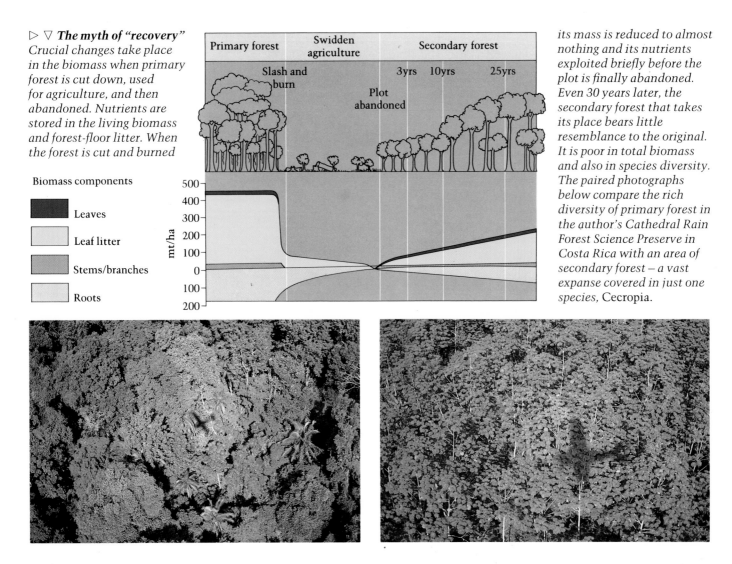

▷ ▽ **The myth of "recovery"** *Crucial changes take place in the biomass when primary forest is cut down, used for agriculture, and then abandoned. Nutrients are stored in the living biomass and forest-floor litter. When the forest is cut and burned* its mass is reduced to almost nothing and its nutrients exploited briefly before the plot is finally abandoned. Even 30 years later, the secondary forest that takes its place bears little resemblance to the original. It is poor in total biomass and also in species diversity. The paired photographs below compare the rich diversity of primary forest in the author's Cathedral Rain Forest Science Preserve in Costa Rica with an area of secondary forest – a vast expanse covered in just one species, Cecropia.

rivers and out to sea in a reckless expenditure of soil fertility. In fact, the leading "export" of most tropical-forest nations is topsoil. A farmer may harvest only two or three crops on the same plot of land before he must move on to fell more forest and begin the destructive and wasteful process over again. That these same people must continue to sustain themselves year after year is too infrequently acknowledged, yet this is the essence of tropical-deforestation issues. Where aboriginals practiced lengthy fallow periods, allowing fertility to build, today's land-hungry cultivators return too soon, recutting and degrading previously used areas, and all too often rendering the plots infertile. Increasingly, there is permanent degradation.

Soon, sheet and gully erosion of nightmarish magnitude rake the land. Studies show that in primary rainforest, even on undulating terrain, the erosion factor is almost negligible. Well under a ton of soil is lost per hectare (2.47 acres) per year. Depending on slope, an identical plot under a dense tea plantation loses 20 to 160 tons; for man-made pastureland the loss is up to 200 tons; and on 70% slopes planted with annual field crops, losses have been measured at 268 t/ha/yr and more.

It is significant that in the past, shifting cultivators lived in balance with the environment as long as the human carrying capacities of the land were not exceeded. The population density allowed fallow land sufficient time to recover – either to return to climax forest or at least to regain sufficient fertility to allow recultivation.

△ The shifting of fields instead of crops is labor intensive as well as wasteful of valuable resources. Felling, burning, planting, and harvesting can take 1,500 man-hours, and must be repeated every few years as the migrant farmer moves on. Here, an Amazonian farmer will grow manioc (Manihot sp.), a starch crop with low nutritional value.

▷ While indigenous tribal swidden agriculture had little adverse effect on the forest biomass, as in this Akawaio swidden in Guyana, the influx of vast numbers of people into the "great green realm" is now far exceeding the biome's carrying capacity.

Certainly these gentle swidden agriculturists are not wantonly or maliciously motivated. But simply by pressure of their overburgeoning numbers, 8.4 million acres (3.4 million ha) of closed tropical rainforest are felled yearly. The cut-over forests resulting from shifting cultivation in recent times cover an area equivalent to 28.5 percent of the remaining closed tropical forests of Africa, 16 percent of those of Latin America and 22.7 percent of the remaining Asian forests. As the slash-and-burn cultivators could not infiltrate the forest so effectively without the logger, their contributions to deforestation are traditionally coupled to give a total of 19.3 million acres (7.8 million ha). It is the logger, however, who opens up Pandora's box by driving his access roads deep into areas of virgin primary forest.

Often when flying over areas of forest in the remote tropics, I have seen the occasional, isolated patch of forest felled and planted, with a rustic shack built on the forest edge. I often wondered how these people penetrated into the middle of nowhere and how, if ever, they would get out. Indeed, it seems they have little need to leave at all. These are bravely independent people who still live in balance with the land, as do the infrequent Indian tribes that can be viewed living near the river's edge in thatch-roofed houses, again surrounded by virgin forest. From my aerial viewpoint they can be seen plying the river in dugout canoes, a tranquil plume of blue smoke telling of women preparing an afternoon meal.

A different sort of black smoke fills the air from the firestorms set by the hordes of unintentionally destructive migrant cultivators and, increasingly, large-scale commercial farming operations.

The grim realities of geometric progression

The agricultural population density of tropical forest areas not yet altered by agriculture is 1 person per 4.1 acres (1.7 ha). Their annual growth rate is 1.58 percent globally. Compare this density with an agricultural area in the United States. Idaho has 1 person per 82 acres (33 ha), and comparable arable land in the tropics holds 2.19 persons per hectare. When we tally the masses of shifting primary forest cultivators at 300 million (the figure rises to 800 million if we include secondary-forest areas as well) and add 160 million more comprising pastoral nomads and rural communities dependent on forest grazing and browsing, we can see this as the major socioeconomic issue of the near future. It already has achieved the dubious distinction of being the world's leading environmental concern.

There are widely varying estimates of the sustainable carrying capacity of tropical forest. From the land of the Hanunoo in Luzon, Conklin (1959) reports 48 people per square kilometer. Freeman (1955) gives us 20 to 25 people for the Iban of Sarawak, and van Buekering (1947) claims 50 people per square kilometer as the top level for swidden carrying capacity. It is worth emphasizing that population densities in tropical forest aboriginal cultures are much lower, varying from 1 (Denevan 1971) to 10 persons (De La Marca 1973) per square kilometer for Campa Indians of the Gran Pajonal Amazonia. Campa cultures today are able, without fertilizers, to sustain a two-to-three-year cycle of agriculture by providing a fifteen-year fallow period for the regeneration of at least minimal nutrient stocks. This is their first priority, irrespective of any ecological concerns they, or we, may embrace. Yet such basic environmental limitations are rarely considered in the misguided resource-development directions of our time.

Problems of haphazard colonization

The plight of the universal peasant is much the same throughout the moist tropics. His prime concern is to provide food and shelter for himself and his family, yet he faces the cruel reality of swidden agriculture – the bleak prospect that the vulnerable habitat that supports him could be reduced to a memory within his own lifetime. The greatest irony of all is that in many parts of the tropics, millions of landless peasants are being directed into rapidly dwindling forest areas by government resettlement programs.

The government of Indonesia, for example, has for several years maintained a zealous colonization scheme attempting to relocate millions of peasants from the overcrowded island of Java to the virgin wilderness of Irian Jaya (the western half of the island of New Guinea) and other outer islands. Such an ambitious undertaking will, invariably, lead not only to the destruction of much of the island's natural habitat, but to the decimation, as well, of some of the most primal aboriginal tribes remaining on earth, through dislocation from their tribal lands and from plagues of disease introduced by the immigrants.

In addition, colonizers typically fall victim to malaria and other lethal diseases for which they are ill-prepared in terms of natural defenses, prophylaxis, or medication. As any benefits to the colonizers will be temporary at best, the trade-offs to the loss of 8.15 million acres (3.3 million ha) over the next five years (on top of the millions of hectares that have already been lost) seem clearly unwarranted.

Several distinctive factors turn up here that are common to many resettlement programs.

1. Java, although extremely fertile, is severely overpopulated, with as many as 5,000 people living on 1 square mile (2.6 sq km).

2. Almost 45 percent of the people who reside in the countryside have no land at all; another 35 percent have insufficient land to produce enough food to support their families.

3. A glaring reason for this predicament is unfair land distribution. One-third of the land on Java is in the hands of 1 percent of the landowners.

4. Many of the new colonists have few farming skills. A 1976 study showed that up to 45 percent of the transmigrants had never grown rice, the staple crop of Indonesia.

The question is not one of whether to employ these people or have them sit idly by, but of *where* to direct them so that they may sustain their lives, and of *how* to prepare them for a measure of success, while at the same time adhering to principles that will prevent the environment from spiraling into irreversible degradation.

Toward that end, a report was issued by the Indonesian government itself at the end of 1986, identifying transmigration as the single largest threat to the nation's forest resources, since 80 percent of the proposed resettlement was directed into pristine rainforests.

As a result of this, and mounting pressure on the World Bank (the major source of funds for transmigration), World Bank's president, Barber Conable stated that both the World Bank and the Indonesian government have decided to scale down the scope of the transmigration by 60 percent. This decision, if put into practice, will reduce the impact of the scheme considerably. Subsequent government budgets have made no allocations of money to further forest clearance for settlement.

The exploitation of Brazilian Amazonia

In December 1966, at the invitation of Brazil's President General Castello Branco, 300 of the most powerful Brazilian tycoons, real estate speculators, and beef barons, boarded the *Rosa de Fonseca*, a luxury cruise ship anchored off the Amazonian city of Manaus. Two years earlier, Branco had proclaimed, "Amazonian occupation will proceed as though we are waging a strategically conducted war." "Operation Amazonia" had been launched.

President Getulio Vargas, during the 1930s, was the first proponent of large-scale Amazonian development. Drawing on his schemes, Branco's chief theorist and point man, General Golbery Couto e Silva, is today the man most responsible for the policies and programs that have evolved in Brazil's Amazonia. Golbery referred to Brazil's "Manifest Destiny" in occupying "the vast hinterlands waiting and hoping to be roused to life." Golbery's central ambition of "inundating the Amazon forest with civilization" would, he surmised, provide a disgruntled population with a nationalistic goal, while "the march west" would people this great green realm with settlers, thereby creating a presence on Amazonia's vast and occasionally contested frontiers.

Through the filter of their own dreams, the entrepreneurs aboard the *Rosa de Fonseca* watched the forest slip by while the general laid out an offer few on board could refuse: tax holidays of 100 percent and for up to 17 years; loans providing subsidized credit at negative interest rates; and land grants of one million acres (404,700 ha), capped off with the promise of roads, airports and hydroelectric projects (the latest, the Xingu Project, will displace a tenth of the Brazilian native population and a quarter million peasants, while the dam will produce relatively small amounts of energy).

What finally evolved was a land rush, which became a handy hedge for investment portfolios against an inflation rate currently at 600 percent. To establish ownership, land was cleared and cattle often unceremoniously dumped on it. Under the fever of the land grab, unprecedented in history, it no longer seemed to matter that others, be it *peones* or indigenous tribes, were there first. For the financiers, the ready remedy to prior occupancy and ownership was the hiring of gangs of *pistoleiros*. Hired for "cleaning or service" by the absentee industrialists, the gunmen insulted, provoked and generally harassed peasants, clergy and organizers alike without discrimination. When these tactics failed to drive the stubborn off their land, the victims were tortured, or murdered. Statistics compiled by the Catholic Church show that over 1,000 innocents had been killed by the gunmen between 1985 and 1989, and this accounts for only three percent of the total estimated incidents. That Chico Mendes, the now-legendary union organizer and martyr to Amazonian deforestation, was only one of that multitude in some way brings home the enormity of the tragedy which continues today.

Yet the ranches created on board the *Rosa de Fonseca* are total failures. One in three of the government-subsidized mega-ranches has since been abandoned, and almost fifty percent have never sold a cow. Despite this, however, given the huge government subsidies, they have all turned handsome profits for the magnates. The real winners in this vast development project are the powerful and influential construction companies and government bureaucracies, the recipients of international lending institution loans.

Today, the tribal groups, backwoods settlers, and rubber tappers have become high-profile allies in an effort to direct protective legislation through the difficult channels of political Brasilia – a terribly steep uphill task, given that those halls are the exclusive domain of entrepreneural club members. In unprecedented cooperation, distant tribes of Kayapo, Yąnomamö, and scores of others, have joined in a solidarity front against the theft of their lands.

It is clear that far more than a demand for fast-food hamburgers has been at work in Amazonia. The voices of the international anthropological community, rights movements, and many others, are now increasingly heard in the outcry against this economically and politically motivated outrage.

The Transamazon Highway

We have come to realize that a road cut through the forest has far more grave implications than the mere removal of a transect of trees. Not only does the artery infuse the region with misdirected agriculturists, breaching the region's integrity, but it is also found that many species will not cross open clearings, resulting in fragmentation and isolation of animal populations.

▷ *Brazilian writer Euclides da Cunha's perception of Amazonia is of a last vestige of Eden, "The last unwritten page of Genesis." That page is now being set in type. The Transamazon Highway is now seen as a vein infusing ill-equipped and unprepared farmers into a hostile hinterland of unproductive soil, and bringing out the broken results — humbled, often malarial families, leaving behind them the wreckage of failed farms.*

Back at its inception, the Transamazon Highway was envisioned as "the solution for 2001." It was not to be. Even if all of Brazil's legal Amazonia were designated as 100-ha (250-acre) parcels, as was the standard lot size along the highway, the entire region would be filled by only 5 million families, or 25 million people. This represents only eight years of Brazil's population growth from 1980 figures of 119 million at a rate of 2.4 percent per year. Although 25 million people are surely significant, this is not "the solution for 2001."

Given that only 4 percent of Amazon soils are fertile, and that only 7 percent of settlers prove successful, the highway is seen by many as a poison vein, bringing in the hopeful destitutes and carting out, for the large part, the same people with broken dreams and bodies. A 12-mile (20-km) wide area of forest all along the new highway has been designated for agricultural development, although the predicted numbers of settlers have not arrived due to the widespread crop failures and severe disease suffered by the original migrants into the area. Settlement names such as Tingo Maria, Jaci Parana, Belo Horizonte, Boa Vista, Vale do Xingu, then a new town named Super Mama (Super Mama?), belie the hardships of life awaiting the new settlers.

The chaotic infusion of settlers into the state of Rondonia by the road BR-364, where paving was funded by the World Bank, saw such lawlessness that in the town of Rolim de Moura in one month of 1984 there were more than thirty deaths by gunshot. In such areas, it is not uncommon for corpses to be left casually bloating in the sun for days! In addition, there are 200,000 Rondonia children who cannot go to school as such facilities are virtually non-existent. The coffee and cacao cash crops, which were to make all this tolerable, were largely decimated by leaf rust and witch's broom.

We now have the benefit of hindsight in evaluating the transamazon colonization which began in 1970. In all, only 7,389 families were established in three model colonies in the following seven years, instead of the goal of 100,000 families expected there by 1974. Low-crop productivity due to low-soil fertility was specifically cited as the principal reason for failure. Typically, a farmer will plant 20 acres (8 ha) of rice annually. Sales of the crop gross only $1,900, considered meager given the high cost of manufactured goods and the necessary wages paid for labor. We shall see that alternatives to haphazard colonization do, in fact, exist, but for the present the world's peasantry, by following the path of least resistance, are relegated to the destructive process of slashing and burning themselves into their own future oblivion.

The cocaine connection

Oddly, the contribution of the illicit drugs trade toward tropical deforestation has in past years largely escaped analysis. However, recent findings by NASA, based on aerial photography, show highly visible coca (*Erythroxylum coca*) growing on an extensive scale in Colombia. Removal of forest to make way for this crop, which is predominantly for cocaine paste, followed by processing to cocaine powder for export to the United States and Europe, is shown to have already seriously silted many of Colombia's bays. "Cocaine has overtaken coffee as Colombia's main export," reports editor Enrique Santos of *El Tiempo*, Colombia's largest newspaper. Coffee, a $1.5-billion export business in 1988, was greatly overshadowed by cocaine's $4-billion turnover in that same year. An estimated 670,000 acres (271,150 ha) of the Peruvian Huallaga Valley alone are under its cultivation. Marc Dourojeanni at the World Bank's

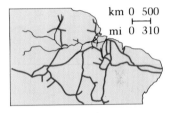

km 0 500
mi 0 310

——— Major highways

△ *The tragic effects of the development of new roads through the virgin forests of Amazonia are dislocation of the indigenous people, and a reduction of the forest itself that already exceeds 15%.*

△ Largely unrecognized, deforestation is another of cocaine's devastating effects, now accelerating as producers attempt to keep up with the demands of the "crack" epidemic. Here, farmers harvest the coca leaves (Erythroxylum coca), destined for clandestine laboratories deep in the forest ◁ where they are converted into the deadly white powder.

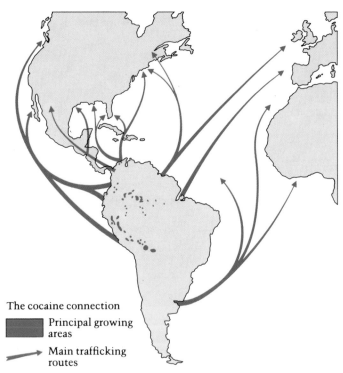

The cocaine connection

▮ Principal growing areas

↗ Main trafficking routes

△ The narcotrafficantes' deadly cargo crosses the globe on wings of money and murder. In a system called "plata o plomo" – "silver or lead" – over 200 judges and supreme court officers, and one presidential candidate, have been ruthlessly assassinated for refusing the bribes of the all-powerful drug cartels.

△ On the filter lies the partly processed coca extract. Below, and in drums behind, are the processing chemicals – noxious, highly caustic compounds which will be dumped after use in the nearest stream, often poisoning the water for many miles downstream.

Latin American Environmental Division, claims that in Peru no crop other than coffee (Coffea arabica) is planted so extensively. Such farms, he maintains, along with exhausted lands abandoned by the growers, areas used by peasants who have fled regions dominated by narcotics traffickers and terrorists, land used by coca growers fleeing police repression, and areas deforested for clandestine landing strips, camps, and laboratories, are collectively the direct or indirect cause of approximately 1.8 million acres (728,460 ha) of deforestation in the Peruvian Amazon and on the eastern Andean slopes. That accounts for fully 10 percent of total rainforest destruction in Peru this century – yet skyrocketing demand for cocaine has been a reality for only a single decade! We need only extrapolate to the rest of the Andean-Amazonian countries to see that the impact is already tragically high – and it is growing at a rate of 10 percent annually.

Beyond the overt effects of deforestation are the insidious consequences to river systems of the dumping of the caustic chemicals associated with cocaine processing. Buenaventura Marcelo of the National Agrarian University in Lima, states the estimated annual volumes of those toxic wastes are "15 million gallons (57 million l) of kerosene, 4 million gallons (15 million l) of sulfuric acid, 16,000 metric tons of lime, 3,200 metric tons of carbide, 1.7 million gallons (6.4 million l) of acetone, 1.7 million gallons (6.4 million l) of toluene and 16,000 metric tons of toilet paper (used for straining)." When cocaine paste is transformed into cocaine hydrochloride, the white powder export familiar to users, ethyl ether and concentrated hydrochloric acid are employed, and these are evacuated into rivers as well, generally in clandestine labs in Colombian and Brazilian Amazonia.

According to recent reports (1989), more than 150 of Peru's streams and rivers are polluted beyond standards established by the World Health Organization, and the effects on plants, fish, and other wildlife in those habitats are, in many cases, severe.

This growing problem has few easy answers. With an enormous market demand on one end, and between $700 million and $1.6 billion in drug profits accruing to the Peruvian economy annually – a sum equal to 30 percent of the country's legal exports – gargantuan incentives are at play. In Colombia, such incentives have produced audacious armed attacks by drug cartel terrorists on the judicial branch of government. Users of the drug could well consider the effects of its use abroad, although we can assume few will be so inclined.

△ *Peruvian troops of a Special Forces faction of the National Guard set off on patrol during "Operation Lightning" in July 1987. The aim of this offensive was to regain control of the Alto Huallaga upland coca-growing areas from drug traffickers and guerrilla groups such as the Sendero Luminoso and the MRTA. US financial support and training aided the operation.*

The cattle connection

An increasing demand in the United States and other developed nations for inexpensive beef for human convenience foods and pet food has had a direct effect on tropical forests by resulting in their conversion to short-life pastures. Thus far a more popular concept in Latin America than elsewhere in the humid tropics, the forest is clear-cut and seeded with aggressive grasses. This would seem innocuous enough, even a logical and productive use of land. After all, the North American West is legendary for its cattle production. The differences between tropical and temperate soils and climates are, however, dramatic. Moderate rainfall and reasonably stable soil fertility in the American West and many other states allow for sustained pastures. The thin, fragile soil and torrential rainfall of tropical-forest areas place them at the

Continued on page 106

THE BIGGEST FIRE LIT BY MAN

An environmental holocaust is currently sweeping the equatorial regions, brutally illustrated by the burning of Amazonia. Described by United States senators as "one of the great tragedies of history," images like the one below have finally awakened the world to the blight of deforestation.

◁▷ *Rondonia*
Over western Brazil the skies are darkened day and night. During the dry season, the forest is put to the torch to make way for unsustainable farming and cattle raising. In the large map opposite, exploitation can be seen spreading out at either side of highway BR-364, laying waste the forest and opening up areas that were formerly sacrosanct Indian tribal lands.

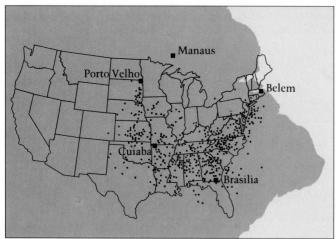

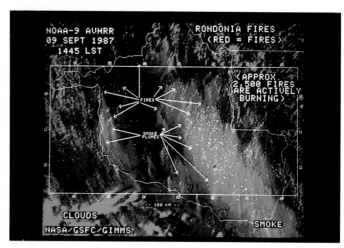

△ **The scale of the burning in Brazil**
The horrifying extent of the assault on Brazil's forests can be seen when the affected area is super-imposed on a map of the United States. The area suffering the brunt of the attack is roughly half that of the entire continental US, and the destruction shows no sign of abating in the forseeable future. In 1988 alone, an estimated 12,350 sq mi (32,000 sq km), an area larger than Belgium, was burned.

△ **Satellite view of the state of Rondonia**
The epicenter of Brazil's firestorm is the Amazon state of Rondonia. In this NASA satellite image some 2,500 separate fires are actively burning and many more are in other stages. At times the smoke was so thick that the airport at the state capital was forced to close, often for days at a time. NASA scientists have also noted "indications that cloud formation may be suppressed in areas where smoke is present."

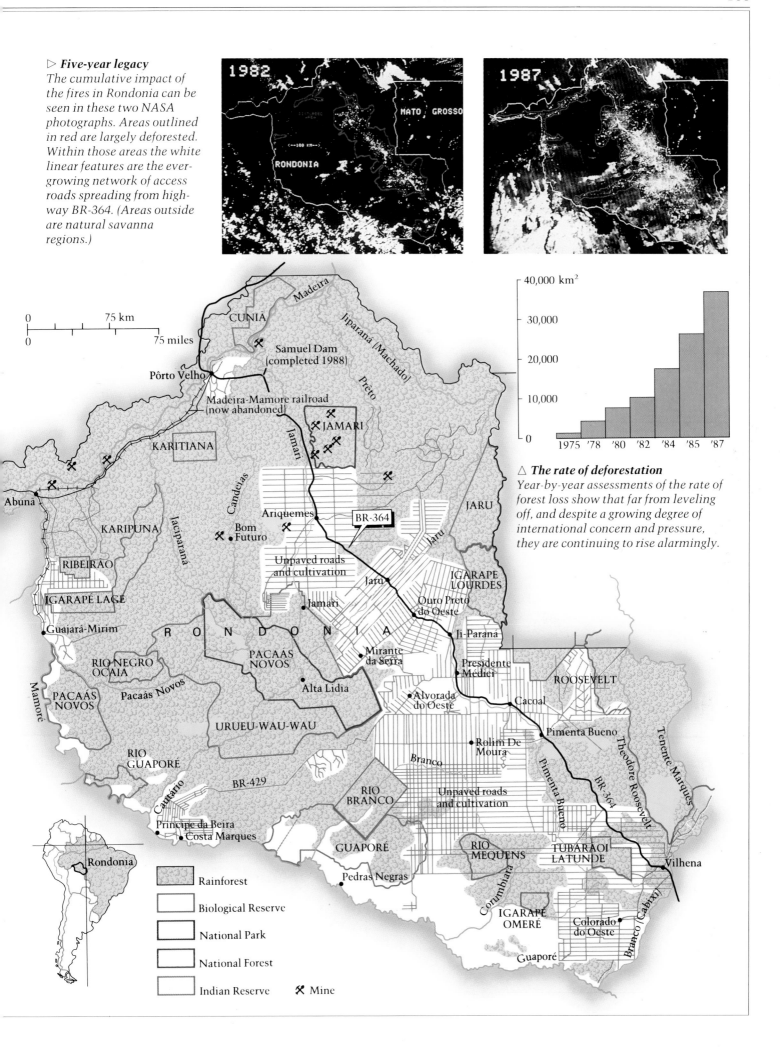

▷ **Five-year legacy**
The cumulative impact of
the fires in Rondonia can be
seen in these two NASA
photographs. Areas outlined
in red are largely deforested.
Within those areas the white
linear features are the ever-
growing network of access
roads spreading from highway BR-364. (Areas outside
are natural savanna
regions.)

1982

1987

MATO GROSSO

RONDONIA

△ **The rate of deforestation**
Year-by-year assessments of the rate of
forest loss show that far from leveling
off, and despite a growing degree of
international concern and pressure,
they are continuing to rise alarmingly.

40,000 km²

30,000

20,000

10,000

0

1975   '78   '80   '82   '84   '85   '87

0   75 km

0   75 miles

Madeira

CUNIA

Jiparaná (Machado)

Samuel Dam
(completed 1988)

Preto

Pôrto Velho

Madeira-Mamoré railroad
(now abandoned)

Jamari

JAMARI

KARITIANA

Candeias

JARU

Abunã

Jaru

BR-364

Ariquemes

KARIPUNA

Jaciparaná

Bom
Futuro

IGARAPE
LOURDES

Unpaved roads
and cultivation

Jaru

Ouro Preto
do Oeste

RIBEIRÃO

Jamari

IGARAPÉ LAGE

R   O   N   D   O   N   I   A

Ji-Paraná

Guajará-Mirim

Mirante
da Serra

Presidente
Médici

ROOSEVELT

RIO NEGRO
OCAIA

PACAÁS
NOVOS

Mamoré

PACAÁS
NOVOS

Pacaás Novos

Alta Lidia

Alvorada
do Oeste

Cacoal

Pimenta Bueno

Theodore Roosevelt

Tenente Marques

URUEU-WAU-WAU

Rolim De
Moura

Pimenta Bueno

RIO
GUAPORÉ

Branco

BR-429

Pimenta Bueno

BR-364

Cautário

RIO
BRANCO

Unpaved roads
and cultivation

Príncipe da Beira

Costa Marques

GUAPORÉ

RIO
MEQUENS

TUBARAOI
LATUNDE

Vilhena

Pedras Negras

Corumbiara

Branco (Cabixi)

Rondonia

IGARAPE
OMERÉ

Colorado
do Oeste

Guaporé

Rainforest

Biological Reserve

National Park

National Forest

Indian Reserve   ✗ Mine

The hamburger equation
Recent research into the real costs of converting Amazon rainforest into cattle pasture has produced some staggering statistics.

Assuming that cattle put on weight at 50kg/ha/year and that they are killed after 8 years, yielding 50% of their total body weight in meat, then each animal will produce 200kg of meat – or roughly 1,600 quarter-pound hamburgers. If one hectare of forest represents 800 tons of biomass, then the environmental cost is half a ton of rainforest per hamburger.

Expressed as forest area, the cost is 67 square feet – more than 6.25 square meters of forest – for every hamburger sold. Consider this against millions of years of forest evolution, and thousands of species now facing the threat of extinction.

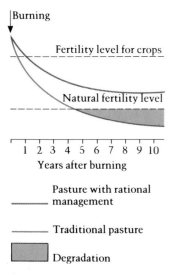

△ Following forest clearance and burning, peak fertility levels plummet. Five years on, pastures are marginal, soon to be abandoned.

opposite end of the spectrum. Tropical pastures have a short life and new areas must be constantly encroached on. This continuing process results in a rate of deforestation third in direct impact after logging and shifting cultivation.

An increasingly large proportion of these commercial enterprises are owned by corporations outside the countries with tropical forests. One of the largest of such holdings included a 540-square-mile (1,400-sq-km) concession in eastern Amazonia, and when this tract of forest was put to the torch it produced the largest single fire ever deliberately created by people!

Extensive industrial logging of Borneo's forests in 1983 left an abundance of debris lying during the dry season of a crucially dry year in which the rainy season was virtually absent. Tropical moist forests, which as a rule are too wet to support a forest fire, can become tinderboxes in such conditions. A fire in the debris area, most probably set by migrant cultivators, went on under these "El Niño" conditions to burn 3 million acres (1.2 million ha) of forest.

Cattle ranching was the cause of 72 percent of Brazil's deforestation up to 1980, and is now the major cause of forest clearance in Costa Rica and many Amazon countries. Road construction is a necessary ingredient of developmental projects of this scale, and is highly destructive in its own right. From 1966 to 1975 this construction accounted for 27 percent of Brazil's deforestation. By 1971, international lending institutions had contributed $3.5 billion toward road and infrastructure development. Further, the World Bank, the United States Agency for International Development (USAID), and other development agencies have provided some $4 billion for beef-production expansion. The journal *Cultural Survival Quarterly* estimates that "at least two-thirds of Central America's arable land is now devoted to cattle production."

Beef is produced almost exclusively for export in these countries, and surprisingly little is consumed domestically. Local consumption is commonly limited to less desirable parts such as the viscera. The average Brazilian, for example, consumes a mere 35 pounds (16 kg) of beef annually; less meat than a domestic cat is pampered on in the United States. Fed on coarse, nutrient-poor grasses, the cattle yield low-quality beef, and it is not surprising that fast-food chains in the United States are the largest importers. One of the most ludicrous aspects of this trade is that some 67 square feet (6.25 sq m) of forest are sacrificed for each standard quarter-pound hamburger. That area of forest would contain roughly 800,000 pounds (362,900 kg) of plant and animal material – much of it comprising species as yet unknown to science.

There are convoluted reasons why conversion of tropical forest to cattle pasture is so ultimately destructive. By its very nature, cattle raising comes with built-in inequities that compute poorly into the lower-economic sector. Such industry promotes the concentration of large landholdings in relatively few hands, and this results in small farmers being displaced from their land, and thus to unemployment and social stratification. The principal factors at play are: the very small labor force employed in cattle production; the large capital and land requirements, which result in consolidation of holdings and eviction of renters and smallholders; and the inability of small landholders to compete in the purchase of land, equipment, and expensive fuels or to obtain capital and credit.

Such dynamics drive the landless in large migrations to urban areas, where they contribute to escalating unemployment, or to new wilderness areas where they contribute to deforestation. And, as production of beef for export

replaces production of staple food crops, protein deficiencies appear in the landless and food imports very soon become necessary.

In the process of deforestation for cattle pasture, the area is often not logged commercially. The rule seems to be, "The less bother the better." Herbicide is applied, and the area is then torched. As a result, 50 cubic meters (1,766 cu ft) of timber per hectare, worth $35 per cubic meter, is flagrantly wasted on 25,500 square miles (66,040 sq km) of virgin tropical forest. The loss to date amounts to over $7.7 billion, an incredible two-and-a-half times Amazonia's total yearly timber sales.

To compound this extravagance, cattle production is the least productive use of the land and the worst environmental alternative in the wet tropics. Stocking rates are surprisingly low at only one animal per hectare. Fertility, and thus profit, often wears out after only three to five years. The soil is commonly trampled to compaction, overgrazed, oxidized, and sun-baked, and toxic weeds move into the pasture and compete more successfully than the grasses, especially as they are not grazed away by livestock. Fertilizer has not been a cost-effective solution. Finally, it takes a full four years before steers are ready for slaughter weighing a scant 992 pounds (450 kg), and the severe epizootic problem is a constant harassment and constraint on productivity: this, after all, is the land of the parasite.

Why invest with such discouraging odds?

Cattle production remains profitable because Latin American countries wish to "open up," and expand their "influence" on, their outer territories. To this end highly attractive financial incentives are offered to investors, which encourages wasteful operational procedures. In Brazil, these include up to 72

△ Land barons in Brazil clear immense tracts of land and then introduce cattle primarily to establish their presence there. Most ranches never sell a cow, but make their profit through inflated land prices. In Brazil, cattle ranching accounts for 30% of all deforestation, and nearly half of this is promoted by government subsidy. There are many who argue that such financial resources should be directed instead at the reclamation of degraded land and development of sustainable agriculture.

percent of the project's costs, and 50 percent of the tax liabilities of the company. While investors have earned up to 250 percent profit on their investments, it is found that the government's real out-of-pocket costs ($1.4 billion) and its loss of tax revenues bring the total fiscal losses to $2.9 billion, "... more money than it would have taken for the government to have just established the ranches itself," reports Robert Repetto of the World Resources Institute. Brazil's agricultural incentives are, in fact, considered by many economists to be one of the leading factors in the country's runaway inflation.

It is precisely these tax breaks and subsidies that have allowed speculators in cattle and farming to profit even as the operations lose money. Roberto Alusio Paranhos do Rio Branco, president of the Business Association of the Amazon, states that nobody would farm Rondonia, now the focus of exploitation, without government incentives and price supports for cocoa and other crops. Yet since 1980, Rondonia's forest cover has dropped from 97 percent to 76 percent, and it is still falling rapidly. As early as 1983, Brazil, recognizing the ecological and economical deficits involved in cattle operations, declared an end to tax benefits for the creation of cattle pastures. Cattle politics, however, caused a reversal of that declaration. Again in 1988, Brazilian government decrees removed the cattle benefits – yet to date they are still a reality.

However, not all the news is bad. In 1987, highly successful broad-based grassroots environmental movements in the United States, coordinated by the Rainforest Action Network, have convinced Burger King (one of the major fast-food importers of Latin American beef) to cease the practice, favorably impacting deforestation at least in Central America. Burger King is to be commended for its leadership in adjusting its operations toward conscionable business practices.

The economics of hunger

Some illuminating facts on world hunger: 450 million people currently suffer from malnutrition, that is one out of every ten people on earth; 12,000 die every day of starvation. Many claim that the major cause of hunger is not food shortage, but rigid artificial economic structures that make food unaffordable to the poor. This includes surpluses that are deliberately left to spoil to keep produce prices up and peasant salaries down. Grain production in India has tripled over the past thirty years, and supplies are available. While the situation has improved greatly since the early 1960s, starvation *en masse* continues. Current food stores would feed every person on earth twice over, but they remain out of reach artificially. Fifty percent of United States food imports come from the Third World, the reservoir of hunger and misery. Such systems, introduced largely by multinational corporations and bolstered by foreign aid, have ensured that small farmers and field workers in Third World nations raise luxury crops expressly for export while their families go hungry. When drought threatens cocoa or crops, they can produce neither food nor income to sustain a family until next season's food harvest becomes marketable.

While it is difficult to ignore these imbalances, and they beg every effort toward correction, many have grave concerns that a simplistic shift of blame for ever-growing starvation onto the political and economic sector avoids facing head-on the human tragedy of unbridled population expansion which is rapidly accelerating beyond the visible means to sustain those lives.

II · INTERNATIONAL LOGGING

What is the place of human beings in the tropical forest biome? Are we inside or out? Are we intruders in the blissful rainforests or are we to consider ourselves part of this vast system? These questions cut to the quick of conservation in the wet and moist tropics. There are no ready black-and-white responses. Yet a moderate shade of gray is emerging out of the hard conglomerate of valiant ecological values on the one hand and fluid monetary incentives created by pressing raw-material demands on the other.

The consequences of logging operations

Tropical timber extraction by international companies obviously has a major impact on the viability of the remaining areas of rainforest. But unfortunately the impact does not stop there. As soon as the loggers leave, slash-and-burn cultivators move into areas of forest opened up by the logging roads. It is important that we realize just how closely the swidden agriculturists are wedded to the logging industry. Without the ingress of logging roads into new forest areas, migrant cultivation would be much reduced, possibly resulting in a more rational, intensified use of the original farm plot. For every 177 cubic feet (5 cu m) of logs removed by exploiters of timber, 2.47 acres (1 ha) are cut and torched by the follow-on cultivators; the implications are not evidenced by a subtly smoking gun, but by a 21-gun salute!

Although hard realities demand a clear differentiation between tropical and temperate exploitive strategies, extractive methods remain dictated by the price tag of each cubic meter of wood. For example, the dipterocarps, a most sought-after Asian forest family, which includes "Philippine mahogany," are currently being exploited to extinction. Temperate trees produce seed yearly, but many tropical species flower and produce seeds infrequently, some only once in thirty-five years. To ignore reproduction cycles in the planning of cutting schedules is to ensure the demise of these and other tree species within a span of only a relatively few years.

Certain species are very sparsely populated. *Aglaodorum griffithii* from Sumatra and Borneo, for example, has been studied by botanists since the mid-nineteenth century, but only about fifty specimens have been located to date. Furthermore, up to 10 percent of rainforest trees have extremely limited ranges, some occurring over as little as a few dozen square kilometers.

As conditions are so constant and hospitable inside the undisturbed forest, tropical tree species (as well as other biotics) have a marked intolerance toward disturbance. Seeds of temperate species survive hot summers and sub-zero winter temperatures, sometimes for periods of many years before germinating. Tropical species, on the other hand, often refuse to germinate after as little as twenty-five days. The author is familiar with several palm species (*Astrocaryum mexicanum, Euterpe oleracea* and others) whose seed has failed to germinate after only four days. Further, certain dipterocarp species require a germination temperature of 73–79°F (23–26°C), yet after the forest is opened by loggers, ground temperature soars to 104°F (40°C).

Continued on page 112

The forests of this planet are no longer to be regarded as the preserve of one industry for the production of a few commodities; rather, they are the habitat of millions upon millions of people whose intricate relationship to the forest must be of primary concern to those who would seek to manage forests more effectively.

THE FOOD AND AGRICULTURE ORGANIZATION OF THE UNITED NATIONS

△ *Every year, 12 million acres (nearly 5 million ha) of closed tropical forests are logged. But because the canopy is interlaced with lianas, cutting 10% of the forest also destroys 30-60% of the noncommercial trees.*

Logging operations commonly target only the high-value commercial species, a gross underutilization that requires the logging of vast areas to fill company quotas. Globally, the forest resource is treated as nonrenewable, and many smallholders sell their logging rights for as little as $78/ha.

△△ Loggers near Korup in southwest Cameroon cut up a massive hardwood trunk.

◁ A tractor operator drags a felled tree in the Atlantic rainforest of Brazil. Mecha-nization of this kind has its own problems: the heavy machines leave a wake of damaged vegetation and compacted soil, promoting erosion and reducing the forest's potential for recovery. Men and oxen hauling logs would be a preferable alternative.

△ An aerial view of the Osa Peninsula in Costa Rica illustrates the results of exploitive operations. Sustained cyclic cutting of forests is still almost unknown in the tropics.

Developing nations in the tropics, often crippled by staggering debts, all too often export their principal asset, their forests. The implications of this shortsightedness are grave. By the end of the century, of the 33 countries that are currently exporters, 23 will have become importers of forest products, and the level of forest products exports will have fallen from $7 billion to $2 billion.

△ A heavily laden truck makes its way through the rapidly diminishing Atlantic rainforest of Brazil, heading for the coast where ▷ the sawn timber will be loaded onto ships for export.
▽ In many parts of the tropics, broad rivers like the Solimões in Amazonia provide one of the main methods of transporting large numbers of logs from interior forest regions to coastal ports.

△ *With latex bleeding from its wounds, another huge forest tree falls to the chain saw having started its life as a seedling about the time Columbus discovered the New World, an event which eventually led to its undoing. Global demand for tropical hardwood is largely responsible for the felling of 19 million trees every day.*

Pollination is also precarious in the forest. In the still interior, very little pollen is carried on the wind. In Brunei only 1 in 760 tree species in 100 acres (40 ha) is wind pollinated, while in Central America each of 40 species of fig relies on a specific insect pollinator. Should disturbance remove a pollinator from the area, the dependent trees will not produce seed. This also removes from the area those animals that rely on the species for fruit, and this in turn may remove other pollinators, required for service to other tree species.

Because of such intricate relationships we can readily understand how fragile this habitat is and why it demands treatment far different from those in temperate zones. We can also see why five species a day, and before long one per hour, are doomed to be expunged from the global genetic reservoir.

In their policy report to the president, the United States Interagency Task Force on Tropical Forests stated: "The world is being confronted by an extremely serious problem with immediate and long-range socioeconomic and ecological consequences as the result of the accelerating loss of forest and vegetative cover in the humid and semiarid lands within or near the tropical latitudes. Further, the community of nations must quickly launch an accelerated and coordinated attack on the problem if these greatly under-valued and probably irreplaceable resources are to be protected from virtual destruction by the early part of the next century."

Their report goes on to say that although United States imports of tropical hardwoods and related products amount to a substantial $430 million annually (1974–1978 figures), in terms of volume and acute dependence these imports are not essential. Such materials amount to only 1 to 2 percent of total hardwoods and softwoods used, or approximately 3 percent of the total hardwoods used in the entire United States.

The task force confirms the severity and immediacy of the tropical deforestation problem, but of course does not condemn logging in the tropics *per se*, as the need for such products is recognized. The force calls for lucid, responsible, and improved tropical forest management to foster a sustained yield. Only in this way can other equally important facets, such as "ecological, recreational, scientific and educational" uses, be developed and sustained as well.

"Cut-and-run" vs. "sustained yield"

It is generally acknowledged that the logging industry could enjoy a longer and more profitable life if it synchronized its consumption to regeneration cycles instead of concentrating on the race it currently runs with competing companies around the world.

By their own axes 10.9 million acres (4.4 million ha) of closed broad-leaved tropical forests are logged annually, while an additional 18.5 million acres (7.5 million ha) are cleared for other purposes, generally agriculture. Roughly 45 percent of this reduction, or 8.4 million acres (3.4 million ha), can be ascribed directly to shifting cultivation, the balance to other population pressures (livestock grazing, repeated burning, and fuelwood collection). The combined causes total 29.4 million acres (11.9 million ha) of forest altered. It should be noted that despite the growing international outcry on the issue, deforestation of the tropics is in no way tapering off or even stabilizing, but increasing dramatically. Brazil's rate, for instance, accelerates at 33 percent per year.

The pitfalls of self-regulation become glaring in tropical logging. Regulations laid down by tropical countries on overcutting and the taking of

undersize trees go largely unenforced. A common, circuitous, but somewhat justifiable complaint of the logging firms is, why should they be charitable by adhering to conservation regulations when other operators secure a competitive advantage by ignoring conscionable harvesting procedures?

A recent United Nations hearing on multinational corporations reveals how the understandably appealing carrot of foreign skills and capital is often eagerly accepted by Third World nations with large balance-of-trade deficits. The price tag on the carrot is often the handing over of enormous tracts of virgin forest, unencumbered by regulation, or a tacit waiver in practice of regulation enforcement.

To be realistic, it should be acknowledged that the industry's major concerns are profit and the uncertainties over ever-changing political conditions in the countries in which their investments lie, the latter specifically causing the retreat of several American firms previously heavily engaged in tropical-timber operations. Yet the political and economic power wielded by the multinationals in the countries they exploit often exceeds and even undermines the governments of these nations. The question is raised: Why have *we* granted the transnational corporations such latitude?

Indonesia serves as a typical example of the logging industry's environmentally counterproductive flexing of its political muscle. With the use of proper cyclic methods, forest regeneration is theoretically possible in 30 years. The Indonesian government requires logging corporations to follow a 35-year cutting cycle, yet it grants them a 20-year lease. Most of Indonesia's accessible forests are already allocated to multinational timber corporations, and within nine years Indonesia is expected to be completely overcut.

It is clear that both the importing and exporting nations have been irresponsibly inadequate in leaving the policy making, policing, and enforcing of regulations to the logging concerns. This could well be a major point of focus in the next decade. If much of this review appears critical of current timber industry practices it is to emphasize that the pivotal point is not whether extracting timber is an admirable endeavor, but rather how extensive tracts of tropical forest are currently being cut down without design, planning, or regulation. There is fault, and it is clearly widely shared.

Two scientists from Weyerhauser, one of the more candid companies that previously operated logging concessions in Kalimantan, Indonesia, studied changes in species composition and growth pattern in old logged-over areas. They found that "whereas many Southeast Asian foresters feel that the select-fell system of tropical rainforest silviculture [taking only desirable specimens of commercial species as opposed to clear-cutting] will successfully perpetuate yields of desired species, others are less convinced." They cite a 1977 study of nine companies operating in Kalimantan which revealed that "none was leaving the required 25 select crop trees per hectare and, indeed, on much of the area there were not sufficient trees at the start to comply with the regulation."

Of 50 companies currently plying the tropical forests, 22 are Japanese. These and other operators generally front the enormous capital investment necessary to build roads and extract timber. By so doing they are given a free hand, with little or no enforcement of regulations by the understaffed forestry departments of the tropical nations. It is apparent that strict attention must now be given from within and without the industry to the grossly wasteful harvesting practices universally tolerated as the *status quo*.

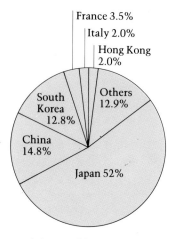

△ *If the world is now a "global village," there is a disproportionate consumption of resources by at least some of its occupants. With barely 7% of the village's population, Japan now consumes a staggering 52% of total tropical timber exports.*

△ *The world is anxiously watching Brazil's plan, backed by Japan's multi-billion-dollar Nakasone Fund, to pave the extension of highway BR-364 through the pristine Amazonian state of Acre. Once completed, this road would link up with the Peruvian road to the Pacific coast port at Lima. Such a link would create a direct export "pipeline" from Amazonia to Japan, with disastrous consequences for the Amazon Basin forests.*

While tropical timber nations will continue to rely on the industrialization of their forest sectors as a means of stabilizing their balance-of-trade deficits, there is a glaring failure on every continent of operation when it comes to realizing the potential rents from logging and timber processing. Typically, the Philippine government in a period from 1979 to 1982, captured only 12 percent of the potential rents available to it, and consequently pursued excessive timber extraction practices to fill the dollar shortfall. Such frugal measures as differentiating revenue charges by timber grade, species, and accessibility, are overlooked in a system dominated by broad uncategorized charges on gross volumes cut.

The world's major forest consumer

A sketch of one nation's harvest and use of tropical wood beggars belief. Although having only one-fourteenth (7.1 percent) of the total global population, Japan receives 52 percent of all tropical logs exported, more such wood than any other nation, and more than twice the amount of all Europe combined. Consumption per capita is also more at 4,273 cubic feet (121 cu m) per 1,000 persons, with Europeans at 1,200 cubic feet (34 cu m) and the United States at 530 cubic feet (15 cu m).

Surprisingly, for a nation known traditionally for its frugality, a conspicuous amount of waste is built into Japan's high-profile overuse. Up to 80 percent of the wood is processed into plywood, most of which is used to make molds for concrete. These are then discarded and burned after only a few uses. Furthermore, coastal mangroves, the removal of which can be proved directly responsible for the serious depletion of Asian coastal fisheries, are used to make chipwood and to grill *yakitori*, a popular chicken dish. In Southeast Asia, natural forests are widely cleared and replanted with "more suitable" wood for the production of *waribashi*, or disposable chopsticks!

Part of Japan's official "foreign aid" is the construction of logging roads into Sarawak and other areas, and these are highly destructive to the Penan and other traditional tribes. Such roads are used solely as a conduit for wood to Japan, and the burden of cost must be repaid by the people of Sarawak. Japan, by use of high tariffs, discourages the importation of any finished products, taking only raw logs and thus ensuring the tropical forest nation's need to export large volumes of timber in order to accrue the necessary balance-of-trade revenues.

At the time of writing, Japan has shaken the global scientific, political, and environmental communities with news of her apparent intention to pave the connection of Brazil's infamous BR-364 highway with the Peruvian road that leads directly to the Pacific coast near Lima. In its short life, BR-364 has already had an enormous impact on the Mato Grosso and caused the destruction of almost 25 percent of the forests of Amazonia's Rondonia region. The proposed new 500-mile (805-km) paved road would go through the comparatively pristine Brazilian state of Acre at a cost of $300 million. One glance at a map will show that it will connect the Amazonian borders of Brazil, Bolivia, and Peru – the major holders of the basin. One can envision logging spurs infiltrating the entire region, and reaching out into Colombia and other northern forest holders.

Researchers estimate that between 15 and 20 percent of the Amazon's primary forests have been cleared in the past two decades. It is also noted that Japan's major source of tropical wood imports is currently Indonesia, where the forests are rapidly approaching depletion. There is a visceral foreboding that should this highway connect the very heart of Amazonia with Pacific shipping access to Japan – the world's number one importer of tropical forests – it would quite literally extract every last commercial log, leaving Amazonia and the last of its traditional tribal cultures disenfranchised and effectively obliterated. It was to the halting of this road that the martyred Chico Mendes dedicated his life. Concerned individuals and organizations worldwide are closely monitoring this assuredly disastrous plan.

Plantation ratios – the critical imbalance

Recent FAO figures indicate the glaring and ever-widening gap between deforestation and reforestation. By the end of 1980, only 28.4 million acres (11.5 million ha) of tree plantations existed. Yearly, an additional 2.7 million acres (1.1 million ha) are planted. Yet, when we compare this to the 29.4 million acres (11.9 million ha) of virgin closed tropical broad-leaved forests removed annually, it becomes apparent that we are a full 1:10 ratio away from keeping pace with deforestation: only one tree is planted for every ten removed from natural tropical forests globally. Individual regions vary widely. In Africa, for instance, the ratio is 1:29, and India's loss of tree cover at 3.3 million acres (1.3 million ha) annually would see most of its remaining forests destroyed by century's end, so meager is the rate of renewal.

ESTIMATED AREAS OF ESTABLISHED PLANTATIONS AT THE END OF 1985
(Areas in thousand hectares)

| REGION | HARDWOOD SPECIES | | | | | | Softwood species | | All species | |
| | Other than fast-growing | | Fast-growing | | All hardwood species | | | | | |
	Total	1981–5	Total	1981–5	Total	1981–5	Total	1981–5	Total	1981–5
Tropical America (23 countries)	796	248	4012	1561	4808	1809	2485	864	7293	2673
Tropical Africa (37 countries)	823	235	896	251	1719	486	692	145	2411	631
Tropical Asia (16 countries)	2425	449	3488	1185	5913	1634	1390	558	7303	2192
Total *(76 countries)*	**4044**	**932**	**8396**	**2997**	**12440**	**3929**	**4567**	**1567**	**17007**	**5496**

ANNUAL RATES OF DEFORESTATION AND PLANTATION BETWEEN 1981 AND 1985

| REGION | ANNUAL RATES OF DEFORESTATION | | | Annual rates of plantation | Plantation to deforestation ratio |
| | Tree formations | | | | |
	Closed	Open	All		
Tropical America (23 countries)	4339	1272	5611	535	1 : 10.5
Tropical Africa (37 countries)	1331	2345	3676	126	1 : 29
Tropical Asia (16 countries)	1826	190	2016	438	1 : 4.5
Total *(76 countries)*	**7496**	**3807**	**11303**	**1099**	**1 : 10**

◁ *Despite the efforts of many governments, and international agencies such as the Forestry Department of the United Nations' Food and Agriculture Organization, the establishment of new plantations lags far behind what would be necessary even to keep pace with current rates of deforestation. Although the replacement ratio for Asia averages 1:4.5, in Africa it is only 1:29; and the world ratio is a poor 1:10.*

While industrial and nonindustrial plantations covered some 17 million hectares in 1985, there are signs now of a global shift away from plantations of relatively slow-growing hardwoods, destined for use as sawlogs and veneer logs, to much faster-growing softwood species.

III · FUELWOOD COLLECTION

The third of our major tropical forest reducers is the demand for fuelwood. Maharaj K. Muthoo, former director of FAO's Forestry Operation Service, states that fuelwood is of such major importance as a forest product that almost two billion people depend on it, consuming 85 percent of all wood produced in the Third World. Of these people, 96 million are unable to satisfy even their minimum needs for heating and cooking, and so prepare only one cooked meal a day, or grow less-nutritious crops which can be eaten raw. An additional 1,052 million are in a deficit situation which demands that they deplete wood reserves when they forage. On average, each person in the developing countries consumes 16 cubic feet (0.45 cu m) of wood a year – roughly the amount First World residents use in paper, for varied and far less vital uses. As most of this material is collected directly by the consumers themselves, these glaring figures rarely appear in national income accounts. Furthermore, while most of this foraging is from open and drier tree formations, the total amount collected is estimated to be over four times the volume of the total world timber trade.

Take India, for example, where over 50 million tons a year are harvested from her forests as headloads. The market value of this necessary produce alone far exceeds the recorded value of the country's entire forestry sector. Brazil's annual fuelwood consumption is estimated at being equal to $3 billion in foreign exchange. This ominous demand escalated sharply at the time of the OPEC increase in oil prices. These effects of deforestation should not be, but often are, overlooked by government agencies and planners when natural resource development decisions are made.

An estimate of significance is that one person may forage sufficient fuelwood from 1.2 acres (half a hectare) of forest yearly without degrading the habitat. It is illogical, however, to suppose that people will keep this rule of thumb in mind when a meal is to be prepared or cold averted. In reality, seven people on the average (in the Himalayan regions) collect wood from an area that size, an impossible burden for sustained use. In point of fact, in many critical areas, saplings are taken in sheer desperation – thus negating any possibility of future regrowth.

The world wood famine

The Worldwatch Institute in Washington, D.C., reports that many of the world's developing nations are entering a "wood famine." These nations export the greatest percentage of their wood at a trifle of its value. Nonfuelwood (industrial) production accounts for 20 percent of the total wood actually removed from the tropical forests, including the drier formations. Only 6 percent is exported. Of the wood produce that remains at home in these countries, 80 percent is used for fuel. In tropical Africa, some 100 million people would fail to meet their needs even by cutting all standing vegetation. Overall, a further 14,126 million cubic feet (400 million cu m) of fuelwood are presently required to make good the deficit. FAO predicts that by the year 2000, unless remedies are installed, 2,400 million people will be

THE WORLD FUELWOOD CRISIS

The world fuelwood famine kindles grave concerns for the developing countries whose people rely on this dwindling resource for cooking and heating.

As forests of all types continue to diminish, in many of the world's poorest areas it now costs more in time and effort to heat the pot than it does to fill it.

REGION	1980			2000
	ACUTE SCARCITY	DEFICIT	TOTAL	ACUTE SCARCITY OR DEFICIT
Tropical Africa	49	131	180	464
Tropical Asia	29	710	739	1,434
Tropical America	18	143	161	342
Total	**96**	**984**	**1,080**	**2,240**

△▷ **The scale of the fuelwood crisis**
Current FAO figures for the years 1980 and 2000 show the numbers of people, in millions, whose fuelwood supplies cannot be maintained. "Acute scarcity" means a lack of even the minimum requirement, while "Deficit" means that needs can be met only by overcutting the resource and degrading the habitat. Here ▷ wood is collected in Guinea.

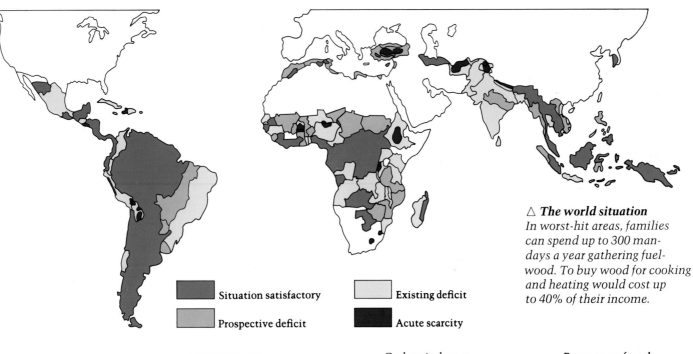

Situation satisfactory

Prospective deficit

Existing deficit

Acute scarcity

△ **The world situation**
In worst-hit areas, families can spend up to 300 man-days a year gathering fuel-wood. To buy wood for cooking and heating would cost up to 40% of their income.

▷ **Fuelwood's share of total energy use**
While the developed world's consumption of fossil fuel gives cause for increasing environmental concern, most developing countries have few options but to use fuelwood as an energy source. Alternatives are too expensive, or simply not available.

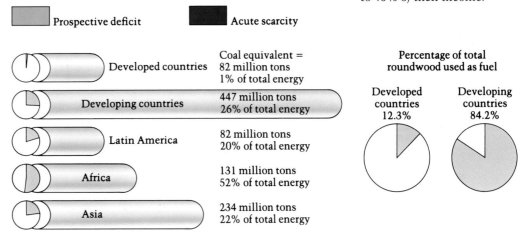

Developed countries — Coal equivalent = 82 million tons — 1% of total energy

Developing countries — 447 million tons — 26% of total energy

Latin America — 82 million tons — 20% of total energy

Africa — 131 million tons — 52% of total energy

Asia — 234 million tons — 22% of total energy

Percentage of total roundwood used as fuel

Developed countries 12.3%

Developing countries 84.2%

vitally involved in a wood famine representing a 33,900-million-cubic-feet (960-cu-m) deficiency – the energy equivalent of 240 million tons of oil a year. As that would represent – even at today's depressed price of about $20 a barrel of crude oil – about $33,000 million per year, it is unlikely the deficit will be met in this way as most developing nations are even now net petroleum importers with staggering foreign trade imbalances. The shortages are now so critical that in some denuded rural areas that were not long ago clothed in forest, a family member must now spend two days foraging for enough firewood to cook one hot meal for the family. Worldwatch alerts us that "it can cost more to heat the pot than to fill it." There are even reports of armed poachers illegally cutting forests to make charcoal to sell in urban areas. Even in Zaïre, a nation with a wealth of forest resources, families on the Bateke Plateau find that the price of charcoal is such that a family requiring two sacks per month can only afford one – at the cost of one-third of a worker's salary.

A resource goes up in smoke

While visiting Calcutta, India, as far back as 1962, I noticed patties of a strange material plastered to wall surfaces. In answer to my inquiry, I was informed that these were cow-dung cakes drying, to be used as fuel: a most common practice, I later found, as there is simply no wood available at all for the masses of this, one of the world's most crowded and certainly most impoverished cities.

A smoky pall of this interesting flavor hangs over many Indian towns and cities as in many other Third World countries, and the practice, unfortunately, is growing. The burning of dung and crop residues robs the fields of much-needed nutrients, and borrowing from Peter to pay Paul causes a continuous downward spiral in harvest yields at a time when, due to population pressures, increased production is demanded. Solid fossil fuels and oil appear to be out of the question as fuel sources due to their high cost. It is estimated that some 400 million tons of dung are burned as fuel in areas where firewood is scarce or nonexistent. The trade-off is highly illuminating. The task force convened to produce the Tropical Forestry Action Plan states that by loss of dung (fertilizer) in the fields, food-grain harvests are reduced by more than 14 million tons. This loss of food is nearly *double* the quantity of food provided annually in aid to developing countries!

▷ *Dung patties drying on a wall in Calcutta. The growing reliance on cattle dung for fuel is robbing the developing countries' fields of desperately needed nutrients. Each ton of dung burned represents a loss of 110 lbs (50 kg) of grain production, and in Asia, the Near East, and Africa, 400 million tons are burned every year. By the year 2000, 250 million people will be burning dung unless village tree-planting schemes are introduced and established quickly on a wide scale.*

IV · THE PAPER CHASE AND OTHER FACTORS

Few would disagree that a more concerted paper-recycling effort than now prevails is due from the developed nations.

The period from 1950 to 1976 saw world paper consumption alone increase from 40 to 160 million tons, a rise more than double that of population growth. This figure is expected to reach 400 million tons by the year 2000 and to double again twenty years later. Of the current total, over 87 percent is consumed by the developed nations.

In standard practice, each citizen of the United States throws away in paper three whole conifer trees yearly. This represents only paper wasted, not the total amount consumed, and means that approximately one billion trees (6,725 square miles or nearly 17,416 square kilometers of forest, an area larger than the state of Hawaii) are being wasted each year by one country alone. In developing nations, the average person uses only 11 pounds (5 kg) each year, but most use less than 2.2 pounds (1 kg), the equivalent of one-half of the Sunday edition of the *New York Times*. (Conversely, one single run of the *New York Times* Sunday edition consumes 75,000 trees.) As profligate use of paper and packaging continues throughout the developed countries, our insatiable demand for raw materials is placing ever-increasing pressure on the forests of the temperate and tropical regions alike.

Mineral extraction

The extraction of mineral resources from forest lands is often accompanied by circumstances that produce far more damage than the mining process itself. The $3.5 billion, 324,000-square-mile (839,000-sq-km) Grande Carajás Project in Brazil's eastern Amazon pursues the exploitation of considerable deposits of iron ore, copper, manganese, bauxite, and nickel. While the principal iron-ore mine has had little impact on the forest since it began production in 1985, a large problem looms in the form of the charcoal-powered smelters which convert the ore into pig iron. The most expedient source of charcoal is the surrounding forest. There are grave concerns that Grande Carajás will duplicate the dismal experience in the Brazilian southeastern state of Minas Gerais, where pig-iron production resulted in the obliteration of two-thirds of the state's forests. It is surprising then that despite international censure, the World Bank continues to support Carajás – a project that will involve the conversion of 12.4 million acres (5 million ha) of forest to croplands, 7.4 million acres (3 million ha) to cattle ranches, and, so far, 3.7 million acres (1.5 million ha) for the smelter charcoal.

Hydroelectrical debacles

It is understandable that tropical nations with major rivers will wish to consider their hydroelectric alternatives. A disturbing pattern emerges, however, of vast projects going ahead without a thorough evaluation at the outset of factors such as the projected longevity of the dam, the actual need for electricity production, environmental destruction, and the displacement of indigenous cultures with few satisfactory options for their future.

In any conversion from one form of land use to another, there will, of necessity, be trade-offs which must be carefully evaluated. All too often the more obvious merits of hydroelectrical projects are, for lack of more tactful description, wanton infusion of capital, commonly out of political expedience. USAID, World Bank, and other international lending institutions have been duly challenged on such policies toward the end of the 1980s. However, the promise of future environmental impacts through major dam projects unfortunately still exists.

Brazil's "Plan 2010" dictates the construction of 136 high dams, twenty-two of them in Amazonia, and will flood a rainforest the size of the United Kingdom. Recent demonstrations against the Altamira Project, part of the plan, by the Kayapo Indians as well as by anthropologists, rankled the government and resulted in the arrests of participants, who carried their concern to the United States. The project will flood almost 2,800 square miles (7,200 sq km) of Indian homeland in the Xingu region.

Various factors conspire to differentiate the feasibility of dam construction in temperate areas and tropical forest regions. Erosion, and subsequent siltation, has been consistently problematical. The ludicrously accelerated obsolescence due to this factor can be easily demonstrated by the example of Colombia's Anchicaya Dam, which lost a full quarter of its storage capacity within only two years of its completion. Another concern is the overgrowth of water-surface vegetation. This matting chokes off primary production, oxygen production, and animal life in that order.

Of major consequence, and a factor regularly overlooked, is that due to unvarying temperatures, the layers within impounded tropical water bodies do not mix. Due to anoxic (oxygen-deficient) conditions, submerged vegetation produces hydrogen sulfide, and this in turn often produces water of such extreme acid content that turbine blades in hydroelectric generating stations corrode, drastically shortening the life of such installations.

In addition to the criticisms levelled at the World Bank for its active support of the Grande Carajás project, that major international finance institution has

Cotingo
Branco
Jari-Paru
Maicuru and
Curuapaneme
Araguari
Cachoeira
da Porteira
Trometas
Negro
Balbina
Tucurui
Santa
Isabel
Samuel
Madeira
Xingu
Ituxiendimari
Jamari
Tapajos
Araguaia and
Tocantins
Manso

● Dams built or under construction
● Dams planned
● Potential dam sites
■ Grande Carajás iron ore project

◁△ **Hydroelectric schemes**
Vast areas of Brazil's forests are being flooded by hydroelectric schemes. The victims are many of the country's indigenous tribes – displaced and forced into reserves, or into territorial conflict with others. Criticisms focus on the politically motivated international bank loans that are used to finance the schemes, and the low output of energy and inappropriate location of many of the projects.

also been subject to widespread censure for supporting Brazil's power-sector investment and development plans with a loan of over $500 million, and with additional loans amounting to a further $1.4 billion currently under consideration. This development plan will include the building of several very large hydroelectric schemes which will completely submerge 61.8 million acres (25 million ha) of forest, the home of some half a million people, and will have a major negative impact on more than half the remaining Indian tribal lands of Amazonia.

It should be especially noted that such projects, funded by the World Bank, commonly *reduce* employment opportunities in rural agriculture, small-scale village industries, and other traditional livelihoods. For example, bank-funded rural electrification projects in Bangladesh and Indonesia have taken employment from millions of women who formerly earned their living husking rice by hand. In the bank's one-step forward two-steps back approach, it is just such displaced rural masses who are then forced to try to cultivate steep hillslopes and other inappropriate areas in an attempt at survival.

Population growth and tropical forests

Global population is expected to double by the year 2020. This, in a world already straining to support its overburgeoning numbers, which now exceed 6 billion souls and are increasing by 227,400 every day. This now brings the population density of the earth to 100 people per square mile. The National Research Council of the National Academy of Sciences, in its report *Research Priorities in Tropical Biology*, estimates that 90 percent of that population growth will have taken place in the tropical Third World. A large percentage of those unfortunates will be relying for their sustenance on slash-and-burn agriculture in tropical forest areas. On that observation, and recognizing that such warnings are written on the wall in blood, Peter Raven, director of the Missouri Botanical Garden and a prominent voice among concerned scientists, in testimony before a congressional subcommittee, stated, "Since [virtually all] the tropical forests will be destroyed during the next 25 years, it is difficult to avoid the conclusion that up to one billion people will be starving to death in the first two decades of the next century."

It is obvious that we cannot simply multiply our current developmental patterns to accommodate such increases in our species' numbers. It is expected that with the starving multitudes will come widespread civil unrest, economic chaos, and war.

It should also be abundantly clear that nothing is more firmly at the heart of the issue than population pressure, and that family planning can in no way be subjugated to more direct causes, such as commercial timber extraction, migrant cultivation, fuelwood collection, or the hamburger connection. It is no mere coincidence that Ethiopia was 45 percent covered with forest in the year 1900, and that 3 percent now remain; and that the population of that country in 1920 was 5 million and in 1987 had reached 46 million.

The population of Madagascar has doubled in the past 25 years, and 90 percent of its forests are now gone. Its 1988 population of 10.5 million is projected to reach 16 million souls by the end of the century, and at current growth rates it will almost triple by 2015. Not only will any hard-won economic gains be lost, but fuelwood supplies by then will be nonexistent, and human beings cannot digest uncooked cereal grains wherever they might materialize from. Already one of the most heavily eroded places on earth,

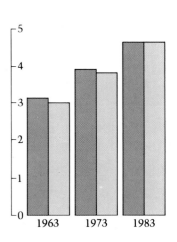

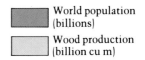

World population (billions)

Wood production (billion cu m)

△ *The connection between population increase and deforestation is clearly shown in this graph, leaving little doubt that those who would seek answers to the problem of tropical deforestation must also address the problem of population pressure – one of the root causes*

COUNTRY (LATIN AMERICA)	Brazil	Colombia	Costa Rica	Ecuador	Guatemala	Guyana	Honduras	Mexico	Nicaragua	Panama	Peru	Surinam	Venezuela
POPULATION IN 1980 (in millions)	118.7	26.7	2.2	8	7.2	0.8	3.7	69.8	2.6	1.8	17.4	0.4	14.9
RURAL POPULATION (%)	39	40	59	58	64	60	69	36	51	50	38	34	25
POPULATION IN 2000 (in millions)	176.5	39.4	3.3	13.6	12	1.2	6.7	115	4.7	2.8	27.3	0.6	23.8
YEAR OF STATIONARY POPULATION	2075	2065	2065	2085	2085	2065	2090	2075	2090	2070	2080	2070	2075
TOTAL OF STATIONARY POPULATION (in millions)	281	60.2	4.8	28.4	24.2	1.8	16	202.6	10.8	4.3	48.8	0.9	38.6

△ **Population in the tropical forest zone**
The projections in this chart show the vulnerability of the tropical developing countries. One half of the region's people are 15 years old or less, and population growth rates continue to rise, putting ever-more pressure on the region's natural resources.

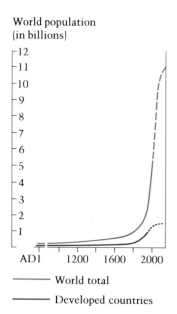

World population
(in billions)

—— World total

—— Developed countries

△ *If runaway population is the disease, then tropical deforestation is one of the main symptoms. An increase of some 80 million souls per year is a reflection of the need of peasant parents in many parts of the world for help on the farm and security in old age.*

Madagascar's topsoil is vanishing eight times faster than Ethiopia's. Given such bleak austerity, it is regrettable, but not surprising, that infant mortality has soared in the last decade (1978–1988) from 75 per thousand live births to a glaring 133 per thousand.

Haiti, in 1920, was 60-percent forested, now 2 percent remains, a major reason for its position as the poorest country in the Northern Hemisphere. (It is said that Haiti would actually qualify as the poorest nation in the world, were it not for its ties with the United States.) Its population in 1920 was 2.1 million and reached 6.2 million in 1987. Similarly, Nigeria, by 2040, will have a population equal to that of the entire present-day Africa. Of all the major environmental debacles plaguing the earth, overpopulation is the greatest. In many respects it is the fundamental disease; most of the other problems are in reality only the symptoms.

It is estimated that 800 million people in rural zones are landless, and that they farm one-fifth of the entire tropical-forest biome, including secondary forests. The death toll for these landless people in times of food shortages is fully three times higher than that for people who own a plot, even one as small as 3.7 acres (1.5 ha).

Large landholdings are certainly one cause of the problem. In Latin America, 7 percent of the landowners possess over 90 percent of the arable land. In the United States, the largest 7 percent of the farms account for only 27 percent of total farmlands. Family plots are much more productive than large operations. In Colombia, the production ratio of small to large is three to one. In this area, sustainable development can be directed toward land reforms and split holdings, and the provision of investment credits and market networks to peasant farmers.

Yet most tropical Third World governments are dominated by the landowning elite, and so the larger percentage of the agricultural budget is allocated to that sector. Consequently the landless continue to seek virgin forest territory. The population of Amazonian Peru has increased in the past several decades from a few tens of thousands to 1.5 million.

The best indicator of industrial pressure on the biome, of course, is the exponential growth of saw mills. In 1959, the Brazilian state of Rondonia had only four saw mills. In 1978 there were 141; in 1981 a total of 250; in 1982 the figure was 387 and in 1985 it was over 600. At present, in Brazil's northern Amazonian region alone there are 3,000 to 4,000 saw mills in operation.

ASIA	Bangladesh	Burma	India	Indonesia	Malaysia	Papua New Guinea	Philippines	Thailand	Vietnam	AFRICA	Cameroon	Congo	Gabon	Côte d'Ivoire	Madagascar	Zaire
	88.5	34.8	673.2	146.6	13.9	3.1	49.1	46.9	54.2		8.5	1.5	0.7	8.2	8.7	28.3
	91	78	78	82	73	87	68	87	78		71	60	68	68	84	70
	141	54	994.1	216	20.8	4.4	76.9	68	87.9		14.2	2.7	0.9	14.8	16.1	51
	2125	2095	2115	2110	2070	2125	2075	2070	2075		2110	2100	2130	2110	2110	2110
	338.2	89.7	1,621.5	388.4	30	9.4	125	102.5	153.4		40.8	10.5	2	47.4	51.1	156.1

Those in the environmental sciences are increasingly concerned that sufficient world resources are not being allocated to the population problem. Even with a somewhat stepped-up family-planning program, and two children per couple, the world is not expected to reach zero-population growth until late next century, maybe even not until the early twenty-second century. This is due to the characteristically youthful population of much of the Third World, where 50 percent of the population is fifteen years of age or younger. (In the United States the equivalent figure is 20 percent.) The future Third World parents are already born! Their children's future may be a bleak one at best. There may be wisdom in evaluating China's recently adopted policy of one child per family. On balance, it should be realized that we have little latitude of choice in this issue, for if we fail to control population, it will, by the most natural and odious of processes, provide its own control.

It is quite clear that given the very high rates of infant and child mortality, parents in developing countries exhibit a very deliberate will to produce more rather than fewer children. A large number of children provides more than just workers in the fields (workers whom the parents could certainly not afford as paid labor); it also provides a degree of insurance against old age.

In this situation it is essential to parallel our efforts to promote birth control with equally determined efforts to increase soil fertility, crop yields, and farm plot productive life. A real decrease in birth rate cannot be achieved until there is real progress in the improvement of food supply, child health, longevity, and overall well-being in the populations of Third World countries. If we can do this, we will, at the same time, be attacking the root causes of tropical deforestation.

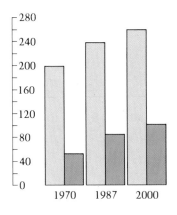

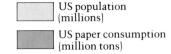

US population (millions)

US paper consumption (million tons)

△ *The United States population produces more waste per capita than any other nation. While less than one-third of all newspapers are recycled, recovering just one run of the Sunday* New York Times *would save 75,000 trees. It is a sobering thought that recycling one ton of paper can save 17 trees, 25 barrels of oil, 7,000 gallons of water, and 3 cubic yards of landfill space.*

Tallies of conspicuous consumption

Given the 10.9 million acres (4.4 million ha) of deforestation by the logger, the 8.4 million acres (3.4 million ha) of forest removal by migrant cultivators (including illicit-drug crops), and 10.1 million acres (4.1 million ha) of conversion to cattle pasture, fuelwood collection and other population pressures such as deliberate burning at forest edges, grazing of forest fodder, plus urban and industrial expansion, FAO arrives at a yearly total of 29.4 million acres (11.9 million ha) of closed tropical tree formations deforested.

In the following chapters, we will look into what is at stake if these imbalances go uncorrected, and consider a range of viable alternatives.

4
WHAT DO WE LOSE?

The action for which our descendants are least likely to forgive us is the loss of genetic and species diversity by the destruction of natural habitats. Unless we curtail our activities in these areas, the effects of the loss of such a large portion of species will have the most serious long-term consequences, of even longer duration than the unthinkable outcome of nuclear war, famine and political turmoil.

EDWARD O. WILSON
National Medal of Science Recipient, Harvard University.

Symbolizing both the harmony and vulnerability of the rainforest biome, a three-toed sloth (Bradypus infuscatus) rests in the branches of a Cecropia tree in the Panamanian forest.

I · BIOLOGICAL DIVERSITY

The whales, the rhinos, the tigers, the elephants, these are the visible tip of the iceberg. But what we're really talking about is the biological impoverishment of this planet.

RUSSELL E. TRAIN
PAST PRESIDENT, WORLD WIDE
FUND FOR NATURE – USA

H. G. Wells once said, "Human history more and more becomes a race between education and catastrophe."

What then does it mean to us when we hear that 46,500 square miles (120,425 sq km) of tropical forest disappear annually; that each year a sector equal to the size of the mountain kingdom of Nepal, along with most of the life that forest supported, is expunged from existence? Are the figures and the problems of tropical deforestation so enormous that they elude comprehension? The speed with which this destruction proceeds threatens to diminish the biome, perhaps irrevocably, even before the limitations of development, and its effects both global and local, are recognized. These factors underlie the scientific community's resolve to declare the effects of tropical deforestation the "sleeper issue of the 20th century."

In this chapter we will bring down to earth just what is at stake should we choose to allow the "habitat holocaust" to continue, and what such a decision will mean to us personally, as well as to the biological integrity of our planet.

The copious productivity of the forest

At the outset it may help to bring our plight into focus to know that the tropical forests are responsible for a conspicuous percentage (up to 69 percent) of earth's biological productivity. Nothing could demonstrate the significance of our dependence on this biome more than to recall the transpiration dynamics of a single large emergent forest tree – pumping some 200 gallons (760 l) of water per day into the atmosphere. Through this process, 1 acre (0.4 ha) of tropical rainforest releases 20,000 gallons (76,000 l) of water into the atmosphere daily for cloud formation; twenty times the amount the sea contributes through evaporation from the same surface area.

Were we to search for a single mechanism to preserve soil fertility; percolate water evenly through the seasons, and so prevent flood, erosion, and drought; release atmospheric water; store atmospheric carbon; cleanse the air; moderate global temperature and climatic balance; beautify the terrain, and support a varied fauna and flora – none could be found to serve better than a tree. The forest is a community of such benefactors and its list of credentials is imposing.

As a self-perpetuating cornucopia, undisturbed and without our management, earth's most productive biome converts ground litter, carrion, and offal to sustain an infinite supply of forest plant and animal produce, including fruit, seeds, berries, nuts, teas, perhaps 80,000 edible plants, fuel, latex, oils, spices, gums, resins, turpentines, varnishes, lubricants, inks, flavoring and scenting agents, drugs, bamboo, barks, polishes, insecticides, cosmetics, clothing, thatch insulation, packing materials, rattan, flowers, soaps, dyes, tanning agents, fish, animals, animal skins, meat, honey, decorative plants, fodder, wood, pulp, paper, jute, and countless other diverse products with a potential market value of many billions of dollars annually. In addition, this priceless resource could serve as the bounteous provider of scientific, cultural, educational, recreational, and aesthetic riches. More incredibly, it can perform

PRODUCTS OF THE RAINFOREST

At the current rate of tropical deforestation we face a cumulative loss of a million species by the year 2000. We already derive a wealth of benefit from the forest resource and can only speculate on the countless medicinals, food, and other useful plants we stand to lose before even knowing they exist.

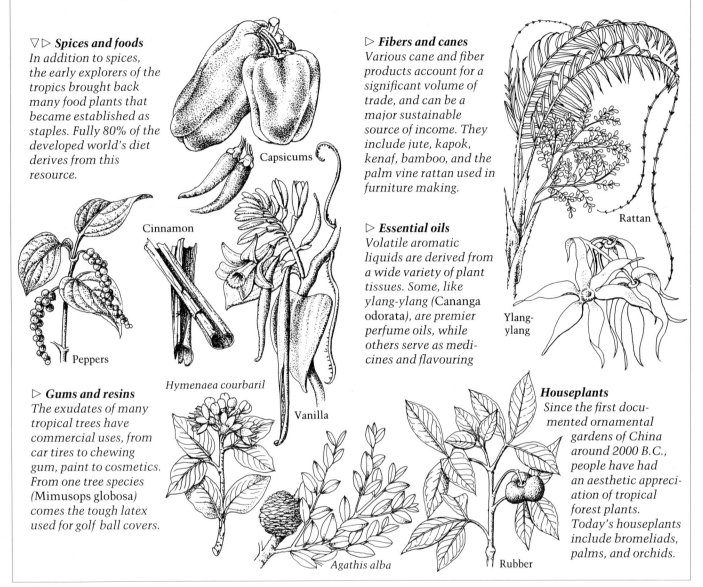

▽ ▷ **Spices and foods**
In addition to spices, the early explorers of the tropics brought back many food plants that became established as staples. Fully 80% of the developed world's diet derives from this resource.

Capsicums

Cinnamon

Peppers

▷ **Gums and resins**
The exudates of many tropical trees have commercial uses, from car tires to chewing gum, paint to cosmetics. From one tree species (Mimusops globosa) comes the tough latex used for golf ball covers.

Hymenaea courbaril

Vanilla

Agathis alba

▷ **Fibers and canes**
Various cane and fiber products account for a significant volume of trade, and can be a major sustainable source of income. They include jute, kapok, kenaf, bamboo, and the palm vine rattan used in furniture making.

▷ **Essential oils**
Volatile aromatic liquids are derived from a wide variety of plant tissues. Some, like ylang-ylang (Cananga odorata), are premier perfume oils, while others serve as medicines and flavouring

Rattan

Ylang-ylang

Rubber

Houseplants
Since the first documented ornamental gardens of China around 2000 B.C., people have had an aesthetic appreciation of tropical forest plants. Today's houseplants include bromeliads, palms, and orchids.

all these varied and essential services at once, *and* render them cost free. Dependent on which course humanity takes in the next decade, or perhaps two, it is probable that at no other time in our history will we risk losing – yet conversely have a better opportunity to preserve – so many vital assets.

Pockets of endemism

Observing the biology of the earth, we find its life-forms diminishing in complexity and number as we move from the tropical rainforest to deserts and into areas of increasingly cooler temperatures in the temperate zone.

Of up to 30 million species that share the planet with us, some 50 percent, perhaps even 90 percent, will be found in the tropical forests. Harvard's Edward O. Wilson alerts us that only 1.4 million species have yet been described, which in the major groups includes, approximately 750,000 insects, 47,000 vertebrates, and some 250,000 plants. Peter Raven brings this fact

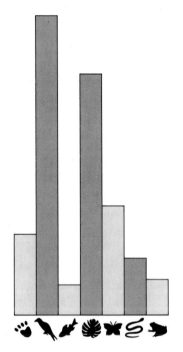

△ *The astonishing species diversity of the tropical rainforest biome is well illustrated by the species count taken in La Selva, a Costa Rican biological reserve of only 1,800 acres (730 ha). The tally of 1,125 species is roughly half as many again as in the whole of California's 158,313 sq mi (410,000 sq km).*

home when he states that "the species-rich tropical rainforest is not one mass of vegetation with species roaming about at will, but a very complex jigsaw puzzle. The pieces of this puzzle are intricate pockets of endemism. Great order reigns here, all subservient to the mutualistic ecologic relations. Man is very much dependent on these relationships himself, whether or not he chooses to acknowledge this."

A poignant comment on Raven's challenge is the sad observation that at least eight animal species that serve as official symbols of their national lands are today on the brink of extinction, and we must note that the American bald eagle is included in that austere membership.

A pocket of endemism is a relatively small area to which the entire distribution of a species is relegated. Examples include the snail darter, Miss Furbish's lousewort, and the mountain gorilla. Such limited range is a common feature of the tropical rainforest.

Under the constant environmental conditions of the tropical rainforests, a large number of species have become so specialized over the millennia that their ranges are restricted to certain niches and often to surprisingly small areas. A single square mile (2.6 sq km) or less is not uncommon for the entire range of a species, and this makes them extremely vulnerable. The spectacular golden toad (*Bufo periglenes*), for instance, discovered in 1964, inhabits a single mountaintop (Monteverde) in Costa Rica. It would take just half an hour with modern logging techniques to completely obliterate this particular gem of creation which took millions of years to evolve.

Such creatures do not serve solely as zoological curiosities or to stimulate natural history tourism. For instance, tetrodotoxin, derived from certain Central American and Caribbean rainforest frogs, is employed as a painkiller and muscle relaxant for victims of neurogenic leprosy and terminal cancer. As an anesthetic it is 160,000 times more potent than cocaine, a fact not lost on Haitian voodoo practitioners who, it was recently discovered, use tetrodotoxin as the primary ingredient in potions designed to create "zombies"! Another unlikely drug is capoten. Derived from a South American viper, it is responsible for millions of dollars' worth of sales globally as a highly effective blood pressure inhibitor.

Species rich and interdependent

While a relatively rich temperate forest may have 20 different species of tree to the hectare (2.47 acres), but more often only two or three, the same-size area of tropical rainforest may have over 200 different species of tree and many thousands of other plant and animal species. A case in point is a single volcano in the Philippines which contains more species of woody plant than the entire United States. Another is a minute 5.4 square-foot (0.5 sq-m) quadrant of ground in the Peruvian lowland tropical forest in which are found the leaves of 50 different species of tree.

This luxuriant diversity has proved to be a severe liability when these forests are exploited. Many major tree species have large, heavy seeds that do not colonize far from the parent tree. There may be only a few in an area of 25 acres (10 ha), and when such a species is selectively logged, or when large areas are clear-cut, too few individuals are left scattered over too wide an area to successfully propagate the species, and extinction may become imminent. This is but one reason why the tropical rainforest, exploited by classical methods, has been referred to as a "nonrenewable resource."

These spectacular flowering trees themselves support a multitude of less conspicuous plants and animals, some of which rely on a specific tree species for their survival, so that the demise of a species can result in a chain reaction or extinction domino effect. Although animals are most often the recipients of public attention when threatened, Raven alerts us that a single plant species can take ten to thirty dependent insect, higher animal, and other plant species with it to extinction.

There will, without a single exception that I am able to cite, be ramifications up and down the food or dependency chain with the demise of any one of earth's species. Paul and Anne Ehrlich, authors of *Extinction*, have likened this to rivets popping out of an airplane you are piloting. The aircraft remains aloft until the critical point is reached when too many rivets have been lost. At that point, disaster is inevitable.

The black hole of extinction

It took 100 million years for the flowering plants to evolve and clothe the earth, yet the past twenty years alone have put a sizeable portion of them in mortal jeopardy. The Threatened Plants Committee of the International Union for Conservation of Nature and Natural Resources (IUCN) has decreed 10 percent (20,000–30,000) of the world's known flowering plants to be "dangerously rare or under threat." This figure is current and will escalate monthly. In his 1979 book *The Sinking Ark*, ecologist Norman Myers estimated that due mainly to the exploitation of the tropical forests, one species per day was doomed to extinction.

In the autumn of 1986, an international conference was convened by the United States National Academy of Sciences. By separate and independently derived sets of calculations, a number of eminent biologists concluded that the extinction rate at that time was "several per day." Within a few years the loss of one species per hour is expected, and Raven projects several hundred per day by the early part of the next century. Myers states that with the currently expected rate of escalation, the unthinkable extinction of one million species by the century's end is "a not unlikely prospect." The great majority of these life-forms will never even have been identified. "This crisis is not about saving a handful of species; it is not an endangered species program," says William Rodriguez, who heads the Botany Department at the Institute for Amazonian Research in Manaus, Brazil. "We are talking about the source of species diversity itself, the machine that cranks them out and ultimately protects us from calamity."

With few exceptions, species have always flourished and waned, each filling its own purpose in its own time. For most, the ultimate destiny is to be replaced by a bright young successor.

Although concerted waves of extinction have certainly occurred in our paleontological past, our current and future losses will be so exponential that the implications are chilling. Average extinction "background rate" has a range of 2.0 to 4.6 families per million years, and may rise to 19.3 during periods of mass extinction (such as the great dinosaur decline, with their kin, and the marine extinctions 65 million years ago). We now expect, within the next two decades, to lose more than 50 families of plants alone, and with them many of the fauna that live with them – making our current rate of extinction over 800 times higher! Michael Soule and Bruce Wilcox have written, "Death is one thing; an end to birth is something else." We can speculate with some

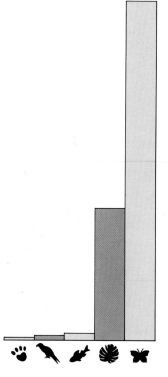

△ *Birds and mammals are highly visible, and we have a considerable fund of knowledge about them. The tragedy of extinction now is that hundreds of species are lost without ever being studied or named. For every bird that disappears, we lose 2 or 3 fish, 35 plants, and about 90 insects: and for every 2 birds lost, a mammal species disappears forever.*

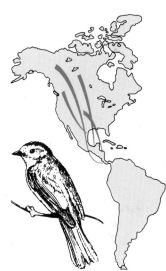

◁ Most people today would count themselves lucky to see a crocodile in its native habitat. Debatable taste for products made of rare skins is often fueled by the species' increasing rarity. Such is the fate of this Amazonian black caiman (Melanosuchus niger).

confidence that as the weeds and vermin outcompete the more useful and aesthetic species we will be looking forward to a world largely dominated by pests and weeds which, by and large, will not be species useful to humanity. Furthermore, it has been extrapolated that as a result of the disturbance of the tropical forest biomass to date, it is unlikely that another *conspicuous* animal will ever again evolve on earth.

Telltale yet widespread effects of Amazonian forest clearance are already showing themselves to be forerunners of more major consequences. One example is the plight of farmers in the American midwest. The recent overburgeoning numbers of crop-destructive insects have been shown to be caused at least in part by a decrease in the country's population of insect-eating birds. Intensive research traced the birds' migration routes (80 percent of them winter in the tropics) and found that their wintering grounds in Amazonia and elsewhere were being deforested. The same holds true for the considerable decline in migratory waterfowl reaching North American summer breeding grounds.

△ Migrating songbirds like this Wilson's warbler (Wilsonia pusilla) are increasingly affected by habitat changes in their tropical winter quarters.

Asia's forests – a focus of concern

If the Amazon presents an escalating scenario of unrestrained exploitation, the situation of the Asian forests is already quite grave. Because their 610 million acres (247 million ha) are most accessible, and because certain of their species (especially dipterocarps) offer great commercial rewards, exploitation has been extensive and intensive. Although the Asian forests cover an area one-third the size of Amazonia they hold one-half the number of species, making the tropical forests of New Guinea, Borneo, Java, Malaysia, the Philippines, Sulawesi, and Sumatra inch for inch the richest area on earth. The very small Bornean state of Brunei contains approximately 2,000 species of tree. The entire country of The Netherlands, seven times larger, has only 30.

These are surely the most quickly receding tropical forests on earth, and as they are spread over hundreds of widely separated islands, a great proportion of their species are endemic. In Papua-New Guinea, 320 out of 670 birds are found nowhere else on earth. Most forests in these areas will be gone in five to twelve years.

◁ Every individual must now take responsibility for the consequences of the choices he or she makes. If we buy curios like these on sale outside Acapulco, Mexico, we create a market for them. The fate of these animals is firmly in our own hands. Without a market, the traders and the hunters who supply them would have no viable business.

Inconspicuous species

How fragile the tropical forest ecosystem is, and how dependent the whole is on its parts, may be demonstrated by a typical interrelationship. Many tree species depend directly on the sole pollination services of individuals of distinct species of hummingbirds, wasps, bees, and butterflies. If deforestation removes from a pollinator's range the last tree that flowers during certain months, then the creature is forced to abandon its territory. The remaining trees in that area will consequently fail to produce fruit, and a variety of herbivorous species dependent on that food source may also succumb, leading to the potential demise of predators who preyed on those species, and so outward through the food web to other plant and animal species.

The majority of the doomed species will slip away into extinction without the fanfare and attention that marks the plight of certain more flamboyant species. Most of these losses will be unknown to science, gone before even being recognized, or their potential service to the biota, and even mankind, noted. We take an arrogant risk when we tamper with this delicate mechanism, casting away small gears and pieces that seem irrelevant to us with our current, relatively rudimentary, biochemical knowledge. In *Extinction*, the Ehrlichs emphasize this by stating, "It seems certain that over 95 percent of the organisms capable of competing seriously with humanity for food or of doing us harm by transmitting disease are now controlled *gratis* by other species in natural ecosystems."

While many would quickly dismiss the potential effects of the disappearance of many insect species, future use of these minute life-forms could have highly significant impacts. For example, Malaysian oil palm (*Elaeis guineensis*) plantations used to require inefficient and labor-intensive hand pollination. Research indicated that a weevil from West Africa, where the palm is indigenous, was responsible for pollination – and so imported insects were released into the Malaysian plantations. They now generate $110 million in savings annually.

Recently the lowly pokeweed was found to contain a snail-killing chemical, and this is now used to battle schistosomiasis, the lethal snail-borne parasitic disease that infects over 200 million people in the tropics. We can be quite sure that in times past no one had much use for the unsightly mold we now know as *Penicillium notatum*, from which the drug penicillin is made, yet today most of us are indebted to the discovery of its amazing properties.

The "Noah principle"

Certainly, though, there are many species that have thus far demonstrated no proven value to man. In these cases David W. Ehrenfeld, Rutgers University biologist, argues for a noneconomic approach to the issue. "Longstanding existence in nature is deemed to carry with it the unimpeachable right to continued existence. Existence is the only criterion of value." Ehrenfeld's ethical justification for species preservation is known as the "Noah principle." Noah admitted into his ark "everything that creepeth upon the earth." No creature was turned away for lack of apparent economic value.

Felix Houphouet-Boigny, president of Côte d'Ivoire, amplifies the "Noah principle" when he states, "Man has gone to the moon but he does not yet know how to make a flame tree or a bird song. Let us keep our dear countries free from irreversible mistakes which would lead us in the future to long for those same birds and trees."

II · A Wealth of Natural Resources

Medicinal Value of Tropical Plants

At various stages in the disintegration of the forest life chain, human beings most definitely suffer. For example, fully 50 percent of the medicines we use are derived from plants, and 25 percent of all prescription drugs have their origins in tropical forests. Should trends of habitat loss continue, by the middle of the next century we can expect to lose 25 percent of all higher plants – approximately 60,000 species.

Although only about 7 percent of tropical plants have been screened for possible usefulness to humans, many of our "wonder drug" botanicals have been used for centuries by primitive tribes. This has "sparked a revolution," says Richard Evans Shultes, director of the Harvard Botany Museum, who reports with enthusiasm that "it crystallized the realization that the plant kingdom represents a virtually untapped reservoir of new chemical compounds, many extraordinarily biodynamic, some providing novel bases on which the synthetic chemist may build even more interesting structures." The simplest bacterium can synthesize more organic compounds in its brief life than can all the world's chemists combined.

Let's take a self-serving look at just one plant-derived class of compounds, our proven friends the alkaloids, used extensively by the medical profession. These versatile and biologically active chemicals are employed as cardiac and respiratory stimulants, blood pressure boosters, narcotics, hallucinogenics, antimalarials, local and general anesthetics, painkillers, muscle relaxants, pupil dilators, tumor inhibitors, and antileukemic drugs, to name only the most prominent applications.

Of the 10,000 or so alkaloids known in 1988, the vast majority have not yet been subjected to critical pharmacological screening. Yet it is known that plants in the tropics are twice as likely to contain these versatile chemicals as those in temperate zones.

ACTIVE COMPOUND	MILLION PRESCRIPTIONS	PERCENTAGE OF TOTAL
Steroids (95% from Diosgenin)	225·050	14.69
Atropine	22·980	1.50
Reserpine	22·214	1.45
Pilocarpine	3·983	0.26
Quinidine	2·758	0.18
Total	**276.985**	**18.08**

△ These 1973 figures show the extent of our debt to the rainforest biome: over 276 million medical prescriptions issued in the US alone were based on just five pure compounds derived from rainforest plants. Of some 3,000 plants now known to possess anticancer properties, no fewer than 2,100 are from tropical rainforests.

The life-saving cinchona tree

Had the cinchona tree (*Cinchona* spp.) of the eastern Andean tropical forest not yielded quinine, this world's tropical, subtropical, and even some temperate climate residents would be laboring under the scourge of unmitigated endemic malaria. (The spread of this mosquito-transmitted disease is in large part the result of tropical deforestation, as removal of the forest canopy brings the mosquito (*Anopheles* spp.) down to ground level and thus into contact with humans.) Even now responsible for more deaths than any other transmissible disease, the horror of malaria afflicts 200 million people worldwide. Over one million die annually in Africa alone.

During recent fieldwork in Zaïre, both myself and a colleague, Roxanne Kremer, came down with falciparum malaria (*Plasmodium falciparum*), the most dangerous of several malaria strains which may be lethal on the first attack. We were in an extremely remote sector of the Ituri Forest and the

△ On Costa Rica's Cano Island, the author picks a Costus *species, widely used by past cultures as treatment for kidney ailments. He also found it remarkably effective as a dentifrice.*

attacks raged day after day, with chills, pain, paralyzing hallucinations, and fever hovering near 104°F (40°C). Fortunately, my son Gandhi, the third member of our party, nursed us both until we could make radio contact with Nyankunde Mission Hospital in the Ituri region, to which safe haven we were subsequently airlifted for treatment.

You may be able to appreciate my profound respect for quinine. Synthetic drugs such as chloroquine, quinacrine, and primaquine were produced only after quinine, and this accomplishment was made possible only by using the original compound as a model. Yet even now an ever-growing number of tropical areas have developed a type of malaria resistant to synthetic chloroquine drugs (the strain we incurred was of this type), and our prophylactic antimalarials are becoming largely ineffective. Physicians therefore are once again using quinine. The multi-faceted quinine is also used in the treatment of headache and neuralgia, for cardiac arrhythmia, as a sclerosing agent in the treatment of varicose veins, as a substitute anesthetic for cocaine, in the treatment of bacteriological infections, including pneumonia, and as a stomachic and labor inducer as well.

▽ *Machiguenga Indians in a remote Peruvian forest presented the author's expedition with a myriad traditionally used forest plants after expedition members had saved the lives of two tribesmen with modern medicines. The cultural exchange was completed when the tribal medicine man, using local herbs, cured the author and others of a severe reaction to black-fly bites when the expedition's medications proved quite ineffective.*

Another plant, the Mexican yam (*Dioscorea* spp.), found only in tropical forests, yields diosgenin used in the manufacture of cortisone and hydrocortisone for the treatment of a wide spectrum of ills including rheumatoid arthritis, rheumatic fever, ulcerative colitis, various allergies, sciatica, Addison's disease, and certain skin diseases. This versatile species is also used in the preparation of various sex hormones, including "the pill." Potential over-the-counter sales of this one product alone exceed $700 million.

As an example of the potential impact on humanity of a single plant, note our current reliance on the nontropical purple foxglove (*Digitalis* sp.), which gives us digitalis, the savior of congestive heart failure. Digoxin from another foxglove is three hundred times stronger, and much faster acting. In America alone, over three million people would expire within as little as seventy-two hours without this plant-derived drug.

△ *A miracle plant from Eden, this* Dioscorea, *half-hidden in the ground litter of the author's Cathedral Rain Forest Science Preserve in Costa Rica, is the source of diosgenin, a compound with a wide range of uses including the birth control pill.*

The cancer connection

Another plant, the rosy periwinkle (*Catharanthus roseus*) from the tropical Madagascan forests, produces 75 different alkaloids. Two, vincristine and vinblastine, have produced a major breakthrough in the treatment of cancer. Chemotherapy involving these drugs achieves 99 percent remission for acute lymphocytic leukemia and 80 percent remission for Hodgkin's disease (and in an impressive number of cases, complete cures) where previously there existed only a 19 percent chance for remission of this dreaded disease. In addition, the two drugs are responsible for 50 to 80 percent remission for several other forms of cancer. The United States Cancer Institute has stated that "the widespread elimination of the tropical moist forests could represent a serious setback to the anticancer campaign."

As the habitat holocaust continues, how do we measure such losses? Noted biologist George M. Woodwell considers this continuing biological degradation to be "one of the great issues of our time, right up with nuclear proliferation, the stability of government, and health care. The ultimate resource is biota – there is no other, and we are destroying it."

*The rosy periwinkle of Madagascar (*Catharanthus roseus*) now gives 99% remission from some forms of childhood leukemia, and is also effective against Hodgkin's disease.*

A CORNUCOPIA OF NEW FOODS

Almost all our food originates from hybridized wild plants. Indeed, most all of us are partaking daily in the bounty of the tropical forests without ever giving a thought to the origin of the foods we eat regularly. Let's simply consider breakfast. Do you like corn flakes? These are made from plants originating in the South American forests. Or do you prefer rice crispies, whose origins lie in the Asian forests? Sugar is from Indian forests; bananas, Asian; pineapple, Venezuelan; hash brown potatoes, not Irish but Andean; orange juice, Asian; tomato juice, Central American; cocoa and chocolate, not Swiss but Latin American; coffee, Ethiopian; tea, Asian; and eggs – even these are derived from the tropical forests, from the Asian jungle fowl (*Gallus gallus*). Meat, milk, or cheese? These are products of cattle descended from the endangered banteng (*Bos banteng*) of the Javan forests. Fully 80 percent of what we eat has its origins in the tropics. In fact, even we evolved there!

Now we see why conservationists have compared the present exploitation and extinction of species for transient benefits to the burning of a Rembrandt masterpiece for an hour's warmth.

△ *Photographed wild in its native Javan jungle, this banteng bull (*Bos banteng*) is the ancestor of our familiar domestic cattle. Without our help he would soon be extinct: without him we have no gene stock for future hybridization.*

Untapped food resources

Humankind's dependence on the tropical forest genetic pool is marked by the little-known fact that 90 percent of the world's food is produced from only 20 plant species and a dangerously few seed varieties, yet many thousands of species are believed to be edible. Through hybridization, a few wild species of one genus have produced a whole range of familiar vegetables – cabbage, broccoli, kale, cauliflower, and brussel sprouts.

Botanical breeding programs turn increasingly to wild plants to find genetic traits that can be integrated into the 20 crop species upon which most of the world's people depend. Some plant hybridizers already warn that the potential for improvement in that minimal number of crop species may be reaching its limit. It is time, they say, to go back into the wild and find new plant species that can be domesticated for food. (So narrow is the tolerance of modern hybrid-crop varieties that a 1.8°F (1.0°C) drop in global temperature could cause rice production to fall by a catastrophic 45 percent.)

In the forests of southern China grows a vine known as the gooseberry (*Actinidia chinensis*). The juice from its fruit, now known popularly as the kiwi, is up to eighteen times richer in vitamin C than orange juice.

From Amazonia, *tucuma* palm fruit (*Astrocaryum vulgare*), has a vitamin A content three times that of a carrot, previously thought one of the best sources of vitamin A. From the same forest, the peach palm fruit (*Bactris gasipaes*) has twice the protein of banana and will produce more carbohydrate and protein per acre than maize. Yet another Amazonian palm fruit, *patauá* (*Jessenia bataua*) has revealed its protein to be comparable to good animal protein, and appreciably better than most grain and even legume sources. In fact, the biological value of its protein is 40 percent higher than that of soybean.

In South America, *guaraná* (*Paullinia cupana*) is a staple food, yet it remains virtually unknown elsewhere. Unbeknown to many, it provides the active

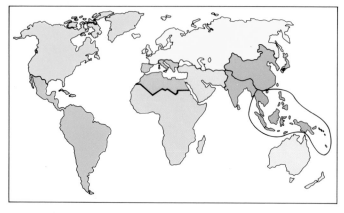

△ **Genetic diversity of plants**
Almost 80% of our food crops are derived from tropical stock, and it is to that biome we must return for the genetic resources we will need if we are to produce new food crops, resistant to disease, insect pests, and climatic constraints, in the fight against world food shortages.

NORTH AMERICA
Sunflower

LATIN AMERICA
Maize
Potato
Sweet potato
Cocoa
Cassava
Tomato
Cotton (lint)
Cottonseed (oil)
Seed cotton (meal)
Tobacco
Rubber

AFRICA
Oil palm (oil)
Oil palm (kernel)
Sorghum
Millet
Coffee

CHINA-JAPAN
Soybeans
Oranges
Rice
Tea

EUROPE-NORTH ASIA
Oats
Rye

MEDITERRANEAN
Sugar beet
Cabbage
Rapeseed
Olives

WEST-CENTRAL ASIA
Wheat
Barley
Grapes
Apples
Linseed
Sesame
Flax

INDIA
Jute
Rice

AUSTRALIA
None

SOUTHEAST ASIA
Banana
Coconut (copra)
Yams
Rice
Sugar cane

ingredient in a very popular over-the-counter herbal weight-reduction remedy. Its caffeine content is three to five times that of coffee, and Brazilians consume over *15 million* bottles of *Guaraná* soda daily.

From the forests of Southeast Asia a previously uncultivated fruit called the mangosteen (*Garcinia mangostana*) is purported to be "perhaps the world's best tasting fruit." But on that point perhaps I would take issue. I recall sampling the most delectable fruit I have ever tasted from a small tree on my Cathedral Rain Forest Science Preserve in Costa Rica. Consuming a small portion and feeling no ill effects, I was anxious to return to the tree early in the morning for much more of the same. The tree, to my enormous disappointment, had been completely stripped by a troop of monkeys during the evening. In my disappointment, I found myself nibbling the monkeys' leftovers, lying half-eaten on the ground.

Although I marked the tree for future identification when in flower, it was subsequently lost when a squatter deforested the very acre on which the tree had stood. In the fifteen-year period since then I have been unable to locate another specimen of the species, and not once have I seen the fruit in a native market. The potential for loss in such a scenario is easily extended to the whole biome.

In the mysterious forests of New Guinea grow 251 tree species that are known to bear edible fruit, yet only 43 have so far been ushered into cultivation. One East Indian tribe regularly uses no fewer than 17 forest plants as a source of fruit drinks – significantly more varieties than can be found on any modern supermarket shelf!

The forests of Southeast Asia and New Guinea have also given us the winged bean (*Psophocarpus tetragonolobus*). With up to 42 percent protein, more amino acids than any other staple vegetable food, and leaves containing up to 20,000 units of vitamin A, it is no wonder the US National Academy of Sciences in 1975 stated, "Of all the plants examined, the winged bean emerged as most capable of relieving protein hunger [in the Third World]."

△ *A wild dwarf pineapple plant (*Ananas *sp.) stands unobtrusively among blooms of red flowering* Neoregelia *in the upland forests of Venezuela. This small and insignificant plant should remind us of the enormous debt we owe the forest. Commercial pineapple cultivation today is a multi-billion-dollar worldwide industry.*

Dessert for some, staple for many

Of great current importance are the staple subsistence crops that feed masses of people in tropical wet areas and which can become a significant export of these Third World nations. High on this list would be manioc (*Manihot utilissima*). As its Latin name suggests, this is a multipurpose, rampantly growing tuberous root with vegetation shooting up from cuttings to 8 feet (2.4 m) tall in only a few months. As a paste, porridge, or meal, boiled whole, or in the form of flour, it serves as a cheap and abundant starch for people who would otherwise starve. We know it in the United States and Europe in the form of tapioca. A single plant can produce 50 pounds (23 kg) of edible root. (Lethal toxins present in the plant are extracted during processing.)

Manioc is known, however, as a "cheat" starch. It contains only 1 percent protein, and few vitamins, and people who rely solely on it for nutrition will surely develop malnutrition and a related scourge of the world's poor – kwashiorkor. We have all seen the pathetic pictures of sufferers of this disease, the sunken eyes, pot bellies, and arm and leg bones covered only in skin. Kwashiorkor kills over four million people, mostly children, every year.

A ray of hope, however, is that First World botanists are now attempting to develop high-protein strains of manioc. Again it is a case of going back to the wild populations of the crop's relatives, usually in virgin habitats, in search of protein-rich varieties with which to interbreed; but the habitats must still be intact or we will have burned our genetic bridges behind us. In actuality, many of the relatives of our common agricultural crops are already being lost to extinction through habitat destruction.

We have seen the tragic vulnerability of disease-susceptible cultivars in the Irish potato famine of the 1840s when over two million people perished, and in the United States corn blight of 1970. These issues transcend academics and strike at the very heart of human survival. A new genetic constitution must be bred into food-crop varieties about every five to fifteen years as diseases infiltrate the plants' defenses. We are now, it is feared, on the brink of losing this flexibility.

Perennial corn – the farmer's dream

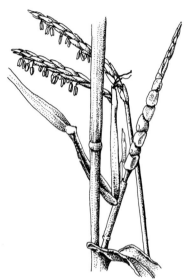

△ The potato blight of 1846 wiped out virtually the entire Irish crop in one season and resulted in the starvation of up to one million people. The recent discovery of an ancient perennial corn in the mountains of Mexico holds promise of new food-crop strains that will be less susceptible to failures of such tragic scale.

△ Rafael Guzman, a young Mexican botany student, and his discovery Zea diploperennis – not only perennial but also resistant to 5 of the world's 7 major corn viruses.

Recently a young Mexican botanist exploring a mountainous area in Mexico came upon a small, high valley, where he encountered clumps of a shaggy cornlike grass. Previously unrecorded in science, this wild grain may soon completely revolutionize the cultivation of corn worldwide.

This priceless discovery was a new perennial species of teosinte (*Zea diploperennis*), a member of the grass family (Gramineae) and a distant relative of annual teosinte, the ancestor of modern corn (*Zea mays*). Such distant relatives of corn may have special value, in this case an almost complete resistance to most of corn's major diseases. While it has been suggested that the new find may lead to the development of a hybrid corn that will send up new shoots each year without replanting, thus saving labor, time, money, and fertility by avoiding the necessity of plowing fields and replanting new seed, this development would produce very low-yielding crops. On the other hand, the above-mentioned disease resistance may in time save enormous proportions of future corn crops.

This new discovery by University of Guadalajara botanist Rafael Guzman, and Hugh Iltis and colleagues at the University of Wisconsin, is but one of scores of new and valuable biological breakthroughs based on utilizing newly discovered genetic material from the earth's remaining natural areas. It is gratifying to know that in 1987 the Mexican government declared the whole mountain range the UNESCO Reserva Biosfera de la Sierra de Manantlan, comprising 350,000 acres (141,650 ha) and ranging from 1,300 feet to nearly 10,000 feet (400 m to nearly 3,000 m). Here a marvelous diversity of plants and animals will be protected.

Vast areas of the world have soils too salty for grain production. By hybridizing with standard rice a variety of wild rice that grows in salt water, scientists are now producing a commercial rice that is perfectly adapted to these regions of saline soils that exist, "unused," globally. (It should be recognized in balance that these areas are not, however, wastelands but valid and precious habitats themselves, supporting rich and varied floras and faunas. They must therefore be used only with care and forethought.)

Geneticists also hope to avert much of the 40 percent loss of food crops currently incurred in the field and in storage through the ravages of pests. They look to the tropical rainforest for cross-breeding stock to induce pest resistance in plants (almost a prerequisite for survival in tropical plants and usually effected by means of "fur," spines, or chemical repulses). The aim must be to develop more permanent *natural* biological controls on pests instead of dependence on extremely toxic chemical poisons that lose their effectiveness in time and have proved to be dangerous to humans and other animals as well as to the target pests. Monetary returns with these methods have yielded an incredible $30 for each $1 outlay, and have increased crop yields exponentially.

Improving animal husbandry

Geneticists also look to the tropical rainforest for improvement of our animal stock. Near the Thailand/Kampuchea border lives a very rare and elusive bovine, the kouprey (*Bos sauveli*). It is presumed to be one of the wild ancestors of the humped zebu cattle used for beef production in many areas of the world. This and other wild cattle such as the gaur (*Bos gaurus*), anoa (*Babalus depressicornis*), and tamarau (*Bos mindorensis*) could markedly increase world beef production by revitalizing domestic breeds in cross breeding. Their habitats, however, have been war-ravaged, defoliated with lethal herbicides, and otherwise disturbed by human activities for a protracted period of time, so that ultimate survival of these creatures will require immediate concerted action.

THE FOREST'S INDUSTRIAL POTENTIAL

Such poignant realities as the poem from *Green Medicine: A Search for Plants that Heal* highlight a dramatic and practical void in global environmental policy and law. Biological diversity has no protection, and no provision for compensation at present. This is unacceptably archaic. Our courts will award judgment to an aggrieved party if his tree is unlawfully cut down, but should a species be exterminated by industrial activity, or to stretch the point for means of illustration, by a wantonly malicious act, there is no compensation, even though typical sales for a plant-based drug are in the neighborhood of $50 million per annum! Even more to the point, daughters, and other souls, like the one in our poem, could die for want of a drug based on a plant that has been extirpated.

From what we have reviewed of wildlife tourism, medicines, and foods derived from the tropical forest, it is apparent that vast potential economic resources remain unutilized. Taking this all-important point into consideration, Charles Peters of the New York Botanical Garden, Alwyn Gentry of the Missouri Botanical Garden, and Louis and Robert Mendelsohn of Yale use a "net present value" to reflect the human tendency to see advantage in taking an "all-at-once" harvest, placing a current value on an infinite harvest, and discounting present monetary value to expected inflation. Their results are illuminating.

Robert Mendelsohn explained to me that not only are tropical forests worth considerably more than was previously supposed, but that the actual market benefits of timber are quite small in relation to other nonwood forest resources. For instance, 2.47 acres (1 hz) of forest will produce, annually, $400 in fruit and $22 in rubber. But as these trees produce every year, the true value far exceeds those figures. For those products alone the net present value is $6,330. In contrast, the one-time nonrenewable exploitation of the plot's timber would net a revenue of $1,000, periodic cutting of selected trees would yield a net present value of $490, while a tree plantation on the same plot would have a net present value of $3,184. Converted to pasture it would yield

I wonder what's around the bend?
  said the explorer.
I wonder what that plant is?
  said the collector.
I wonder what's in it?
  said the chemist.
I wonder what activity it has?
  said the pharmacologist.
I wonder if it will work in this case?
  said the physician.
I hope she lives!
  said the father.
Please God!
  said the mother.
I think she'll be all right in the morning,
  said the nurse.

GREEN MEDICINE: Search for Plants that Heal (1964) by Margaret Kreig.

less than $2,960, or less than half the value of the fruit and rubber that could be judiciously cropped from the climax forest. Climax forest used in this way would go on to serve humankind and the environment indefinitely. Rattans alone, collected in Old World tropical forests, generate a global trade totaling $4 billion.

In his Earthscan briefing document *What Use is Wildlife?*, Norman Meyers suggests that the United States may even be more crucially dependent on foreign plants and animals for food, medicine, and industry than on foreign oil. Their importance cannot be underscored strongly enough.

The Brazilian oil tree

Examples of this legacy appear daily in scientific journals, and several recent discoveries even go so far as to promise to augment fossil-fuel oil supplies.

One article entitled *Brazilian Tree Pours Pure Diesel Fuel*, tells of University of California chemist Melvin Calvin's discovery in Brazil not long ago. He was taken into the Amazon Forest by an Amazon Indian and shown a 100-year-old, 100-foot (30-m) tree called the copa-iba (*Copaifera langsdorfii*). A plug in a bunghole drilled in the tree's trunk was removed, and a beautiful golden oil issued forth. Although certain plants in the euphorbia family are known to have the ability to reduce carbon dioxide to hydrocarbon compounds, none literally pours oil like the copa-iba.

Calvin reported that this oily sap was used as a base for perfumes and a healing ointment for cuts. But "nobody realized it was diesel fuel until I got there this year." He added at a presidential address that the Brazilians have already "put [the sap] in a car directly out of the tree, and it ran fine." He added jokingly, "You don't even need an oil company." Calvin was awarded the Nobel Prize for his discovery.

It is now known that such a tree will yield approximately 5 gallons (almost 20 l) of the sesquiterpene hydrocarbons from a single bunghole in two hours, and that it can be retapped at six-month intervals. Thousands of tree seedlings have already been planted by the Brazilian government for later distribution to warmer areas in the United States, and the current update declares that fully 20 percent of Brazil's diesel fuel is now supplied from the tree.

Yet another Amazonian oil tree of significant future industrial application is a swamp-growing palm, *Mauritia* sp., whose large seeds contain an oil which maintains its lubricating qualities at extremely high temperatures. French investigators are in the process of utilizing this characteristic in military and high-altitude weather rockets.

Tropical Third World futures

Perhaps the most immediate incentive for tropical governments to regulate and sustain their forest resources is provided by a historical review of one of the nations that failed to do so. Once among the world's largest tropical log exporters, Nigeria in 1964 exported 27.3 million cubic feet (773,000 cu m) of timber. The nation's exports have, however, recently diminished to 2.1 million cubic feet (59,500 cu m), due mainly to increases in domestic consumption – a growing trend in Third World countries. While earning only $6 million in 1985 from *exports* of all forest products, Nigeria spent $160 million on *imports* of those same products! While thirty-three Third World nations are currently net exporters of wood, that figure will drop to twenty within the coming decade.

III · ATMOSPHERIC STABILITY

It is estimated that the tropical forests are responsible for a major proportion of the earth's biological productivity. This, of course, represents a vast yearly intake (through photosynthesis) of carbon dioxide, which is stored in the form of carbon in the trees' tissues. Not long ago, the alarming results of the most vital ongoing scientific research were revealed. It is possible that over the long term no discovery to date will have a more profound effect on our well-being or the state of our planet.

Since 1958, Charles D. Keeling of the Scripps Institution of Oceanography has conducted a continuous monitoring of atmospheric carbon dioxide from a research station in Hawaii. Other records have been kept by other researchers representing many governments, sampling air at the South Pole, in Australia, at Point Barrow in Alaska, and on Long Island, New York, as well as at many other locations. The amassed data point to one overriding conclusion.

The CO_2 connection

Biologist George M. Woodwell of Woods Hole Research Center states, "In the century and a quarter since 1850, human activities have increased the amount of carbon dioxide in the atmosphere of the earth from 270 parts per million or less to slightly more than 330 parts per million. Perhaps a fourth of the total increase has come within the past decade. By the year 2020, if present trends continue, the amount of carbon dioxide in the atmosphere could approach twice the current value." The majority of the increase has been attributed to the burning of fossil fuels and to tropical deforestation.

The significance of deforestation in the "greenhouse gas" (GHG) buildup can be underscored thus: although only 30 percent of the earth's surface is composed of land, primary production by terrestrial vegetation is slightly more than twice that of the oceans. Further, there is five-hundred times more carbon locked up in land plants than in all the marine ecosystems combined. Dramatically, the carbon held in trees roughly equals the amount in our atmosphere.

While there is nothing in future scenarios to suggest that people will ever be running amok for want of oxygen, or succumbing to lethal concentrations of carbon monoxide, the most conservative estimate's bottom line has us very much paying the piper on this debt, and at dates not far into the future. There is ample justification for current anxieties that we may be ill-equipped to meet these payments as they come due.

The recent findings of a "dry extraction" method developed for analyzing the air bubbles trapped in ancient polar ice were sobering. A team of French researchers from the Laboratoire de Glaciologie et de Geophysique de l'Environnement shows that during the Ice Age 15,000–20,000 years ago, CO_2 constituted 0.016 percent of our atmosphere. Today that portion has risen to 0.033 percent!

As these data were being assimilated, yet another discovery of equal import was confirmed in their wake. Paul Crutzen, a spokesman for the National Center for Atmospheric Research (NCAR), in Boulder, Colorado, reported that

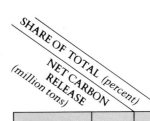

SHARE OF TOTAL NET CARBON RELEASE (million tons)		SHARE OF TOTAL (percent)
Brazil	336	20
Indonesia	192	12
Colombia	123	7
Côte d'Ivoire	101	6
Thailand	95	6
Laos	85	5
Nigeria	60	4
Philippines	57	3
Burma	51	3
Peru	45	3
Ecuador	40	3
Vietnam	36	2
Zaïre	35	2
Mexico	33	2
India	33	2
Others	337	20
Total	**1,659**	**100**

△ Estimates of various nations' release of carbon into the atmosphere as a result of deforestation show Brazil far in the lead. These 1980 figures are in the middle of the estimated range. Tropical forests of the world lock up about 55% of total biomass carbon, while temperate and boreal forests account for about 33% overall.

△ *The aftermath of forest burning in Amazonia. The carbon held in trees is roughly equal to that in the atmosphere, and land vegetation holds some 500 times as much carbon as all the marine ecosystems combined. As this data has only recently come to light, it is not surprising that the CO_2-climate connection is only now gaining the credibility it deserves.*

there is also, presently, an alarming buildup of carbon monoxide (CO) in our atmosphere. According to NCAR, the major source of this gas is an increase in the burning of vegetation around the globe. Cutting and burning of the tropical rainforest looms out in this study as a major culprit along with fossil-fuel use.

Atmospheric decay

Scientists of NCAR have conducted intensive probes into the Amazon rainforest in search of the causes of these escalating gas imbalances. "We had always thought the southern hemisphere would be pristine because there is so little industry," states team member James Greenberg. "But we found as much carbon monoxide over the Amazon jungles as over US suburbs – that was a big discovery." The major source? The slashing and burning of the Amazon Forest.

The effects of carbon monoxide build-up promise to be severe, but not because the gas is toxic, as concentrations will not reach those extreme levels. However, future consequences could include suffocating runaway killer smogs, more severe than the historically lethal London smogs that were caused by the burning of coal. The carbon monoxide produced by burning vegetation is three times the amount caused by the burning of fossil fuels, Crutzen reports, and the dense smogs which may result are expected to be long-lived phenomena.

It appears that the amount of carbon monoxide released by burning vegetation is twenty times higher than was previously estimated. Atmospheric chemists of the National Center for Atmospheric Research have discovered that the reaction rate of CO with the hydroxyl radical (OH) is twice as high as was previously assumed. "That meant a large source of CO was lurking somewhere, undiscovered." The chemists explain that "OH cleanses the lower atmosphere by reaction with nearly all pollutants." (Quite a useful radical to have in your employ.) An excess of CO, however, will surpass OH and allow the pollutants to build.

Robert Watkins of the National Aeronautics and Space Administration (NASA), which monitors the upper atmosphere by satellite, virtually puts a cap on any fence-walking dialogue. Watkins stated in a June 1986 *Newsweek* article that "global warming is inevitable – it's only a question of magnitude and time." The EPA goes on in the same science report to project rises of between 2 feet and 12 feet (0.6 m to 3.7 m) in sea levels by the year 2100, and claims that a 3-foot (0.9-m) rise expected by 2030 would poison irrigation sources and bleed into the drinking water supplies of many cities worldwide, as well as flooding huge tracts of densely inhabited coastal land.

In a July 1988 statement following accelerating drought and agricultural crop failures, James Hansen, climate expert at the NASA Goddard Institute of Space Studies, testified to the Senate Energy Committee that the rise in average global temperature for this year so far was 0.72°F (0.4°C) relative to known temperatures for the period 1950–1980. Hansen stated he was 99 percent certain (there is never 100 percent certainty of anything, he clarified) that greenhouse gases are responsible for the warming trend. Drawing on figures for the preceding 100 years, he continued that the 1980s alone show a 1.17°F (0.6–0.7°C) increase, and the five warmest years in the last century.

Presently a growing coalition of scientists has declared serious concern that the longer regulatory action is delayed, the more severe and irreversible will be the impact of these changes on world climate and our ability to feed ourselves; and this could be the legacy we bequeath to our children.

The "greenhouse effect"

The "greenhouse gases" have been an atmospheric reality since our planet formed and stabilized eons ago. They have, however, been regulated by earth's steady-state systems, and without the presence of these gases the planet would be approximately 54°F (30°C) colder.

Although still only trace gases in our atmosphere, GHGs are playing an ever-more critical role in controlling our climate. CO_2, CO, and chlorofluorocarbons (CFCs), absorb radiant energy at infrared wavelengths, continuously trapping more heat as the GHG concentration rises. This has caused a global warming phenomenon we now know as the "greenhouse effect."

Continued on page 146

THE GREENHOUSE EFFECT

Is humanity viewing the tunnel at the end of the light? There are many in the scientific world who now believe it is. While ignorance may have excused us in the past, we are now fully aware of the consequences of our actions and the future of the global habitat is in our own hands.

△ ▷ *Point of attack*
The major sources of green-house gases (GHGs) are the industrialized regions of the world, but reducing current output will be difficult, and slow. A more promising attack could, however, be made on forest burning, already contributing 35% of the CO_2 released.

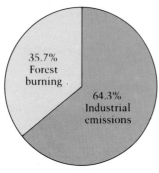

35.7% Forest burning

64.3% Industrial emissions

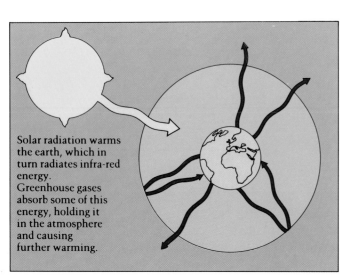

Solar radiation warms the earth, which in turn radiates infra-red energy. Greenhouse gases absorb some of this energy, holding it in the atmosphere and causing further warming.

◁ *The greenhouse effect*
Human impact on the environment has greatly impaired our planet's equilibrium and its ability to compensate effectively. The sun's radiation warms the earth which then itself releases energy as infra-red radiation. The increasing buildup of GHGs, however, is deflecting ever-greater amounts of that energy back to earth creating a heat trap. It is now known that chloro-fluorocarbons (CFCs), a group of gases recognized in

1974 to destroy atmospheric ozone, also trap thermal radiation 10,000 times as effectively as CO_2, so compounding the problem. With currently projected increases in world population, even if we double our energy efficiency and reduce our use of CFCs, total output of greenhouse gases will still be increasing at a dangerous pace.

▷ Turning up the planet's thermostat

Temperature increases will not be uniform over the earth's surface. The polar regions will probably warm three times as much as the global average, resulting in changes to wind patterns which will have profound effects on agriculture. For example, with a rise of 7°F (4°C) by the year 2030 (a temperature increase never before experienced by the human species) many of the mid-latitude grain-producing regions – the "bread-baskets" of the world – could become arid.

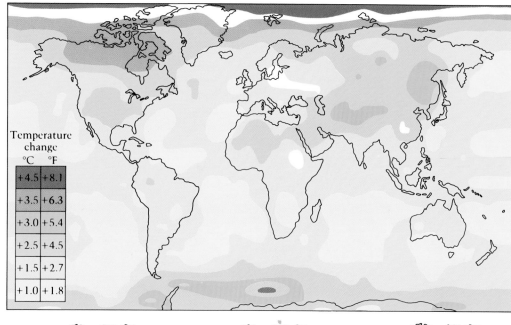

Temperature change	
°C	°F
+4.5	+8.1
+3.5	+6.3
+3.0	+5.4
+2.5	+4.5
+1.5	+2.7
+1.0	+1.8

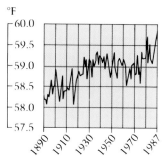

1950-1980 average

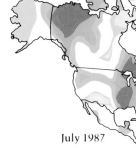

July 1987

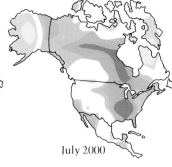

July 2000

July 2030

△ Record warmth

Records of average global temperatures show an inexorable rise through the present century. Most scientists agree that the trend started with the industrial revolution, but the past 20 years have shown a marked acceleration.

△ An endless summer?

In a scenario entitled "The endless summer," the green-house effect will pro-duce a rise of between 3°F (1.7°C) and 8°F (4.4°C) over the next 50 years. Even at much lower rates of 0.2°F (0.1°C) per decade, which may appear small, the

changes are 10 to 20 times greater than those typical of the transition from the last Ice Age to the post-glacial period. One consequence of the scenario could be a 50% reduction in rainfall in America's grain belt – shifting prime production north into Canada.

Temperature increase

°C	°F	°C	°F
−3.0	−5.4	1.0	1.8
−2.0	−3.6	2.0	3.6
−1.0	−1.8	3.0	5.4
0.0	0.0	5.0	9.0

▷ Flood scenarios

The maps on the right show the kind of impact that major sea-level changes could have on some of the world's most densely populated low-lying coastal regions. In the case of Bangladesh, a 10-foot (3-m) rise would affect most of that country's population.

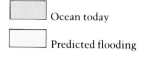

Ocean today

Predicted flooding

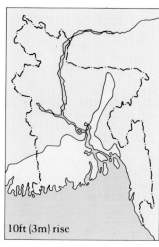

10ft (3m) rise

Bangladesh

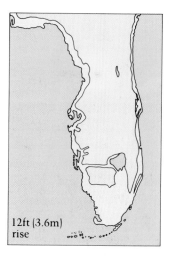

12ft (3.6m) rise

Florida, USA

10ft (3m) rise

Netherlands

It appears likely that as the net concentration of CO_2 doubles its current 350 ppm some time before the year 2050, temperatures will rise 2.6–9.7°F (1.2–4.5°C) – even using conservative figures. Other published statistics are almost 300 percent higher on the upside, higher than the human species has ever experienced; and if this does not appear at first glance to be meaningful, the lower figure is a more dramatic change than we have experienced in the past 10,000 years. A very conservative 1.8°F (1°C) increase alone could cause an 11 percent decrease in United States corn production and reduce by over $268 million the gross income of spring-wheat farmers. In 1988 alone, the early phases of the drought resulted in $2 billion in losses to American farmers – and that represented only nine weeks without rain! Further, such temperature increases could last a millennium, or more.

At only 3.6°F (2°C), calculations predict a scenario of doubling the frequency, extending the formation area, and increasing the power of hurricanes – perhaps by 50 percent! (Hurricane Gilbert, in 1988, was the most violent on record, producing wind velocities in excess of 200 mph (320+ kmph). Coinciding with that, it is expected that precipitation over the American grain belt will be reduced by 50 percent. As ocean currents descend and rise, bringing up nutrients from uncustomary depths, food-fish production will also fall off, reports Carl Wunsch of the Massachusetts Institute of Technology. Clearly, the potential exists for a severe loss of food production from both land and sea at a time when global population will be doubling in thirty years and then tripling its present figures.

William Kellogg of the National Center for Atmospheric Research warns that polar temperatures are expected to rise at three to five times the average world rate. Thus, substantial climate change is expected to occur if world temperatures rise by only a degree and a half centigrade, a fact ignored by those apparently unable to respond to this potentially catastrophic issue.

Herman Flohn, founder of the Institute of Meteorology at the University of Bonn, offers a historical perspective and a realistically bleak future scenario. He states that "the European revolutions of 1789 and 1884 occurred after a succession of years with bad weather, bad harvests, and high cereal prices ... what has happened can happen again," and he is intense in his belief that "this risk is unacceptable and must be avoided even at very high cost."

The greenhouse effect is suspected, in turn, of contributing significantly to desertification, the phenomenon we have all observed in news and documentary reports. As deserts grow and consume former agricultural areas, we are simultaneously faced with the prospect of the world's growing population relying on these areas to produce additional sustenance. Multitudes perished in the recent Sahelian tragedy, in areas that have in the past supported agriculture or livestock grazing, but have become arid due to climatic fluctuations compounded by overpressure on the land.

The great carbon sink

Researchers have shown that tropical rainforest is responsible for the highest net primary production of carbon per unit area to be found on earth. This is particularly striking as tropical forest covers less than 7 percent of earth's landmass. As the rainforest is destroyed, this carbon is no longer captured but, conversely, is released into our atmosphere.

Estimates have emerged on this impact. In 1987, Brazil alone burned some 50 million acres (20 million ha) which included 20 million acres (8 million ha) of primary tropical forest – ominously up from the 5 million acres (2 million ha) of primary tropical forest burned in 1986. Brazil's fires in 1988 covered an area of forest the size of West Germany.

Woods Hole Research Institute assigns a yearly production of 5.6 billion tons of carbon to the burning of fossil fuels and from 1 to 3 billion tons (we will use 2) to deforestation, for a total man-made atmospheric carbon contribution of 7.6 billion tons annually. The carbon sinks of the oceans and forests absorb some 4.8 billion tons, leaving 2.5 to 3.0 billion tons excess yearly. Of this, Brazil's share alone is 500 million tons, or 20 percent of the total excess.

Global temperatures for the past two decades are the highest since records have been kept. The Congressional Record of July 1988 highlights Senator Timothy Wirth's testimony that the global warming phenomenon is "the most significant economic, political, environmental, and human challenge of the next decade and well into the next century for all of us."

The melting of the ice caps

Mankind now faces an unprecedented dilemma. GHGs, until recently benign trace gases in the atmosphere, are now widely recognized as deeply implicated in the potential melting of the polar ice caps.

Of all the earth's fresh water the largest single amount is locked up in the six-million-square-mile (15.5-million-sq-km) West Antarctic ice cap. Stephen Leatherman of the University of Maryland's Center for Global Change reflects recent qualified estimates which question the likelihood of the West Antarctic ice sheet melting in the next 100 years, and put the upper limit of probable sea level rise at 9.8 feet (3 m) but probably considerably less, primarily from the melting of alpine glaciers and the Greenland margins. Leatherman points out that we have already experienced a one foot (0.3 m) change over the last century. The authors of low-range findings, however, point to "horrendous" uncertainties in this field and state that by adding up all known contributions to the current sea level rise, they cannot match the observed rise of about 1.3 millimeters per year. Should less conservative estimates prove accurate, and the West Antarctic ice sheet melt (and few deny the possibility), it would liberate 6.5 million cubic miles (27.1 million cu km) of water. Scientists predict that coastal cities such as Washington, D.C., as well as low-lying states such as Florida, would be permanently inundated. If tropical deforestation and fossil fuel burning continue at the expected rate, the melting of West Antarctica could conceivably occur: the current debate is not how – but when?

It is hoped that a global agreement can be reached on a "Law of the Atmosphere as a Global Commons." However, results of meetings held so far do not give much cause for optimism: one recommendation advised that planners of installations near the sea should at this time "allow for the risks of sea level rise."

Arctic sea ice, on the other hand, is only 7 to 18 feet (2.1 to 5.5 m) thick, and given a worst-case scenario, the melting of this ice and that of Greenland may be a more serious threat than the melting of Antarctic ice. Flohn, at the University of Bonn, warns that an ice-free Arctic Ocean would most probably lead to displacement of earth's climatic zones by 250 to 500 miles (400 to 800 km), drastically changing freshwater supplies and agricultural productivity. Ocean fish production will diminish at a time when the resource will be

NEWSFLASH: DATELINE 2030

The formerly disparate nations of the Middle East, North Africa, and the United States meet in emergency session in Cairo to discuss a common cause – runaway heat! Most delegates report more than four weeks of temperatures over 130°F (54°C), yet no resolve is established on a plan to envelop major metropolitan areas in air-conditioned domes. The hole in the ozone layer, first detected in the 1980s and now referred to as the ozone blowout, has been proven responsible for a 7 percent skin cancer mortality worldwide.

The major part of most national defense budgets is now allocated to the protection from plunder by masses of refugees of the remaining tropical forests, which now comprise only 1.5 percent of the earth's surface. Major shifts in world power have resulted from similar shifts in major grain-growing areas – this aggravated by several major nations having to finance, at staggering cost, sea walls around the perimeter of their national coastal boundaries.

Not all these projects have been successful. Holland is completely underwater, as are Bangladesh and many Caribbean and Indonesian islands. The Mississippi River has a distinct reverse flow at high tide – its overflow has turned the entire delta, along with most of the US southeastern gulf area, into an enormous infertile brackish marsh.

The state of Florida is likened to a mausoleum presenting a particularly macabre specter. Deserted hotels on Miami Beach, as well as state-of-the-art techno-exhibits of the Epcot Center and Disney World, are saltwater tombs.

While almost one billion have perished from starvation, as former agricultural areas wither in unprecedented heat, many millions more have, for the past decade and a half, been on a relentless trek northward – a tragic spectacle, infinitely dwarfing the sub-Saharan droughts and famines which, almost fify years ago, gave a warning of far greater catastrophes to come.

△ *Flight of fancy – or closer to the truth than comfort would admit? At this stage no one can say with any certainty, but this is the kind of future that some are predicting the world could face if the international community fails to address the problems of global imbalance that now face us.*

heavily relied upon. Presently, 800 million people are on the brink of starvation. It would be logical to assume that the effects of spreading deserts and reduced food production will mean the end for these numbers and more.

It is known that polar ice is an absorber and therefore a reservoir for a wide variety of atmospheric pollutants. There is scientific concern that should the ice melt, it will liberate these stored pollutants, many of which, like chlorofluorocarbons (CFCs, which contribute to warming), can further exacerbate ozone depletion, now an anxiously studied phenomenon in Antarctica and over the North Pole.

Enter the "albedo effect"

To add to the problem we also have the "albedo effect." This phenomenon, which is an increase in solar reflection due to deforestation, will directly alter global patterns of air circulation, convection, and wind. Climatologists warn of a rainfall decrease in equatorial zones, an increase in rainfall for areas between 5 and 25 degrees north and south of the equator, and decreases in areas between 40 and 85 degrees latitude in the north. Due to its large ocean masses, the Southern Hemisphere may be spared substantial changes. It is expected that the hardest-hit area will be the world's breadbasket, the grainlands of the United States and Canada.

On the cutting edge of the greenhouse effect's impact on agriculture, Duke University's research provides additional warnings. While crops such as sorghum and maize, categorized as C–4 plants, will grow only slightly more rapidly due to increased atmospheric CO_2, weeds known as C–3 plants, often associated with those crops in the field, grow much faster under increased CO_2 influence, creating a highly unfavorable competitive advantage. In addition, another (and quite unexpected) effect is a marked increase in insect damage to crop plants resulting from changes in leaf composition at higher

CO$_2$ exposure. These changes result not only in a lowering of plant defenses but also in decreased nutritive values in plants and vegetables which, we can expect, will present deficits in human nutrition.

The hydrological cycle

Aside from the release and build up of gases, there is also the added factor of particulate matter from man's forest burning being suspended in the troposphere, resulting in still greater decreases in rainfall. In addition, deforested soils, such as pasture, absorb less than one-tenth of the water absorbed by forest, and this results in runoff. Thus, 90 percent of the water exits the cycle and becomes unavailable for return to the atmosphere. Climatologists now have ample evidence that approximately one-half of the total precipitation in the Amazon Basin is transported by winds from the Atlantic Ocean. The remaining 50 percent is provided by evapotranspiration from the forest itself. In the rainforest proper (compared with other forest forms, and savanna) the figure for evapotranspiration may be as high as 75 percent of total rainfall. There are now great anxieties that the continued reduction of forest cover by man's activities will reduce rainfall on that forest in a continued downward spiral that could soon fall below the minimum required to support the forest formation, and so effectively seal its fate.

The lungs of the planet

We know that green plant parts contain chlorophyll, which has the exclusive talent of capturing a percentage of the sunlight that reaches them. This energy is used to break down water into hydrogen and oxygen during daylight hours, and also to produce starch and sugar by collecting carbon dioxide from the atmosphere.

Chlorophyll appears to have evolved on earth over approximately the last two billion years, as decomposition products have been identified in rocks containing algae of that antiquity. Before that time our atmosphere contained virtually no oxygen. It is generally accepted that almost all of the oxygen in the earth's atmosphere has been produced over the last two billion years by biological activity, mainly from photosynthesis by plants. This would explain, in part, why other planets' atmospheres are so radically different.

Our crucial dependence on plants may be further acknowledged by our efforts to grow them successfully in a weightless environment, because plants will be essential in providing astronauts not only with food but also with oxygen during possible future interplanetary flights.

Because of the uninterrupted biological activity of tropical rainforests, the constant availability of water, the direct and high intensity of light that reaches these forests, and the fact that they contain the largest terrestrial biomass on earth, it is not surprising that the tropical rainforest is credited with the greatest gas exchange of all earth's habitats.

It is estimated that the global tropical rainforest produces $15,300 \times 10^6$ tons of oxygen per year, or 28 tons per 2.47 acres (1 ha). Although this is a huge amount of oxygen it is approximately the amount consumed during vegetative respiration and by small organisms through concomitant decomposition and decay. The volume of gas exchange, however, is monumental. A significant percentage of this exchange emanates from the faunal-rich humus of the forest soils. Through this exchange, the atmosphere is cleansed of significant quantities of pollutants, which otherwise could build to toxic levels.

IV · A Dwindling Land Resource

▽ Behind the dramatic image of the demarcation between the silt-laden Amazon and the clear dark waters of the Rio Negro near Manaus, Brazil, lies a somber warning. Such is the level of erosion now caused by deforestation that by the year 2000 the amount of topsoil available for use, per person, will have been reduced by 32%, with a consequent loss of crop production of 15-30%.

Tropical forests form new soils even as they prevent erosion, another factor of prominent concern which should be considered, but most often is not, when decisions are taken on converting forest to other land uses. By a sponge effect they release a sustained flow of water during dry seasons and prevent flooding in wet seasons, thus protecting watersheds over immense areas. A closer look at the Amazon, the mightiest river in the world, will illustrate this.

Remarkably, the Amazon River contributes nearly one-fifth of all the fresh water that flows on earth. From its mouth, 5 trillion gallons (23 trillion l) of nutrient-rich water rush into the Atlantic every day. Mightier than any other river, its output would fill Lake Ontario in three hours. The volume is such that it colors the ocean 20 miles (32 km) out to sea, and vastly reduces the ocean's salinity for more than 200 miles (320 km). Its nutrients, which are fed upon by plankton and form the base of a food chain up through the big fish, are carried by currents into the Caribbean, from where the Gulf Stream delivers them along the Atlantic coast all the way to the Grand Banks of Newfoundland. Thus, some of the most fertile fishing grounds in the world are fed directly by the Amazon.

Flood and soil loss – the twin scourges

The Amazon is only one of many scores of major tropical forest rivers that empty into the oceans around the world. When watershed forest is cut, the land is eroded and rivers are loaded with silt, resulting in far more than the normally forest-regulated nutrient load reaching the seas. One might assume that this excess would lead to a greater bounty in fish harvest. The overload of nutrient, however, causes plagues of algal blooms which remove oxygen from the water, creating a decline in fish numbers on an enormous scale.

Siltation also causes the death of coral reefs, which are responsible for building and holding coastal land. With the decay of these basic life-support systems, imbalances occur in the food chains of the ocean, as well as the recession of coastlines. This is blatantly contrasted by the fact that the undisturbed forest is so efficient in its thrift that concentrations of certain nutrients in the streams that drain from these areas have been found to be actually *lower* than the concentrations in the rains falling onto them.

The truly massive erosion caused for the most part by tropical deforestation can be illustrated by the following. To match the transportation of topsoil caused by erosion, every person on earth would have to load 4.9 tons of soil, and then cart it to and deposit it in the nearest body of water – every year! Instead of the regulated, constant year-round flow that results from the "sponge effect" of forest cover, deforested streams and rivers now alternately swell to disastrous flood or shrink to no flow at all. This is compounded by the die-off of biological activity in silted rivers.

▽ *For its entire length across a ridgetop in the eastern Colombian Andes, a freshly cut pipeline route has created a deep gash in the forest cover. Already the steep slope is eroding. Within a year, sheet and gully erosion will have stripped it to bare rock.*

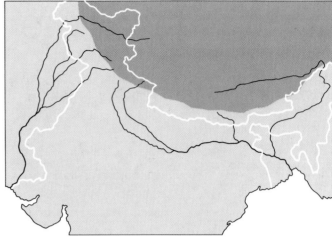

The deforestation of the Himalayas has resulted in devastating erosion downslope and into the lowland plains, even into India. During rains, unchecked flooding has wiped out agriculture and swept entire villages away, causing tragic death tolls. Presently, it is reported that no one sleeps at night in these regions when it rains – and no wonder. In Bangladesh, such floods have resulted in yet-uncounted numbers of dead and 25 million homeless, leading researchers there to declare, "We are no longer dealing with disaster events, but with disaster processes."

The Independent Commission on International Humanitarian Issues alerts us that between 1960 and 1980 the number of people suffering from flooding tripled. In India, one in twenty people are at risk, while during the dry season the other edge of the double-bladed axe of deforestation, drought, takes its toll. In the single Indian state of Maharastra, denuding of watersheds has resulted in the drying up of water supplies in 27,000 villages, up 6,000 in the past five years alone.

While humankind could manipulate its current dependencies on such things as fossil fuels, tropical wood, hydroelectric power, and the like, it is inconceivable that our species could flourish without the largess of earth's topsoil – the basis of our culture. Toward the close of the 1980s, earth is losing each year, through erosion, 25.4 billion tons more topsoil than it produces! This same soil is the very namesake of our planet.

Research emanating from Nigeria shows that cassava (*Manihot esculenta variegata*), one of many crops that leave previously forested soils prone to erosion, when planted on mere 1 percent slopes caused average losses of 8 tons of topsoil per acre per year. On 15 percent grades the loss was 88 tons per acre, at which rate the topsoil would be totally depleted within a decade, but before which (perhaps in only two years) declines in crop yields would dictate abandonment of the site in favor of a fresh plot of forested land.

The mid-1980s brought global attention and concern to the drought and famine in the African sub-Saharan region, where multitudes perished before our eyes on television screens. Although diverse factors contributed to this tragedy, deforestation through overgrazing and fuelwood gathering measured highly. It is known, for instance, that less than a century ago, Ethiopia's surface was 50 percent clothed in forests of various types; today only 3 percent of such cover remains. The direct result is the loss of 269 tons of topsoil per hectare, that's 1,600 million tons per year. Need we ask if Ethiopia can afford that loss? Although worldwide sympathy was given to the country's

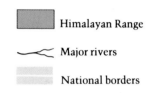

Himalayan Range

Major rivers

National borders

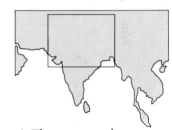

△ *The water catchment area of the Himalayan Range has lost 40% of its forest cover and is now the greatest single ecological hazard on earth in terms of numbers of people involved. The Ganges plain alone is home to 500 million people, and inundation is an inevitable feature of life. Year by year the floods become more severe. In one year some 65,700 villages were flooded, 2,000 people drowned, 40,000 cattle were lost, and property damage ran to more than 2 billion dollars.*

◁ *Another high-profile ecological tragedy – the highlands of Madagascar are bare and scarred where once there was lush forest and a wealth of endemic wildlife.*

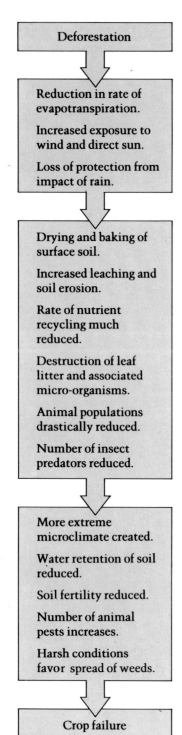

Deforestation

⬇

Reduction in rate of evapotranspiration.

Increased exposure to wind and direct sun.

Loss of protection from impact of rain.

⬇

Drying and baking of surface soil.

Increased leaching and soil erosion.

Rate of nutrient recycling much reduced.

Destruction of leaf litter and associated micro-organisms.

Animal populations drastically reduced.

Number of insect predators reduced.

⬇

More extreme microclimate created.

Water retention of soil reduced.

Soil fertility reduced.

Number of animal pests increases.

Harsh conditions favor spread of weeds.

⬇

Crop failure

△ *Downward progression from deforestation to total crop failure or land exhaustion is an inescapable consequence of short cycle shifting cultivation and cattle raising on tropical-forest soils.*

immediate needs, such as the lack of grain, as was necessary, of course, almost nothing was done to address urgent priorities such as reforestation. Toward this lesson we must, in retrospect, weigh the full meaning and future implications of the wisdom of "an ounce of prevention." Harold Sioli cautions us in relation to the ever-expanding effects of erosion in Amazonia, "There is a danger that the region may develop into a new dust bowl."

1,000 years for the forest's return

In most instances following the disturbance of climax-forest cover, a secondary succession will become established. Such healthy healing will usually follow aboriginal cultivation, where conversion involves reasonably small areas, where terrain permits, compaction has not occurred, and weedy growth is not deflected.

The popular concept, however, of climax forest moving back quickly and regaining the land is altogether false. Secondary-plant species that tolerate the sun create impenetrable thickets, more like the grade-B movie version of "jungle." Where you never use a machete in virgin forest, you often cannot move without one in secondary growth. A chaotic mockery of the former ordered magnificence takes hold. The great majority of the original plants and animals that inhabited the climax forest cannot tolerate this alien environment. Due to the quick seed cycles of the secondary-forest species, rodents move in, and following them comes a rise in the population of snakes.

Only if conditions permit, and a large enough seed reservoir of original forest is left standing nearby, will the successive generations of secondary species slowly die off and permit the original flora to return to a reasonable semblance of climax growth. This process probably requires 200 years at a minimum, but perhaps 1,000 years or more pass before the forest is restored. Beyond this, however, is the concern for the regeneration of large tracts where the nearest source of climax species seed is some kilometers away. For such cases, *The Ecology of Sumatra* speculates a time scale of "hundreds if not thousands of years" for regeneration. Due to the very intense competition for scarce nutrients and light in these forests, it appears that trees in some temperate forests grow even faster than trees in the primary tropical wet forest.

Green mansions to red desert

Once primary forest is removed, the prognosis for the future depends on several factors. When secondary growth is deflected by human disturbance, succession is, of course, retarded. We now increasingly see in areas where the clay subsoil is abused by cattle or machinery – compacted, leached by rain, and parched and baked by the tropical sun – that not even aggressive grasses will grow again. In fact, where cement is unavailable or unaffordable, the laterite soil itself serves very effectively for the construction of airstrips and roads. We have managed to create useless, barren, red deserts where bountiful luxuriance once flourished.

An apt illustration of the permanence of the void that may result is that the bricks used to build the Angkor Wat temples in Kampuchea (Cambodia) were made from the red laterite forest clay. The temples still stand after more than 1,000 years, through war and weather. Incredibly, the forest in the Angkor vicinity was widely cleared and then abandoned in 1431. In the time that has lapsed, some 560 years, the forest still has not returned to a climax state. The

◁ *The slow process of healing begins on a clear-cut patch of hillside in Panama. First to show are light-loving species such as* Heliconia *and* Cecropia *which will mature into secondary forest and provide essential cover for the primary-forest species that will follow. Recovery to mature primary forest will take hundreds, more probably thousands, of years.*

botanically informed will likewise find the composition and structure of the Mayan Petén Forest, near Tikal, somewhat short of climax – and it was abandoned some 1,200 years ago. In "Local Effects of Tropical Deforestation" in *Conservation Biology: The Science of Scarcity and Diversity*, Carl F. Jordan states that the high levels of species diversity and the complex food webs of the original forest may take a great deal longer to return than we may anticipate, or indeed may never return at all if the disturbances have caused important extinctions.

Mounting pressure from an ominously expanding world population is putting severe stress on the tropical forest biome. This current situation holds a clear parallel to an ancient tragedy, and, as it is said that "he that does not pay heed to history is condemned to repeat it," we might profit from a brief review of a historical puzzle.

The mystery of the Mayan collapse

The Mayan civilization in northern Guatemala was at its peak just over 1,000 years ago, and supported some five million people. Then, within a relatively short span of three or four generations, there occurred a total collapse that is to this day one of the great mysteries of historic times.

New archaeological evidence now indicates that environmental degradation caused by overpopulation and mounting pressure on the fragile tropical ecosystem may have been its undoing. According to field studies conducted by the University of Florida and the University of Chicago, the Mayan population in the Guatemalan rainforest grew slowly over seventeen centuries and took 400 years to double until its collapse around A.D. 800. (By contrast, it now takes 20 years for the population to double in some developing countries.)

Direct evidence of forest abuse comes from a study of soils in lake beds in the major Mayan population centers of northern Guatemala. Extremely high levels of phosphorus in the lake sediments can be explained only by overwhelming soil erosion that would have placed an "undoubtedly severe" strain on the Mayan agricultural resource, thus causing the inevitable catastrophic decline.

This has not been transient in effect, as some of the Mayan farmlands still have not recovered full productivity more than 2,000 years after intensive use by the Mayans. Nothing similar to these effects holds true for temperate areas where soils are deep and rainfall is more moderate. There, climax conditions return several times faster, and animal populations are more adaptable to human intrusion.

△ *This ruined Mayan temple in the Petén Forest of Guatemala, is a monument to an advanced civilization capable of sustaining a population of five million on agriculture and the utilization of the natural forest. The abrupt end of this ancient culture may have been caused by population growth, leading to stress on the land, a critical fertility loss, and the enforced dispersal of the Mayan people.*

We recall the atmospheric nitrogen-fixing capabilities of *Rhizobium* as well as the ability of mycorrhizal fungi to transfer soil nitrogen and insolubles such as phosphorus and zinc directly to tropical forest tree roots in exchange for sugars. These unique "door-to-door" mechanisms account, in part, for the rapid uptake of nutrients and minerals in the tropical forests. This is also one of the reasons for the biome's vulnerability to disturbance. Once the tree cover is gone, the sun has direct access to the soil, whose formerly moist 77°F (25°C) temperature now soars to a dry hard-baked 115°F (46°C). At these temperatures, and with exposure to ultraviolet light, the soil chemistry degrades and mycorrhizal and many other fungi and decomposer organisms perish. Under those relatively sterile conditions, small twigs lie about on the ground unchanged where previously whole trees decayed and were recycled in fairly short order.

If the tropical forests have been described as trees growing in a desert, the statement refers primarily to the limited nutrient budget. A survey of soil types by the Brazilian government agency RADAM (Radar Imagery for the Amazon) found only 10 percent of Amazon soils fertile enough to support agriculture. (Certain other estimates are as low as 4 percent.) It is easy to see how these fragile assets are quickly lost in an agricultural system dependent on the illusive paradox that persists to this day – that such great forests could only be supported by the richest of soils!

V · The Human Resource

Public Health and Deforestation

"Disease is the retribution of outraged Nature" – Hosea Ballou. Never before has this dictum had more meaning than in the theater of deforestation in the moist tropics. Due largely to a lack of preplanning we are now witness to the creation of death traps in newly colonized areas, just as was the case with the Aswan and other dam construction sites which caused the spread of dreaded schistosomiasis, the snail-borne parasitic disease. This disease now spreads widely to other countries in the tropics and subtropics due to the effects of deforestation and colonization, both of which create favorable breeding habitats for the parasite.

The hazards of unplanned colonization

Recolonization schemes are motivated by a variety of stimuli. Concentrations of landless people seeking work, which may not be available in urban areas, are a vivid reality. Often the cause of landlessness is a highly inequitable system of land tenure. The status quo is most easily maintained by the wealthy and those in power by shunting the landless off to forest frontiers, often with the added incentive of peopling loosely held border areas to establish a national presence. Not infrequently, the shifting courses of jungle rivers move national boundaries. Brazilian villagers have awakened in the morning as Colombians.

A look at the well-documented before-and-after disease levels in the Amazon Basin as a consequence of the development of the Transamazon Highway is indicative of conditions in the wet tropics globally in the wake of deforestation and colonization.

Amerindians have long adapted to endemic diseases, and have prevented them, in large part, by their adaptation to conditions of life over the 20,000 years they have inhabited the tropical forests. The recent colonization of the Amazon, however, has facilitated the spread of virulent diseases and organisms. As "modern" medicine is rarely, if ever, accessible to the indigenous peoples, and their resistance to the new diseases is incredibly low, the toll they pay in debilitating illness and death is tragic. This is not to say that the colonizers themselves are in any way equipped to cope with the diseases they unwittingly bring with them. Actually, their activities create the conditions necessary for the spread of the diseases, but they at least do have some naturally acquired resistance to many of the diseases they transport. These immigrants into the forest, on the other hand, are often quickly brought down by alien forest diseases to which they have no built-in immunity.

The disease cycle

As the tropical forests are shattered by careless and unplanned agriculture, so is the population dealt an insufferable and devastating dose of misery. The power tools at the shifting cultivator's disposal encourage an easy assault on the forest, and result in him opening up areas far larger than are needed to feed

△ *For the Grande Carajás project, thousands of imported workers will be housed in the new town of Carajás, where sadly they are likely to provide a human reservoir for many tropical diseases.*

his family and provide a modest reserve for sale. Finding it easier to move on and repeat this process every two years than to practice a more intensive, updated form of agriculture, he lays bare immense areas of virgin forest. This begins the deadly cycle. Animal habitats are destroyed, sending predators and insect-eating birds elsewhere. As a result, the opportunistic rodents, destroyers of crops and reservoirs of disease, multiply and move in.

Puddles, road ruts, drainage ditches, even the ever-present auto tires and discarded tin cans of settlement areas, provide inviting pools of stagnant water, previously rare in virgin forests except in bromeliads and the odd crotches high in trees. (These natural sites in any case generally kept mosquitoes high in the canopy and safely out of human contact.) The village sites are now perfect for the breeding of domestic insects and lethal microorganisms. Enter the settlers' cattle, chickens, and dogs to the scene, most handy hosts for the vectors, and you have sprung the death trap. While disease is rarer in remote areas, agricultural settlements are generally infested. When traveling in these areas, whenever possible, I prefer to camp in the deep forest rather than run the risk of contracting disease under the roof of a colonizer's house.

Combating these diseases goes on grudgingly, but every inch won is a hard-fought battle. Long-term use and misuse of agricultural pesticides has largely backfired by killing nontarget bird and bat populations, thus increasing insect infestations. In one sample area of the Amazon (Altamira) it was found that malaria infected over 15 percent of the population. Over 200,000 Brazilians are afflicted with leprosy, of which only 61 percent receive treatment. That represents a horrifying 40.2 leprotics per 1,000 inhabitants of Amazonia; this, despite the fact that effective drugs are available for terminating infection and effecting cures.

A fascinating if repulsive parasite, the adult human bot fly (*Dermatobia hominis*) is a New World tropical forest resident. It resembles an extremely large bumblebee, both visually and in its threatening movements, and for this reason mammals, including human beings, are instinctively intimidated by this conspicuous creature. But it is not the fly but its larvae that should be feared, as they grow into large and painful maggots under human skin.

Humans, and certain other larger mammals such as peccaries and jaguars, serve as necessary intermediate hosts for the human bot fly. As mammals are not abundant in the tropical forests, the numbers of these bot flies have never been very high as they require the hosts for the completion of their life cycle. The introduction of masses of cattle into the American tropical forest areas, however, has brought an unnatural bounty of hosts for this deep-forest insect. The result is that where human parasitization by the bot fly was formerly rather a rarity, in cattle country it is now often a prominent public health reality. In fact, I was parasitized by seven larvae at one time.

Humans are also palatable targets for ascaris worms (familiar to many people as the 2-foot-long (0.6-m) roundworms that inhabit their pet dogs). These infest 90 percent of patients examined on the Transamazon Highway (Sucam). Indeed, the lack of planning of this road charted it directly through the main focus of a black-fly vector area. The fly (Simuliidae) is the carrier of an insidious parasitic larva, and the building of the road is likely to lead to an epidemic of onchocerciasis, causing blindness in hundreds of thousands of Amazonian inhabitants.

At present, an estimated 18 million people suffer from the disease, which threatens another 85 million people globally according to World Health Organization officials. The parasite (*Onchocerca volvulus*) causes eye lesions, and up to 20 percent of the population of heavily infested areas of Africa, and now Mexico, and Central and South America, are permanently blind as a result. Onchocerciasis is one of the leading causes of blindness in the Third World. In some villages of West and Central Africa, 60 percent of people over fifty-five years of age are either completely or partially blind as a result. Long chains of people of all ages can be seen linked together, holding onto sticks or a rope, and led by a sighted child. Hydroelectric projects are primary causes of the spread of river blindness as the fly finds the fast-moving waters of the raceways of dams ideal breeding spots. Similar raceways are created by logjams that build up downstream of discontinued logging operations.

Adult worms are 2 feet (60 cm) in length, and humans are the only known host. Great promise now lies in a new drug, mectizan, developed from ivermectin which is currently used in domestic animals to combat other parasites.

Research, and the development of an effective pharmacopoeia of drugs for such tropical maladies, generally lag far behind even the most minimal requirements, as the destitute millions who are afflicted are seldom able to pay the price of such exotic drugs. It is particularly heartening in this instance

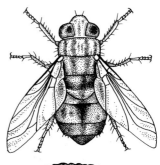

△ *The human bot fly* (Dermatobia hominis) *is a largely unrecognised but rapidly growing public health threat in moist tropical areas. Eggs laid in the skin develop into larvae that burrow deep and are difficult, and risky, to remove as they contain toxins. Public information campaigns like the one illustrated above, from Mexico, are still all too rare.*

△ *River blindness* (Onchocerciasis) *is a tragic disease now spreading due to logging operations and the building of dams in many tropical areas.*

to learn that Merck, the company that developed mectizan, has announced that it will be donating the drug for distribution to Third World sufferers in cooperation with the World Health Organization. Such philanthropy should be emulated by other pharmaceutical firms.

In Amazonian Brazil, the 1980s have brought record-breaking epidemics of a recurring viral disease called oropouche, which can cause inflammation of the tissues around the brain. This coincides with Brazil's influx of colonizers into the region. Health officials have linked the epidemics to huge piles of cacao husks, a result of cultivation, which hold pools of water ideally suited to the breeding habits of the flies that spread the disease.

Man-made pockets of pestilence

△ *Puddles and road ruts in the squalid conditions of many tropical settlements provide an ideal breeding habitat for disease-carrying insects.*

Malaria is a growing global concern rather than a receding one. Increasingly, the anopheline vectors are developing resistance not only to the drugs used in prevention and therapy, but to insecticides as well. Faced with such frustrations, and limited public health resources, authorities in malarial areas are becoming resistant to the further long-term expenditures required by extensive antimalaria programs. The specter of a full-scale malaria epidemic is brought nearer by the continually increasing settlement of the tropical zone, and by tropical deforestation, both of which are creating new endemic foci for this essentially man-made disease.

As *Anopheles* mosquitoes prefer sunlight and standing water, the dark virgin forest is relatively free of these vectors. Tree felling brings the mosquito, an upper-canopy species, down to the ground and into contact with people. As the forest is altered, sun infuses the area, and rutted roads and drainage ditches, stagnant ponds created by logging equipment, and hauling scars in the earth, all provide a ready supply of habitats for mosquito breeding. These are precisely the areas unsuspecting settlers are sent to, and it is here that the anopheles wait with cryptic patience for the colonizers, who have little or no malaria resistance. In 1969, Peru reported 3,168 cases of malaria and a mortality rate of 0.3 persons per 100,000. In 1980, reported cases hovered around 80,000 with a mortality of 4 persons per 100,000. In Brazil, matters are far worse: in the state of Rondonia alone, considered an environmental holocaust, 240,000 cases were reported – fully 20 percent of the state population. (The town of Ariquemes, south of Porto Velho, has the dubious distinction of being "the world's malaria capital.") Even these figures are expected to escalate, and as a vivid example of the real potential of this disease, we have only to look to Central Africa where one out of every four children perishes from malaria.

Dengue fever, as well as its more severe form, dengue hemorrhagic fever, strikes about 100 million people annually through much of Asia, Africa (where I contracted it), and the Southern Hemisphere. The disease, which has eluded attempts at a vaccine, strikes mostly children, and can cause fever, internal bleeding, shock, and death. In Asia it is spread by *Aedes albopictus*, which has developed a strong preference for water-holding auto tires. The United States has imported millions of such tires in past decades for retreading, and with it the mosquito responsible for dengue as well as yellow fever and other tropical diseases. As a result, *A. albopictus* has now infiltrated seventeen southern US states as well as regions of South and Central America. The Centers for Disease Control in Atlanta, Georgia, are presently concerned about the very real threat of a US dengue-fever outbreak.

THE LAST OF THE FORAGING PEOPLES

Anthropologists have long recognized the world's remaining aboriginal cultures as endangered species of the highest significance. Such tribes, who derive their sustenance through hunting and gathering, exist with perhaps just a few exceptions only within the insulation and isolation of the tropical forests. A host of climatological and environmental calamities, many occurring over the past decade, appear to be effectively communicating to us that we are not, in fact, separate from the rest of the species with which we share our planet but rather that our actions are accountable to the balance of nature and that we cannot hope to establish a viable equilibrium outside earth's natural systems. Perhaps the most striking perception an observer of culturally isolated tribes acquires is of their profound atunement to and reverence for their environment, to the point of integrating it into their culture, lore, and religious practice. There is so much that we can learn from these tribes.

A disappearing human resource

The reference to aboriginal cultures is in need of some definition, as most people outside the professional anthropological disciplines perceive these tribal people as unevolved beings – virtually prehistoric. Whether viewing documentary films, photographs within this book, or the rare experience of personal contact with these cultures, there is a quite common and almost instinctive tendency to assign them an almost mystical splendor; the "noble savage" as it were. There is nothing new in this perception. In April of the year 1500, the Portuguese explorer Pedro Alvares Cabral, destined for India, was blown too far to the west and arrived in Brazil where he was stunned by people as beautiful as birds, living in harmony with nature. "Their innocence is as great as Adam's," Cabral exclaimed.

The author admits he has been as deeply impressed by our forest relations as anyone, and cannot here dispel the "myth" of the "noble savage" as he has, by and large, found him noble. There is a reality, however, that is lost on most casual observers. First, these people are not throwbacks or living fossils, but evolved, intelligent beings functioning in complex societies of their own making. Cultures that exist exclusively on hunting and gathering will be an extreme rarity today, and this is not due primarily to their dilution by civilization.

Agriculture sprang up almost spontaneously in various areas around the world, oddly at around the same time – some 10,000 years ago. Before this time, man's way of life on earth was more commonly one of hunter-gatherer. It would surprise many that evidence indicates that the European Cro-Magnon clans engaged in elaborate networks of trade between 28,000 and 10,000 years ago. This suggests the practice was common for a great many "hunter-gatherers" over the past 12,000 years, according to one current anthropological theory. As aboriginal populations increased, the need for village gardens of varying degrees manifested itself, and the people became more specialized hunter-gatherers. In addition, even the most isolated tribes had some degree of communication and trade between them, which tended to homogenize the various aspects of agriculture.

In another category are certain tribes of Asia and Africa which do not engage

in agriculture, but have, even in the distant historical record, maintained symbiotic trading relationships with other tribes which produce cultivated carbohydrates in exchange for the hunter-gatherer's excess forest bounty. The Pygmies are just such a people. That these cultures have existed and grown in a relative vacuum until recent decades should be a matter of great relevance to us. As an integral part of the forest ecosystem, they may be studied with great practical benefit to humanity.

It should be known that we are rapidly losing this profound cultural resource, and that simultaneously, as a result of victimization by forest exploitation, these people very much want to take an active role in their destiny – demanding self-rule and legal title to their traditional tribal lands. Without such documents, these cultures are constantly vulnerable to the whims of government and industry. Prominent University of Michigan field anthropologist Magdelana Hurtado's research revealed that of 257 such groups in Venezuela, only one, the Karina, held legal title to their lands – and that was in the form of a colonial grant dating from the 1700s.

The impact of assimilation

An unacceptably high percentage of the traditional tribal people who do survive the immediate effects of invasion of their lands, and forced transportation to relocation settlements or reservations, die in plagues of new diseases such as tuberculosis, influenza, parainfluenza, measles, mumps, rubella, poliomyelitis, and the common cold, to which they have no natural resistance. Moreover, it is readily apparent that the survivors of this morbid gauntlet of assimilation into the modern world all too often become the dregs of civilization, riddled particularly with alcoholism and venereal disease, often unable, even in the long run, to adjust to and become useful members of the new society. While this might seem a loaded appraisal, the plethora of well-documented scenarios contrasting before-and-after situations speaks in almost unredeeming negatives.

From epidemiological data gathered by UNESCO, certain relationships clearly exist between observed declines in public health, and forest removal. UNESCO's Tropical Forest Ecosystems Report sums up its findings with the following conclusions: "Semi-nomadic hunter-gatherers are relatively little affected by malaria and other vector-borne disease. Their nutritional status is also generally satisfactory. Settlement appears to bring a deterioration of health. Man-made changes in the forest create situations favoring transmission of malaria, intestinal parasites, schistosomiasis and other water and vector-borne infections."

Immediately apparent to any visiting lay person or medical anthropologist is the relatively uniform excellent physical and mental health, and general well-being, that the traditional people so commonly display. There are, of course, various virulent tropical diseases that do take their toll and effect a population control. Many studies have shown, however, that these tribes do not seem to suffer many of the fatal degenerative diseases with which we in the developed world are afflicted in epidemic proportions. Arteriosclerosis and its related heart attack, high blood pressure, stroke, and diabetes, are the number one killers in our society. Most of us will eventually die of one (or a combination) of these diseases, while the conditions are largely absent in archaic cultures. That Nathan Pritikin based his longevity diet on that of the

Continued on page 166

△ Blending the magic of the forest into religious and cultural practices, a Yąnomamö medicine man, assisted by another tribal member, has ebene, a powerful hallucinogen prepared from the virola vine, blown into his nasal passages. After suffering violent nausea the man then symbolically drew an evil spirit from the chest of a seriously ill child – an act of such passion and conviction that it will remain forever in my memory.

◁ Is this the last glimpse of Eden? This Yąnomamö girl is so completely a part of her forest home near the headwaters of the Orinoco River in Venezuela that it is difficult for the few who know this fiercely independent people to visualize one separated from the other.

A window to our past. The insulation and isolation of the tropical rainforests have provided vital refuges for the few remaining pristine human societies. Will we choose to protect this unique resource or squander the opportunity in a headlong rush to rape the forests for a quick flush of nonsustainable profit? We can learn much from forest people about utilizing the forest without degrading it.

◁△ After taking the drug ebene, a Yąnomamö man recovers in his house, built from, and filled with, produce of the forest. Nearby △ a young woman continues weaving. The hunter ▷ stands proudly with an ocelot he has killed with his longbow. The Machiguenga boy ◁ from the Peruvian jungle is making a hunting arrow.

△ *The revered Yąnomamö chief Ciacho Awar A-Teri performs "big talk" at a tribal gathering. Recently, Yąnomamö homelands in Brazil were invaded by gold-seekers, and lives were lost to violence and disease. Sadly, the trouble has now spilled over to their Venezuelan stronghold.*

traditional Tarahumara tribe of northern Mexico's rugged hill country is a splendid example of applied anthropological study.

A repository of knowledge

The erosion of these cultures, principally through deforestation, entails the very real and major loss for global society of literally thousands of years of diverse traditions, languages, and philosophies, as well as vast unwritten catalogs of botanical, animal, and mineral pharmaceuticals and foods. Invading agriculturists are, to be conservative, having a very difficult time finding any meaningful measure of success in developing sustainable colonization in the moist tropics. As the interior-forest people of these zones have evolved, out of sheer necessity, an infinite understanding of the ecological interdependencies and resources available there, and moreover, how to ply them without degrading the environment, there is ample justification to view them as professors emeritus.

A single village in the north of Thailand, for instance, makes use of 295 varieties of plant for food, and 119 separate plants for medicine. (It is noted that many indigenous remedies, such as the oils used to remove stomach parasites, are impressively effective while carrying none of the severe side effects of Western prescription pharmaceuticals processed from those primary source materials.

The World Health Organization is presently searching for new and improved contraceptives, and many scientists believe the best possibilities yet may be found in primitive tribal preparations, many of which are said to be both safe and effective. On the same line of inquiry the National Biological Institute reports a spermicide used by a tribe made from active ingredients found in a forest tree. Altogether, as far as is known to date, over 3,000 plant species are used by forest tribes for purpose of antifertility.

The revolutionary protein-rich winged bean (*Psophocarpus tetragonolobus*) and the giant wax gourd (*Benincasa hispida*), which are now dramatically upgrading diets in over 50 countries and are predicted to put a significant dent in world hunger in the future, were found being used by forest tribes in Southeast Asia.

How did we come to discover quinine, used by millions of people globally to treat malaria? The answer is that South American Indians were found using the bark of the cinchona tree (*Cinchona* spp.) medicinally.

A survey, though grossly incomplete, shows evidence of at least 4,000 plant species in Indonesia alone that have served the area's native people. Yet less than one in ten of these are used widely today by modern cultures. Leaves of more than 1,650 tropical forest plants have been found to be "highly nutritious," yet very few are presently in use outside the forest biome. How many plants are thought to be edible? Well over 80,000!

A unique and comprehensive study in the Philippines contrasts the total diet of a forest tribal person with that of a peasant inhabiting an area where the forest has disappeared. All the food consumed by one person of each group was weighed and recorded, meal by meal, for a full year. The results significantly illustrate the large gaps and imbalances in the foods consumed as one is removed from forest-subsistence conditions. As these cultures are forced from isolated independence, they move toward a state of exploited dependence; this is a transition some Latin American social scientists have termed marginalization.

Eons of insulation shattered overnight

Regardless of how these cultures may ultimately enhance our lives, the vigorous and self-sufficient lifestyles of these tribes are abruptly reversed when the loggers enter their ancient tribal lands. "Not so," says Charles W. Bingham, past senior vice-president of Weyerhaeuser, one of the leading timber operations plying the tropical forests until political instability made such ventures insecure. According to Mr. Bingham, "Any major investment brings major changes in the economic arena, and those changes tend to translate gradually into social change ... I am sure we do disrupt primitive societies ... I believe this is *cultural enrichment* [author's emphasis], however, not disculturalization. I do not believe disease, poverty, and illiteracy are inalienable human rights, or that primitive societies should be forced to remain primitives, simply to provide museum pieces for their more affluent world neighbors' entertainment."

▽ *In an echo of human prehistory, a New Guinea highland medicine man infuses village life with his mystical rituals. Though still using stone axes, the tribe is in many ways rich beyond our comprehension. The young girl ▽, adorned in paints of earth tones, reflects the health and harmony of a people to whom heart disease and most degenerative diseases are virtually unknown.*

When Columbus reached the Americas, between six and nine million Indians occupied Amazonia. In the Brazilian Amazon in 1900 there were 230 traditional tribal groups numbering some one million people. Today, only 143 groups remain (a rapidly diminishing figure), and their total population of less than 50,000 is dwindling at an alarming rate. For example, in 1969 some 700 Suruí Indians were contacted "officially" for the first time in Brazilian Rondonia. By 1974 fully half had died – most of them from influenza and measles introduced by settlers. Since then, and despite the fact that in 1976 the Suruí tribal territories were recognized and delineated, the area has been heavily invaded by colonists, who quite illegally – yet with impunity – have driven a road right through Suruí lands.

In an atmosphere of developmental imperatives that fuel deculturalization, tribal groups are too often seen as impediments. "When we are certain that every corner of the Amazon is inhabited by *genuine* [author's emphasis] Brazilians and not by Indians, only then will we be able to say that the Amazon is ours," – the words of a discredited member of Brazil's former military junta, 1982. Classical episodes see government-authorized road-building, cattle ranching, agricultural, logging, or mining projects penetrating long-honored tribal lands. After a series of unhonored commitments by government authorities, conflicts inevitably result, not always instigated by the Indians but frequently by the commercial-interest groups themselves.

Unfortunately, there is nothing at all unique about this tragic scenario. Imbued with imperial traditions, tropical forest nations, often obsessed with what they perceive as a toothless control of their hinterlands, encourage their exploitation, most often at the expense of the human rights of their resident tribal groups. We need look no further than the treatment of North America's native peoples, and the treaties of the past century to the present, to see that this is not just a Brazilian characteristic.

The tribes share a common frustration when faced with an omnipotent political machine. They themselves are not often considered full citizens, even if they were the country's original residents. After becoming aware that they have been the victims of psychological sleight-of-hand, often after "carrot-and-stick" pacification attempts, some tribes attempt combative defense. But to no avail. For what few soldiers they can repulse with spears and arrows, vengeance comes swiftly from the air. Machine guns and bombs are the common form of retaliation. The Indians are relentlessly pursued. Villages are burned, and any flicker of smoke from a cookfire in the forest is attacked by aircraft. In a commendably candid 1968 investigation initiated by the Interior Ministry into Brazil's Indian Protection Service, findings revealed "widespread evidence of corruption and sadism, including the massacre of whole tribes by dynamite, machine guns, and sugar laced with arsenic." However, attitudes can change, and recent enlightened Brazilian policy now metes out few reprisals if Brazilian citizens are killed by aboriginal tribespeople when trespassing into legal Indian tribal territory. On the other hand, I am not aware of any arrests and convictions of Brazilians for the deaths of Indians killed by willful trespassers on Indian lands.

Brazil's Villa Boas brothers, Orlando and Claudio, who were famous for their initial pacification work, and often mentioned for the Nobel Peace Prize, now refuse on moral grounds to pursue the practice because of the pattern of violence that almost invariably followed. Orlando has recently said that "an integrated Indian is no longer an Indian, but just a lesser citizen of the

△ *In a wary first contact a remote band of Peruvian Machiguenga Indians are aware for the first time of a world beyond that of their forest home. Their garments, "manchakintsi," are woven from wild cotton and are the result of six weeks of proud work by the women. In the lower photograph a young man returns home after crossing a swollen river.*

Brazilian nation." In despair over the quintupling of the Brazilian population in his lifetime, and the vast numbers of those shunted into Indian lands, he cryptically states that "all we can do is pick up the hat of a drowning man and marvel that we lived to witness the last days of Eden."

The tribal-rights advocacy organization, Cultural Survival, informed me that in 1988 alone more than 200,000 Third World indigenous people were killed, and that over two million were forced to flee for their lives, leaving behind shelter and gardens. As aboriginal peoples fade, ghostlike, before the invasion of their tribal homelands, governments in many tropical lands march headlong into development schemes, a great many of which prove to be economic as well as ecological catastrophies.

Although there are exceptions, such as the protection afforded the Tasaday tribe's ancestral rainforest in Mindanao in the Philippines, the general attitude of many tropical governments is to treat aboriginal people as a nonentity, or worse, as a national embarrassment. Such is the case, for example, with the Pygmies in Zaïre, Cameroon, and Gabon, where many bands are forced by decree to wear "civilized" clothing and to work on road construction. Vast numbers have perished from introduced alien diseases. Similarly, in Brazil, only fifty-three Asurinis Indians are left, the balance of the tribe destroyed by intruders to their homeland. Anthropologist Berta Riberiro states, "They want no more children; they know they are finished."

△ Perhaps the most gentle of the world's people, the Pygmies of Africa live a nomadic yet highly ordered life, even while the forest around them is shrinking. Their mutualistic relationship with the Bantu people outside the forest hints at the possibility of coexistence on a wider front between such pristine cultures and our own.

The 1987 Malaysian government's expropriation of the native lands of Sarawak forest tribes, and their subsequent handing over as timber concessions to logging companies, sparked the resistance of tribal members, who blockaded the loggers' access roads. Subsequent arrests, and the illegal detention of the forest people, precipitated demonstrations at Malaysian consulates around the world and investigative missions by human rights and environmental groups.

If there are, understandably, economic sacrifices to be made by home governments in honoring tribal sanctity, these may be balanced by a format of supportive aid. Such a policy would be consistent with viewing these cultures as a common universal treasure, at the very least as precious as any other endangered species and deserving of the protection that only an enlightened international agreement can afford them.

By their very nature these tribes are typified by a lack of political power, with little chance to participate in a meaningful way in the decisions that decide their fates. This facilitates the processes of ancestral land expropriation, economic exploitation, and ensuing violence. An avenue is open for governmental agencies, assisted by First World funding, to allow the tribes the self-determination to adapt at their own pace and to do so with a dignity they are accustomed to, but which is all too often denied them.

In 1854, Chief Seattle said, "What is man without the beast? If all the beasts were gone, man would die from a great loneliness of spirit. For whatever happens to the beasts happens to man."

The chief's words are as true today. The human being is as rightfully part of the global environment as any other species. Should we not, therefore, make a proper and lasting place for *all* other plants and animals to coexist with us, instead of degrading the very fabric of life? Such considerations go far beyond moral or ethical assertions. Many of those now living on the brink will perish. Others will move in to take their place on the margins. And if we take no action, it will simply be a matter of time before we too face the abyss.

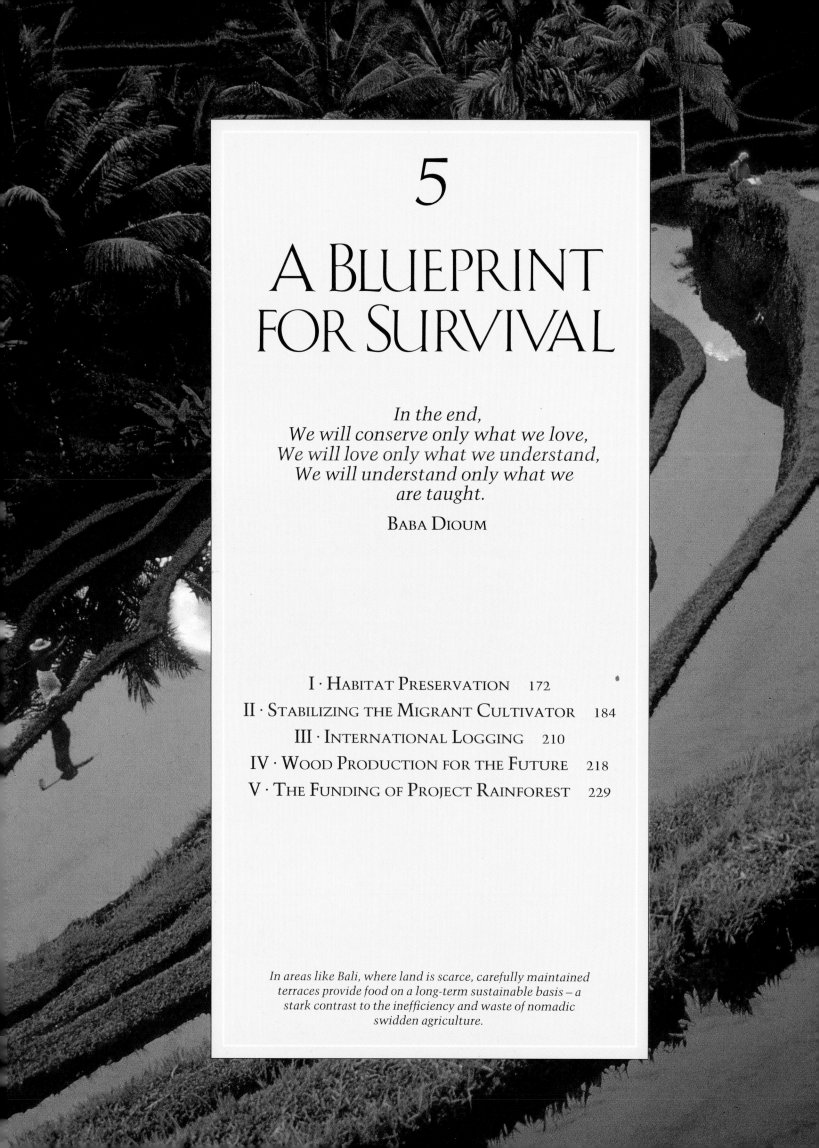

5

A BLUEPRINT FOR SURVIVAL

In the end,
We will conserve only what we love,
We will love only what we understand,
We will understand only what we
are taught.

BABA DIOUM

In areas like Bali, where land is scarce, carefully maintained
terraces provide food on a long-term sustainable basis – a
stark contrast to the inefficiency and waste of nomadic
swidden agriculture.

I · HABITAT PRESERVATION

There is a consensus among conservationists and scientists that nowhere can the conservation dollar be stretched further than in the tropical forests through habitat preservation. By the end of 1988, however, barely two percent of the tropical forest biome had been set aside as conservation areas. The goal still remains very much ahead of us.

NEWMAN

A lily pond, so a French riddle goes, contains a single leaf. Each day the number of leaves doubles – two leaves the second day, four the third, eight the fourth, and so on. Question: If the pond is completely full on the 30th day, when was it half full? Answer: On the 29th.

The global lily pond in which over 5.6 billion of us live may already be well over half full. Clearly population stabilization must be the highest and most immediate international priority. Tropical deforestation and its consequences are but one of the results of overpopulation, and it is unlikely that environmentally oriented advancements will remain permanent without finally stabilizing or reducing global numbers.

The World Commission on the Environment and Development, in its report *Our Common Future* (the Brundtland Report), states, "Humanity has the ability to make development sustainable – to select paths or progress to ensure that it meets the needs of the present without compromising the ability of future generations to meet their own needs."

The author is one of many who feel humanity is empowered to preserve the many crucial values held in the tropical forest biome. We hope to illustrate in this chapter that the aims of controlling population growth, addressing global hunger, and achieving sustainable levels of wood production, while simultaneously striving to conserve vast portions of our biosphere are not contradictory, but are by necessity complementary.

Applied technology

We know that with applied use of our advances in technology we can increase the productivity of land in use, and that the sun must set on the tropical norm of rotation of fields. Agriculture, animal husbandry, and the logging industries in the tropics must leave behind the inefficiencies and wastefulness of the recent past.

Many parts of the humid tropics are quite unsuitable for sustained agriculture and, as we have seen, attempts to utilize these areas can quickly lead to permanent degradation of the site. In other areas, however, as demonstrated in parts of Indonesia, Thailand, Brazil, and Rwanda, productive forms of agriculture have been developed which have retained the fertility of the original forest soil. Such areas leave more options open to development. It cannot be the objective of enlightened conservation to preclude development from future planning, but a thorough review of alternatives can assure that the best possible course is charted so as to maximize the forest's ability to provide. That we are not currently doing this is emphasized by the fact that although tropical forests comprise 80 percent of earth's terrestrial vegetation, the global trade in tropical forest products represents only 4 percent of the market.

Stemming the tide of extinction

While preserving habitats and their resident species *in situ* will come at enormous cost, it is sobering to first consider the alternatives of attempting to preserve species as separate entities, in many cases outside their natural habitats (*ex situ*). These measures might include an *Endangered Species Task Force* assigned to the collection and germination of seed, and the transportation of animal and plant species from areas under exploitive pressure to appropriate "safe port" habitats, while ensuring that exotic transplants (if that is the case) will not be detrimental to their new environments. Although such a program would naturally be expensive, some of the cost might be saved by incorporating a curriculum for academic credit utilizing students or lay volunteers, as has been applied to other scientific fields. No finer example could be found of this hands-on approach than the field courses run by the indefatigable Mildred Mathias, Professor Emeritus at the University of

◁ "*Operation Rescue, 1971.*" *Aware of the high degree of endemism among tropical species, and the threat of extinction facing so many of them, the University of Papua New Guinea launched a major salvage operation when the Segeri Plain was flooded as part of a hydroelectric plan. I was pleased to have participated in this rescue, in which thousands of plants were collected for study.*

California, Los Angeles. Often working under the auspices of the Organization for Tropical Studies, this pioneer biologist leads students and interested laymen on crash field courses to the forests of Central and South America. Among her former students are scientists, administrators, and decision makers far more aware than those of even a decade ago of the huge potential of tropical forest conservation.

It should be acknowledged that in many cases, species possessing commercial value increase in market demand sharply as those species move closer to extinction. Such species require heroic efforts in the black-market place of origin and at the export destination, as well as in the habitat, in order to effect their survival. The rhinoceros and African elephant, both now under the most serious threat from poachers, are classical and highly topical examples.

There are many situations, however, in which the remaining natural population is already too small to ensure continued survival of the species. In such cases a captive breeding pool may be the only alternative, with the goal of re-releasing animals into suitable habitats when and if increases are realized, while holding back a captive breeding pool as a hedge against failure.

Because of high costs and space limitations, this kind of program would seem to be extremely limited in scope. William Conway of the New York Zoological Garden considers that a population as small as 50 to 100 specimens of a given mammal species may be adequate as a breeding stock, but he warns that he has estimated that only 100 mammal species could be maintained in such a manner even if fully one-half of all American zoo capacity was put to this purpose. Naturally, the ideal situation is to make national parks profitable, since it has already been shown in Kenya that a maned lion is almost four hundred and fifty times more valuable as a living tourist attraction than it is as a hunting trophy.

In some cases, however, such as the European bison (*Bison bonasus*) and Pere David's deer (*Elaphurus davidianus*), the only surviving individuals reside in zoos. These species walk a tightrope. Ironically it was war and flood that annihilated the last of Pere David's deer from its wild habitat in China at the turn of the century. Bred in England since that time, a breeding stock was sent back to China not long ago.

Clearly, however, gene banks should be maintained for as many endangered species as possible in case the more natural and practical measures ultimately fail. The seeds of many plant species can be kept viable at 5 percent humidity and −4°F (−20°C) for long periods. You may call such facilities "frozen zoos" and "iceberg botanical gardens," but their time, unfortunately, has come. Yet given acts of God or man, such facilities as the Fort Collins Seed Laboratory (Colorado), the Northwest Germ Plasm Repository (Oregon), and the Potato Station (Wisconsin) offer a priceless if precarious insurance.

At best, however, such arrangements conserve the species but not the interactions between them that are so essential to healthy ecosystems. There can be no doubt that the greatest economy both in species preservation and the environmental dollar will be in the maintenance of holistic, biotic communities in the wild.

I doubt if anyone better appreciates the merits of preserving intact habitat, against the finances and energies required in bringing back a forest already gone, than Daniel Janzen, the "dean of tropical biology" who, with the able assistance of his colleague Winnie Hallwachs, has virtually single-handedly not only generated financial support for the preservation of the rare dry-forest

△ *In an FAO-sponsored study program, an Indian forester records the breast-height diameter of a tree. Research and monitoring activities like these are essential to management of global forest resources.*

region in Guanacaste in Costa Rica, but is now actually regenerating the forest, largely by hand, on the large areas of degraded pasture that surround the remnant undisturbed habitat.

Environmental triage

Guanacaste is an extraordinary example of what motivated people can achieve, but many heroic, understaffed, and underfinanced conservation organizations are forced to use a form of environmental triage. This strategy, as proposed by Smithsonian Institution's Thomas Lovejoy, identifies certain areas for priority over others, even though they too may be imminently threatened. The priority rating is awarded when various uncommon and vital factors cry out for immediate action. Traditionally these areas were defined where the habitat contained an "important or highly visible endangered species," such as the orang-utan, for example. Also high on the priority list should be areas of great evolutionary diversity, such as the Pleistocene "refugia" which have been and are still being identified globally.

The agonies of triage can be jolting. Yet out of at least a decade and a half of strategy formulation and encouraging successes in certain sectors, there is emerging an *espirit de corps*, more so internationally in recent years, and a belief that such uphill fronts can, in fact must, be conquered – that the alternatives are unacceptable.

If it is true that no one single factor is responsible for the growing optimism, the combination of several broad strategies of integrity does promise adequate returns if implemented widely. Take, for instance, the dual goals of preserving indigenous cultures as well as tribal forest territory.

An ideal solution to the problem of the limited financial resources available to establish and maintain tropical forest parks exists in having the tribal peoples themselves patrol and maintain their own homelands as national parks, reporting to senior officers employed by national parks departments. This, of course, keeps inviolate both tropical forest habitat *and* the tribal lands. The Kuna Indian Forest Park in Panama is an outstanding example of this arrangement. Funds generated from visiting scientists and tourists are used to support the park, which is the first in the world to be created by an indigenous group.

The Philippine discovery of the Stone Age Tasaday tribe on the island of Mindanao, and the subsequent establishment of the Tasaday Preserve, in the neighborhood of 114,000 acres (46,000 ha), was, we would hope, a harbinger of positive future paternal attitudes toward indigenous peoples worldwide.

Costa Rica – the pilot project

Here we might take heart in the Costa Rican example. This remarkable country covers only 19,575 square miles (50,695 sq km) or roughly the area of Denmark, but it has one of the richest biological heritages of any nation in the world. It contains 850 bird species, of which fewer that 140 migrate. This avifauna contains more bird species than exist in the whole of North America north of the Tropic of Cancer. Plant species total in excess of 12,000, with orchids numbering over 1,200.

As a result of decade-long conservation efforts on many fronts, Costa Rican leaders, many subsequently the recipients of international conservation awards, have protected in some form or other approximately 26 percent of the country's national territory, with 22 parks and preserves – fully 8 percent of

△ *In establishing the Cathedral Rain Forest Science Preserve on the Osa Peninsula in Costa Rica, I inadvertently cut off the only access of an American logging firm to a vast area of their Pacific coast forest holdings. The ensuing bitter battle resulted, eventually, in the expropriation by the state of the firm's entire holding – much of which is thankfully now protected by the Corcovado National Park. The Costa Rican government enjoys wide recognition as a prominent world leader in tropical forest conservation.*

the area being designated as national parks. Proportionately it is among the very top nations in total area/preserve ratios. (By comparison, the United States has only 1.5 percent of her area so dedicated.)

In 1977, while receiving a much deserved international conservation award in Washington, D.C., then Costa Rican president Daniel Oduber attested that he believed that "when nations have shown little or no respect for the environment, and where the natural environment has been ruined or lost in an over-hasty and uncoordinated exploitation of the earth's resources, human relations inside these nations are also likely to be characterized by a lack of respect for individuals and for human rights."

How much is "adequate" habitat?

There is a mounting hue and cry to preserve adequate habitat in order to conserve a high percentage of the biotic community in various distinct ecosystems, and while it has been conservatively suggested that no less than 10 percent of the world's tropical forest should be set aside as protected areas, this figure, we will see, may be much too low.

Lowland rainforest, preferred by loggers and cultivators alike, is more biologically active than other tropical forest types and warrants a proportionately larger percentage of installed preserves, yet it is essential that representatives of the full range of tropical forest habitats be identified for protection according to priorities which include endangered or threatened species, comparatively rare forest formations, imminent threat of development, escalating habitat degradation, and so on.

Many tropical forest animals exist at very low densities and require large territorial ranges. The select fruit trees that form the base of their food chains are also often widely distributed in very low numbers. To ensure the survival of adequate gene pools of animal and plant species we must accept that huge tracts of protected land will be required.

Recent research gives us some rough-cut estimates of minimum reserve sizes. It is often anticipated that areas surrounding preserves (and their buffer zones) will be disturbed or cleared, effectively creating "conservation islands", and the theory of island biogeography states that the number of species in each of these islands will fall, as the carrying capacity has been reduced, until it reaches a new equilibrium. Even here, questions arise over the merits of conserving an area with one massive preserve compared with the benefits of preserving an archipelago of "islands." Some argue that specific target species may be preserved on each of a number of islands comprising the same volume of habitat as the alternative mega-preserve. The consensus, however, seems to favor the sound ecological concept of preserving entire biotic communities (as far as funding and resource allocations will allow). Justifiable scientifically, logistically, and economically, it enjoins us to conserve whole working relationships; that is, ecologically dependent entities. In so doing, larger preserves will salvage more species; moreover, these communities are aesthetically and scientifically more significant than their components. This integrated holistic scenario would convincingly argue that life-forms cannot prosper long if removed from their biotic contexts.

With this in mind, how can we, in planning the earth's tropical forest preserves, keep our species losses to a minimum? First, of course, we know that the larger the islands of tranquility, the more ecologically stable they are, and the fewer will be the losses over time.

The golden toad (Bufo periglenes) perfectly exemplifies the fragility of endemism. The toad's sole habitat on earth is the wooded peak of Monte Verde in Costa Rica, which could be deforested in a matter of hours with modern logging equipment.

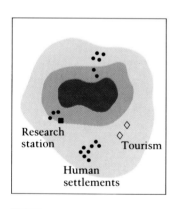

■ Core area

▨ Buffer zone 1

☐ Buffer zone 2

△ *A popular and effective form of reserve consists of a totally protected core area surrounded by buffer zones in which scientific research and limited human activity is permitted.*

According to biologists Michael Soule and Bruce Wilcox at the University of California at San Diego, no large mammals have been known to evolve into new species on islands smaller in area than 232,000 square miles (600,800 sq km) – an order of magnitude larger than any existing national park.

"Evolution is in trouble," Soule warns, adding that we can look forward to a "biological holocaust without precedent." Although the prospects for evolution appear to be fading fast, the main scope of today's conservation efforts in the tropical forest biome is to preserve extant species.

Ensuring a minimum breeding pool

Field zoologists have verified the extensive ranges certain animals require in order to forage successfully. Estimates of the minimum populations required to ensure a viable breeding pool also indicate the size some preserves need to be. Different species, of course, vary widely. Certain butterflies, for instance, in order to collect enough amino acids from specific kinds of nectar, need in excess of 39 square miles (100 sq km). Hornbills, it appears, need 5,000 individuals to maintain population equilibrium, and this population requires an area of between 770 and 3,900 square miles (2,000 to 10,000 sq km). Tigers, on the other hand, need a breeding pool of only 400, but the area of forest necessary to support this group may be as large as 15,000 square miles (almost 40,000 sq km). When the tiger's hunting range is restricted by agriculturists, the great cat is known to prey on people and their livestock.

△ A viable breeding pool of tigers (Panthera tigris) requires a large area of forest, and as that habitat is encroached upon by man and his livestock, tigers and some other great cats may turn on them as prey. This tigress, at Tapak Tuan, Sumatra, was trapped just minutes before this picture was taken. She had eaten three men, one of them just four hours earlier, and with those appetites firmly established she could not be re-released. Her destination was a Sumatran zoo.

On the smaller scale, World Wide Fund For Nature's Minimum Critical Size of Ecosystems project outside Manaus, Brazil, illuminates certain specifics. Within local forest-clearing operations, natural forest plots of varying sizes were left intact, and have since been intensively cataloged and studied. Thus far, the results show that a 2.47 acre (1 ha) plot isolated in a large cleared area became severely sun-scorched on its periphery, and wind blown and desiccated well into the interior, grossly affecting the forest. In one heavy storm the plot was virtually leveled as a consequence of the typically shallow-rooted structure of lowland wet forest.

A 25-acre (10-ha) "island" fared somewhat better, but was unable even to support a colony of army ants, which range over a 75-acre (30-ha) area.

A 250-acre (100-ha) area supported the army ants but not the ant-following birds, including woodcreepers (Dendrocolaptidae) for example, that depend on them for opportunistic feeding. As we would suspect, many bird species chose to fly out of this size "island." A mitigating positive factor in this example was the presence of a "corridor" of virgin forest running from the isolated plot to a more extensive area of undisturbed habitat. Conversely, when even narrow strips are cut across such corridors, the ant-followers disappear.

A 3.9-square-mile (10-sq-km or 1,000-ha) plot resulted in a more normal bird population, but larger predator and prey species such as tapir and jaguar were absent. The larger mammals are also responsible for creating water-holding "wallows," on which many smaller but no less crucial species are dependent.

On "islands" of nearer 40 square miles (100 sq km or 10,000 ha), certain species, such as capuchin monkeys (Cebus sp.), will still range far beyond the area, and Norman Myers suggests that parks of at least ten times this size will be needed to ensure stable populations of such animals. A viable breeding population of jaguars is not expected to reside in an area of less than 1,900 square miles (5,000 sq km) given their known breeding behavior.

Continued on page 180

UNDERSTANDING THE RAINFOREST BIOME

It has been said with some justification that we are currently burning our bridges before we can even cross them. The tropical forests represent the world's last great repository of plant and animal life – a resource of such promise for the good of mankind that its study and preservation is vital.

▽ **Detailed habitat studies**
We can conserve a habitat
only if we understand it.
Studies on Barro Colorado

*Is., Panama, measured the
density and the biomass
contribution of the main
resident mammal species.*

△ **High-level scientists**
*Canopy biologist Donald
Perry pioneered many new
techniques of access and*

*movement. Julian Steyermark
discovered 97 new species in
1988, and over 2,200 in his
lifetime.*

RESIDENT MAMMALS	no/km²	kg/km²
CARNIVORES		
Felis pardalis (ocelot)	0.14	2
ANTEATERS		
Tamandua mexicana (Mexican anteater)	5	20
Cyclopes didactylus (fairy anteater)	37	13
INSECT-EATERS/OMNIVORES AND FRUIT AND INSECT EATERS		
Marmosa robinsoni (mouse opossum)	55	3
Dasypus novemcintus (9-banded armadillo)	8	28
FRUIT AND SEED EATERS		
Sciurus granatensis (squirrel)	300	75
Heteromys anomalus (spiny pocket mouse)	67	5
Oryzomys sp. (rice rat)	434	22
Dasyprocta punctata (agouti)	46	92
Proechimys semispinosus (spiny rat)	350	105

RESIDENT MAMMALS	no/km²	kg/km²
FRUIT-EATERS/CARNIVORES AND FRUIT-EATERS/OMNIVORES		
Philander opossum (4-eyed opossum)	27	37
Didelphis marsupialis (opossum)	45	45
Cebus capucinus (cebus monkey)	16	42
Tayassu tajacu (peccary)	16	373
Nasua narica (coati mundi)	24	72
Eira barbara (tayra)	3	12
FRUIT-EATERS/BROWSERS		
Alouatta palliata (black howler monkey)	80	440
Agouti paca (paca)	26	208
BROWSERS		
Bradypus infuscatus (3-toed sloth)	123	393
Choloepus hoffmanii (2-toed sloth)	25	108
Tapirus terrestris (tapir)	0.53	139
Mazama americana (brocket deer)	2	30

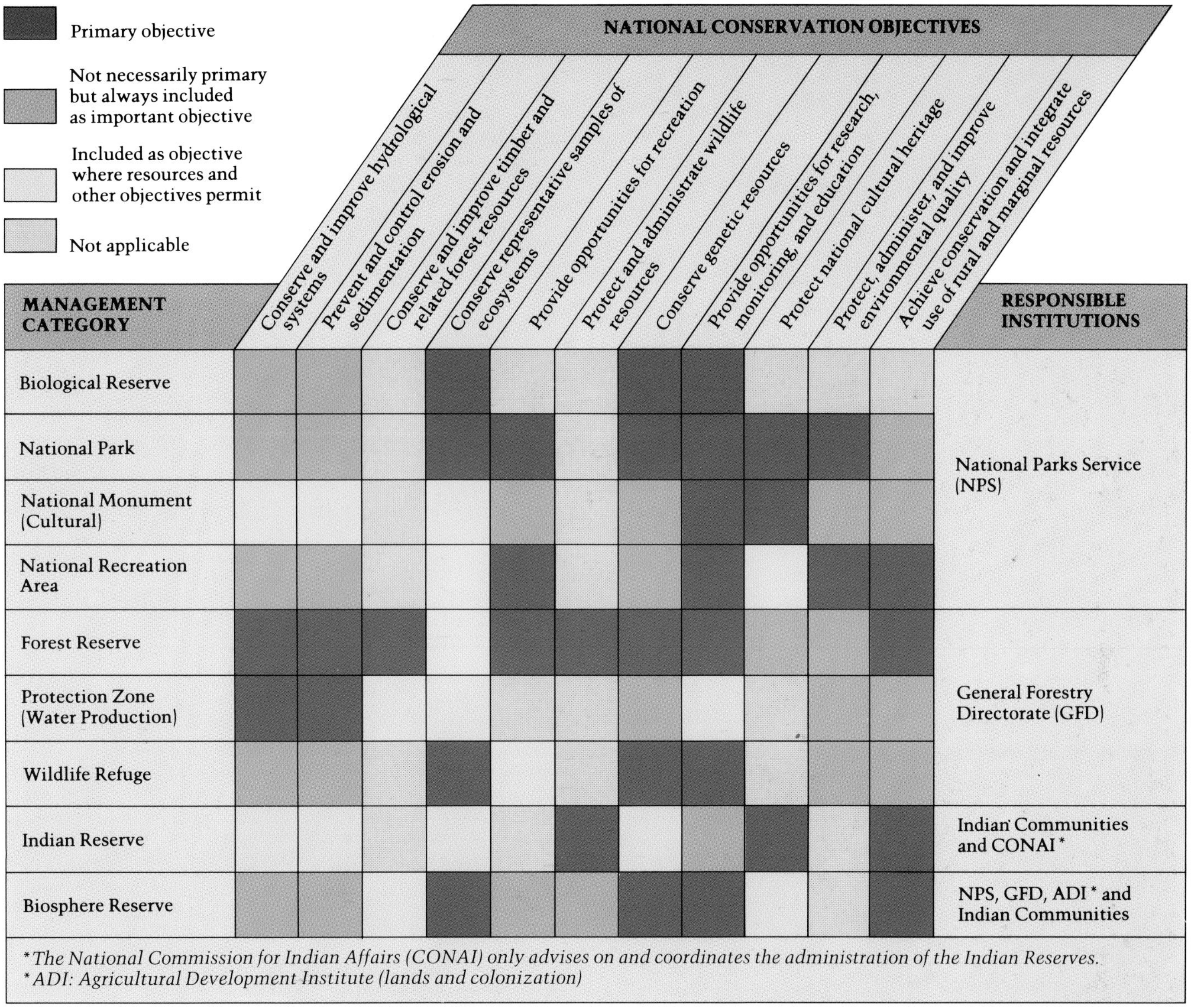

Legend:

- ■ Primary objective
- ▨ Not necessarily primary but always included as important objective
- ▢ Included as objective where resources and other objectives permit
- □ Not applicable

NATIONAL CONSERVATION OBJECTIVES

Column headers (left to right):
1. Conserve and improve hydrological systems
2. Prevent and control erosion and sedimentation
3. Conserve and improve timber and related forest resources
4. Conserve representative samples of ecosystems
5. Provide opportunities for recreation
6. Protect and administrate wildlife resources
7. Conserve genetic resources
8. Provide opportunities for research, monitoring, and education
9. Protect national cultural heritage
10. Protect, administer, and improve environmental quality
11. Achieve conservation and integrate use of rural and marginal resources

MANAGEMENT CATEGORY	RESPONSIBLE INSTITUTIONS
Biological Reserve	National Parks Service (NPS)
National Park	National Parks Service (NPS)
National Monument (Cultural)	National Parks Service (NPS)
National Recreation Area	National Parks Service (NPS)
Forest Reserve	General Forestry Directorate (GFD)
Protection Zone (Water Production)	General Forestry Directorate (GFD)
Wildlife Refuge	General Forestry Directorate (GFD)
Indian Reserve	Indian Communities and CONAI*
Biosphere Reserve	NPS, GFD, ADI* and Indian Communities

*The National Commission for Indian Affairs (CONAI) only advises on and coordinates the administration of the Indian Reserves.
*ADI: Agricultural Development Institute (lands and colonization)

△ **Conservation planning**
National Parks are often seen solely as strictly protected nature reserves, but with proper planning, other elements can often be incorporated, including human use, research, watershed management, and other national and global conservation objectives. The chart shows the categories of protected wild area used in Costa Rica.

▷ **Minimum critical size**
These 1-ha and 10-ha plots in Amazonia, surrounded by clear-cut areas and in some cases linked to virgin forest by corridors, form part of a Brazilian-American study of minimum effective reserve sizes carried out by WWF.

Plant species are somewhat more difficult to quantify. Oxford University botanist T.C. Whitmore, author of *Rain Forests of the Far East*, has estimated that in order to perpetuate many tree species, a reserve of significant genetic diversity would require at least 5,000 trees inhabiting an area of between 6.6 and 52 square miles (17 to 135 sq km). Whitmore concludes, "The prospect is frightening."

The "island effect"

By analyzing the species loss of oceanic islands separated from the mainland 10,000 years ago at the end of the Ice Age, we can estimate fairly accurately the minimum "island" park size for average intents and purposes.

A practical translation for conservation use tells us that if 90 percent of an extensive virgin forest area is disturbed, leaving 10 percent intact, we can expect to preserve no more than half the species in the island. Loss will be rapid in the initial period. If the area of preservation is increased tenfold, survival rate for species will double. These figures indicate that unless you desire to trade off, by protecting specific target species, it is far more advantageous to preserve one large area than to conserve two of half its size.

A realistically based anxiety will be the forecast that whatever the final amount of tropical forest biome we settle for, say 15 percent, this area will suffer from the inevitable erosion of invasive deforestation and be reduced in time. Just as a good many tropical forest parks established in the past have been eroded away, we can reasonably expect pressure to increase in proportion to the biome's diminishing size. It is far better that a 30 percent biome be whittled to 20 percent than a 15 percent biome be slashed to a meager 5 percent.

Such a scenario is already a reality in what have become referred to as "paper parks." Such "parks" are often, in reality, little more than the good intentions of the undeveloped tropical nations that decree them, and are mandated without the funding necessary for their patrol and protection. Many "paper parks" fall not only to the hordes of squatters, but also to more organized exploitation as government heads are conveniently turned. These are gossamer forests that blow away like the paper they were born on. Good intentions must be followed by priority funding for genuine protection.

Charismatic species as campaign leaders

In many specific instances, intensive fund-raising campaigns may be centered on well-known or appealing animals or even plants, while also keeping as a primary target the conservation of the habitat that supports these popular life-forms. In this way countless less charismatic, unrecognized, or even unknown species have greatly improved chances of survival. It will be this holistic approach that will keep the broadly intertwined ecological relationships intact.

Many of the most "spectacular" animals are at the top of the food chain and are less likely to suffer mass extinctions via the domino principle than many of the less visible species that receive a more subdued public support. Again, this "web of life" may be preserved only by extensive preserves, which include, ideally, entire watersheds.

Yet the situation is circuitous. Can the world afford to lose a spectacular animal such as, for example, the African mountain gorilla? Obviously, in order to ensure the survival of this endangered species, a very large part of its forest habitat, the Virunga Volcano Range, must be preserved.

△ *The gorilla is one of our closest relatives: 99% of its DNA is the same as ours, and its blood is barely distinguishable. To many, the brutal killing of this superb creature is close to homicide – often for the sake of "trophy" heads and hands to be sold to undiscerning tourists.*

THE MOUNTAIN GORILLA PROJECT

Discovered only some 100 years ago, the mountain gorilla now has a population of about 310. Given the huge problems of aiding the recovery of a species whose numbers dropped as low as 239 in 1979, the Mountain Gorilla Project (MGP) is one of the most heroically successful conservation stories of recent years. Far from being a hostage to destiny, this charismatic creature played a key role in its own campaign, his poster image firing widespread public support. Through Carl Akeley, George Schaller, Dian Fossey, and the MGP, the gorilla has helped preserve its own unique montane habitat, although it is still under threat.

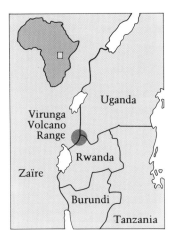

◁▽ **Home of the gorilla**
The mountain fastness of the Virunga Volcano Range straddles the wild borders of Zaïre, Rwanda, and Uganda. Cutting the greatest swath through the highland home of Gorilla gorilla benegei *is the human population, using the land for agriculture, wood-cutting, and grazing livestock. By controlling rainwater runoff, the forests protect downslope farms.*

◁ △ **Habitat pressures**
Generally gentle and contemplative by nature, gorilla groups often gather at the forest's edge to stare in disbelief as trees are cleared to make way for fields. MGP rangers assist tourists and mount constant patrols against poachers who plague the gorillas, forcing them higher and higher into the mountains, where damp and cold conditions can often lead to pneumonia.

▷ **Gorilla behavior**
A fierce glare shows this silverback male perceives my camera as a threat. He beats his chest at me in a deafening display, and, not quite satisfied with his efforts to humble me, he shakes a bamboo plume full of rainwater – but douses himself instead.

△ *Roxanne Kremer created a high level of Brazilian and Peruvian government awareness and widespread public support for her Pink Amazon River Dolphin project (PARD). Now, International Dolphin Day (26 June) is dedicated to this engaging and fearless creature.*

△ *In a poignant letter written just a month before his murder, Chico Mendes wrote, "I wish no flowers after I die, for I know they would be taken from the forest. All I want is that my murder will serve to put an end to the impunity enjoyed by the criminals... who, since 1975, have killed more than fifty persons like me, rubber-tapper leaders dedicated to defend the Amazonian forest." Since his death, Chico's wife, Izla, has carried on his campaign to save the forests of Acre and beyond.*

Many such gallant species exist and can be brought into the service of conservation to ultimately effect their own survival. 'Roxanne Kremer's Preservation of the Amazon River Dolphin (PARD), a project of the International Society for the Preservation of the Tropical Rainforest (ISPTR), has been highly successful in that regard. Prior to the project, only a small minority of the global lay public was aware that in parts of the Amazon and Orinoco river system there exists a river dolphin (*Inia geoffrensis*) that is actually bright pink in color and so tame it can be called to a canoe quite easily. Sadly, this is one reason for the dolphins' precarious survival profile, as fishermen destroy them effortlessly for their sexual organs and eyes, which are sold as *macumba* magical amulets in certain Latin American countries (and as an item of minor export to France).

Kremer has secured recognition in Brazil and Peru for this endearing dolphin, which now has an International Dolphin Dedication Day (26 June) in its honor and a safe haven in the River Dolphin Preserve at the mouth of the Yarapa River, a tributary of the Amazon, outside Iquitos, Peru. In this tightly knit scenario we see the enhanced potential for survival of an important species, the preservation of portions of its habitat, and a crucial realization by the governments and people of Brazil and Peru that the pink dolphin is attracting tourist and science revenues, both locally and internationally.

Multiple-use forestry for people

Tropical forest reserves can in many cases be put to multiple use as a much preferred alternative to destruction. In addition to providing gene pool perpetuation, watershed protection, tribal culture insulation, tourism, and educational uses which will result in enthusiasm for conservation, other less conventional uses may also be allowed. These may include selective forestry, game cropping, and use by local people for fruit and other forest product gathering. Buffer zones of no disturbance may surround or be imbedded in these areas of light disturbance. In many areas the more the resident population is integrated into the forest reserve the more chance the forest will have for survival in the long run: far more so than under the protection of typically inadequate ranger patrols. This concept is recognized by, and central to, the Man and the Biosphere (MAB) Reserve System.

Toward the realization of those concepts, the Brazilian government announced the formation of four rubber and Brazil nut "Extractive Reserves" in the state of Acre totaling more than 700,000 acres (283,000 ha), thus setting a global precedent in sustainable forest use.

These brilliant successes are earned only through the most determined efforts. In that Amazonian state of Acre, 120,000 of the 380,000 residents are *seringueiros*, or rubber tappers and their dependents. Their Rural Worker's Union believed in a "just social development" of the Amazon, while respecting and protecting their long-term source of products, foods, and medicines. Led by the internationally acclaimed Francisco (Chico) Mendes, a rubber tapper whose heroic demonstrations, with union support, were so successful against cattle ranchers' attempts to denude the forest, local people have now ensured that only 133 acres (54 ha) of the 3,000-square-mile (7,800-sq-km) Xapuri township were deforested in 1988. To this day Acre has lost only 4 percent of its forests, and the *seringueiros* maintain a higher standard of living harvesting the sustained bounty of the forest than do the slash-and-burn farmers who plant crops.

Three days before Christmas of that year, Mendes was murdered by shotgun, one of a great many to die for the cause in Acre. While the cattle ranchers responsible have been arrested, Mendes' martyrdom has immeasurably strengthened the Brazilian people's conservation tenacity.

Even now, some Brazilians still hold the view that they have a legitimate right to the Amazon. Outspoken environmentalist José Luzenberger, by contrast, considers the Brazilians themselves to be outsiders when they enter the region with their development plans. "This talk of, 'We can do with our land exactly what we want' is not true," says Luzenberger. "If you set your house on fire it will threaten the homes of your neighbors."

◁ While the cattle baron power structure that killed Chico Mendes is still destroying vast tracts of forest, yielding a meager $47/ha for six years at best, rubber tapping leaves the virgin forest unscathed, and yields $50/ha indefinitely.

▽ The gathering of Brazil nuts from virgin tropical forest accounts for 50% of household income in some areas. Attempts to establish plantations failed, however, because the trees' pollinator lives only in primary forest.

II · Stabilizing the Migrant Cultivator

The government tells us that we need more grain. They encourage us to plant corn for the country. I want to cultivate this land that is now forested. Yet they also tell us we can't cut down the trees. Sure the trees are good too, but what should a man do? You can't do both things at once.

PEASANT FARMER,
Puriscal, Costa Rica, 1979.

Some 800 million people in Third World rural areas, the majority from tropical forest countries, are landless or nearly so, and jobless as well. Caught also between cultures, these unfortunates are at the mercy of the whims of nature and government. During periods of food shortages the death rate of these millions may be three times higher than those like our friend the Puriscal peasant who, fortunate by comparison, owns a mere 3.7 acres (1.5 ha) of land.

Possibly the most compelling single reason for continued reliance on the extravagantly wasteful practice of slash-and-burn agriculture is the formidable inertia behind the practice which is now solidly ingrained in the culture of tropical peasantry.

In recognizing the crucial and timely importance of sustainable development, there is a growing concentration on identifying and producing manageable and realistic agricultural alternatives to swidden agriculture, which policy makers agree must be replaced with more frugal and efficient systems, given that the supply of fields for rotation is very limited and the loss of the tropical forest biome is, for a host of reasons, unacceptable.

For the herculean task of upgrading the practices of traditional peoples, nongovernmental organizations (NGOs) and government agricultural outreach programs can be armed with a surprising array of effective alternatives. Make no mistake, those extension services are not just another color on the palette; they are the very artists that man the brushes. Acknowledging the issues and values in the balance, there is a growing opinion that this new technological data base offers the highest potential return to humanity and the best chance for the maintenance of healthy and productive ecosystems.

The fertile varzeas

It is known, for example, that the seasonally flooded "varzea" forests of the Amazon can sustain agriculture indefinitely without the use of expensive fertilizers, as supplies of rich silt and vegetation debris are delivered free of charge by the rivers every year without fail. Indeed, any reference to the seasons in the vicinity of the Amazon is a reference to high water or low, with a water-level difference of 30 feet (9 m) separating the two. Imagine looking up and seeing alluvial flotsam in tree branches that high! Not only can these varzeas be permanently farmed, but for fast-maturing crops such as corn or beans, production levels are also outstanding.

It now appears that varzeas are also significantly enriched by a high potential for nitrogen fixation, and some sites have recorded values as high as 176 pounds per acre annually (200 kg/ha/yr). Through three crops a year, rice yields of 18 tons per hectare are achieved, whereas outside Amazonia the yield on irrigated land is only 3 to 4 tons. With abundant organic nutrients delivered free of charge, the varzeas can sustain agriculture as rich as any along the fertile Nile.

Pioneering tropical entomologist Terry Erwin has patterned a raised-bed garden on ancient Mayan techniques in a swamp forest in Tambopata, Peru.

Known as the Amazon Gardening Project, the prototype bed, surrounded by a moat for drainage, is filled with the super-rich swamp forest muck that retains such rich fertility. This soil is harvested at small cost to the forest, and the one-tenth of an acre (less than ½₅th of a hectare) garden is expected to feed four families over an extensive period. Development here can be less destructive and is able to take the pressure off more fragile upland forests where crop production is a constant drain on the resource.

Although carbon–14 dates lead us to believe that human activities became established along the margins of the South American continent between 23,000 and 20,000 years ago, direct evidence of occupation by Neolithic aboriginal peoples at Abrigo do Sol, a rock shelter in the south, is dated at 10,500 B.C. to the present time. (Flattened baked clay balls were found here, strongly suggesting the *bolas*, the hunting device in use on the Argentine pampas when the area was first visited by Europeans.)

The earliest European explorers in Amazonia vividly reported a much more advanced and affluent culture living along the varzeas than existed in the terra firme forests. The nutrients of the annual siltation fed a rich aquatic food chain which culminated in caimans, manatees, turtles (which in lieu of refrigeration were reportedly corralled for use when needed), as well as strikingly large and abundant fish. Farming produced copious harvests. Two crops of maize were grown each year, a variety of manioc was developed that matured in six months to avoid inundation, and wild rice was harvested and fermented into wine. This rice and the profusion of other aquatic grasses attracted large flocks of water birds which further enriched the lives of the varzea occupants. Large numbers of turtle eggs were pressed into oil to preserve meats. Why such diverse productivity escapes the modern descendents of those people is exemplified by their persistent use of inappropriate crops such as cassava, whose roots rot with the slightest flooding.

█ Flooded area

– – – – Limits of drainage basin

△ △ *The "Ribeirinhos" who farm the floodplain of the Amazon form a bridge between traditional Amerindian understanding of the region's natural diversity and the limited view of recent settlers. With its rich alluvial deposits, delivered free every year, the region offers sustainable crop and tree produce yields. One tree alone, the Açai palm* (Euterpe oleracea) *can yield fruit worth $136/ha/yr indefinitely.*

▷ *The river's seasonal flow is the calendar for varzea farmers. High flood (May-July) is the period of scarcity when stored foods are relied on. As the flood recedes, wild rice plants root on the lakesides. The peak time for hunting, and for gathering forest foods, is during low water (October-December). Crops of rice, maize, and manioc are harvested before the waters rise again.*

Jan	Feb	March	April	May	June	July	Aug	Sept	Oct	Nov	Dec	
												Rainy season
												Flood period
												Manioc
												Maize
												Wild rice
												Turtles, fish

△ ▷ *The fertile varzeas can support ten times the population of terra firme forests. Covering some 24,000 sq mi (62,000 sq km), these alluvial zones can support villages of 2,500 people (Tapajos) compared with 300 (Omagua) in the terra firme. Silt-enhanced productivity is the key. Turtle ranching produces 440 times as much meat as upland cattle, while rice yields of 3.2 tons/ha/yr are remarkable even by world standards.*

With all this potential on the horizon, a word of caution is necessary. Because of the nutrients that support such rich fisheries, care must be taken to avoid the serious consequences of overexploitation of the varzea. The indigenous peoples have long understood what we have only recently learned: that approximately 75 percent of the commercial fish of the Amazon are dependent on fruits and seeds and other organic material which falls into the water from the forest at high-water periods, during which time even piranhas switch to a diet of rubber tree (*Hevea brasiliensis*) seeds. A great many tree species, in turn, are dependent on the fish for germination of their seed. For this reason, attuned Amazon residents who do cut wood leave the forest intact at the water's edge to protect these crucial relationships.

Fisheries are, in fact, the most important source of animal protein for Amazonians. But mismanagement of this resource is now outstripping the yield, which is currently very noticeably on the decline. For this reason, both the avoidance of overexploitation and the regulation of fishery activities are urgent priorities. Yet there are plans for neither. Tom Lovejoy astutely points out that although rice culture in the varzea far exceeds fish production in weight, it does not do so in protein value. He suggests that provision be made to support rice and fishery production, and even fish culture, but that floodplain parks are an essential investment as well to protect the vital river community.

There is no reason, save for excessive numbers of people, which would stretch the limits of the resource, why sustained integrated development should not be possible without the need for the lengthy fallow periods necessary in terra firme forests. It should be further observed that continued overexploitation of the Amazon terra firme forests will result in higher and less regular flooding – with disastrous consequences for the varzea cultivators.

It is encouraging that the Brazilian government has recently proclaimed that 50 percent of the land bought for development in its Amazonian region will be left in its natural state. Biologists in various fields are now determining which tracts are ecologically most crucial and which may be exploited with minimal impact on Amazonia's gene pool.

Sustained agriculture, the elusive goal

It is a popular misconception that the Amazon Forest and other major tropical forests are homogeneous regions with similar terrain, soil, and rainfall characteristics. As a result, agricultural plots are given out indiscriminately.

An expert on tropical forest soils, Pedro Sanchez of North Carolina State University finds that about 8 percent of Amazonia has naturally fertile soil, and that 75 percent more is cultivable. These well-drained acid soils, he states, are the same as those found in the southeast United States, and will support continuous crops with proper care. In work in the Peruvian Amazon, Sanchez and others have sustained three crops per year for seven years, with yields comparable to any other area in the world. This has been achieved by the careful application of fertilizers and lime, and with a crop rotation of certain varieties of corn, dryland rice, soybean, and peanuts. A good payback of $5-worth of crops for each $1 in fertilizer has been achieved. (Other research, however, shows lower levels of fertility and indicates that lime and other additives can run off into water sources, neutralizing the acid pH. This has created favorable breeding conditions for the snail necessary to the life cycle of schistosomiasis, and a rapid rise in the occurrence of this dreaded disease has followed.)

Scientists working on the Tropical Soils Research Project are carrying out studies in Peruvian Amazonia where they claim extended areas exist where the subsoil differs from the lateritic clay so typical of large parts of the Amazon Basin. Here, the agricultural methods described above can give a much more continuous yield, and also increase the yearly gross income of a native farmer from US$750 to US$5,100, giving a 612 percent return on capital investment. Currently, however, farm credit in rural areas is scarce at best, and application of the all-important fertilizer is impossible without it. This leaves a gap that can only be filled by creative aid targeted at the remote farmers, in other words by an exercise in bankrolling success.

Something might be said of farmers transporting topsoil, along with leaf debris with its biological activity, from surrounding natural forest to their farm plots as nourishment and subsoil cover. Field studies would indicate whether this was a rob-Peter-to-pay-Paul practice or whether an extensive forest could readily regenerate its litter (and, if so, how often this potentially renewable resource could be tapped).

SOIL CONSTRAINT	MILLION ACRES	MILLION HECTARES	% OF AMAZON
Nitrogen deficiency	1,080	437	90
Phosphorus deficiency	1,077	436	90
Aluminum toxicity	946	383	79
Potassium deficiency	934	378	78
Calcium deficiency	746	302	62
Sulfur deficiency	692	280	58
Magnesium deficiency	689	279	58
Zinc deficiency	578	234	48
Poor drainage and flooding hazard	287	116	24
Copper deficiency	279	113	23
High phosphorus fixation	190	77	16
Low cation exchange capacity	175	71	15
High erosion hazard	96	39	8
Steep slopes (>30%)	74	30	6
Laterization hazard if subsoil exposed	52	21	4
Shallow soils (<50 cm deep)	7.4	3	<1

△ *Leached by tropical storms for eons, many of the red and yellow soils of the Amazon Basin were laid down 180 million years ago when the great southern continents first began drifting apart.*

Farming to simulate nature

The time is long overdue for us to take note of the natural and reproducible processes that occur when forest is disturbed, and to apply them to our own agricultural practices.

This innovative yet obvious method of retaining fertility reproduces the natural regeneration cycle that under favorable conditions takes place on deforested land. A *sustained-yield agro-ecosystem* is designed to mimic instead of resist forest succession, by using plants useful to humans at each stage of the cycle. First to appear after a burn is the herb community, and so this plan utilizes food crops analogous to the natural herb plants, such as pineapple (*Ananas comosus*), sugar cane (*Saccharum officinarum*), and beans (*Phaseolus* spp.). Year two brings pioneer trees naturally, and so the farmer is instructed to introduce cashew (*Anacardium occidentale*), bananas (*Musa* spp.), and papaya (*Carica papaya*) which could be productive for 5 to 10 years. Simultaneously, food and cash-crop tree species that correspond to primary forest trees are introduced. Such long-lived favorites as peach palm (*Bactris gasipaes*) are planted, from which not only fruit but also palm heart may be harvested on a sustained basis as the tree produces suckers when cut. This highly prolific native Amazon species provides one of the basic aboriginal staple foods. It remains productive from its eighth year to its fiftieth, with an annual crop of up to 150 pounds (68 kg) of versatile and nutritious fruit. Brazil nut (*Bertholletia excelsa*) and rosewood (*Tipuana tipu*) may also be planted, and when these become senile they may be felled and the process repeated as the fallow period would be sufficient to allow a natural return of fertility.

In addition, the following garden candidates were shown, in field trials in Panama by the Smithsonian Tropical Research Institute, to perform with high productivity in soils of low fertility: arrow root (*Maranta arundinacea*), tuber-bearing yam (*Dioscorea bulbifera*), Mexican yam bean (*Pachyrhizus erosus*), again the versatile peach palm (*Bactris gasipaes*), hardy banana clones (*Musa* spp.), a shade-tolerant, soil-covering vine (*Desmodium ovalifolium*), and leguminous shade trees (*Erythrina* spp. and *Gliricidia sepium*) for nitrogen capture.

▷ *Simulating a natural forest succession after the initial clearance, this managed system of garden and field crops, pig forage, and forest species, replaces natural forest vegetation with analagous plantings of greater economic value. Incorporating a commercial tree species such as paraiso (Melia azedarach) would give an additional long-term cash return.*

A *corridor system* formerly used in highly populated areas of Africa, employed 30- to 150-foot (9- to 46-m) strips cut through old growth forest and planted with crops. Close proximity to the forest edge ensured leaf-litter enrichment and soil protection, and when the plot was abandoned, seeds and mycorrhizae quickly repopulated the cut. We should presume that biotic diversity was maintained at a level sufficient to prevent excessive competition from pests. This was a successful method of agriculture but one that fell into disuse as soon as production of cash crops demanded continuous use of the land.

Because agriculture must not be discouraged in the wet tropics, it is considered imperative that a significant proportion of migrant cultivation should be directed into areas of seasoned secondary forest.

Although there is need for much additional research in this area, it has been shown that shifting agriculture is not significantly less stable on secondary forest than on primary forest provided the fallow period is long enough. Tests in Amazonia suggest that 14–21 years fallow is sufficient to regenerate soil fertility. Conversely, return to short-fallow secondary growth is unproductive, and can permanently incapacitate the land.

It is ironical that while virgin tropical forest is being depleted by swidden agriculturists, there exist an astounding 591 million acres (239 million ha) of fallow or previously cut closed-canopy forest, much of this standing as mature secondary growth, ripe for agricultural use or reuse.

△ *The incandescent coral tree (*Erythrina *sp.) seen here in the Central Valley of Costa Rica, probably inspired the intermixing of food crops and such nitrogen-fixing species. The tree is a deciduous legume, often used as a shade tree in coffee plantations, and its ability to fix nitrogen at up to 40 kg/ha/yr makes an invaluable contribution to sustained productivity.*

Untapped potentials for agriculture

Bamboo culture in much of the tropics has been largely ignored, yet there is evidence that would recommend it strongly. Moso bamboo (*Phyllostachys pubescens*), for instance, has long been a staff of agriculture in China, where 5 million acres (2 million ha) are planted. It is surprising then that it is extremely scarce outside China and Japan. One of the fastest-growing and largest of the bamboos, it reaches 80 feet (24 m) in height and 7.5 inches (19

△ *Bamboos, the world's fastest-growing plants, are an excellent source of building material, pulp, and edible shoots, yet their cultivation is conspicuous by its rarity outside China and Japan.*

△ *The babacú palm (Orbignya martiana) is another multiple-use plant that thrives on poor soils and has great potential as a plantation tree and as a shade tree in agroforestry mixed-planting systems.*

cm) in diameter. Its reputation as timber, pulp, and splitwood is second to none, as is the quality of its edible shoots. Among its greatest assets, however, is Moso's tolerance, perhaps almost preference, for very poor red clay soils, the curse of tropical forest agriculture. Further, it thrives on deforested mountain slopes, often regarded as wastelands and long discarded as sterile, where it prevents erosion, excludes weeds, and regenerates readily after clear-cutting.

The remarkable babaçú palm (*Orbignya martiana*) is so versatile that its fruit yields oil, feed and fertilizer cake, flour, charcoal, methyl alcohol, tar, and acetic acid. Some palms have yielded up to half a ton of fruits per year. It is noteworthy that its seeds can simply be strewn in degraded areas and they will sprout and grow so effectively that as they mature it is difficult to clear them, even with fire and machete! The huge fronds are harvested for an inexhaustible source of coal-like fuel. This palm's industrial potential appears unlimited.

Intensifying productivity

As yet we have seen no one single answer to the problem of extending the productivity of the slash-and-burner's plot. Research directed in this area, however, has been fruitful. The answers will no doubt lie in combinations of techniques tailored to the needs of specific locations. But one thing is certain: they will be far removed from the old regimen of corn and cassava.

Extremely impressive are the results of the Peruvian Amazonian tests on the Improved Yurimaguas Technology developed by the Tropical Soils Research Program of North Carolina State University (NCSU) and Peru's Ministry of Agriculture through its National Agricultural Research and Promotion Institute (INIPA).

On level and well-drained ultisols, although these soils are deficient in most nutrients, five crops a year were achieved by *intercropping*, or the growing of several different crops simultaneously. Forest was cut and burned in 1972, and as of 1985 (the date of the report) twenty-five consecutive crops of an upland rice/peanut/soybean rotation had been successfully harvested.

The system is dependent on fertilizer and lime, without which the yields declined to near zero after the third crop rotation in control tests. The main aspect of note, however, is that the system is as economically feasible as it is productive, bringing in a $2.91 net return for each $1 invested in the purchase and transportation of fertilizer and lime (at 1977 Yurimaguas prices). The NCSU/INIPA team report that the Improved Yurimaguas Technology gave the highest net revenue per hectare return (600 percent) to a corn/peanut/corn rotation. On a 3.7-acre (1.5-ha) farm, using an initial investment of $180 (half borrowed at 64 percent interest) and the family labor alone, the annual net income was a very healthy $2,797 compared with an average farm family net income for the region of $750.

△ *Biointensive gardening systems in the Philippines achieve high levels of sustained productivity on plots of only 540 sq ft (50 sq m). All debris is composted, crop diversity and close planting helps to reduce the spread of weeds, and the roots of plants that have been removed are left in the ground to add humus.*

Another strategy of promise comes from the International Institute of Tropical Agriculture in Ibadan, Nigeria. In this technique, tree roots are left intact after felling, and a soil-protective, nitrogen-fixing perennial legume (*Mucuna*) is planted immediately after clearing. This is left to its enriching capabilities for one or two seasons before annual crops are planted. Crop residues are used as mulch. In addition, appropriate grass or legume crops such as *Panicum maximum, Pueraria phaseoloides*, and *Mucuna utilis* may have to be grown specifically as mulch material. Crop selection must focus carefully on those species and varieties that are adapted to soils of low fertility, low pH, and aluminum levels that are toxic, characteristics typical of many tropical moist forest soils.

Nitrogen depletion, we can see, is one of the major constraints on sustained agriculture. It is no surprise then to find that nitrogen-fixing plants are a major feature in many productivity-enriching schemes. So generous are the amounts of nitrogen fixed from the air and made available to crops by certain legumes, that trials in Rwanda (*Project Agro-Pastoral de Nyabisindu*) using *Crotalaria* spp., *Tephrosia vogelii*, and *Cajanus cajanas* as a legume fallow, incorporated at 10 months, have increased maize yields more than four times compared to control plots with no addition of fertilizers.

It will be obvious to any home gardener that the addition of the legume crop not only enriches the soil but also improves soil stability, water retention, absorption, and access to air. These are all high priorities, none of which can be acquired through use of chemical fertilizers.

It will be very difficult for those readers in the southeastern United States, and other areas afflicted by the fiercely aggressive kudzu vine (*Pueraria* spp.), to appreciate that a tropical variety is used as an effective ground-covering, nitrogen-fixing legume and intentionally planted with crops such as plantain (*Plantago* spp.). Additionally, it has been used successfully as forage for pigs and other livestock in tests conducted in Progresso, Panama.

△ *Kudzu (*Pueraria *spp.), a prolific weed outside the the tropics for ground cover, to suppress other invasive plants to protect the soil, and as a source of nitrogen and nutritious animal fodder.*

Near the Brazilian Amazonian town of Tomé A,çu researchers are studying the surprisingly successful sustained agriculture of a Japanese community which has farmed there for half a century. Seemingly, these people have succeeded under the adverse conditions that most commonly result in short-life, traditional slash-and-burn agriculture. Their highly intensive system first employs quick-growing rice, cotton, and beans, which are then integrated with moderate-lived perennial vines such as passion fruit (*Passiflora edulis*) and black pepper (*Piper nigrum*). These are then followed by trees planted for fruit and latex, and on the trees are grown epiphytes such as vanilla bean orchid (*Vanilla fragrans*). So intensively frugal is their methodology that the residue from the black pepper processing is applied to the garden as an insect control! More than any other single factor, this colony's attitude, attributing immeasurably high value to a given plot of land (as in their homeland where it is the scarcest of commodities), has given rise to a highly productive labor-intensive form of sustained agriculture.

Another system of managed crop rotation is currently undergoing trials in parts of New Guinea. Following the harvest of food crops, one of the fast-growing nitrogen-fixing tree species (*Casuarina papuana*) is planted. During this time there is a return of nutrients to the soil. The trees are then cut for firewood, leaving the branches and leaves (slash) containing a concentration of minerals to decompose and return to the soil. During this same period, other plots of seasoned secondary forest are reused for farm crops, retarding the natural tendency to move into virgin forest.

Most slash-and-burn cultivators, however, expect maximum returns for a minimum amount of effort, and so move on to greener pastures (virgin forest) as soon as more effort is required. This is not to say that the swidden agriculturist's life is an easy one, or that he is essentially slovenly. Quite the contrary: these people are among the world's hardest working. Indeed, an FAO study reveals that it takes an average of 86 man-days to fell and burn each hectare of climax forest. The gross waste of the biomass is simply inherent in swidden agriculture, the method of long-standing habit. It incorporates not a single modern agricultural principle or advantage. Slash-and-burn agriculture supports only a paltry 7 persons per square kilometer (0.39 sq mi). Compare this to successful areas of permanent cultivation such as the Tonkin Delta which supports 354 times as many people per square kilometer without putting excessive pressure on the land resource.

The unexploited land resource

Soil maps prepared by the United Nations Educational, Scientific and Cultural Organization (UNESCO) were analyzed by a group at the Wageningen Agricultural University in The Netherlands. Results show that a surprising amount of cultivable land remains unused in the tropics worldwide. Argentina, for example, has the same amount of cultivable land as India, with only 4 percent of India's population. Brazil, which now farms 116 million acres (47 million ha), has 124 million acres (50 million ha) of savanna that is suitable for wheat and soybean production after aluminum-rich soils are treated, and this without infringing at all on the ecologically fragile Amazon Basin where agricultural potential is marginal at best.

MIT, in extrapolating available data, shows that each new hectare of land brought under cultivation will produce 0.9 metric tons of cereal grain. At FAO's minimum nutritional standard of 1,600 calories per day, this will feed 5 people. If the land is irrigated, 3.5 metric tons or four times the nonirrigated yield can be realized. It is estimated that 2.71 billion acres (1.1 billion ha) are available for crops through irrigation, enough to feed 10 billion people at twice FAO levels. Yet, there is a tragic vulnerability in such a scenario. Should every available global niche be occupied by the agriculture necessary to support 10 billion people, and all habitats reduced accordingly, any vagaries of climate, encroaching desertification, or other effect of global warming, will produce devastating poverty, misery, and death.

Edible giants and miniatures

There is every reason to expect that as investigations continue into innovative crops to complement the impoverished selections available to swidden agriculturists, the developed world's limited selection of twenty or so main crops will also expand.

From the Asian tropics comes the surprising giant wax gourd (*Benincasa hispida*), which holds great promise in upgrading tropical field production. It grows so fast (one inch (2.5 cm) every three hours at peak) that four crops yearly can be achieved. When mature, the gourd weighs 77 pounds (35 kg) and measures over 6.5 feet (2 m) long by more than a yard (1 m) in diameter. Its juicy pulp can be eaten at any stage of development, and this mammoth vegetable can be stored for a year, even in the humid tropics, thanks to its thick protective skin.

Recent experiments show that giant kelp (*Macrocystis pyrifera*) may have growth rates of up to 3 feet (0.9 m) per day. Farmers use this alga as fodder for goats, sheep, and other stock, but palatable varieties can also be grown for human consumption as anyone fortunate enough to have sampled Japanese seaweed soup or seaweed-wrapped *sushi* can testify. It is also lauded nutritionally. *Principes*, the Journal of the Palm Society, reports a recent hybrid Indonesian coconut palm (*Cocos nucifera*) that promises to quadruple nut production.

China has made other innovative and practical strides. Azolla (*Azolla* sp.), a floating aquatic fern, reacts symbiotically with a blue-green alga (*Anabaena azollae*) which resides in the fern's leaf cavity, where it fixes atmospheric

△ *Where cultivable land is scarce, as here in tropical China, there is a growing emphasis at community and government level on crop intensification, increased crop diversity, natural pest control, terracing, and other measures to improve land husbandry and maximize productivity.*

nitrogen. The Chinese grow 3.5 million acres (1.4 million ha) of *Azolla*, which produce the annual equivalent of at least 100,000 tons of nitrogen fertilizer. The fern is then plowed into rice fields. By this method alone the Chinese have increased their rice yields by 158 percent!

A new process called Green Crop Fractional can produce leaf proteins, salt, sugar, lipids, and vitamins that may be directly consumed by man. By rupturing or bruising plant stems, inflorescences, pods, and other plant parts, these nutrients are released as flowing juices in enormous quantities. Palm toddy, an intoxicating tropical native beverage, is produced by fermenting this sugar-rich syrup. Although this would represent an extreme latitude in intensifying productivity, the tropical forest may potentially produce at least as much food in an undisturbed state as when it is felled to produce crops. This, in fact, is the very essence of rubber tapping.

When the conquistadores first came to Mexico, they found the Aztecs using a blue-green alga as their main source of protein. Fully 60 to 70 percent of its bulk is high-caliber protein, and it flourishes in saline, even alkaline, water, producing food in arid lands unsuitable for other agriculture. A mere 2.47 acres (1 ha) can yield 187 pounds (85 kg) of protein a day. Until recently the alga (*Spirulina platensis*) was apparently used in modern times only by villagers around Lake Chad in Africa.

Plant geneticists are now working on a strain that will tolerate magnesium. *Spirulina* could then be grown in seawater, a development that would have the potential to significantly impact world hunger. I have found great advocacy among nutritionists for supplementing the diets of sub-Saharan drought-famine victims with *Spirulina* where there was no cultural resistance to its consumption. The plant extract was also administered as a "vitamin" supplement with considerable success.

Of special note in this context is the winged bean (*Psophocarpus tetragonolobus*), whose beans, leaves, shoots, tendrils, and buds are among the world's richest sources of protein, amino acids, and vitamin A. The plant, therefore, has great potential to save the eyesight of multitudes of mal-nourished Third World children. Furthermore, the bean's enlarged tuber is not only protein-rich and extremely tasty, but is also of higher food value than Irish potato, sweet potato, or manioc.

Do as the Lacandon do

The integration of traditional field crops with the highly promising new crops, tree plantations, and use of all available forms of by-product forage, will undoubtedly aid in curbing encroachment on new land. Moreover, neighboring undisturbed forest will act as a gene pool to recolonize the vacated plots with indigenous species and will also serve the resident farmer as a storehouse of food and materials. Incoming agriculturists must be taught what these resources are and how to locate them, and the main source of this invaluable information is, of course, the tribal forest people.

An example of a semi-archaic people who engage in agriculture as well as hunting and gathering are the Lacandon Indians of the Mexican Chiapas Forest. On a single hectare they plant up to 80 food and raw material crops. In addition, they ply the nearby forest for as many as 100 varieties of wild fruit and other foods, 20 species of fish, 6 varieties of turtle, 3 types of frog, 2 species of crocodile, 2 kinds of crab, 3 types of crayfish, and 2 species of snail. And this is by no means the limit of the (renewable) resources they exploit.

Known as "milpa" gardens, the Lacandon's 1.2-acre (0.5-ha) plots of intensely managed land reportedly produce a quarter metric ton of corn and an equal weight of root and tree crops annually. The rich plots last five to seven years (up to 300 percent longer than less intensive swidden plots) so that a single farmer may need only clear as little as 25 acres (10 ha) in his lifetime. In addition, as these diverse farm plots are left to fallow, the secondary vegetation that takes over will contain many plants attractive to animals, thus creating an agriculturally based game farm of sorts which will continue to supplement the nearby farmer.

The very antithesis of the broadly diverse Lacandon method of land use is the conversion of tropical forest to cattle pasture which, on a like-size plot to our "milpa" above, will produce less than 9 pounds (4 kg) of beef. Such enterprises are typified by a small labor force and large landholdings, displacing peasant farmers to wilderness areas and so perpetuating destructive deforestation practices.

Small landholdings yield far higher returns than larger farms, as farming families have all hands in the field maximizing production. This is especially so in the tropics. Even so, an unsponsored study covering 83 countries found that roughly 3 percent of landowners control 79 per cent of the farmland. These inequities call for cutbacks in cattle-enterprise credit (a welcome recent development in Brazil) and an imposed ceiling on the size of landholdings.

More efficient animal husbandry

There is no agricultural application that produces less sustenance per unit area than cattle grazing. Highly significant data from Cornell University show that a switch in emphasis from beef to chicken production would produce a 50 percent saving in energy. Further, if American beef production shifted from grain to grass feed, a saving of 135 million tons of grain a year could be realized; that is ten times the yearly consumption of the American population. This surplus grain, valued at $20 billion, could theoretically feed the world's starving and take pressure off the virgin tropical forests while simultaneously realizing a 50 percent energy saving. In addition, if 50 percent of our animal protein were supplemented by plant protein (as is widely advised for cardiovascular fitness) an extra 50 percent in energy could be saved

◁ The perilous decline of wild crocodile populations through hunting and habitat destruction gave birth to the concept of the crocodile farm. In the early 1960s, conservation laws and natural scarcity forced up the price of skins, making such farms commercially viable. Now, the farms produce meat and skins for sale, and many also breed rare species for return to the wild.

in its production. The use of tariffs to raise the price of imported beef is an obvious device at our disposal. As cattle are unlikely to completely disappear from the tropical scene, there is an environmental trade-off to switching from beef production to intensified dairy production, which relies on smaller herds and a more stable market.

Higher yields than cattle grazing can also be realized by the use of multispecies forage, the food supply regime responsible for the high wildlife-carrying capacity of African savannas. In this uniquely biologically sound regimen, nature is mimicked by incorporating pigs, chickens, ducks, fish, and domesticated native wildlife such as tapirs (*Tapirus* spp.), deer (Cervinae), crocodiles (*Crocodylus* spp.), banteng (*Bos banteng*), capybaras (*Hydrochoerus hydrochaeris*), and others. By taking advantage of the full spectrum of sustainable aquatic and terrestrial fodder and live feed, an increase in production can be achieved that will far outstrip its antithesis, the concentration on cattle and its rapidly depreciating food source.

Manure from the livestock will provide the fertilizer that is largely lacking in primitive agriculture, and this can be a major factor in increasing the life span of the farmer's plot many times over. Introduction of dry-season grasses can boost the life of the plot even further. An added bonus is that the domestication of forest animals can relieve the pressure of overhunting of these species in the wild.

There appears to be considerable success in Panama in green-iguana (*Iguana iguana*) ranching. Providing a traditionally prized food, and valuable skins for export, the iguanas are raised in a variety of trees that are also useful to the farmers, who harvest the fruit while the lizards eat the leaves. Early reproduction, the fast growth rate, and the iguana's tendency to remain around the release area, even after it has been reforested, commend this program which produces impressive results in undisturbed forest as well.

Agroforestry – the new land ethic

No practice more typifies the ushering in of *intensified* land use, as opposed to *extensified* land use, than the practice of *agroforestry*. This process mimics primary forest structure and species diversity with a multistoried network of trees and shrubs bearing fruits, nuts, fibers, medicinals, and beverages, as well as providing fuelwood and marketable timber. Chickens, pigs, fish, and other livestock provide additional sources of food – all on a self-sustaining basis. Falling leaf litter added to livestock feces helps enrich the fields, thus

▽ *A popular variation on the* taungya *method of cultivation uses coconut palms (*Cocos nucifera*) as shade trees and producers in their own right. For up to 8 years, space permits the planting of annual or short-term perennial crops; from 8 to 25 years the palm cover dominates to the exclusion of herb or shrub species; but from 25 years onward the high elevation of the canopy again allows understory species such as cocoa (*Theobroma cacao*) to grow.*

prolonging the life of the plot and reducing the traditional imperative to move on. Not only does the above prescription render the peasant farmer and his family well fed and more affluent, but also – and very importantly – it means he is stable on his land, in contrast to the role of the involuntary nomadic slash-and-burn farmer who rotates fields of forest instead of crops. In test programs, title may be obtained to colonized land after a minimum five-year tree crop establishment, which again encourages peasant farmers to take up permanent residence. Trees mature and are marketed through credits, tax incentives, and grants.

These measures are not utopian: they have been proven entirely practical. Tests in Nigeria show a cash income per farmer of $200-$300 per year from the trees alone. The agroforests cost only $200-$350 to establish, compared to $800 if trees were planted directly. By turning profit back into fertilizer and pesticides, the cultivator may then quadruple his harvest of food and remain stable on his farm.

The conservator of forests of the Sabah Forest Department reports on the progress of a 1979 agroforestry project utilizing 54,000 acres (21,850 ha) of logged-over dipterocarp forests. This outstanding program is unusual in that it promotes regeneration of the commercially valuable dipterocarps (and other fast-growing hardwoods) where sampling reveals inadequate natural regeneration. In addition, cocoa (*Theobroma cacao*) is widely planted between the timber trees. It is anticipated that the income from the cocoa crop alone will cover the costs of the entire project.

It should be stressed that unless opportunities other than forest farming are made available, that sector will continue to grow faster than the balance of the national population. And yet sustainable agriculture must be seriously addressed in response not only to the nutrient self-sufficiency of the people, but also to the national balance of trade. Aside from innovative applications, the selective use of traditional crops such as cocoa, which is particularly suitable for agroforestry as it is not deleterious to the soil, accounted for $778 million in exports for Brazil in 1986. Developing countries must strive for the optimum mixture of sustenance crops and export crops.

Intensified agroforestry – the linchpin of sustained development

It is with well-earned gratification that we may finally feel we have techniques and technologies with which to stabilize agriculture in the moist and wet tropics. Although the discipline of agroforestry has only recently been studied in depth, we may now evaluate some of the first hard data on those highly intensified agroforestry systems. The jury is out. For the first time, we may realistically appraise the outstanding benefits that await the swidden agriculturist should he choose to intensify his production capacities and remain on his plot. This, against the very real and considerable losses he suffers annually in labor, produce, and fertility as he continues the rote habit of migrant cultivation.

While researching the comparative benefits of the new, integrated, agricultural strategy, I was greatly encouraged by the many researchers in diverse disciplines who contributed their data to the analysis. (See explanatory notes in Appendix 3, on page 244, referring to the comparative chart on pages 202–205.) Their enthusiastic consensus indicated that such a comparative analysis was long overdue and would serve as a useful tool for decision makers involved in the issues of tropical deforestation and sustained development.

△ *A major step toward*
sustained productivity can
be achieved by planting
Leucaena leucocephala *in*
garden plots. This fast-
growing tree produces huge
amounts of fuelwood,
pulpwood, and timber;
animal fodder from its
foliage, and human food in
the form of pods, young
leaves, and seeds; and at the
same time provides good soil
erosion control, shade, and
crop protection. Just as
important, this legume is
also a prodigious fixer of
atmospheric nitrogen.

We are advised that as a migrant cultivator moves into ten-to-twenty-year fallow secondary forest with nonmotorized hand tools (steel axes, machetes, etc.) he will expend 50 man-days (400 man-hours) felling, preparing slash for torching, and burning 2.47 acres (1 ha). In primary forest the labor rises to 86 man-days, or 688 man-hours. The entire process, including planting and harvesting, will require 1,588 hours. This is no small expenditure of energy and is consistent for most grain-crop annuals, whether corn (*Zea mays*), or rice (*Oryza* spp.).

With even a most simplified agroforestry plot, one incorporating only corn and *Leucaena leucocephala* for its nitrogen-fixing capacities and fuelwood, corn production was 4,400 pounds (2,000 kg) per hectare. Corn production for the first year was the same for the slashed-and-burned plot, but soil loss was 20 tons per hectare for the short-cycle shifting cultivation while it was only half that for year one on the nonintensive agroforestry plot. Year two sees production on the shifting plot drop to 2,700 pounds (1,225 kg) as soil loss increases to 25/tons/ha/yr, the last year it will marginally pay to farm the plot. But here the *Leucaena* kicks in for the agroforester: his soil loss is reduced to 2 tons/ha/yr while his plot is producing 3,400 pounds (1,542 kg) of corn. By year three the migrant is back to square one with some 1,588 man-hours of labor, cutting primary forest, while our agroforester has frugally gone to between 5 and 8 hectares of surrounding forest for renewable supplies of mulch, replacing the phosphorus and other essential nutrients his corn crop has removed. In addition, his *Leucaena* now produces 4,400 pounds (2,000 kg) of wood, cut 3 inches (8 cm) above the ground to induce further sprouting for fuelwood, and an additional 5,500 pounds (2,500 kg) of foliage for mulch, which will give a net return of 500 pounds (227 kg) of nitrogen for soil enrichment., At the same time, his soil loss is only 0.75 tons/ha/yr. He can maintain this production of corn and *Leucaena* into a 25-year horizon with labor dropping to 300 man-hours per year.

World Wide Fund For Nature's dendrologist, Gary Hartshorn, counsels that through new shoot growth, the prudent farmer can expect to continue to crop the original level of harvest of *Leucaena* indefinitely.

Even greater efficiency, in terms of labor, soil loss, and production, is realized by *intensifying*, that is, by incorporating, in a simplified example, corn, papaya, and oranges, which produce into perhaps the fortieth year, and laurel trees (*Cordia alliodora*) as a timber cash crop. A look at the chart on pages 202–205 shows labor dropping to 40 man-hrs/yr, as the high labor factor of weeding is now markedly minimized, soil loss is down to 0.3 tons/ha/yr as the mulch and crop protect the soil, and income increases to $2,690 per hectare, more than thirteen times the migrant's best year. As a benchmark, cattle produce $47/ha/yr. We now move to a facet of intensification that can inject a true measure of prosperity.

The ultimate protein source

Given human nature, attempts to change traditional food production systems to more intensified methods often meet with resistance. But if it can be demonstrated that a new plant or technique will provide a bounty of produce, especially with less physical effort, it is likely to take hold in peasant agriculture. This is especially so if agricultural extension services are provided during the transition period. Families observe their uncles' successes and abundance of produce, and will be quick to copy any successful innovation.

Possibly nothing has more merit in this category than fish aquaculture. Where proliferation and naturalization by exotic species is a risk, the introduced fish must be contained artificially, or selected indigenous species used in their place. Ponds are dug and extension services – important to the program's success – supply seed fish, often the highly succcessful tilapia fish (*Tilapia* spp.), and expertise.

One of the tilapia's preferred foods, aside from algae, are termites, an especially abundant commodity in the forest. Three nests a week of high-protein termites are fed to the fish, which also eat a great variety of vegetable matter. The fish usually prosper and multiply – as do the farmers.

Assisted by my organization Africa Tomorrow – an advocacy group of entertainment-industry people, legislators, and scientists directed toward nutritional self-sufficiency in the sub-Saharan region – tilapia fish-farming has gained widespread acceptance as a step toward long-term sustained developmental strategy in regions where even a minimal water supply can be relied on throughout the year. This includes semi-marginal drought areas in the sub-Saharan region, as well as the moist and wet zones. (Modest, yet ever-expanding projects, resulting from Africa Tomorrow's indoctrination programs, presently feed several thousand villagers in the tropics.) The technology is as yet underapplied. It has enormous potential as judged by successes in Rwanda, Nigeria, Jamaica, Thailand, and other tropical nations, and can be critically important to stabilizing land use in areas where swidden agriculture is the norm.

Especially significant is the strong tendency of peasants to remain on the land after investing their labor in pond construction, and after banking marketable reserves of fish protein. This, in turn, encourages the acceptance – even the pursuit – of more such intensive methods of farm-plot cultivation and animal husbandry. In Zaïre, during a tour of inspection of tilapia ponds instituted by the Peace Corps, parades were held honoring Loret Miller-Ruppe, the corp's director. Cloth tilapia flags were flown on the streets signifying the people's enthusiasm for this new source of protein.

In China, the Philippines, India, and Togo, synergistic interactions have increased farm production markedly. There, swine and chicken enclosures are constructed directly over fish ponds so that animal wastes drop directly through a grated floor. In this intensified system, manure is also collected and placed in chambers where anaerobic fermentation produces methane gas which, in turn, is employed to heat buildings, produce light, and, of particular merit in the tropics, power refrigerators. The solid sludge then remaining in the biogas reactor, as it is called, is used in the fields as fertilizer. The liquid residue (*caldo*) is used in the cultivation of a nitrogen-fixing alga that, in turn, produces a protein-rich feed for the swine and poultry – thus completing a highly efficient closed cycle of productivity.

△ It is impossible to overstate the potential of fisheries combined with agriculture as a means of improving the diet and economic well-being of forest people, and of simultaneously stabilizing migrant populations and removing a major cause of deforestation. Carp fisheries in India △ △, like the tilapia farms of Panama △, can add US$7,985 per hectare per year to family incomes.

Integrated agroforestry and aquaculture

The International Center for Aquaculture at Auburn University is reporting compelling results following more than five years of fish-culture projects in Rwanda, Jamaica, Panama, and a CARE project in Guatemala.

Ponds were hand dug with an average water area of 4 ares (0.04 ha) in Rwanda and 2,200 square feet (204 sq m) in Guatemala. The smaller pond is the more feasible for family construction: larger ponds are often communal in construction and operation, involving many families. The former required 53 man-days (at 8/hr day), less than that required to fell and burn a hectare of forest. Clay soils serve excellently. In many cases, ponds can be glayed, a process promoting algal growth in water. This involves draining the pond and allowing the algae to seal the surface and dry in. Given the edge-effect of many smaller-sized ponds, leading to enriched crop planting on the levees, and proportionately superior tilapia production, the smaller size is the more logical family choice.

Pond maintenance requires some 488 man-hours per year and involves putting in crop residues and manures, culling fish, etc. (For consistency, we extrapolate production figures for a one-hectare pond.)

Fish (*Tilapia nilotica*) production was 1,760-2,200 pounds per acre per year (2,000-2,500 kg/ha/yr) and exceeded 3,500 pounds per acre per year (4,000 kg/ha/yr), on only moderately intensified ponds in Guatemala. Those incorporated only some 20 chickens over a 2,200 square foot (200 sq m) pond. Manure and chicken feed (animal and/or green) which subsequently falls into the pond, increases production of plankton, which is the natural food of tilapia. (Yields in the range of 7,055-8,800 pounds per acre per year (8,000-10,000 kg/ha/yr) were reported in the Jamaica project when the fish were fed rice, wheat, or chicken meal. However, for our purposes we will keep with the easily affordable start-up pond scenario without extensive feeding, even though the more capital-intensive method has a premium return on investment.) It is an indication of the project's success that by the end of 1987, Moss reports 2,365 ponds were operating, serving more than 7,000 Rwandan families and producing 22 tons of marketable fish during that year.

In addition, farmers were growing crops on pond levees, benefiting not only from pond moisture during the dry seasons but also by applying the enriching pond mud to planting beds, and so also increasing traditional crop yields.

Spread over 25 years (although ponds dug 40 years ago are still quite operable), the net present value of the return on the investment was 21,197 FRW (Rwanda monetary unit) ($258). The "average" farm family has an income of 55,441 FRW ($676), of which coffee, the universal crop, contributes 4,023 FRW ($49). While the net returns for fish were negative for the first two years, returns exceeded costs for years 3 to 25. In fact, the net benefit investment ratio was 17:1 (1:0 is considered acceptable). By another measure, the internal rate of return for the farmer's investment yielded 41 percent: excellent justification for the project as it is considerably better than the opportunity cost for capital, which is almost 15 percent for Rwanda.

We note that gross returns per acre are almost five times that for beans and almost twice that for rice production. Further, fish farming enjoys a harvest every fifteen weeks and has no defined season so harvests can be planned to coincide with periods of low crop productivity. In the grand plan to stabilize agriculture and improve income/nutrition in the tropical Third World, fish in aquaculture admirably succeeds in injecting cheap, high-quality protein where the propensity did not previously exist. The price of fish is relatively high, yet compares favorably when measured against other protein sources; and while fish comprises 35 percent protein, beef comprises only 23 percent.

At this point we can readily appreciate the security and stability that eludes the migrant cultivator not presented with these alternatives. Should we now fine-tune such an operation and introduce pigs, goats, turtles, and so on, we see just how little there is to recommend the slash-and-burn methods of the migrant farmer.

Don Moss of Auburn's International Center for Aquaculture is our leading advisor on this technology, and he has astutely identified why fish farming has not proliferated as widely as it clearly deserves. While the national and international funding institutions, such as US-AID and the World Bank, clearly acknowledge the merit in fishing aquaculture (AID has, in fact, funded the majority of such projects), such projects compete directly for funds with other traditional agriculture projects whose feet are, frankly, firmly placed in the revolving door of grant machinery. It takes great patience to make headway in such circumstances. Moss and staff, by their impressive track record, are apparently in the process of mastering the art.

Here I must add something a little more insidious to this soup. It is not a well-kept secret that the AID agencies clearly prefer projects of high monetary value to smaller projects, regardless of returns, which would often make the smaller-unit projects far more commendable. The reason is apparently that it requires the same funding/staff time to oversee the $70,000 fish aquaculture project as it does to administer the $7 million blockbuster. There is an ever-growing consensus that a time for change has come.

△ Quite unlike the illusory fertility of tropical forest soils, floodplains such as that of the Amazon sustain a large biomass of aquatic life, especially fish. This is the most important source of animal protein for local, rural and urban populations. There is cause for concern, however, that deforestation, consequent silting of rivers, overfishing, and the building of dams are depleting this otherwise infinitely renewable food resource.

Continued on page 206

TOWARD SUSTAINED PRODUCTIVITY

While sustained productivity is widely recognized as environmentally sound and desirable, this comparative chart demonstrates that there is every reason for the migrant cultivator to adopt these new technologies entirely on their own merit. Sustained extraction of rubber, nuts, fruit, and game can yield US$1,000 ha/yr without degrading the forest, while fish, turtle and game farming can produce twenty times the income with only minimum disturbance. By contrast, cattle ranching in tropical forest regions yields a meagre $47 ha/yr. (See Appendix 3.)

TYPE OF AGRICULTURAL ACTIVITY Showing labor input (man-hours/ha/year), quantity, and value of produce (lbs/ha/year; $US/ha/year), and soil loss (tons/ha/year).	YEAR 1	YEAR 2	YEAR 3	YEAR 4	YEAR 5	YEAR 6
SHORT-CYCLE SHIFTING CULTIVATION Growing corn only, on 1-ha plots cleared in primary forest.				Plot abandoned at end of year 2: cycle then		
Labor (man-hours/ha/yr) 688 hours to clear new plot every 2 years, plus 900 hours annual input of labor on planting, weeding, and harvesting.	1,588	900	1,588	900	1,588	900
Quantity of corn produced (lbs/ha/yr)	4,400	2,700	4,400	2,700	4,400	2,700
Value of corn produced ($US/ha/yr)	200	123	200	123	200	123
Soil loss (tons/ha/yr)	25	25	20	25	20	25
NONINTENSIVE AGROFORESTRY Growing corn and *Leucaena* on 1-ha plot (using renewable natural fertilizer – manure, mulch, and slash).						
Total labor (man-hours/ha/yr)	1,650	700	500	400	300	300
Quantity of corn produced (lbs/ha/yr)	4,400	3,400	4,000	4,400	4,400	4,400
Value of corn produced ($US/ha/yr)	200	155	182	200	200	200
Quantity of *Leucaena* produced (lbs/ha/yr). (From year 3 onward = 4,400 lb of wood for fuel, plus 5,500 lb of foliage for mulch.)	0	4,000	9,900	9,900	9,900	9,900
Net return of nitrogen to the soil (lbs/ha/yr)	0	1,000	1,500	1,500	1,500	1,500
Soil loss (tons/ha/yr)	10.0	2.0	0.75	0.70	0.60	0.40
PARTIALLY INTENSIFIED AGROFORESTRY Growing corn in year 1, papaya in years 1-3, and oranges in years 1-25+. Laurel trees (*Cordia alliodora*) utilized to best advantage with shade-tolerant perennials, for mulch, poles, fuelwood, and eventual sale for timber.						
Total labor for clearing (man-hours/ha/yr), Amortized over 5 years to conserve soil.	1,088	1,000	700	600	500	100
Value of laurel crop ($US/ha/yr). Trimmings taken in years 6-12; mature trees cut for sale in years 18 onward.	0	0	0	0	0	100
Value of crops ($US/ha/yr): Corn (yr 1), papaya (yrs 2/3), oranges (yrs 3-25+)	150	1,000	1,000	270	330	465
Soil loss (tons/ha/yr)	1.00	0.40	0.30	0.29	0.25	0.20
CATTLE PASTURE On manually cleared 7% slopes in primary forest.						
Labor (man-hours/ha/yr)	928	50	50	50	50	50
Live-weight cattle production (kg/ha/yr)	50	50	50	43	37	16
Value of cattle production ($US/ha/yr)	47	47	47	40	35	15
Soil loss (tons/ha/yr)	20	5	5	5	5	5

Multispecies agroforestry

Shifting cultivation requiring 1,588 man-hrs/ha/yr yields only $200 in the best (first) year of its two-year cycle, and the price is a huge drop in soil fertility. Partially intensified agroforestry can yield $2,690 a year, with labor falling to only 40 man-hrs/ ha/yr and topsoil loss no greater than in the natural forest. When fish aquaculture is added, formerly migrant cultivators are already moving from mere subsistence toward comparative affluence – with no detrimental impact on the forest.

YEARS 7/8	YEARS 9/10	YEARS 11/12	YEARS 13/14	YEARS 15/16	YEARS 17/18	YEAR 19	YEAR 20	YEAR 21	YEAR 22	YEAR 23	YEAR 24	YEAR 25

repeated on new primary forest plot.

YEARS 7/8	YEARS 9/10	YEARS 11/12	YEARS 13/14	YEARS 15/16	YEARS 17/18	YEAR 19	YEAR 20	YEAR 21	YEAR 22	YEAR 23	YEAR 24	YEAR 25
1,588 / 900	1,588 / 900	1,588 / 900	1,588 / 900	1,588 / 900	1,588 / 900	1,588	900	1,588	900	1,588	900	1,588
4,400 / 2,700	4,400 / 2,700	4,400 / 2,700	4,400 / 2,700	4,400 / 2,700	4,400 / 2,700	4,400	2,700	4,400	2,700	4,400	2,700	4,400
200 / 123	200 / 123	200 / 123	200 / 123	200 / 123	200 / 123	200	123	200	123	200	123	200
20 / 25	20 / 25	20 / 25	20 / 25	20 / 25	20 / 25	20	25	20	25	20	25	20

YEARS 7/8	YEARS 9/10	YEARS 11/12	YEARS 13/14	YEARS 15/16	YEARS 17/18	YEAR 19	YEAR 20	YEAR 21	YEAR 22	YEAR 23	YEAR 24	YEAR 25
300	300	300	300	300	300	300	300	300	300	300	300	300
4,400	4,400	4,400	4,400	4,400	4,400	4,400	4,400	4,400	4,400	4,400	4,400	4,400
200	200	200	200	200	200	200	200	200	200	200	200	200
9,900	9,900	9,900	9,900	9,900	9,900	9,900	9,900	9,900	9,900	9,900	9,900	9,900
1,500	1,500	1,500	1,500	1,500	1,500	1,500	1,500	1,500	1,500	1,500	1,500	1,500
0.30	0.20	0.20	0.20	0.20	0.20	0.20	0.20	0.20	0.20	0.20	0.20	0.20

YEARS 7/8	YEARS 9/10	YEARS 11/12	YEARS 13/14	YEARS 15/16	YEARS 17/18	YEAR 19	YEAR 20	YEAR 21	YEAR 22	YEAR 23	YEAR 24	YEAR 25
90	80	70	60	50	40	40	40	40	40	40	40	40
400	700	900	0	0	1,000	1,200	1,300	1,400	1,500	1,600	1,700	1,700
780	990	990	990	990	990	990	990	990	990	990	990	990
0.15	0.12	0.10	0.09	0.08	0.07	0.05	0.04	0.03	0.03	0.03	0.03	0.03

Pasture abandoned as no longer productive and infested with toxic weeds.

TYPE OF AGRICULTURAL ACTIVITY Showing labor input (man-hours/ha/year), quantity, and value of produce (lbs/ha/year; $US/ha/year), and soil loss (tons/ha/year).	YEAR 1	YEAR 2	YEAR 3	YEAR 4	YEAR 5	YEAR 6
UNSUSTAINED LOGGING One-time fee paid to colonist by logging company: no replanting undertaken.						
Value ($US/ha)	78					
Soil loss (tons/ha/yr)	5.0	1.0	0.5	0.1	0.05	0.03
TERRACED CULTIVATION Growing corn on 40% slopes in primary forest on eastern Andean foothills.						
Labor (man-hours/ha/yr) 688 hours to clear forest cover, plus 500 to build terraces (year 1); then annual input of 800 hours cultivation labor and 30 hours terrace maintenance.	1,988	830	830	830	830	830
Value of corn produced ($US/ha/yr)	190	190	190	190	190	190
Soil loss (tons/ha/yr)	2.0	1.0	0.6	0.6	0.6	0.6
NONTERRACED CULTIVATION Growing corn on 40% slopes in primary forest on eastern Andean foothills.						
Labor (man-hours/ha/yr) 688 hours to clear forest cover (year 1); plus 800 hours cultivation labor in years 1 and 2. Plot then abandoned.	1,488	800	Plot abandoned at end of year 2:			
Value of corn produced ($US/ha/yr)	170	80				
Soil loss (tons/ha/yr)	200	160	80	50	25	20
FISH AQUACULTURE (IN ASSOCIATION WITH AGROFORESTRY) Area of pond is 4 ares (0.04 ha), but for ease of comparison production figures are given per hectare.						
Labor (man-hours) 500 hours to dig, prepare, and stock pond (year 1); then 488 hours annual labor input on pond maintenance, and feeding and harvesting the fish.	988	488	488	488	488	488
Quantity of fish produced (lbs/ha/yr)	1,144	2,200	4,500	5,500	7,000	8,800
Value of fish produced ($US/ha/yr)	0	0	4,082	4,990	6,350	7,985

SUSTAINED EXTRACTION FROM PRIMARY FOREST

		YEAR 1	YEAR 2	YEAR 3	YEAR 4	YEAR 5	YEAR 6
Fruits, nuts, etc.	Labor (man-hours/ha/yr)	560	560	560	560	560	560
	Value ($US/ha/yr)	650	650	650	650	650	650
Latex collection	Labor (man-hours/ha/yr)	63	63	63	63	63	63
	Value ($US/ha/yr)	50	50	50	50	50	50

BUSHMEAT EXTRACTION, FOREST ANIMAL FARMING

		YEAR 1	YEAR 2	YEAR 3	YEAR 4	YEAR 5	YEAR 6
Bushmeat collection	Labor (man-hours/ha/yr)	50	50	50	50	50	50
	Value ($US/ha/yr)	40	40	40	40	40	40
Wild crocodile skins	Labor (man-hours/yr)	220	220	220	220	220	220
	Value ($US/yr)	150	150	150	150	150	150
Capybara farming	Labor (man-hours/ha/yr)	500	500	500	500	500	500
	Value ($US/ha/yr)	0	560	560	560	560	560
Turtle ranching	Labor (man-hours) 500 hours to dig 4-are pond then annual input of 1,200 hours feeding, harvesting. For ease of comparison, all production figures are given per hectare.	1,700	1,200	1,200	1,200	1,200	1,200
	Value ($US/ha/yr)	0	0	600	1,000	1,200	1,400

	YEARS 7/8	YEARS 9/10	YEARS 11/12	YEARS 13/14	YEARS 15/16	YEARS 17/18	YEAR 19	YEAR 20	YEAR 21	YEAR 22	YEAR 23	YEAR 24	YEAR 25
	0.03	0.03	0.03	0.03	0.03	0.03	0.03	0.03	0.03	0.03	0.03	0.03	0.03
	830	830	830	830	830	830	830	830	830	830	830	830	830
	190	190	190	190	190	190	190	190	190	190	190	190	190
	0.6	0.6	0.6	0.6	0.6	0.6	0.6	0.6	0.6	0.6	0.6	0.6	0.6

land may require 20-100 years fallow to regenerate adequate fertility.

	YEARS 7/8	YEARS 9/10	YEARS 11/12	YEARS 13/14	YEARS 15/16	YEARS 17/18	YEAR 19	YEAR 20	YEAR 21	YEAR 22	YEAR 23	YEAR 24	YEAR 25
	488	488	488	488	488	488	488	488	488	488	488	488	488
	8,800	8,800	8,800	8,800	8,800	8,800	8,800	8,800	8,800	8,800	8,800	8,800	8,800
	7,985	7,985	7,985	7,985	7,985	7,985	7,985	7,985	7,985	7,985	7,985	7,985	7,985
	560	560	560	560	560	560	560	560	560	560	560	560	560
	650	650	650	650	650	650	650	650	650	650	650	650	650
	63	63	63	63	63	63	63	63	63	63	63	63	63
	50	50	50	50	50	50	50	50	50	50	50	50	50
	50	50	50	50	50	50	50	50	50	50	50	50	50
	40	40	40	40	40	40	40	40	40	40	40	40	40
	220	220	220	220	220	220	220	220	220	220	220	220	220
	150	150	150	150	150	150	150	150	150	150	150	150	150
	500	500	500	500	500	500	500	500	500	500	500	500	500
	560	560	560	560	560	560	560	560	560	560	560	560	560
	1,200	1,200	1,200	1,200	1,200	1,200	1,200	1,200	1,200	1,200	1,200	1,200	1,200
	1,600	4,000	10,000	20,000	20,000	20,000	20,000	20,000	20,000	20,000	20,000	20,000	20,000

A slightly different turn on agroforestry is the technique known as *alley cropping*, which offers a practical alternative to slash-and-burn. This method leaves rows of forest trees standing as hedgerows between rows of agricultural crops. The trees protect the soil from erosion, provide a rain of nutritious leaf litter which suppress weeds, serve to lower soil temperature, reduce evaporation, provide fuelwood, and serve as supports for vine crops.

In addition, as trees along the hedgerow mature, they may be judiciously sold, allowing seedlings to develop and replace them. This all adds up to the magic words "sustainable development," the ultimate goal in the tropical deforestation arena.

Encouraging success stories

○ In Costa Rica, beautiful coral trees (*Erythrina poeppigiana*) are used in agroforestry plots to shade rows of coffee and banana plants and to fix nitrogen at a density that yields 4 metric tons of extremely rich erythrina forage (dry weight) every six months.

○ We look with optimism to the recent successes of agroforestry in China and Korea, where shifting cultivation for the first time in world history has been stabilized and made productive without encroaching on virgin forest. China's aim is to have 30 percent of the country under tree cover, and her commitment to achieving that goal is evidenced by the fact that of the 300 million acres (122 million ha) currently under forest, as much as 99 million acres (40 million ha) are man-made forests created over the past 37 years. The rate of tree planting has recently been stepped up to 20 million acres (8 million ha) per year, and the authorities expect to reach 20 percent tree cover by the century's end.

○ Korea is working toward filling every available niche with trees. Slogans are posted such as "Love Trees, Love Your Country" and more than one-third of the national land area is now planted with trees less than 10 years old. Village forestry associations have been established in almost every village. An *esprit de corps* has succeeded where an order to plant might have failed. Privately held, unproductive hillsides are either donated for use, or 10 percent of the profit, where formerly there was none, goes to the owner. The benefits of availability of wood and profit have boosted the average family's income by 15 percent, and all this money goes directly to the peasant, not to moneylenders, big landholders, or government officials.

○ Support for village woodlots, agroforestry schemes, and environmental rehabilitation has been provided by the World Bank, FAO, AID, the United States State Department, the US Congress, and the Canadian and Swedish governments under project titles such as Forests for Local Community Development.

○ During the 1980s sub-Saharan drought, the Treepeople, a southern California conservation corps group, transported from the United States over 6,000 appropriate-species fruit trees. In a community effort involving a host of African countries, the trees were planted successfully and are now producing fruit, to the sustenance and delight of their new owners.

○ Over 3,500 improved wood stoves were built in Senegal, principally by women: 77 percent were still in use several years later.

○ Uganda's logging residues, once wasted, are now converted into charcoal, and the resulting output of charcoal has risen from 200 to 63,700 tons per year.

○ Even in Haiti, one of the areas hardest hit by deforestation, effective use of

△ *Private enterprise bore fruit in spectacular fashion in 1986 when the US organization Treepeople acquired more than 6,000 surplus fruit trees that would otherwise have been incinerated by American growers and, with freight donated by Pan Am and Cameroon Air, airlifted the trees to Ethiopia, Kenya, Tanzania, and Cameroon. In addition to cropping many tons of fruit, the people of those areas have also benefited from the many thousands of new trees propagated from cuttings from the original stock.*

networks of nongovernmental organizations has resulted in the planting of more than 10 million seedlings – double the number planned.

○ In Nigeria, maize production increased from 1,100 pounds (500 kg) to 4,410 pounds (2,000 kg) per 2.47 acres (1 ha) by mulching with nitrogen-fixing *Leucaena* tree leaves. Agroforestry programs in Senegal have increased millet and sorghum production from 1,100 to 2,200 pounds (500 to 1,000 kg) per 2.47 acres (1 ha) by using *Acacia albida* trees in fields.

○ Village farmers in Gujarat, India, realizing the extra income to be generated by planting trees for pole production, increased seedling distributions from 17 million to an impressive 200 million plants per year.

○ Another social forestry program in Uttar Pradesh, India, far exceeded the program's goals by planting degraded forest areas and farm forests with 8 million seedlings. In the process the scheme employed people for 17 million workdays – including 4 million days for women.

○ In parts of Nepal, family income quadrupled after manure sufficient for a second annual crop was amassed by use of increased fodder from planted grasses, and by tethering livestock. The scheme also produced an abundance of fuelwood from multipurpose tree planting.

○ One of the most resourceful schemes to date has been established with great success by the Paper Industry Corporation of the Philippines, in conjunction with loans from the World Bank. Farmers rent, say, 25 acres (10 ha) of deforested land through a 75 percent loan; 20 acres (8 ha) are planted in pulp trees and 5 acres (2 ha) are used for food and livestock production. The farmer then receives the entire first year's food production. Trees are grown and sold to the pulp mill after 8 years, providing earnings to tenant farmers of $2,600 per 2.47 acres (1 ha), an enormous income for these people. While at the same time reducing deforestation considerably, the company can obtain 40 percent of its required pulpwood from the farmers, where previously the Philippines had imported $30 million worth of paper pulp annually.

Without minimizing the specter of ongoing forest recession, these stunning successes point perhaps to a ray of hope in the dark jungle of apathy that has dominated development/deforestation until now. As consumptive land use comes increasingly under the scrutiny of the bright lights of world attention, intensified production methods become first more palatable, then profitable. As a litmus of this propensity, parks and preserves worldwide have *doubled* their area within the past 15 years: they now total more than 3,000 and cover more than one billion acres (400 million ha), including several crucial tropical forest areas.

Arresting and reclaiming eroded lands

We have previously addressed the enormous problems resulting from erosion when tropical forests are removed. Gully erosion, one of the more formidable yet common forms, can remove topsoil immediately and etch a canyon 70 feet (21 m) deep in 50 years in steep, rainy regions such as Nepal.

Such a loss of fertility can be appreciated by looking at the geological history that preceded that 70-foot-deep sterile canyon. Fifty-one years before, a protective forest resided on that slope of the Himalayas. The mountain range, through the pressures of plate tectonics, grows some 1.5 inches (4 cm) every 10 years. But even as they rise up, ice, frost, and water conspire to wear the mountains down. This natural process in turn serves to transform the parent rock (which contains dramatic ancient seabed fossils) into soil.

It takes, in fact, thousands of years to produce even 0.4 inches (1 cm) of precious soil from such weathering, a painfully slow process. Population pressures accompanied by overgrazing, crude farming, and wood abduction, none on a sustained yield, have resulted in the denuding of slopes at higher and higher elevations.

A manageable equation dictates a single cow or buffalo per person grazing up to four times as much land area as the family cultivates. Present realities, however, show the impact of animal grazing to be much greater – not as a result of greed, but of necessity. Population grows simultaneously with the elimination of fertile areas by the thief called erosion. The hungry move further upslope for more fuel, pasture, and garden space, perpetuating the tragedy in geometric progression for those downslope, all the way to the plains of India.

As gargantuan as this morass appears it is now quite possible, with concerted and dedicated effort, to reverse the effects of such erosion and reclaim the land in an acceptable time span. Formerly, in Nepal, cost-prohibitive barbed wire was used to protect critical areas containing young trees which would otherwise have been grazed by cattle. Under the present program, people are allowed into the forest, *but not their stock*; the forest grasses are cut and carried back to the cattle as feed. Dung now stays at home where it is used to enrich the fields, increasing the harvest by up to 20 percent.

When the Nepalese-project people and their stock were forcibly kept out of the forest by foresters, the latter became the enemy of both. The compatible-use program, however, has indoctrinated the villagers into a positive, friendly, and productive attitude whereby they too have become protectors of the land

▽ These meticulously maintained rice terraces in Bali show conservation land-use at its best. On unprotected mountain slopes, soil losses are as high as 300 t/ha/yr where an acceptable loss rate would be 1 t/ha/yr. With this system, soil loss is as low as 0.6 t/ha/yr on 40° slopes, and the land has been in stable production for centuries.

that feeds their stock. Moreover, an innovative reforestation project has also been implemented using fast-growing pines to protect and build the soil, after which broad-leaved trees naturally take hold. Only 11 years after the pine planting, a very healthy mixed forest now stands. The villagers, who were the labor force in the planting, receive three-fourths of the wood the forest produces, a welcome source of income and fuelwood.

In the case of our 70-foot eroded canyon, and other areas like it, these were seeded with strong, aggressive grasses and appropriate trees with pugnacious root systems. Grazing was prohibited and the degraded area has become stabilized in a matter of years.

Finally, a planting method known as *tied ridging* has been established in the fields. Planting vegetables and other crops in a raised grid pattern prevents run-off, preserves the soil surface, and eliminates the necessity for applications of fertilizer.

While such documented progress in tropical Third World agriculture and forestry exists, the results are often obscured by the litany of unchallenged problems in these arenas. Such projects offer infinitely fertile grounds for concerted International Development Bank investment.

Although prevailing conditions in tropical and temperate regions differ, it is interesting that the greater portion of eastern North American forests were removed during colonial settlement and subsequent periods of extensive farming. It is encouraging that with the implementation of modern intensive methods, adopted in the United States since then, less land has been needed for cultivation, allowing for the present return of vast areas of natural forest – and that despite large population increases!

▽ *Abused and eroded hillsides can be healed and stabilized by terracing them and planting with nitrogen-fixing ground-cover species and multi-purpose trees. Livestock are excluded: fodder is taken to them in lower-elevation fields and their manure is carried back to the terraces. Once stable, the terraces are put to productive use by intercropping.*

III · International Logging

Timber mining is a short-sighted strategy for unlike petroleum and minerals, forests need not be exhausted. They are a renewable resource and should be conserved for use in perpetuity.

Maharaj K. Muthoo
Director, Forestry
Operations Service, FAO-
United Nations

As we have noted, the two main causes of tropical deforestation are archaic and wasteful forms of agriculture (including cattle production) and logging. Food must and will be grown in these difficult regions, and it is hoped that in the preceding pages we have shown that not only does a new direction appear both possible and feasible, but also that we have no option but to pursue these directions with the single-mindedness of those with their backs to the sea. With exactly the same determination we must also approach our alternatives to the present course of tropical timber extraction.

It is by now apparent that the tropical forests are repositories of unique and irreplaceable ecological assets as well as undeveloped natural resources. Far from utilizing integrated strategies to make optimal use of this precious biome, the inherent opulence of the forest has led us instead to wanton misuse, as is evidenced in the results of its exploitation.

Improving our forestry practices

▽ In Tobago, coconut palms (Cocos nucifera) produce nuts, copra, fiber from refuse, and fuelwood from senile trees. The trees benefit from cattle dung.

According to FAO figures, hardwood forests, both moist and dry, cover 7.3 million square miles (19 million sq km) of the world's surface. Only 4.6 million square miles (12 million sq km) of these are tropical moist forests, and of this amount only 3.86 million square miles (10 million sq km) remain of undisturbed, closed broad-leaved tropical forests, the focus of commercial

attention. Yet, because the developed nations have come to value the aesthetic and recreational merits of their temperate forests, the tropical forests are now targeted to satisfy most of the worldwide demand for hardwoods. If proven silvicultural and intensive management techniques were practiced such as "complete-tree utilization," output from commercial hardwood forests in the United States alone, for instance, could be doubled.

It is worth reemphasizing that American imports of tropical timber and produce represent only 2 percent of the total hard- and softwoods used, and so if these imports are more than a convenience, they are somewhat less than vital. Further, enlightened conservation today is not aimed toward condemning logging in the tropics but toward improved tropical forest management, so that the equilibrium of a sustained yield of timber may be realized. Yet a highly visible fact emerges. Although timber exploitation is proceeding at a rampant pace in the Amazon Basin and Southeast Asia, and experimental sustained-yield management projects such as the Malaysian Uniform System and the Celos Silvicultural System show promising results at this stage, only two commercial operations in the Amazon Basin (Bolivia's Chimanes Permanent Production Forest, initiated in 1987, and the Colombia Bajo Calima Project begun in 1960) are currently engaged in attempting intensive or sustained-yield management!

The Bajo Calima Project, although hampered by log poachers, has succeeded in prohibiting heavy equipment from the forest (sky cables are used for extraction) and in keeping viable virgin forest, with its vital seed reservoir, less than a kilometer from clear-cut areas. (Other plots are selectively logged.)

Toward bringing direction and synchronicity to so optimal a plan, and filling a long-standing vacuum in the timber industry, the International Tropical Timber Organization (ITTO) was formed in 1987. It is the first international commodity agreement with a conservation mandate, and the 42 country members (including the United States) ply 60 percent of the world's tropical forests and reflect 95 percent of the global trade in tropical timber. Their priorities, as reflected in research and development on improved forest management and reforestation for sustained timber production, may now be on the way to being ratified, as members have recently voted to appropriate $1.1 million toward integrated forest-based development in Brazil's western Amazonian state of Acre. In an effort to avoid the environmental catastrophe resulting from overdevelopment in the neighboring state of Rondonia, Brazil is contributing double matching funds ($2.2 million) to the study of *sustainable* economic use, which includes logging, rubber extraction, and other enterprises that allow continued use of the forest by indigenous peoples. Similar studies have been approved by ITTO in Bolivia and Peru.

An obvious responsibility of such a consortium would be the coordination and enforcement of cutting schedules. Although a cut-and-run mentality currently dominates the field in the tropics, such schedules, geared to 35-year cycles, have the potential to produce a sustained yield indefinitely. Under the status quo, the political power these multinational corporations wield in the countries in which they operate often exceeds that of the national governments of those nations, and as such it is "business as usual." As a union, the ITTO has the potential (with guarded optimism) to represent a major positive political force for sustained development within the industry. To date, however, there has been concern that its emphasis has been weighted heavily toward development, while neglecting habitat and tribal lands conservation.

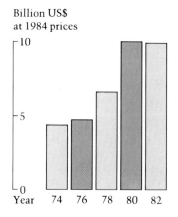

△ Total imports of forest products by developing countries are rising sharply, and a growing dependence on imported goods and materials is pushing the balance-of-trade figures of these countries into ever-more serious deficit.

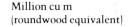

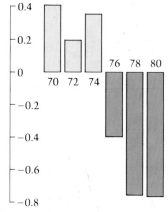

△ Nigeria's net trade in forest products reveals that while formerly a significant exporter of sawnwood, panels, pulp, and paper, that country now imports more than $210 million of forest products annually. This is roughly the value of the 2.5 million tons of grain the country now has to import.

The "Faustian bargain" in forestry

The answer to the question, "Is obsolescence built into current tropical forestry management?" still rests on decisions that are yet to be taken by international commercial operations. By direct effect, sustained commercial yield means sustaining corporate longevity as well as forest products well into the future, when demands for those materials will be ever-more pressing. Current trends clearly indicate an avoidance of that future reality, given that it is financially more expedient in the short term to concentrate on harvesting the "standing crop." Loss of biological diversity, propensity for global climatic imbalances, and, even more surprisingly, re-entry (reharvest) time for cut-over forests are all too often not taken into consideration.

Some of this thinking has a convoluted justification. Why, for example, should one company take an admirable lead by adopting long-range and conscionable practices to ensure sustained yield, only to see competing companies harvesting at the old, high-profit cut-and-run rates? It's not difficult to recognize powerful economic disincentives at play here. Yet, as a function of self-preservation, the industry has a good many reasons to close ranks on a common policy designed to sustain long-term yields.

False predictions of tropical timber shortages

The upsurge in demand for wood materials (principally pulp) beginning at the close of World War II has evolved into a full-blown lust for "green gold." While the international trade in forest timber came to 7,345 million cubic feet (208 million cu m) in 1975 and climbed to 7,451 million cubic feet (211 million cu m) in 1985, in 1987 – the most recent year for which figures are available – the trade in forest timbers reached 8,299 million cubic feet (235 million cu m). Total volume trade can be projected to reach 10,594 million cubic feet (300 million cu m) by the year 2000. These figures quickly dash the widely quoted expectation of a marked reduction in availability of timbers, especially those from the tropics. Although precise statistics do not exist, P. A. Wardle, senior forestry economist in FAO's Forestry Department reports that a fair approximation of the exports from "tropical countries" would be 1,435 million cubic feet (40.638 million cu m) in 1975, 1,419 million cubic feet (40.186 million cu m) in 1985 (the decrease being due more to market recession than to any difficulties in supply), and 1,647 million cubic feet (46.646 cu m) in 1987. It would seem that extraction methods and logging road technology can largely mitigate the problems of working far inland and in difficult terrain, although eventually the operators will meet the inevitable final restriction – the finite nature of the forest resource itself.

The future, therefore, remains uncertain. A World Resource Institute/World Bank/United Nations Development Programme Report predicts that "by the

▽ Forest resources are increasingly being "mined" as nonrenewable resources, bringing ever-more remote areas under exploitation. Figures in these charts reveal for the first time that world timber trade is not declining, as had been forecast, but continues to increase – and will do so far into the future, with extra costs of extraction from remote areas being passed on to the consumer.

WORLD TIMBER TRADE (thousand cubic meters)			
PRODUCT	1975	1985	1987
Roundwood	100,943	106,264	117,433
Sawnwood and sleepers	86,955	85,981	94,919
Wood-based panels	20,542	19,101	23,025
Total	208,440	211,346	235,377

EXPORTS OF "TROPICAL COUNTRIES" (thousand cubic meters)			
PRODUCT	1975	1985	1987
Non-coniferous logs	33,867	26,658	28,670
Non-coniferous sawnwood	4,537	7,954	10,223
Plywood	2,234	5,574	7,753
Total	40,638	40,186	46,646

end of the century, the 33 developing countries that are now net exporters of forest products will be reduced to fewer than 10, and total developing country exports of industrial forest products are predicted to drop from their current level of more than US$7 billion to less than US$2 billion." Current depletion is now evident as lowland forests are virtually exhausted in once-leading exporter nations such as the Philippines. Only for a few more decades will Africa and Latin America be able to fill the market demand before their commercial stands are thinned, raising supply costs. Nations rich in "green gold" would benefit substantially by recognizing the steady demand for their assets and planning for sustained supplies rather than short-term profit.

We would hope that ITTO, as an "OPEC-ization" of tropical hardwood, will facilitate moves toward these countries increasing the price of hardwood exports, for which they are currently being grossly underpaid. We could then look for an increase in foreign exchange and a decrease in exported timber.

While this arrangement would have an inflationary effect on fine furniture and hardwood paneling (and even paper products), the market adjustments and consumption patterns should not be traumatic, and far fewer of these luxuries could well be consumed without affecting the quality of our lives. Such a trade cartel will, at the same time, serve to improve the standard of living in Third World tropical forest countries, reducing in part their need to overexploit their timber resources. The trade-off would seem far more than equitable.

Toward sustained timber yields

As primary forests grow more remote and less economically rewarding, timber companies will be enticed to turn an eye to reworking areas cut some years ago and since grown over. Many quite valuable timber species exist in secondary forests. They are fast-growing and light, are part of a less perplexing species mix, and due to their light-tolerance they exist in several stories. Of 240,000 acres (97,130 ha) of secondary forest in Puerto Rico, for example, one-fourth had the 100 pole-size trees per hectare of commercially useful species deemed essential for a viable logging venture. There are also certain advantages in cropping secondary forest as opposed to plantation forest. Although the former are not as productive, their exploitation involves neither high initial costs nor the downside risks of plantations, and there are well over a hundred times the amount of ever-maturing regrowth areas lying idle.

While data to date on the natural regeneration of specific preferred industrial species from cropped forests is scant, there is evidence that natural cycles could produce reasonable returns. Experimental plots at Curua-Una in Brazil, the oldest such data available from the Amazon (1955), show that commercially valuable primary forest species, such as *Goupia glabra*, will regenerate naturally after harvesting to the extent that a perpetually sustained yield could be expected. Although this was a FAO-SPEVA (Brazil) bilateral project, the information was not widely disseminated. Unfortunately, this is a common scenario. Economic, agronomic, and ecologic failures have often been perpetuated because research data has been institutionally withheld.

In areas of gently rolling slopes, such as parts of Amazonia, a very promising method of harvesting known as *strip cutting* is gaining in recognition. A strip of trees is first clear-cut parallel to a stream on a hill contour. A few years are allowed to pass until naturally seeded saplings begin to appear. At this point, another strip is clear-cut above the first, and the process is repeated. This method has several solid ecological principles behind it to sustain the yield.

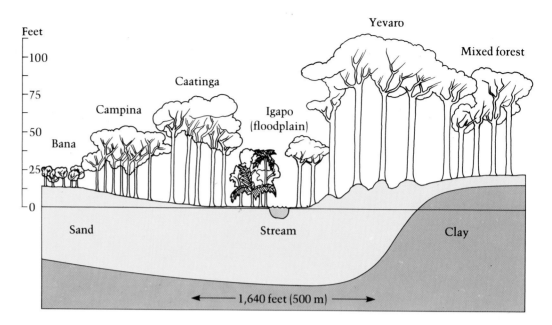

△▷ *Amazonia's rainforests do not comprise a single homogenous type: widely differing formations are found according to the terrain and underlying soil. This example is from San Carlos de Rio Negro in the northern Amazon Basin. Exploitation of the forest should take account of such variation. Cultivation, for example, is impractical on nutrient-poor sand podzol soils where the usual forest type is the stunted* bana, campina, *or* caatinga. *These sand forests produce blackwater rivers as tannins from decaying vegetation pass easily through the sand. Forest management has more potential in the productive* yevaro, *while limited but nutrient-rich* terra roxa *soils have high potential in some areas.*

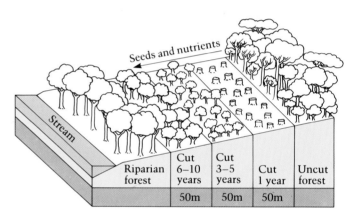

▷ *Strip cutting is one method by which valuable timber can be extracted sustainably, especially on undulating terrain. Mature forest left intact on the uphill side provides a source of seed for natural forest regeneration, while gravity feeds leaf litter and nutrients into the logged strip. Line planting of other useful tree species and crops may be integrated.*

The first cut, now regenerating, is flushed with nutrients from the now barren upslope cut, and the saplings readily take up this material — so conserving the scarce nutrient capital. In addition, cut areas are moderate in size and are naturally reseeded from the seed reservoir of the surrounding climax forest. Both these advantages are absent in large, traditionally logged (clear-cut) areas. Further advantage can be taken of litter availability, fertility, and soil stability by the implementation of line planting of commercial tree or crop species in conjunction with strip harvesting.

The Congressional Office of Technology Assessment (OTA) states that by improved wood-processing methods, along with finding markets for species and sizes currently unused, much of the pressure on tropical forests could be lifted. A case in point is the recently developed press-dry paper-making process which facilitates the use of wood from different species.

Modernizing Third World forestry practices

There are available to the loggers a number of procedures that can effectively reduce the destruction of the forest through extraction excesses. They will, of course, add to the cost of the operation, and this, no doubt, will be reflected in the retail price in the country of import. However, even if such increases are calculated as acceptable, we face a critical challenge.

Procedures that have been suggested include severing the lianas that bind the crowns of desired trees to those of noncommercial species before felling.

By doing this, the noncommercial tree will no longer be dragged down as the target species is felled. Logging damage could be reduced by 20 percent, and is easily worth the added cost of $2 per tree, which would amount to approximately 2 cents on each cubic meter of log exported. The selective liana cutting would also avoid the possible extinction of liana species threatened by the indiscriminate killing of all vines (as many as 2,000 per hectare) as is practiced in some overly "managed" forests.

Biologists hired by the corporations may work to salvage plant and animal specimens in an "operation rescue" as the logging or dam flooding proceeds. As well as saving individual specimens, such operations provide an opportunity for scientists to study endangered and unknown species for description and possible subsequent transplant. A few of the more scrupulous commercial collectors of rare plants engage in collecting at logging sites, as these plants would be largely doomed at any rate. Levying fees for such lucrative collecting could well defray the expense of the biologists' salaries.

Helicopters can be employed to lift out tree boles as an alternative to the highly destructive hauling practices that obliterate a high percentage of noncommercial species *en route*. Although this will add considerable cost to the process of extraction, helicopters and balloons *are* used successfully by timber corporations in the northwest United States: why then are we not exporting these conscionable practices? Light-aircraft reconnaissance flights can be useful in identifying commercially valuable tree species and marking them, and can also provide an efficient way of locating ecologically significant ecosystems which can then be spared or impacted lightly by corporate activity. Such measures would have an important positive impact on public relations.

Certain ecological practices are now followed quite routinely in the United States, such as keeping felling operations 650 feet (200 m) from bald eagle nests during the nesting season. Such restraint is not applied in the tropics for similarly endangered species. Environmental impact reports – the norm in developed nations – are rare exceptions in the tropics, and even when they are implemented the burden of proof is left to conservation interests. Although controlling pollution output from logging mills alone adds 15 percent to operational costs, it has been noted that American consumers who bear these costs have not lobbied for reduced conservation efforts. In fact, timber sales have remained unaffected by such price increases.

In this context it is worth noting that the developed nations, the United States in particular, are often accused of criticizing developing countries for overexploiting their forests while doing little to conserve their own forests and woodlands. While such comment is not without some justification, the fact remains that United States forestry programs, besides reseeding and other reforestation methods, plant over six million trees every year. As a result, the US has some 730 million acres (295 million ha) of forest – more than existed 70 years ago – and a thriving, growing, forestry industry.

Unutilized forest products

The forests contain a myriad fruits, nuts, drugs, bamboos, barks, scents, perfumes, resins, gums, waxes, turpentine, latex, tannins, alkaloids, rattans, beeswax, palm fibers, and exotic plants for export, as well as fodder for cattle and other livestock – all of which is left unexploited. These products and many more could be salvaged during a logging operation, and in many cases

△ *The considerable contribution of sustained forest food production is often overlooked in the evaluation of national production statistics.*

△ *Business is brisk in the busy Lingala market in Zaïre, with numerous varieties of protein-rich beans for sale, all produced by sustainable methods.*

△ *In the parts of Zaïre where timber exploitation has not yet raped the soil, cultivation often takes advantage of forest fertility and shelter.*

could open up a vast cornucopia of forest wealth generally known as "minor forest products." The fact that Sarawak (one of the few tropical countries to even attempt an exploitation of these assets) exported $31 million worth in one year shows that the potential here is certainly not "minor."

The total use of the products of a lumber operation will greatly assist in lessening the impact on undisturbed forest. Indeed, the main constituents of wood are lignin and cellulose, and both go virtually unused! Possible applications are numbered in the thousands, from innovative plastic production to fertilizers, oil well drilling dispersals to synthetic textile manufacturing. Furthermore, a storehouse of energy and fuel is being recklessly squandered in the haste of exploitation.

A single ton of tropical dry wood can yield 660 pounds (300 kg) of coal-like residue, 3.7 gallons (14 l) of methanol, 20 gallons (76 l) of wood oil and light tar, 3.2 gallons (12 l) of creosote oil, 66 pounds (30 kg) of pitch, 2 gallons (7.6 l) of esters, and 14 gallons (53 l) of acetic acid. Along with this, 4,944 cubic feet (140 cu m) of gas may be extracted, which can then be used to power the equipment extracting these useful distillation products. It is estimated that in the tropical forest's yearly new growth alone, the available energy matches half the world's present consumption of energy of all forms combined.

K. F. S. King, former director of FAO's Forestry Department, described present forestry practices as "primitive, costly and wasteful." Norman Myers' analysis of tropical forests as "overexploited and underutilized" also typifies the current global response to the lack of thrift in logging practices.

We also find a plethora of vastly underexploited and virtually unutilized materials that may be substituted for wood. For instance, the frugal Chinese derive 50 percent of their pulp from fibrous crop waste materials. Some of these are available in overwhelming annual supply, such as straw (885 million tons), bagasse, which is the residue of crushed sugarcane (55 million tons), bamboo (30 million tons), reeds (30 million tons), and expired coconut trees (1 billion tons). In the United States, pulp derived from these readily available sources amounts to a mere 1 percent. Many other similar sources are disposed of, and at considerable cost.

Increasing the price of lumber artificially by way of tariffs paid to tropical governments to aid conservation efforts will also serve to encourage the industry to utilize substitute pulp sources, and would also have a favorable impact on the balance-of-trade deficits of tropical nations.

The government of the Philippines has recognized the critical importance of sustaining forestry there by restricting the export of unprocessed logs by banning logging in all provinces with less than 40 percent cover, and by legislating that one tree per month be planted by every male over the age of ten. Similarly, Thailand as of 1989 has a total ban on logging, even in plantations, and has increased imports to feed its furniture-making industry. Throughout the region, countries are drastically reducing their exports of raw logs – and in many cases are eliminating such exports completely.

Enforcement of international responsibility

Gallup polls show that worldwide opinion is overwhelmingly in favor of seeing more done to conserve wildlife and threatened species, and although the world sees its species as a "global heritage" it has had great difficulty asserting this in the face of the concept of national sovereignty. Thus, conservative parities paid to developing countries can be effective and palatable door-openers to those nations wherein the bulk of earth's species exist. This concept is not a new one, but it needs expansion.

In force today are several international trade agreements on endangered species, and their nesting, mating, and calving sites. They include special treaties offering protection for whales, sea turtles, migratory birds, and other species whose survival wholly depends on the real concept of "global heritage." The tropical rainforest could logically be accorded equal if not priority protection.

Such is the legacy of the 1972 Stockholm Conference, guaranteeing sovereign rights yet not the right to "cause environmental damage to states beyond the limits of national jurisdiction."

Paul W. Richards, Emeritus Professor of botany at the University College of North Wales, Bangor, views the conservation of the tropical forests as "beyond the unaided resources of the poorer developing countries, so it is important that the conservation of tropical forests should be treated as an international as well as a national responsibility."

Cross-regulation of the International Tropical Timber Organization (ITTO) in field activities may be administered through the currently operating United Nations Code of Conduct under the United Nations Commission on Transnational Corporations. In this way, environmental muscle may be enhanced, and the logging industries be relieved of the impractical and unsatisfactory responsibility of policing themselves.

Although the United States Securities and Exchange Commission has considered moral regulations, in personal communication with that office, the general counsel relayed to me that he felt that such activities were not within the jurisdiction of the Securities and Exchange Commission. When asked if, hypothetically, it was disclosed that a company listed with the exchange dealt primarily in unlicensed elephant ivory, or to give a more extreme example, traded in illicit drugs, Amy Goodman, deputy associate director for disclosures, informed me that corporate activities *per se* were not a concern of her office and that it would be left to the discerning public whether or not to trade in such stock issues.

IV · WOOD PRODUCTION FOR THE FUTURE

If you plan for one year, plant rice. If you plan for ten, plant trees. If you plan for one hundred years, educate mankind.

KUAN-TZU

Because of their imports of paper products, many developing countries are even now hovering on parity in their import and export trade balance of total wood products. When the forests are gone, they are expected to plummet into a paralyzing trade deficit. In Third World countries, forest products, including fuel, never enter into the market economy, even though the dependence on them is acute. It is difficult to foresee just how the poorer countries will afford to replace these necessities with imported foods, goods, and fuel.

Already, symptoms of shortages are manifesting themselves. In place of wood, concrete and steel are being used for railway sleepers, transmission poles, and furniture. Needless to say, these materials are expensive and in short supply, and so offer no solution in the long run.

In one state in India, huts are needed for landless laborers. This requires 765 million bamboo stems. Only 4 million stems are produced yearly. Had the forests not been destroyed, this renewable resource could easily have filled the needed quota.

We now know that areas allotted to plantations of fast-growing tree species will produce ten times the wood per year that natural tropical forests do, and seven times the production of managed natural forests. Although the answer to *unlimited* sustained harvests still looms in the future, unanswered, the plantation scheme, especially on mature second-growth land, has the potential to relieve the pressures on our remaining virgin tropical forests. Emerson wrote, "The creation of a thousand forests is in a single acorn."

Tackling the greenhouse effect

Gregg Marland of the Oak Ridge (Tennessee) National Laboratory is concerned with technological alternatives at our disposal (in 1988), for actually removing *meaningful* quantities (5 billion tons) of carbon annually from the atmosphere in order to avoid adverse changes in our global climate. Such schemes, he notes, as stimulating the growth of existing forests, and so increasing their yield and atmospheric carbon intake, would be an enormous expense. This expenditure, however, says Marland, "needs to be compared with the costs of other approaches to dealing with atmospheric carbon dioxide or of coping with the attendant changes in climate." Reforestation, he states, would appear to have potential as one of the significant components in addressing this major concern. Woods Hole Research Institute has estimated that 772,000 square miles (2 million sq km) of reforestation will lock up 1 billion tons of carbon annually until that forest reaches maturity. (The current annual excess of carbon is estimated at 2.5 to 3.0 billion tons.)

Now, an ominous reality. By extrapolating recent research findings that in lowland rainforest there are an average of 232 trees per acre over 4 inches (10 cm) in diameter at breast height (DBH), we can now calculate the actual number of trees felled daily in the deforestation of the tropics – a body count, if you will. While credible estimates are given as 100 acres per minute and more, we have averaged the data and used a conservative figure of 57 acres (23 ha) per minute, or almost one per second. Perhaps nothing can better bring

home the grim reality of human activities than the following figures. I was awed while multiplying trees per acre to find this represented 13,224 per minute, 793,440 per hour, and 19,042,560 trees per day felled! (And this may yet prove to be only half the true rate.)

One can begin to perceive the tragic momentum of greenhouse gas accumulation. By George Woodwell's findings, it will take 2,316,000 square miles (6 million sq km) of reforestation to bank the excess of 3 billion tons of atmospheric carbon annually. In tropical forests, at least, that is the equivalent of 348 billion trees: instead we decimate 7 billion annually (not including other habitats).

Simply stated, given the expected gross increase in global population, and its attendant reliance on fossil fuel, truly meaningful cutbacks (and conversion to other energy sources in that sector) are justified and expected. The question is, will we achieve them in the necessary time frame? Can we not at this time begin to chart a course of global action to reduce tropical deforestation and begin budgeting the implementation of plantation schemes worldwide as the first line of defense against global warming? Lastly, in view of the statement by atmospheric scientists in Toronto at the recent World Conference on the Changing Atmosphere that "humanity is conducting an uncontrolled and globally pervasive experiment whose ultimate consequences could be second only to a global nuclear war," is our present course – "do nothing – attempt at a later date to adjust to projected global warming" – really the decision we want to commit to?

△ *In the front line of what has been likened to a "World War III" – the global struggle to retard the greenhouse effect – these* Eucalyptus *seedlings being prepared for planting out in Brazil's Turmalina Reforestation Project will help absorb excess* CO_2 *while contributing to soil and forest conservation.*

With his characteristic constructive optimism, Norman Myers argues that while the task is gargantuan, there are, in fact, some 640,000 square miles (1,657,000 sq km) of watershed in dire need of reforestation in order to protect topsoil and stream flow. Fuelwood production demands some 220,000 square miles (570,000 sq km) of plantations, and for commercial timber we need at least an additional 40,000 square miles (103,600 sq km). Adjusting for overlap, we can immediately justify reforesting 800,000 square miles (2,072,000 sq km) at the very least. Tree planting can be averaged at $160 per acre (0.4 ha), which translates to over $120 billion or $12 billion annually for a 10-year campaign.

Should we find additional justification necessary, India's losses in crops and damage due to Ganges River flooding caused by the denuding of the Himalayas is $1 billion per year. Sea-level rises expected due to the greenhouse effect will carry a bill estimated at up to (and possibly exceeding) $100 billion on the US eastern seaboard alone. Agricultural buttresses to seawater infusion will cost up to $23 billion in the United States. Other costs associated with losses in the agricultural sector will most probably exceed that figure.

As what may be the first action to physically address the greenhouse effect, the American Forestry Association, during International Rainforest Week (9–16 October 1988), announced its resolve to see 100 million trees planted in the United States by 1992. During a press conference on the program, in which I was a participant, urban afforestation was revealed to have additional significance to its role as a carbon absorber. As a shade-provider for homes, and as a reducer of the city "heat-island" effect, even a minimal planting of trees can reduce the use of air-conditioning, resulting in an average saving of 1,000 kilowatt-hours annually, which translates into a reduction of 1,000 pounds of carbon burned.

The establishment of plantations of aggressive, fast-growing tree species will absorb greenhouse gases as well as helping to fill the wood pulp vacuum. In addition, once industry is better geared to make use of *all* species and wood sizes, as with newly developed wood-chipping machines, even the initial harvesting of second-growth forest stands may become financially rewarding.

Assuming an average annual growth rate of 530 cubic feet (15 cu m) per 2.47 acres (1 ha) in plantations, 85 percent of the developing countries' demand for industrial timber (projected to the year 2000) could be met by converting 82 million acres (33 million ha) of the existing logged-over areas into fast-growing plantations. In order to meet ever-growing demands for fuel and water resources, as well as stabilizing soil, Worldwatch Institute estimates that at least 321 million acres (130 million ha) of trees must be planted worldwide by the year 2000.

In view of these projections, international opinion would surely view the halcyon days of unrestrained commercial plunder of tropical forest resources as archaic. Despite the cost trade-off of perhaps more than $250/ha, plantations of realistic scale must be planned, and their costs absorbed at retail level.

Fast growers and new "supertrees"

At this time we can be encouraged by the species available to us from man-made forests. Pines and other conifers for softwoods, and eucalypts for hardwoods, make efficient and traditional starters. Their growth, though considered rapid in temperate regions, is dramatic in the moist tropics. There are, however, other tree species less known or largely unrecognized that possess an unparalleled pulp source potential. Some of these are pioneer species whose growth rates make even pines and eucalypts seem slow. It is to these in combination, depending on site-specific conditions, that our hopes turn for satiating the world's demand for wood produce. A tropical plantation of 193 square miles (500 sq km) produces over 35 million cubic feet (1 million cu m) of marketable timber annually, ten times the natural forest yield.

More important today than construction timber is the growing need for soft, pale timber used for its cellulose and fiber content. Some secondary-growth trees meet this criterion and many also grow in pure stands naturally. This is an important feature when considering species for plantation use, as species that grow dispersed in the wild often fall prey to insect and fungal attack when planted in dense monoculture stands. Seed availability is good, and seed germination is as high as 98 percent in some species.

Furthermore, if the the Third World tropical timber exporters wish to prolong and optimally sustain their source of foreign trade advantage, a determined effort must be made now for reforestation. The necessary expenditure and coordination, which must include plowing back a percentage of profit, establishment of tree-seed nurseries, and distribution of seedlings to remote areas, is presently largely (90 percent) lacking. A showcase project for emulation in this field is the FAO-Honduras Comayagua Plan.

Aracruz Florestal, a progressive Brazilian paper company, has demonstrated startling success in doubling its plantation yields through genetic improvement of its eucalyptus stock by (1) importing new African seed to replace low-yielding Brazilian stock, and (2) selecting genetically superior trees which were then cloned.

It is an important concern, however, that as plantations are harvested, a great amount of nutrient in the stock will be removed, severely damaging fertility and future output. A potential solution here is the integrated planting of nitrogen-fixing legumes to be plowed back. (With close monitoring, even a partial harvesting of these as a vegetable crop is possible.) It is known that certain crops, such as oil palm (*Elaeis guineensis*), pejibaye palm (*Bactris gasipaes*) and other palm fruits, cocoa (*Theobroma cacao*), rubber (*Hevea brasiliensis*), and coffee (*Coffea arabica*), can produce indefinitely on deforested land. These crop-producing trees serve as protective cover for the soil, and the harvest of the fruit alone has minimal impact on the nutrient budget. You will note that all the above are perennial crops and, although they are affected by a variety of diseases, they closely mimic the natural forest structure and so protect the soil.

For pulp production a small plant called kenaf (*Hybiscus sabdariffa*) yields up to 23 tons per hectare, as much as some fast-growing hardwoods and five to seven times as much pulp per hectare as pine trees.

Of extreme promise are trees which performed well in a Smithsonian Institution project in Panama under very poor soil conditions. Topping those rigorous trials were the following: wattle (*Acacia auriculiformis*), madre del cacao (*Gliricidia sepium*), shrubs such as *Desmodium gyroides*, *Tephrosia candida*, and townsville clover (*Stylosanthes guianensis*), and creeping vines such as tropical kudzu (*Pueraria phaseoloides*) and *Desmodium ovalifolium*. Of these, only *G. sepium* and *S. guianensis* are native to the neotropics.

Certain plantation candidates have growth rates that have earned them a place in the *Guinness Book of Records*. Certain species of bamboo

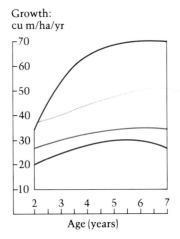

Growth:
cu m/ha/yr

Age (years)

——— Performance of selected cuttings in 1981 trials.

——— Performance of seedlings from South Africa and Zimbabwe, 1974–78.

——— Performance of seedlings from original Brazilian sources, 1967–73.

△ *Brazilian paper company Aracruz Forestal increased its* Eucalyptus *plantation yields more than 250% by genetic improvement of its imported stock. It is easy to see how such fine-tuning methods could create future significant advances in plantation productivity.*

▷ Plantations of African oil palms like this one in the Amapa state of Brazil will be productive far into the future. Like other tree crops, rubber, cocoa, coffee, and peach palm, for example, the mature palm trees will mimic the natural forest, providing soil protection and shade for other plants. As only fruit and latex are taken out, nutrient loss to the system is minimal.

(Gramineae), giant members of the grass family, have been clocked at a phenomenal 36 inches (91 cm) in 24 hours, reaching a height of 100 feet (30 m) in three months. That world record was calculated to represent a speed of growth of 0.00002 mph (0.00003 kmph). Among the fast-growing trees, *Albizzia falcata* grew 35 feet 3 inches (10.7 m) in 13 months, and *Eucalyptus deglupta* grew to 100 feet (30 m) in less than six years. The use of eucalyptus has become controversial in recent years, and considerable care is required in assessing each potential site for suitability for planting with the tree. Very high rainfall is an essential requirement since the tree is exceptionally efficient in taking up water, and unless supplies are abundant it will repress other nearby vegetation. However, eucalyptus plantations are very productive, allowing several successive crops to be harvested from the rapid growth of new shoots, while in suitable conditions fodder and certain palm crops can be planted between the rows.

Gmelina arborea, one of the fastest-growing trees known, is from Asia, and plantations of this species have already been harvested in Brazil and elsewhere, where they perform well on the more fertile soils. Even in extensive areas of poor ferrasols or oxisols, such as cover most of the Amazon Basin, small patches of better soils exist. It is found that a proportionately large percentage of successful farmers owe that success to their ability to recognize those micropatches.

Another Asian species *Anthocephalus chinensis* has a growth rate of 7 to 10 feet (2 to 3 m) per year and a relative in the same genus, *A. macrophyllus*, grew even faster in trials on Java and seems to tolerate poor growing conditions.

Our familiar friend the *Cecropia*, from the American tropics, has also performed well in test plantations. This should be no surprise as the trumpet tree, as it is known, is a secondary-growth tree and springs forth in forest clearings with a speed that can almost be seen.

The mountains of Guatemala are among the few areas in the tropics where conifers (Coniferae) grow indigenously, and some species offer great potential for use in monocultures and other man-made forests. The rapid destruction of these trees in their native habitat, however, threatens to preclude their future use as cultivated species.

Another fairly recent introduction, the *Leucaena*, has been hailed as the "tree that does everything." (This, unfortunately, includes escaping cultivation and, under certain conditions, establishing itself in the native flora.) A native of Mexico and Central America, in cultivation it is said to yield more wood than any other hardwood, and is an excellent fiber source, as well as being a strong and attractive lumber. Its vegetation is a delectable, high-protein animal feed, and its pods and young leaves are gaining favor as a human food source as well.

As a fast grower (growing out of reach of livestock within six months), it is economical as a fuelwood and has 70 percent of the heating value of fuel oil when turned into charcoal. As a nitrogen fixer it does sterling service in reforestation schemes, producing 1,100 to 1,500 pounds (roughly 500 to 700 kg) of nitrogen per kilogram per hectare per year – twice as much as a close competitor *Acacia mearnsii*. In short, a "tree superstar."

Of enormous promise also is *Paulownia*. Known to the Chinese for several centuries, it numbers among its many attributes extremely fast growth, and a light and strong timber that dries easily and has an aesthetically pleasing grain, does not warp or crack easily, has excellent insulation properties, and is suitable for both furniture and plywood. Its leaves are nitrogen-rich and so serve well as fertilizer, and they also make good fodder. The *Paulownia* has a deep root structure and so avoids competition with many crop species by drawing on moisture and nutrients from deeper levels, making it especially suitable for alley cropping or intercropping. Apparently it is so undemanding regarding its soil preferences and quality that Chinese forestry departments use it to cover areas damaged by extensive mining.

Protracted yields from these and other candidates will relieve much of the burden now carried by the tropical rainforest, and their rapid growth assures their volume intake of atmospheric carbon. However, it is well to bear in mind that ecologically these plantations are barren lands compared with natural forests, as they support little of their wildlife and basically none of their botanical diversity. Strong emphasis should be placed on the establishment of such plantations on mature secondary-growth areas, a commodity in long supply in the moist tropics.

Conservative figures for the average global reduction rate of tropical forests range from 0.62 to 2.0 percent annually; however, it is interesting to note that in Asia, where population pressures are the strongest and the natural forests are receding the quickest, the plantation ratio is 1 tree planted per 4.5 removed, where globally the ratio is only 1 to 10. The conditions that prevail in Asia have apparently forced a more rigorous replanting program out of necessity. Even so, these areas are still critically wood starved.

To underscore the importance of individual endeavors, in Rwanda scattered trees planted by individuals collectively total half a million acres (200,000 ha), representing more than the country's combined remaining natural forests and all her state and communal plantations. Village planting programs have found most success within a structure highlighting personal ownership of each tree planted, rather than in regimens where rural people are employed simply as laborers. CARE's message to villagers is an uncompromising, "This is your tree. If it dies it is your loss. If it survives you reap the benefits."

△ The corridor system harvests timber in a line cut through old-growth forest. Here, near Pimenta Bueno in Brazil, mahogany, a highly prized commercial species, is replanted. Taking advantage of the canopy shade and leaf-litter nutrients, the new trees will be ready for cutting in about 30 years.

The FAO further reports that reforestation is not taking place in the main areas of current deforestation, a situation that could be remedied by making replanting programs a requirement of logging contracts. But what of the mode of operations of large-scale logging/planting operations on virgin forest?

"Jarilandia"

Even recent history gives us some useful hindsight. Let's examine the "Jari Project." Oil tanker billionaire Daniel K. Ludwig, the head of National Bulk Carriers, owned 3.9 million acres (1.6 million ha) of virgin Amazon Forest, an enormous private holding that lies in the northeast basin and is the size of Connecticut. At great cost (US$1 billion at the end of 1981), Ludwig built a floating wood pulp processing factory in Japan and towed it halfway around the world to install it on the Jari River, a tributary of the Amazon. Called "Jarilandia" it was a woodcutter's Mecca in the heart of the rainforest.

Much of his climax holdings have been clear-cut and replanted with fast-growing tree species, a financially intensive program with a distant break-even point.

Should sustained yield prove possible, such schemes could prove a prudent environmental trade-off to continued exploitation in the remaining tropical forests. Criticism has been leveled at Ludwig on the grounds that such plantations should be encouraged only on seasoned secondary forests and fallow farmland. Yet both the environmental community and the timber corporations still watch and wait for the eventual outcome of this continuing jungle drama.

Although the best results on intensively studied Jari plots planted with *Gmelina arborea* produced 8 and 12 tons/ha/yr, average large-scale plots studied throughout Jari produced less than 6 tons/ha/yr. Pine, on the other hand, produced 12 to 16 tons/ha/yr.

A final verdict at this time would be premature; however, certain current events are worth reporting. While *Gmelina arborea* was planted initially, and the prophesied pests did arrive, a timely dry spell, along with insecticides, effected control. It was found that much of the area's soil was not suitable for *Gmelina*, so *Eucalyptus deglupta* and *Pinus caribaea* were planted some time into the project.

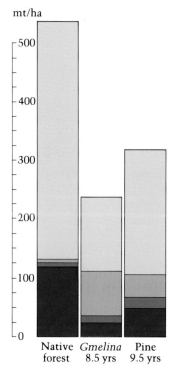

mt/ha

Native forest   *Gmelina* 8.5 yrs   Pine 9.5 yrs

Biomass components

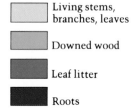

Living stems, branches, leaves

Downed wood

Leaf litter

Roots

△▷ *It is still too early to offer a verdict on whether or not Jarilandia is a fair environmental trade-off. The spotlight of global concern still focuses on the short-comings, sacrifices, and triumphs of this bold plantation scheme, and a vast area of Amazonia is at stake. It is clear from the graph above that the native forest has a far greater biomass than plantations of faster-growing commercial species. However, if the plantation can be managed sustainably, its output of Gmelina (right) and pine is potentially very high indeed.*

Jari properties

△ Jari Enterprises, the billion-dollar gamble 217 mi (350 km) west of Belem and some 5,000 sq mi (13,000 sq km) in extent, cost Daniel Ludwig over $3 million in land purchases alone and over $1 billion overall. The objectives include a large integrated sawmill and pulp mill, a port on the River Jari, a railroad system, hundreds of miles of roads, extensive rice production in the varzea, cattle and water buffalo ranching, and the mining and processing of kaolin. To this ambitious end a complete new town, Monte Dourado, was built from scratch: it now houses an immigrant population of more than 30,000 people.

◁ The single most costly item in the Jari scheme was this 30,000-ton floating pulp mill, built in Japan for $400 million and towed halfway round the world. We must wait to see whether this bold idea represents a new phase of intensive use of natural resources, or a monument to unbridled ambition and technological folly.

The Jari kraft pulp factory has a 750 metric tons per day capacity, and in 1985 still depended on logs from climax forest to supplement the input from its plantations. In addition, significant losses in calcium and other essential nutrients may require a replacement cost of $100/ha/yr.

The Jari mill did turn out salable pulp, and supported 40,000 people, including an influx of area merchants, but the project required an additional pulp mill just at the time the world's money market collapsed and wood demand dropped due to the reduction of new housing starts in the United States in response to high interest rates.

"Ludwig's luck" may have taken a wrong turn on the turbulent waters of the Jari River. The additional hundreds of millions of dollars required could not be found for a still unproved project, especially since the Brazilian political climate began to turn against Ludwig as well. Environmentalism has growing support in the shifting political sands of Brazil and Ludwig was attacked vehemently as an American imperialist exploiting the country. As "Jarilandia" was still losing millions of dollars after 15 years, Ludwig sold out to a Brazilian consortium in 1982.

We are now privy to Jari's balance sheet as it is still operational. In 1985, the International Society of Tropical Foresters named Jari among the top 100 agribusiness firms. In 1983, it reported a $2.1 million operating profit, a modest return of 0.2 percent on its initial $1 billion investment and 0.8 percent return on its subsequent $280 million Brazilian investment.

We are, of course, more interested in the long-term feasibility of large-scale tree plantations than in the waning fortunes of an entrepreneur. Only time will tell, but as wood prices rise, as they seem likely to do in the long run, even more cost-intensive schemes deploying the missing ingredient – fertilizer – will come into play, making tree plantations more attractive in their production and as an investment. That wood *must* be produced is exemplified by the continued poaching of trees in virgin forests. In Thailand alone, 30 to 40 forest guards are killed in gun battles each year.

Peter Raven states that "as a matter of self-interest and national security, all temperate, developed countries ought to begin to contribute substantially to the development of sustainable productive agricultural and forestry systems in the tropics."

Taungya – *family-project reforestation*

Another reforestation scheme seems even more suited to socioeconomic conditions in the tropics. The traditional *taungya* plantation system requires industrious land-hungry cultivators – people in long supply in the Third World, of course. Allotted an area of forest (in the past virgin, but now preferably old second growth) which is first cut, stumped, and torched, the farmer cultivates the plot for food crops for the family unit and for surplus which is sold for cash income. Plantation seedlings are introduced into the agricultural crop and are weeded for at least one year so that they are well established at the time the cultivator moves on to establish another plot.

This method was widely used to establish extensive plantations of teak (*Tectona grandis*) in Southeast Asia. Such systems not only have the wide support of agronomists and range-management officers in foreign countries but are also supported by the principal protagonists of the forests – the people of the land.

A variation of *taungya*, used in West Africa and called "farming for pay" or "departmental *taungya*," enjoys the following features:

1. The farmers employed are recruited as wage-paid employees of the forest department.

2. Land hunger is not a prerequisite.

3. The forest department owns both the farm crop and the trees.

4. There is no allocation of individual farm plots.

We can see that selected species will grow even on impoverished sites, especially when combined with nitrogen fixers, and so the potential for production is considerable, especially as Indonesia, for instance, has more abused land lying fallow than it has areas of productive forest. A representative of the Tropical Forest Institute of the United States Forest Service in Puerto Rico has calculated that if all the deforested lands were reforested, the resulting production would meet all the world's wood and pulp demands.

Fuels for the masses

Worldwatch Institute alerts us that one-half of all wood cut in the world is for firewood for cooking and heating, and that more than one-third of humanity still relies on wood for fuel. These vital needs are often ignored in public statistics but put awesome pressure on the world's vegetation. In some areas, such as Java, home gardens supply a fair share of family-firewood demands. More often, however, this is not the case, and until agro-forestry becomes much more prevalent this demand will remain a serious drain on standing forests.

An alternative to unrestrained wood depletion will be the dissemination of inexpensive but efficient wood-burning stoves to replace the wasteful open fires used by the bulk of the two billion people who rely on wood fuel. In the poorer countries, fuelwood provides over 90 percent of the total energy consumption. So grave is the situation that in some areas people are cutting back on the use of vegetables that require cooking.

△ Surprisingly simple yet effective technology can be used in areas of fuelwood shortage to make optimum use of whatever combustible material is available. Lever-operated presses can convert sawdust, chaff, and other waste into fuel brickettes for domestic use, and can be made wherever there is basic metalworking skill.

◁ The equation "1 ton of charcoal = 212 cu ft (6 cu m) of wood" shows how wasteful is the process of charcoal making. Some traditional methods waste up to 60% of the wood's energy value. Yet fully 80% of all wood removed from tropical forests is used for fuelwood or for conversion to charcoal.

SOLVING THE FUELWOOD PROBLEM

TACTICS	• Increase productivity of existing resources	• Create new resources	• Improve fuelwood distribution	• Improve conversion technologies	• Find substitutes for fuelwood
TECHNIQUES	• Introduce better management • Protect over-worked areas • Subri conversion technique • Utilize 'waste'	• Individual planting • Village woodlots • Strip plantations • Shelter belts • Block plantations	• Organize marketing cooperatives • Improve transport • Provide storage • Investigate import/export	• Improve charcoal production • Improve and disseminate wood stoves • Improve cooking habits	• Subsidize kerosene, bottled gas, coal • Investigate biogas • Investigate solar energy • Rural electrification

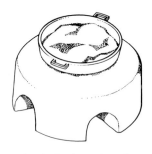

△ This baked-mud-and-sand fire enclosure, used in Senegal, can drastically reduce the energy waste of cooking on an open fire.

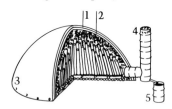

△ Simple technology like this earth kiln greatly improves charcoal-making efficiency. Sand (1) and straw (2) retain heat; air vents (3) promote even burning, and $75-worth of oil drums provide chimney (4) and tar trap (5).

△ Uganda's logging waste, once discarded, now yields 63,000 tons/yr of charcoal.

Most primitive stoves use only 10 to 15 percent of the heat generated. Efficient stoves made mostly of mud can use 40 to 65 percent of the heat, and sell for only $5. The use of solar stoves in the tropics, where sun is the major commodity and is cost free, holds great promise. Although the stove cost would be in the $30 to $50 range, long-range savings would be spectacular.

In the foothills of the Himalayas a practical family-size dung distillery (biogas reactor) has been introduced with positive results in wood conservation. This, unfortunately, is only the tip of the iceberg. The World Bank has calculated that even with widespread future availability of wood-conserving stoves, solar cookers, and biogas reactors, certain areas will have to be reforested at fifty times the present rate if firewood demands in the year 2000 are to be met. In Pakistan, as a harbinger of things to come, there has been a 500-fold increase in wood prices in recent years due to domestic shortages.

As all activities involving meaningful quantities of wood must be analyzed, even India's cremation practices loom as significant. In a country where most deceased are, by religious dictum, consumed on funeral pyres, the amounts of wood consumed are remarkable. Foresters, and a private organization (in Gujarat), are now trying to promote use of a process of cremation that reduces wood consumption from an average of 992 pounds (450 kg) to only 353 pounds (160 kg), a substantial saving for the family as well.

"Whose hand is on the chain saw?"

Virtually all waste material can be recycled into paper, fiberboard, particle wood, and molded products, and may be combined with plastics to form super-durable products with which we are already quite familiar, like the common yellow screwdriver handle, eyeglass frames, and so on.

The intimidating question is, Why is the United State's recycling rate only 23 percent and Great Britain's 62 percent? The annual bill the United States receives for the disposal of this paper material alone is $590 million. (Imagine the habitat this money could purchase.) Government regulations on recycling may be necessary in lieu of public enthusiasm. Clearly it would prove frugal for a government-sponsored incentive program to pay a bounty for collected and recycled paper out of trash disposal revenues saved.

Environmentalists and project developers need not work in conflict but rather are much more likely to benefit by mutual cooperation to coordinate and greatly enhance each other's goals at the least expense to economic expectations and global integrity.

V · The Funding of Project Rainforest

Of all the major problems facing the world today, global scientific opinion places tropical deforestation among the very highest priorities. Toward the end of the 1980s, a number of world conferences on the changing atmosphere were held in Toronto, Villach, and Bellagio where *Developing Policies for Responding to Climatic Change* was issued. The "Bellagio Report," corresponding to US Senate hearings on global warming, called for priority action to "further reduce deforestation, which is a source of CO_2 and other greenhouse gases, and increase both tropical and other forest areas, which absorb CO_2."

While statistics are available, quantifying the area of new forests required to absorb the global excess of CO_2, the author is unaware of the budgeting of any public sector program, however preliminary, toward implementing preventive or corrective strategies. We can state with confidence that the ounce of prevention, in this case preserving existing tropical forests, will come at a small fraction of the costs necessary to effect the "cure." While the bill for either will be enormous, to date not a cent has been allocated!

Quite the contrary. Over the past decade the World Bank has been under siege by diverse environmental organizations as well as by members of the scientific community, for what they consider the bank's ecologically irresponsible approach to funding destructive projects within the tropical forests. It is not without irony that these activities have contributed directly to global warming, and that allocating funding for these projects has never been problematical.

In 1985 alone, the World Bank made $16 billion available in loans to developing countries, of which $2.3 billion was funded by the leading four multinational development banks (World Bank, Inter-American Development Bank, and the development banks of Asia and Africa). Much of this funding has, in the past, been applied to such ecologically disastrous projects as hydroelectric dams of dubious benefit and short project life, built at the expense of large tracts of virgin tropical forest and in direct infringement of the ancestral lands of aboriginal tribal groups. Many project loans were clearly politically motivated, project feasibility being a secondary consideration. This was compounded by the visibly growing delinquency of debt repayment. In addition, of the approximately 2,500 personnel employed by the World Bank, only one was a tropical ecologist.

In addressing these concerns in personal correspondence with the World Bank, the US Department of State's Bureau of Lands and International Environmental and Scientific Affairs, and the US Department of the Treasury, I, among others, received an acknowledgment of the validity, in part, of the accusations, and assurances that attempts would be made to build-in necessary safeguards and an ecological conscience in future projects. A 1986 march on Washington by environmental groups was partly responsible for the World Bank issuing a declaration of intent to change their operational attitudes and policies.

Yet due to ever-mounting public concern, there is reason to believe that aid for tropical forestry may indeed be entering its Cinderella years. The 26 major

FUELWOOD AND AGROFORESTRY
Summary of needed investments, 1987–91

AFRICA	US$ mill
Botswana	15
Burkina Faso	25
Burundi	20
Cape Verde	15
Chad	14
Ethiopia	40
Kenya	48
Lesotho	10
Madagascar	30
Malawi	24
Mali	30
Mauritania	16
Niger	20
Nigeria	50
Rwanda	30
Senegal	25
Somalia	15
Sudan	35
Tanzania	30
Uganda	15
ASIA	
Bangladesh	52
China	250
India	500
Nepal	30
Pakistan	40
Sri Lanka	30
LATIN AMERICA	
Bolivia	25
Brazil	400
Costa Rica	15
El Salvador	10
Haiti	15
Peru	25
Total *(32 countries)*	**1899**

△ *The Tropical Forestry Action Plan indicates that considerable investment will be required to move the developing countries toward self-sufficiency.*

STRENGTHENING
INSTITUTIONS FOR
RESEARCH, TRAINING,
AND EDUCATION
*Summary of needed investments,
1987–91*

ACTIVITY	US$ mill		
	LATIN AMERICA AFRICA	ASIA	
Fuelwood and agroforestry	68	100	155
Land use on upland watersheds	52	30	233
Forest management for industrial uses	43	141	140
Conservation of forest ecosystems	25	48	29
Total	188	319	557

△ *If the industrialized nations fail to invest in developing countries, short-term economic imperatives will inevitably result in continued massive global deforestation. Nowhere is investment more urgently needed than in strengthening national institutions.*

development assistance organizations have increased their budgeting for forestry programs from $606 million in 1984 to $1.1 billion in 1988, and that trend appears to be a growing one. Toward ensuring that this course would be followed, President Reagan, in the closing months of his administration, signed into law a resolution that environmental conscience be, in effect, a criterion for evaluating future projects.

The reverse side of that same coin opens an enormous span of opportunity for the World Bank to take positive action for both the global environment and its occupants. The bank is able to produce the funding necessary to create the "wings" with which to fly in appropriate technologies for sustained development to the fields of peasant agriculturists. NGOs and Third World country peoples' corps, with World Bank funding, can be these "wings". Such programs can be molded perhaps after President Roosevelt's highly effective Civilian Conservation Corps (CCC) which created employment as well as healing large areas of degraded American environment. Time will tell whether the World Bank and others are willing to back recent convictions with significant funding. In the interim, it may be constructive to search the records for examples that may serve as models for future investment for development.

It should be especially noted that while funding is made available for the creation of areas for new forests to avert the bleak future threatened by continued global warming, these ventures should be viewed realistically as developmental in scope as they will create much-needed employment for great numbers of Third World citizens.

As the issues of tropical deforestation are essentially social and economic, remedies must not be divorced from the realities of farm-plot life extension, seedlings for woodlot planting, facilities for providing uncontaminated water, education on environmental protection and proper use of toxic chemicals, and provision of family planning services. It is out of those seeds that global habitat preservation will germinate, and it is likely that such approaches will prove far more economically expedient than encircling tropical forest parks or gorillas with armed guards.

OFFICIAL DEVELOPMENT ASSISTANCE (ODA) TO TROPICAL FORESTRY IN 1988

The figures are broken down by Tropical Forestry Action Plan (TFAP) activities, and by technical assistance (TA), mainly in the form of grants, and investment (I), generally in the form of loans.

FIELDS OF ACTION	DONOR COUNTRIES				DEVELOPMENT BANKS				UN ORGANIZATIONS			
	TA	I	Total	Total %	TA	I	Total	Total %	TA	I	Total	Total %
	US$ mill				US$ mill				US$ mill			
Forestry in land use	98.2	51.8	150.0	24.7	1.3	12.6	13.9	6.5	4.8	45.2	50.0	26.6
Forest-based industrial development	39.0	113.6	152.6	25.2	13.2	133.2	146.4	68.9	19.1	44.7	63.8	33.9
Fuelwood and energy	75.4	22.5	97.9	16.1	1.2	11.7	12.9	6.1	2.0	45.2	47.2	25.1
Conservation of tropical forest ecosystems	46.5	3.8	50.3	8.3	1.8	18.2	20.0	9.4	4.4	8.8	13.2	7.0
Institutions	133.9	21.6	155.5	25.7	1.7	17.7	19.4	9.1	13.4	0.4	13.8	7.4
Total	393.0	298.7[1]	691.7[1]	100.0	19.2	193.4	212.6	100.0	43.7	144.3	188.0	100.0

1) Includes an undetermined US$ 85 million, 13.5% of the total, from the Federal Republic of Germany.

Breaking new and promising ground, two companion pieces of US legislation were signed into law in 1986 that provide $2.5 million toward programs and education in reducing impact on the tropical forests (S–1747) and to protect species diversity (S–1748). This creates a foundation, it is hoped, on which to build a meaningful support system well into the next decade.

In direct response to pressure from the scientific and environmental community, President Jose Sarney of Brazil declared in 1988 that there would be a suspension of tax credits and other incentives that formerly propelled many of the most destructive developmental projects. Cattle ranching in particular will be far more limited, and directed to more appropriate areas. It is reported that the new policy was instigated because of criticism by the World Bank and the Inter-American Development Bank of Brazil's poor environmental and human rights record. Regardless of the threat of the loss of international funds, we would hope Brazil's new direction has the best of intentions. Such policy changes by the largest holder of tropical forest kindles a degree of optimism. Sarney's intentions have been stated to include a ban on the export of (unprocessed) logs and the subjecting of future agricultural and industrial projects to rigorous environmental controls.

Converting debt into habitat assets

World debt in 1988 stood at near US$1 trillion. Toward the end of 1989 Brazil's debt alone was $111 billion. Interest payments are so steep that Third World nations under the gun of debt are now paying more to the lending nations in interest payments than they receive in aid. In 1986, that margin was exceeded by $29 billion.

At the annual meeting of the Organization for African Unity in 1987, 50 member states in requesting amnesty on $200 billion in debts stated that "the problem is not one of liquidity but of a complete inability to pay." Such debt, of course, serves to entrench environmental disaster by ensuring that Third World nations step up their exploitation of tropical forests in their desperate

FOREST MANAGEMENT FOR
INDUSTRIAL USES
*Summary of needed investments,
1987–91*

AFRICA	US$ mill
Cameroon	20
Congo	20
Ghana	10
Côte d'Ivoire	75
Liberia	15
Nigeria	35
Uganda	25
Zaïre	10
ASIA	
Burma	30
China	285
India	190
Indonesia	50
Malaysia	40
Pakistan	20
Papua New Guinea	15
Philippines	40
Thailand	35
LATIN AMERICA	
Argentina	100
Brazil	325
Chile	50
Colombia	45
Costa Rica	15
Ecuador	20
Guatemala	15
Jamaica	10
Mexico	90
Peru	30
Venezuela	25
Total *(28 countries)*	**1640**

	TOTAL			
TA	I	Total	Total
US$ mill			%
104.3	109.6	213.9	21.2
71.3	231.5	362.8	36.0
78.6	79.4	158.0	15.7
52.7	30.8	83.5	8.3
149.0	39.7	188.7	18.8
455.9	**636.4[1)]**	**1092.3[1)]**	**100.0**

EXPECTED INCREASES IN OFFICIAL DEVELOPMENT ASSISTANCE TO FORESTRY TO 1995			
DONOR GROUP	EXPENDITURE 1988 (US$ mill)	EXPECTED ANNUAL INCREASE%	EXPECTED ANNUAL INCREASE US$ mill (first year)
Countries	691.7	> 6.3	> 44
Development Banks	212.6	> 16.0	> 34
UN Organizations	188.0	about 1.5	about 3
Total	**1092.3**	**> 7.5**	**> 82**

△ *While there are some who criticize the Tropical Forestry Action Plan's emphasis on forest management, the plan does enable us to identify critical funding vacuums. Industrial use of wood is essential in the developing countries – and must be undertaken on a sustainable basis.*

◁ *Over US$1,000 million was generated in official development assistance to tropical forestry in 1988, and based on the growing global recognition of the impact of deforestation, there is guarded optimism now that essential funding will be found to promote sustainable forest use.*

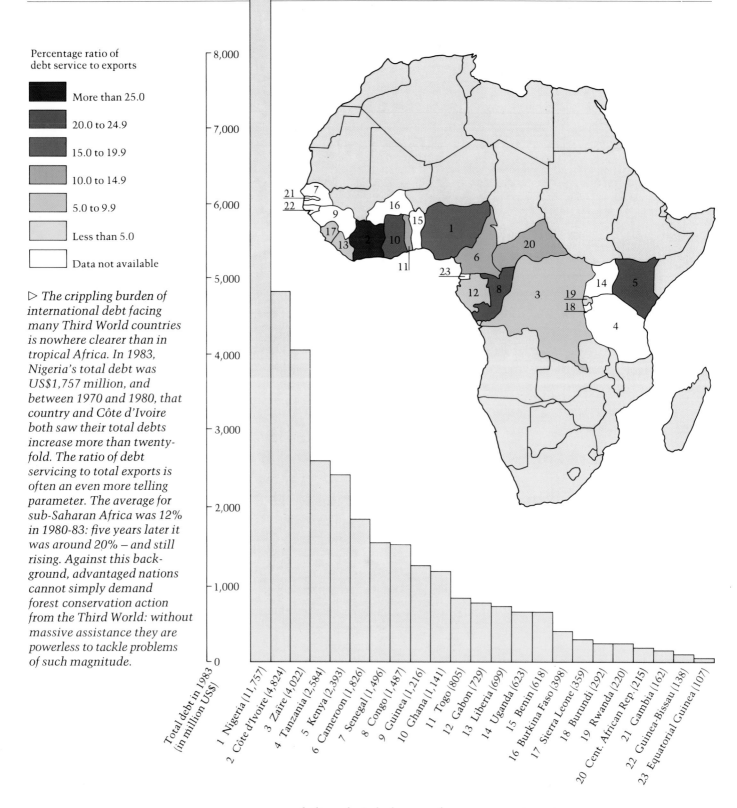

Percentage ratio of
debt service to exports

More than 25.0

20.0 to 24.9

15.0 to 19.9

10.0 to 14.9

5.0 to 9.9

Less than 5.0

Data not available

▷ *The crippling burden of
international debt facing
many Third World countries
is nowhere clearer than in
tropical Africa. In 1983,
Nigeria's total debt was
US$1,757 million, and
between 1970 and 1980, that
country and Côte d'Ivoire
both saw their total debts
increase more than twenty-
fold. The ratio of debt
servicing to total exports is
often an even more telling
parameter. The average for
sub-Saharan Africa was 12%
in 1980-83: five years later it
was around 20% – and still
rising. Against this background, advantaged nations
cannot simply demand
forest conservation action
from the Third World: without
massive assistance they are
powerless to tackle problems
of such magnitude.*

Total debt in 1983
(in million US$)

1 Nigeria (11,757)
2 Côte d'Ivoire (4,824)
3 Zaïre (4,022)
4 Tanzania (2,584)
5 Kenya (2,393)
6 Cameroon (1,826)
7 Senegal (1,496)
8 Congo (1,487)
9 Guinea (1,216)
10 Ghana (1,141)
11 Togo (805)
12 Gabon (729)
13 Liberia (699)
14 Uganda (623)
15 Benin (618)
16 Burkina Faso (398)
17 Sierra Leone (359)
18 Burundi (292)
19 Rwanda (220)
20 Cent. African Rep. (215)
21 Gambia (162)
22 Guinea-Bissau (138)
23 Equatorial Guinea (107)

attempts to stabilize their balance-of-payments situation.

In the later 1980s an admirable program evolved in which portions of the enormous and ever-burgeoning multinational investment bank debt incurred by Third World nations are "written off" in return for the debtor nations' elevation of negotiated areas of tropical forest habitat to permanent national-park status. Additional credits (albeit insufficient) are allocated for long-term maintenance, patrol, and infrastructure development of such areas, monitored by the international environmental community to ensure that something much more substantial than "paper parks" emerges.

This plan has a number of obvious merits:

1. A significant number of such multinational loans are made for political reasons, to secure or maintain allegiances in strategic Third World nations, and so the debt comes with the territory, so to speak. Further, the expectation of repayment in full has appeared to be little more than a posture.

2. The weight of unrealistic unrepayable debt creates an unhealthy atmosphere between debtor and creditor and so may subvert the intent of the original generosity.

3. The trade of preserved habitat for debt credit satisfies both parties and in effect is a repayment in kind that otherwise probably would not have materialized.

4. This scenario presents an exceptional opportunity for the World Bank and other multinationals to enhance their tarnished image by supporting environmentally constructive projects. Recognizing that survival of species is not simply Rwanda's or Brazil's responsibility, but an international one, presents US-AID, the World Bank, and other international lending institutions a golden opportunity to invest in a Third World country's future by solidly bolstering its tourist revenue, in many cases the country's principal long-term asset.

In July of 1987, Conservation International announced a precedent-setting historical negotiation with the government of Bolivia. A "debt for nature swap" was agreed upon by the conservation organization and the Bolivian government whereby areas totaling more than 3.7 million acres (1.5 million ha) adjacent to the Beni Biosphere Preserve, were given conservation status. The transaction was facilitated by Conservation International purchasing US$650,000 of Bolivia's debt at a discounted rate of $100,000. In addition, Guillermo Jusliniano, minister of agriculture and peasant affairs, is designating $250,000 (local currency) for the administration, protection, and management of the Beni Biosphere Reserve, which supports 13 of Bolivia's 18 endangered species. (Since this ground-breaking venture, other "debt for nature swaps" have been consummated by WWF, Nature Conservancy, and other national and international organizations.)

The role of the trade cartel

As a trading group with strong market focus, there is reason for optimism that the ITTO can effect price increases while reducing the bulk of exports and allow parities to operators for conservation. An acceptable 2 percent tax on hardwoods imported into developed nations would raise over $200 million for application to conservation. Such strategies have been put to use in mitigating the adverse effects of many industries, but on somewhat less than global scale.

Another purpose of such a cartel would be to promote raw log processing into sawn wood, veneer, or plywood before export. Finished veneer, selling from $120 up to $4,000 per cubic meter, could amount to $4 billion of extra revenue for tropical countries annually.

Importing countries, on the other hand, have been quite overt in their intentions by levying heavy protective import tariffs on processed wood while leaving raw logs duty free. While it would be naive not to recognize a country's desire to enhance its own economic advantages, a new environmental ethic will demand some adjustment to such rigidly self-serving policies, especially where such trade restrictions are shown to have an overt deleterious effect on crucial environments.

In addition, it has been suggested that a global tax on activities such as deep-ocean mining of manganese nodules could yield well over $800 million as we move into the last decade of this century. With larger proportions paid by major exploiters, these funds would go into a common world coffer for use in tropical forest preservation as well as perhaps in an antidesertification campaign, both related issues geared to world hunger.

A 0.1 percent *ad valorem* tax on internationally traded oil would raise $100 million per year for such global emergency projects. Expand this tax to all goods traded internationally and the figure soars to $1 billion. In this spirit, Saudi Arabia at one point considered a contribution of a 1-cent-per-barrel tax on oil that would accrue $200-$300 million to the United Nations Environment Programme.

The beginnings of international cooperation

The presidential committee of the US Interagency Task Force on Tropical Forests "firmly believes that US efforts, meshed efficiently with those of other nations and international organizations, can make a difference."

I was among the American delegation to Moscow in April of 1987, negotiating the US-Soviet Cooperative Initiative on Tropical Deforestation. Brent Blackwelder and I represented our own organizations, the Environmental Policy Institute and the International Society for the Preservation of the Tropical Rainforest respectively. Also represented were the Audubon Society, the Global Tomorrow Coalition, the Natural Resources Defense Council, the Environmental Defense Fund, the Nature Conservancy, Wildlife Conservation International, Sierra Club, and the National Wildlife Federation.

▽ *Kenya's globally publicized sacrificial torching of $3 million-worth of illegally held tusks hopefully signals the beginning of the end of the international trade in African elephant ivory. In 1988, 1,600 elephants were killed in Africa every week: in 1990 only about 626,000 remain. An unusually united international outcry culminated in the species being placed on "Appendix I" of CITES – the Convention on International Trade in Endangered Species – and with that action, some 90% of the world market for elephant ivory was closed. This successful campaign gives some justification for optimism that the cause of species and habitat conservation is now gaining ground.*

It is now widely recognized that an international effort, with First World nations providing resources and orchestration, will be necessary to ensure positive developments in tropical, moist Third World countries. It is uplifting to report that the Soviet Union, although not involved in exploitation of tropical forests to any degree, nor having any such forests in its own territory, realized the global impact of tropical deforestation and embraced the US-Soviet cooperation on those issues in a gratifying and precedent-setting initiative. Subsequently, 72 members of the US Senate successfully petitioned both President Reagan and General Secretary Gorbachev to include the issue on the 1988 Summit agenda, an effort from which evolved the joint mandate of a bilateral study of "the climate of tomorrow and environmental change."

When 1,600 delegates of 60 nations attending the Fourth World Wilderness Conference, and a league of scientific institutes and societies, passed formal resolutions in support of the initiative, the United Nations Environment Programme declared the cooperation, "One of the few reasons for optimism on the tropical deforestation front." There are strong hopes that such a cooperative effort involving sustainable development, Man and the Biosphere preserves, population stabilization, and other facets, may significantly contribute to mitigating world problems and provide a nucleus for an ever-broadening international *esprit de corps* – a global signal that if former confrontationists are now joining together in cooperation, the time really has arrived when these global issues can be addressed with genuine resolve.

Sanity in global priorities

In 1988, during negotiations to solidify the Draft US-USSR Cooperative Initiative on Tropical Deforestation, Academician Vladimir Sokolov, representing the USSR Academy of Sciences, stated that in order to fund the proposed five-year project in a Third World country, the respective nations "should make the transfer from missiles to tropical forests." Such a scenario bears examination.

The world's nuclear armament reserves now stand at over 50,000 weapons, whose capability for destruction is equal to 1,300,000 bombs of Hiroshima magnitude (roughly 2.5 tons of TNT for every woman, man, and child on earth). Few would deny that such stockpiles represent, in military jargon, an "overkill" of ludicrous proportions. Try comparing our spending on weapons with our investment in the environment. The world's weapons budget is more than $1.4 billion per day: the United Nations Environment Programme's budget is less than $30 million *a year*. That figure is $10 million less than the 1981 cost of a B–1 bomber.

A small portion of the $500 billion annual bill for the global military budget (incredibly, a figure greater than the entire income of the poorest half of the world's population) would channel more than ample reserves into sustainable development, habitat preservation, and greenhouse gas absorption.

Costa Rica, while opting not to maintain an army, has in the trade-off 26 percent of its land under parks and reserves, one of the world's lowest illiteracy rates, most effective social programs, and excellent national health care. Immediately apparent to any visitor is that in place of soldiers bristling with automatic weapons, are bright-faced children in freshly pressed clothing going to and from school. The nation boasts a 93 percent literacy rate, and these same children look forward to a life expectancy of 75 years – a truly staggering contrast to the general perception of a Third World country.

△ The US-Soviet Cooperative Initiative on Tropical Deforestation was drafted in Moscow between the USSR Academy of Sciences and a coalition of ten major US environmental organizations. I was head of the US delegation, and found a strong esprit de corps among those involved, a recognition on the part of the two great powers of the uphill task of arresting tropical deforestation, and a determination – with the active participation of the developing nations – to implement the extensive programs needed to achieve preservation of the earth's tropical forest inheritance.

Think globally – act locally

It is argued that species are the "heritage of humanity," and that "in the United States twice as many people visit zoos and aquariums each year as attend baseball, football, hockey, and basketball games."

A Gallup poll shows that three-fourths of the people of both developed and developing countries want to see more effort and money expended in protecting wild species, and many feel a definite and instinctive responsibility for species in foreign lands "as part of humankind's common heritage." On the other hand, the exploiter views this common heritage more as a "common property resource," up for grabs to the first comer. Myers makes an illuminating observation when he points out that "a live animal is common property, a dead one readily becomes private property." This holds true for exploited habitats as well, and whereas a sullied body of water or polluted air can possibly be restored in time, species extinction is irrevocable.

Apparently, the inherent bond between humans and their biological inheritance is woven so deeply into their makeup that the intergovernmental organization comprising the drought-stricken states of the West African Sahelian Zone (CILSS) repeatedly listed wildlife conservation in its priorities for developmental projects and foreign aid. Thus far, such aid has not been forthcoming from the international community.

ACTION PLAN FOR THE CONCERNED INDIVIDUAL

1. Letters and other communications from individuals and organizations to government representatives are the most direct and effective way of expressing your concern over the issues of tropical deforestation. Also write to the World Bank, AID, United Nations agencies, and other international development bodies, demanding that their projects within the tropical forests are not environmentally destructive. It is interesting to note that in expressing your concern to legislators, one-to-five letters on an issue will generally elicit a form letter; five-to-ten letters elicits a legislative assistant's response; more than ten letters will most often compel the legislators themselves to respond personally. You should address your correspondence to:

President,
The World Bank,
1818 H Street, NW,
Washington, D.C. 20433

Administrator,
US Agency for International Development,
320 21st Street, NW,
Washington, D.C. 20532

President,
Inter-American Development Bank,
1300 New York Avenue, NW,
Washington, D.C. 20005.

Conversely, should you be fortunate enough to visit a tropical forest park or region in a foreign country, take the time to write to the minister of parks, the Forestry Department, the Department of Tourism, or the country's president, to say how impressed you were with the experience and urge the conservation of these resources. One such positive letter has more impact than several negative messages.

2. Lobby against your government's support, financial and otherwise, for certain short-sighted and highly destructive colonization schemes which move masses of ill-prepared people into tropical forest wilderness areas (e.g., Brazil into its Amazon Forest; Indonesia into Irian Jaya). On the positive side, implore that methods at our disposal be taught and implemented to sustain the tropical peasant farmer on his land (e.g. terracing of fields, agroforestry, tilapia fish farming, and other practical measures).

3. Be personally involved in efforts to ensure that timber extraction in the tropics proceeds through the employment of sustainable and environmentally sound harvesting methods (e.g., strip harvesting, reforestation of plantation species in cut areas, etc.). Many fast-food chains do not import beef raised in tropical forest pastures – patronize them.

4. Give your support to the following conservation organizations working in the tropical forests:

Concerned members of the public should be aware that they do have real and effective opportunities to express their anger at species depletion, and to demand appropriate action on the part of their elected representatives.

Renowned zoologist George Schaller, involved in the preservation of the endangered giant panda among other species, crystallizes the gravity of the challenge when he states, "A failure to preserve the panda would be a serious moral blow to the human spirit, an indication that even an aroused consciousness, scientific wisdom, and dedication may not be enough to save humankind from ecological doom."

Yet humankind has met great challenges before and its course is not inexorably set and inflexible. If some part of the same energies spent in mindless exploitation are rechanneled into implementing enlightened conservation programs, constructive aid policies, and the linchpin around which lasting success will turn – sustainable agricultural and wood-producing practices – there is no reason why the tropical forests and the human species cannot coexist – each sustaining the other through the ages.

By so doing, we may still avert a descent into a maelstrom of irrevocable deforestation. While the historic opportunity to embrace that challenge is before us, we should be well aware that the decision is now fully ours: we must choose between temporary opulence and perpetuating life.

The International Society for the Preservation of the Tropical Rainforest,
3931 Camino de la Cumbre,
Sherman Oaks, CA 91423. (The author is president and co-director of this organization.)

The International Union for Conservation of Nature and Natural Resources,
Ave. Du Mont Blanc,
CH–1196,
Gland, Switzerland.

The World Wide Fund for Nature (formerly World Wildlife Fund),
1601 Connecticut Avenue, N.W.,
Washington, D.C. 20009 (and other WWF organizations in other countries worldwide).

Environmental Policy Institute,
218 D Street, S.E.,
Washington, D.C. 20003.

The Nature Conservancy,
International Program,
1785 Massachusetts Avenue, N.W.,
Washington, D.C. 20036.

The African Wildlife Foundation,
Mountain Gorilla Project,
1717 Massachusetts Avenue, N.W.,
Washington, D.C. 20036.

5. Continue to educate yourself and others around you about this wonderfully rich environment. Know that each of us is, in part, responsible for these forests becoming the *earth's first endangered habitat*, and use conscience in modifying your behavior to prevent its extinction. Recycle paper and other forest products whenever possible; avoid adding to market pressures by being an abundant or unnecessary consumer of these products; refuse a paper bag when shopping whenever possible; and see that these practices are contagious.

Don't purchase furniture or products constructed of woods such as mahogany, teak, and tropical wood veneers if they come from natural tropical forests instead of tree plantations. Substitute these with cedar, bamboo, pine, willow, and ash.

6. Gather data on tropical deforestation and conservation. As you accumulate knowledge on "the sleeper issue of the 20th century," schedule talk programs and perhaps slide shows at schools, clubs, and religious centers. As the media, as well as the public, are now increasingly primed on the issues, solicit press, television, and radio coverage. Schools at all levels should be encouraged to include such information in their curricula. See listing in bibliography section for available films, support, and classroom materials.

7. *Know that you personally can make a difference.*

CONCLUSION

CONCLUSION

If a man takes no thought about what is distant, he will find sorrow near at hand.

CONFUCIUS

Through the course of this book we have perhaps come to embrace and appreciate a timeless and copiously productive habitat. Viewing the tropical rainforest as an integral organism, itself regulated by an intricate network of symbiotic dependencies, it is evident that this biome is a vital organ in the maintenance of our planet's integrity. It is also evident that many of our escalating activities today in the tender tropical arena will be quite permanent, but that an organ transplant will not be a future option.

As we have seen, the fabric of mutualistic relationships that keeps our system healthy are so interwoven that as tropical deforestation progresses, atmospheric, climatic oceanographic, and public health imbalances, already manifest, measured, and rapidly escalating, presently promise to produce some of the gravest consequences of historic and assuredly prehistoric times. At the present rate of plunder, the tropical rainforest will be virtually extinct not far into the twenty-first century. Thus, today the tropical rainforest is the earth's first endangered habitat of global consequence.

Ostensibly, this grim, rock-hard actuality looms on the very near horizon ... within our lifetime! It is no wonder that the scientific community has issued the most solemn forewarnings, which include naming it "the sleeper issue of the 20th century," and "the act our descendants will least forgive us for."

As perhaps now five species per day, and within a few years, one species per hour, pass into extinction due to tropical deforestation alone, we face the bleak prospect of losing over one million species by the end of this century. It is time for procrastination to end and the era of the new environmental ethic to dawn. As environmental philosopher Aldo Leopold wrote, "A land ethic changes the role of *Homo sapiens* from conqueror of the land community, to plain member and citizen of it. It implies respect for his fellow members, and also respect for the community as such." Such an ethic demands an understanding of the consequences of our activities, along with a respect for life that will allow other species to coexist with us in their natural, preordained state in spite of the temptations of economic expediency.

It is just as evident that conservation on a global scale cannot afford to divorce itself from socioeconomic imperatives, which themselves do not exist in a vacuum. Given no viable alternatives, the ever-growing land-starved masses will home in on the opulent tropical forests like heat-seeking missiles and obliterate them far more effectively and permanently than any armaments, logging equipment, or botanical defoliants yet devised!

We can be justified in feeling that we now have the necessary agricultural technologies to keep the family-unit farmers on their land and fed. Together with sustained timber extraction methods, population-stabilization programs, revisions of archaic and destructive import-export policies, and constructive hands-on aid principles, we can, in fact, relieve the intolerable burden of pressure presently focused on the tropical forests.

In a good many instances this involves increasing the direct and tangible benefits of the forests for the people of the tropical areas through integrated resource management. The forest that is relied upon to produce a sustained livelihood by many will enjoy a far healthier prognosis for survival. Unless these golden keys are applied to the door, famine, unlike any we have seen, will infuse these masses as the last of the tropical forests are finally slashed and burned.

Leopold framed his principles in Sand County, USA. They are even more applicable in the pantheon of the equatorial rainforests. Fascinating and informative fossil evidence reveals the past and brings it to life. The rise, transformation, and fall of species is always a matter of intricate checks and balances; always in response to the sensitive nuances of the earth and beyond into the universal environment. So that even when, as one theory suggests, an asteroid hit the earth and blanketed the upper atmosphere with dust, excluding a significant portion of the sun's rays and causing temporal die-off or reduction of vegetation, life in this natural laboratory was able to adjust. The dinosaurs may finally have failed, but in the grand scheme of things this was of no great consequence as mammals, many equally dynamic, replaced them as the dominant life-forms. Today, however, many question whether our earth systems are flexible enough to fill such evolutionary gaps again.

We would do well to try, difficult as it may be, to keep our own existence on earth in perspective. For illustrative purposes, should we condense the 3.5 billion years of the existence of life on earth into a single calendar year, humans — understand this — came on the scene only during the latter part of the last day of that year!

If, in this very current part of our infinitely short history, we appear rather a rash and perhaps arrogant species, all our impulses are not poorly founded. Our desire to taste and consume the resources of our planet date back to a time when such assets were thought to be infinite. Only recently have we come to realize, for instance, that land that can hold the greatest biomass on earth, the tropical rainforest, cannot sustain a large human population dependent on conventional agriculture. We also learn, not without making painful mistakes, that these fragile forests cannot continue to be a convenience to temperate regions as the cornucopia of low-cost products, harvested by boom-town methods that are simply no longer applicable. Yet if it is judiciously preserved, this yielding womb can issue forth from its reservoir a never-ending plethora of goods, medicines, and food, while at the same time regulating earth's systems as it was meant to do — at no cost and in perpetuity.

Should we reduce and squander our diversity today, however, we will reduce in as great a measure the alternatives and options available to our children and grandchildren or, like Aldo Leopold's tinker, who does not fully comprehend the pocket watch he attempts to fix, we save all the gears of our biological fabric, ensuring us the full spectrum of possibilities for the immediate as well as the far distant future. Variety does indeed seem to be the spice of life.

Yet even as we probe the corners of our universe for any humble sign of life, we have unconsciously taken earth's most fertile gene pool for granted. However miraculous (yet sterile) the images are that return from these space voyages, the beauty of Saturn's rings, the gaseous spheres with volcanic moons, it remains unlikely that we will ever lay cameras on anything remotely of the caliber or fertility of the planet earth.

Perhaps it will be that realization, brought about by the maturing of space-age exploration, that will usher in a reborn respect and even the awe that earth and its diverse systems deserve.

So dependent is the whole on the parts that the very energy mechanism that drives the cells of the human body is derived from small structures descended from the ancient bacteria given to us some 3.5 billion years ago. Then did photosynthetic lodgers, born of the primal blue-green algae, integrate with plant forms of rainforests and other habitats to bequeath to all of us the oxygen in our atmosphere, which now supports the conglomerate of species that includes us. The fact that the tropical forests are responsible for a highly significant portion of earth's biological productivity is no small consideration and concern.

Those who perceive this issue as a moral responsibility are urged to refer to the previous chapter for direction on how to respond personally. An insignificant effort? On the contrary, it is found that nothing has a more profound influence on policy makers than concerned citizenry asserting their well-founded opinions in personal communications. This principle is perfectly expressed by Edmund Burke who wrote, "No man makes a greater mistake than he who does nothing because he can do only a little."

Are we survivors? As Lewis Thomas puts it, "The survival of the fittest does not mean those fit to kill, it means those fitting in best with the rest of life." Will man use the technology at his command to keep his numbers in bounds, or to blindly increase them – the very cause of his potential demise? It is abundantly clear that these are basic questions that need committed response now if we are to have any chance of solving our problems in the tropical forests and other habitats at our mercy. It may be time now to acknowledge that a critically sullied atmosphere, causing potentially permanent climatic shifts, is an obscene litmus to our activities.

The most significant question to which we can address ourselves today is, Will *Homo sapiens*, a single species on a planet we share with a multitude of other species, endorse a notion that our appetites and directions are so preferential as to exclude the great balance of creation on earth? This may be the very epitaph of a species which became oversuccessful and has already purchased a one-way ticket aboard the train bound for extinction.

If we are today operating on a one-step-forward, two-steps-back approach to environmental management, we should be well advised at this time that the pace of that treadmill is ever quickening. Just how nimble is humanity? At just what point will we be cast off the runaway machine of our own making?

I choose rather to believe that the spark of humanity is inherently worthy, intelligent, and resilient enough to choose an enlightened alternative that will maximize our potential and preserve our dignity while protecting the fellow creatures with whom we share this miracle called life, whether or not many of them can be of direct benefit to us.

The inquiry, "If the success or failure of this planet, and of human beings, depended on how I am and what I do; how would I be? What would I do?" is answered by the ancient Chinese proverb, "If we do not change our course, we will end up where we are going!"

◁ *The intelligence behind the eyes of this Indonesian silver langur (Presbytis cristata) seems to search our souls for some understanding of humanity. Is this elegant primate, one of perhaps a million species that may vanish into extinction, imploring us to carefully consider the alternatives to the continued felling of the global tropical rainforest?*

APPENDIX 1   EDUCATIONAL RESOURCES

STUDENT AND TEACHER AIDS

● Teacher's Guide: *Rainforests – Kids for Conservation.*
A 14-page booklet geared for grades K–12 with interesting facts, maps, activities, flash cards, glossary, and list of organizations. Available from: Education Department, Marine World Africa USA, Marine World Parkway, Vallejo, CA 94589. Phone: (707) 644–4000, ext. 433.

● Filmstrip and Teacher's Guide: *The Vanishing Forest – The Crisis of Tropical Deforestation.*
An in-depth filmstrip that tells the story of tropical rainforests, the threats they face, and the efforts to save them. Meant for grades 4 to adult, it comes with a filmstrip, cassette, and an illustrated guide. Available from: Knowledge Unlimited, Inc., P.O. Box 52, Madison, WI 53701. Phone: (800) 356–2303 or (608) 836–6660.

● Video and Curriculum Booklet: *Our Threatened Heritage.*
An 18-minute video (with curriculum materials designed for use with high school students or in training workshops) about tropical rainforests, their ecology, and reasons they are threatened. Contact: National Wildlife Federation, International Program, 1412 16th St., NW, Washington, DC 20036. Phone: (202) 637–3776.

● Teacher's Resource Guide: *Rainforests – A Teacher's Resource Guide.*
This very thorough and up-to-date 28-page resource guide was compiled and designed by Lynne Chase of Southern Regional High School in Manahawkin, New Jersey. Available from: Rainforest Action Network, 301 Broadway, Suite A, San Francisco, CA 94133. Phone: (415) 398–4404.

● Student Action Group Manual: *Creating Our Future Manual.*
This manual was created by high school students for students. Available from: Creating Our Future, 398 North Ferndale, Mill Valley, CA 94941. Phone: (415) 381–6744.

● Environmental values education guide: *Environmental Education about the Rain Forest* by Klaus Berkmuller.
Scientific information along with sensitive examples that illustrate real-life ethical, aesthetic, cultural, scientific, ecological, and economic value choices. Published by IUCN/WWF. Available in English or Spanish from: Wildland Management Center, School of Natural Resources, University of Michigan, Ann Arbor, MI 48109. Phone: (313) 763–1312.

RAINFOREST FILM LIST

● **Banking on Disaster**, 78 minutes, 1988
This film documents a burgeoning human and environmental disaster in the rainforest: the World Bank-funded road through the forested state of Rondonia in Brazil, where landless families flock to clear rainforest and farm on the fragile soils. The film follows one frontier family over a period of years as their plot of land loses its fertility, and documents the disastrous consequences of this project, both on the Amazonian rainforest and its indigenous peoples. Suitable for grades 9 through adult. Available from Bullfrog Films, Oley, PA 19547. Phone: (800) 543-FROG.

● **Blowpipes and Bulldozers**, 70 minutes, 1988
This video tells the story of the Penan tribe of Borneo in Malaysia and their desperate ongoing fight to save the rainforest homelands from the Malaysian logging companies. It also tells the story of Bruno Manser, a Swiss who lives with the Penan and helps them in their struggle. Described by John Seed of the Australian Rainforest Information Center as a "devastating film, a tour de force," it will inform and motivate an audience on this issue in general. Available from Bullfrog Films, Oley, PA 19547. Phone: (800) 543-FROG. Also available from Gaia Films, RMB 116 Blue Knob, Nimbin NSW 2480, Australia. Phone: (066) 89 7236. FAX (066) 89 7287.

● **Emerald Forest**, 90 minutes, 1985
Available at local video rental stores.

● **Keepers of the Forest**, 28 minutes
What rainforests are, their current and potential uses, and what's destroying them. Looks at the ancient forest practices of the Lacandon Mayans and how indigenous peoples can help us to find workable solutions to problems confronting the rainforests. Available for sale and for rent in ½ inch, ¾ inch, and Betamax video formats. Write: Keepers of the Forest, c/o Norman Lippman, 7745 Mohawk Pl., St. Louis, MO 63105. Phone: (314) 725–3313.

National Geographic Videos
Rainforest, 60 minutes, 1983
Journey to the dense tropical rainforests of Costa Rica, home of captivating creatures such as poison arrow frogs, leaf-cutting ants, and howler monkeys. Excellent information on the ecology of the rainforest.
Tropical Kingdom of Belize, 60 minutes, 1986
This film beautifully illustrates the fascinating range and diversity of life inhabiting the rainforest, while also touching briefly on the problem of deforestation.

The above films are sometimes available for rent from local video stores. They are available for sale from Vestron Video, P.O. Box 4000, Stamford, CT 06907. Phone: (203) 978–5400.

● **Our Threatened Heritage**, 19 minutes, 1988
Ever feel overwhelmed by the enormity of the tropical deforestation rainforest issue? *Our Threatened Heritage* explains the main problems involved and describes what is being done to reverse current destructive trends. A comprehensive introduction, it comes with a curriculum booklet designed for high school students. Available from National Wildlife Federation, *Attn*: Noel Gerson, International Programs, 1412 16th street, NW, Washington, DC 20036. Phone: (202) 797–6800.

● **Planetary Update**, 30 minutes, 1988
The Boulder Rainforest Action Group at Colorado University wrote and performed in this short, witty, and sweet introduction to the crisis of the earth's rainforests that is as entertaining as it is educational. Equal parts hair-raising facts and belly laughs from the point of view of two aliens from another galaxy. Great for young and old alike. Write KSRG Productions, P.O. Box 986, Boulder, CO 80306. Phone: (303) 744–8325.

● **Rainforest Rap**, 6 minutes, 1988
A group of kids perform a rap, singing about diversity, deforestation, and how to get involved in the rainforest issue. Fun for all ages. Accompanied by an educational packet. Available from the World Wildlife Fund, P.O. Box 4866, Hamdon Post Office, Baltimore, MD 21211. Phone: (516) 444–3132.

● **Research to Protect the Tropics**
This diverse film discusses the major problems with tropical development: global climatic change and the disruption of the carbon cycle, loss of biodiversity, firewood availability, pasture conversion and agroecology, hydroelectric development, population, and education. Filmed in the Brazilian Amazon, Costa Rica, Ecuador, and Honduras. An amateur film but well done; research oriented. Available from Charles Goldman, Environmental Studies Department, UC Davis, Davis, CA 95616. Phone: (916) 752–1557.

● **Earth First!**, 59 minutes, 1987
This Australian film documents the efforts to protect the last remaining Australian rainforests. Extraordinary footage of the beauty of the rainforest is contrasted with dramatic newsreel documentation of the efforts to preserve these areas through civil disobedience and demonstration. An amateur film excellent for an activist audience. Available from Educational Film and Video Project, 5332 College Ave., Ste. 101, Oakland, CA 94618. Phone: (415) 655–9050.

● **Environment Under Fire: Ecology and Politics in Central America**, 30 minutes, 1987
This film includes interviews with top Central American and US environmentalists while documenting environmental destruction in the tropical forests, mountains, hillsides, and agricultural fields of Central America. It is a powerful education and organizing tool to show the intimate links between poverty, war and environmental destruction. Available from Environmental Project On Central America (EPOCA), c/o Earth Island Institute, 300 Broadway, Ste. 28, San Francisco, CA 94133. Phone: (415) 788–3666.

● **Equatorial River: the Amazon**, 22 minutes, 1987
The Amazon is the biggest river system on earth, and flows through the world's largest tropical rainforest. The film shows how the water and nutrient cycles work in the Amazon Basin, and provides a fundamental understanding of the interrelation of elements in this enormous and threatened ecosystem now seen to be so vital to our planet. Suitable for grades 7 through 12. Available from Bullfrog Films, Oley, PA 19547. Phone: (800) 543-FROG.

● **Into Darkest Borneo**, 72 minutes, 1988
An Australian film crew's mission to find the Penan, one of the last tribe of hunter-gatherers in Southeast Asia, changes from an adventure trek through the rainforest (with Penan guides leading the way) into an impassioned account of the Penans' efforts to save their forest through direct action. Available from the Rainforest Action Network.

● **Korup: An African Rainforest**, approx. 40 minutes
Beautiful documentary, filmed over five patient years, on the ecology of a primary rainforest in Cameroon in Central Africa. For distribution information contact: Anthony Morris London, Ltd., 6 Goodwin's Court, St. Martin's Lane, London WC2N 4LL. Phone: 071–836–0576.

● **Mayan Rainforest Farming**, 29 minutes, 1987
The tropical rainforests are being destroyed at an alarming rate for lumber production, cropland, and cattle pastures. In nearly all cases the result is massive erosion, and often desertification. But there is a different way. Around the last capital of their former empire, Mayan farmers continue a sustainable form of agriculture. Imitating the

rainforest itself they grow a variety of vegetables and nonfood crops in the shade of their fruit trees. Available from Bullfrog Films, Oley, PA 19547. Phone: (800) 543-FROG.

• **The Business of Hunger**, 28 minutes, 1986
When the "Green Revolution" sent seeds, fertilizers, and farm machinery to the Third World, food production rose – not for local consumption but for large-scale agriculture, largely owned and controlled by outside corporations and geared toward export. This film focuses on peasant agriculturalists being forced off their lands onto less fertile rainforest lands and finally into the city slums. Distributed by Maryknoll Media Relations, Gonzaga Building, Maryknoll, NY 10545. Phone: (914) 941–7590, ext. 308.

• **Replanting the Tree of Life**, 20 minutes, 1987
An inspiring reminder of the essential part trees play in our lives and in the life of the planet. The film covers a broad range from how trees purify the air we breathe and process the water we depend on, to pointing out the central place trees and tree symbols have played in different cultures, including our own, throughout history. Available from Bullfrog Films, Oley, PA 19547. Phone: (800) 543-FROG.

• **The Temperate Rainforest**, 16 minutes, 1982
Examines the characteristics and ecology of the beautiful British Columbian coastal rainforest, and in a powerful, but understated manner, makes the case for its preservation. Suitable for grades 7 through 12. Available from Bullfrog Films, Oley, PA 19547. Phone: (800) 543-FROG.

APPENDIX 2 TROPICAL TIMBERS AND DOMESTIC ALTERNATIVES

Compiled by the Rainforest Action Network

The international trade in tropical timbers is a growing threat to the future of all tropical forests. Several countries that once maintained lush forests have depleted them to the point where they must now import wood. Commercial logging in the tropics as it is practiced today cannot provide long-term ecological or economic sustainability. However, there is much potential for sustainable timber harvesting in temperate forests.

It is encouraging to note that two timber importers are marketing tropical woods harvested on a sustained basis from the Palcazu Project in Peru. They are Luthier's Merchantile, P.O. Box 774, 412 Moore Lane, Healdburg, CA 95448, and the Ecological Trading Company, 1 Lesbury Road, Newcastle upon Tyne NE6 5LB, UK.

The demand for tropical timbers continues to rise because it is generally less expensive and also because of its unique qualities. Low costs for tropical timbers are a result of several factors, including lower wages for workers in producer countries, government subsidies and trade policies that keep timber prices low, and forestry policies that encourage short-term financial returns and damaging, low-cost harvesting methods. Temperate alternatives to tropical hardwoods are available that are comparable in beauty, workability, and durability.

The following information comprises lists of tropical hardwoods to avoid and alternative domestic timbers.

TROPICAL TIMBERS TO AVOID

Common name	Scientific name	Origin
Apitong	*Dipterocarpus* spp.	Malaysia, Thailand, Philippines
Banak	*Virola* spp.	Central and South America
Bocote	*Cordia elaeagnoides*	Central and Sourh America
Bubinga	*Guibourrtia demeusii*	West Africa
Cocobolo	*Dalbergia retusa D. hypoleuca*	Central America
Cordia	*Cordia* spp.	Central and South America
Ebony, African	*Diaopyros* spp.	Africa
Ebony, Macassar	*Diaopyros celebica*	East Indies
Goncalo alves	*Astronium fraxinfolium*	Brazil, northern South America
Greenheart	*Ocotea rowdioea*	Central America
Iroko	*Chlorophora excelsa*	West Coast of Africa
Jelutang	*Dyera costulata*	Malaysia, Brunei
Koa	*Acacia koa*	Hawaii
Lauan	*Shorea* spp.	Philippines
Mahogany, Honduran	*Swietenia macarophylla*	Central and northern South America
Mahogany, Philippine	*Shorea* spp.	Philippines
Meranti	*Shorea* spp.	Malaysia
Andaman Padauk	*Pterocarpus dalbergioides*	Andaman Islands
African Padauk	*Pterocarpus soyauxii*	Central and west tropical Africa
Purpleheart	*Peltogyne* spp.	Central and northern South America
Ramin	*Gonystylus* spp.	Indonesia, Malaysia
Rosewood, Honduran	*Dalbergia stevensonii*	Central America
Satinwood	*Chloroxylon swietenia*	India, Sri Lanka
Teak	*Tectona grandis*	Indigenous to India, Burma, Thailand, Indo-China, and Java. Planted in East and West Africa and West Indies
Virola	*Dialyanthera otoba & gordonifolia*	Central America and Venezuela
Wenge	*Milletia laurentii*	Zaïre
Zebrawood	*Microberlinia brazzavillensis*	Gabon, Cameroon, and West Africa

NORTH AMERICAN ALTERNATIVE TIMBERS

Common name	Scientific name
Ash	*Fraxinus americana*
Basswood	*Tilia americana*
Beech	*Fagus grandifolia*
Birch	*Betula papyrifera*
Butternut	*Juglans cinera*
Cherry	*Prunus serotina*
Cottonwood	*Poplus* spp.
Cypress	*Taxodium distichum*
Douglas Fir	*Pseudotsuga menziesii*
Elm	*Ulmus* spp.
Black Gum	*Nyssa sylvatica*
Red Gum	*Liquidamber styraciflua*
Hackberry	*Celtis laevigata*
Western Hemlock	*Tsuga heterophylla*
Hickory	*Hicoria* spp.
Sugar Maple	*Acer saccharum*
Soft Maple	*Acer* spp.
Red Oak	*Quercus* spp.
White Oak	*Quercus* spp.
Pecan	*Hicoria* spp.
Ponderosa Pine	*Pinus ponderosa*
Yellow Southern Pine	*Pinus* spp.
Yellow Poplar	*Liriodendron tulipiferia*
Sitka Spruce	*Picea sitchensis*
Sycamore	*Platanus occidentalis*
Black Walnut	*Juglans nigra*

APPENDIX 3   TOWARD SUSTAINED PRODUCTIVITY

Explanatory notes to chart on pages 202–205

A great many variables have been brought together within the framework of this synthesis. As such, figures for man-hours, production, and soil loss are not precise for all conditions and locales, but are designed to fall within acceptable ranges. While the author draws on hard data for initial and final years, for some examples the figures were extended by extrapolation, in concurrence with researchers in the field.

SHORT CYCLE SHIFTING CULTIVATION

Production and soil loss (Pimentel 1989; El-Swaify 1990; Bainbridge 1990: all pers. comm.). Slopes of 7% used here. Acceptable level of topsoil loss is less than 1 ton, but perhaps 0.5 tons/ha/yr (Lal 1988). Soil loss of 20 to 25 tons/ha/yr not unusual in Amazon Basin oxisols (El-Swaify 1990: pers. comm.). Figures for manual clearing, no tillage, were 0.4 t/ha/yr. Crawler tractor/tree pusher – conventional tillage – produced 19.6 t/ha/yr in African scenario (Lal 1981). Loss of topsoil on 7% slope in primary rainforest (Ivory Coast) was 0.03 t/ha/yr, but on bare ground loss was 138 t/ha/yr (UNESCO 1978). Slopes of 20% (Peru) produce 26 t/ha/yr soil loss on bare ground, but 4.6 t/ha/yr under annual cropping, while with alley cropping on 15% slopes, soil loss was 1.2 t/ha/yr and under forest cover the loss was 0.7 t/ha/yr (Alegre 1989). The prescription for intensified agriculture makes allowance for copious mulch until crop species provide soil cover.

NONINTENSIVE AGROFORESTRY

All above references. Corn/*Leucaena* production is representative of best-case scenario of adequate selection for soil fertility (7% of Amazon Basin) and conscientious soil mulching. *Leucaena* production (Pimental and Hartshorn 1989; Lal 1990; all pers. comm.). Labor for *Leucaena* trimming estimated at 36 man-hrs/ha year 2 and 48 hrs/ha at years 8–25 (Lal 1990: pers. comm.). Tree component must be appropriate to site; i.e. *Leucaena* is not acceptable for highly acid soils (El-Swaify 1990; pers. comm.). An increase in maize yield of about 1.4 t/ha/yr was observed in association with hedgerows of *Leucaena*, with or without fertilizer (Watson and Laquihon 1985). Shading, root competition, and immobilization by mulch are among factors reducing maize yields in alley cropping treatments, especially in vicinity of trees, compared to nonfertilized controls where subsoil is extremely low in nutrients and cations (Szott 1987). *Leucaena* hedgerows are, however, a positive factor in erosion control (Lal 1989).

PARTIALLY INTENSIFIED AGROFORESTRY

Corn, papaya, and orange agroforest figures are from Chanchamayo, Peru (Villachica *et al.* 1990). Annual incomes vary quite widely according to market availability. Corn price is based on 22 lbs per US$1.00 (US$ 0.04545 pèr lb). Direct costs of production are variable. Figures given are gross. Figure of $653/ha/yr for 25-year-old fruit tree swidden plot allowed to fallow. Labor perhaps 40 hrs/ha/yr. This $ figure represents close access to market geared to produce (Tamshiyacu Village/Iquitos Market). This also represents plots converted from 6–7 year old secondary plots which are far from returning to maximum fertility (Padoch, DeJong, and Unruii 1985). Start-up labor estimated at 20% more for mixed agroforest than short cycle shifting cultivation (Buol 1990; pers. comm.; labor estimates Bainbridge, Gleissman 1990; pers. comm.). Labor for clearing intensified agroforestry plot spread over 5-year period to conserve soil (Nair 1990: pers. comm.). The literature and experience in agroforestry is less than complete. Laurel tree's (*Cordia alliodora*) self-pruning and narrow crown recommends it strongly as timber species in agroforestry. Years 6 to 12 increasingly yield US$ 100–900/ha/yr in trimmings. At harvest, around 18–25 years, 150 trees/ha can be 18″-20″ DBH (diameter at breast height); and market value, where such quality wood is scarce, can be $100–$150 per tree (Budowski and Borel 1990: pers. comm.). While perennials and fruit-tree crops may possibly be sustained and increased over a 25-year period without inputs, annuals, including grains, will require inputs for sustained or increased yields. The payback – in increased produce to costs – can, however, be amply rewarding (see text) (Sanchez 1982; Lal 1990: pers. comm.). Inputs of nutrient need not be purchased, but gleaned sustainably in the form of litter from surrounding forest as in the Kayopo system (Hecht 1989; Gleissman 1990: pers. comm.). A 1-ha garden can be littered from a 5–8-ha area of primary forest (Wilkin 1987). Areas of high rainfall in S. China have carried out productive sustainable agriculture for some 4,000 years without nonrenewable inputs – using green, animal, and human manures only (Gleissman 1990: pers. comm.). Maturing agroforestry plots are a consistent and often growing source of wild animal products not reflected in the analysis.

CATTLE PASTURE

Soil loss rough estimates for land/cattle speculator less likely to mitigate poor pasture practices on 7% slope (Sanchez, Buol, and Bainbridge 1990: pers. comm.).

Root-rake/tree pusher used in clearing land reduced labor to 192 man-hrs/ha but increased soil loss from a potential low of 0.4 t/ha/yr in manual clearing to 19.6 t/ha/yr in year 1 (Lal 1981). For Amazon Basin oxisols, soil loss can be 20 t/ha/yr for manual clearing and considerably higher for machine clearing where the potential for gully erosion is now a factor to consider, especially in overgrazed situations (El-Swaify 1990: pers. comm.).

Year 1 – 928 hrs estimated to manually fell, burn and establish pasture (Buol, Gleissman 1990: pers. comm.). Cattle pasture requires 50 man-hrs/ha/yr for maintenance, once established (Nations, 1990: pers. comm.).

TERRACED AND NONTERRACED CULTIVATION

Eastern Andean slopes of 40% used here. Terraced fields here are manured (green, animal, or human) (Winterholder 1990: pers. comm.). Andean terraces on even eastern slopes date back some 1500 years and have been producing sustainably for several hundred years with minimal soil loss (streams and rivulets run clear below terraces after rain storms), (Treacy 1989; Denevan 1990: pers. comm.). Slopes from 7% to 40% of equal length increase soil loss 10 times. Terraces reduce erosion some 100 times, and fallow may not be necessary (El-Swaify 1990: pers. comm.). Unterraced 49% slopes in Burundi eroded 150 t/ha/yr under corn (Roose, 1988).

Value of produce for western slopes (Treacy 1989). Rough estimated yields for eastern Andean slopes for terraced and nonterraced fields (Sanchez, 1990, and pers. comm.). Maintenance of terraces estimated at 6% of construction labor, which is some 500 hrs (Buol and Bainbridge 1990: pers. comm.). US$650/ha in wages to construct terraces (Hooper and El-Swaify, 1988). Cost of bench terracing $175 per ha but doubled return of yams in nonterraced field (Sheng 1989). Hillside ditches, however, reduced erosion by 80% and were 25% the cost of bench terracing (Sheng 1988). On slopes of 40% in Trinidad terraced pineapple field soil loss was 0.4 t/ha/yr (Gumbs *et al.* 1985). Soil loss on nonterraced land can reach 286 t/ha/yr and more on 70% slope of 164 ft (50 m) length. Unterraced fields of Huri Thung Choa, Thailand, required a period of 20–100 years fallow after only several years of cultivation (Hurni 1985).

FISH AQUACULTURE (IN ASSOCIATION WITH AGROFORESTRY)

See text (Moss, Moehl, Pompa and Frobish 1990, and pers. comm.). Price based on US$2.00 per kg, 1988. Small ponds, 26 by 33 ft, can produce an annual income of $600 (Barrau and Djati 1985). Note that in years 1 and 2, although fish are being produced, there is at this stage no cash return to the farmer.

SUSTAINED EXTRACTION FROM PRIMARY FOREST

Research was conducted on white sand forest formation. Richer soils and forests can be expected to produce even richer harvests (Peters, Gentry, and Mendelsohn 1989).

BUSHMEAT EXTRACTION AND FOREST ANIMAL FARMING

Bushmeat, crocodilian skins, turtle, and capybara ranching (Nations and Coello Hinojos 1989; Bailey 1989: pers. comm.). Not known if harvest of 2 crocodilians/ha/yr is sustainable.

BIBLIOGRAPHY

Any book on a subject as vast as the tropical rainforests of the world and sustainable development within these regions, must draw on the work of many other authors, in many disciplines and in many lands. To list them all would be impossible, yet even this selected bibliography runs to several hundred entries. Therefore, to assist the reader we have listed the various publications under a number of thematic headings for ease of access. References will be found listed in alphabetic order of main author, under the following headings:

Amazonia
Botany
Cattle production

Climate and the greenhouse effect
Conservation
Deforestation
Forest resources
Fuelwood
Historical perspective
Plantation forestry
Population
Public health
Sustainable agriculture
Sustainable and unsustainable logging
Traditional cultures
Tropical forests – general
Zoology

AMAZONIA

"Amazon Research and Training Program News." *Amazon Research Newsletter*, No. 9, (September 1983.)

"Amazon Viewpoints." *Calypso Log*, Pub. of the Cousteau Society, (March 1982.)

Amazonia. Edited by Ghillean Prance and Thomas E. Lovejoy. Pergamon Press, (1985.)

Amazonian Rain Forests. Edited by Jordan, C.F., Springer-Verlag, (1987.)

Anderson, Anthony, B. "White Sand Vegetation of Brazilian Amazonia." *Biotropica*, Vol. 13, No. 3, (September 1981.)

Campbell, Robert. "A Timely Reprieve or a Death Sentence for the Amazon." *Smithsonian*, (October 1977.)

Caufield, Catherine. *In the Rainforest*. Alfred A. Knopf, (1985.)

Dobert, Margarita. "The Amazon Forests Revisted." *Tropical Forests*, Vol. 2, No. 3, (1985.)

Freed, Kenneth. "Amazon Jungle Mocks The Treasure Seekers." *Los Angeles Times*, (6 May 1983.)

Goodland, R. J. A. and H. S. Irwin. *Amazon Jungle: Green Hell to Red Desert*. Elsevier Scientific Pub. Co., (1975.)

"Greatest, Oldest, Richest, Largest, Last." *Calypso Log*, Pub. of the Cousteau Society, (March 1982.)

Hecht, Susanna and Alexander Cockburn. *The Fate of the Forest – Developers, Destroyers, and Defenders of the Amazon*. Verso, (1989.)

Murphy, Richard C., William Vogel, and Charles Eilers, *The New El Dorado: Invaders and Exiles*. Cousteau/Amazon Teachers' Guide. Turner Program Services, Atlanta, Georgia.

Oyens, Pieter de Marez. "Where Trees 'Make' Rain, The Amazon Basin." *Focus*, World Wildlife Fund – U.S., Vol. 5, No. 6, (November/ December 1983.)

Schreider, Helen and Frank. *Exploring the Amazon*. The National Geographic Society, (1970.)

Sterling, Tom. *The Amazon*. Time-Life Books, (1973.)

Werner, Dennis. "Trekking in the Amazon Forest." *Natural History*, (November 1978.)

BOTANY

Allen, Paul H. *The Rain Forests of Golfo Dulce*. Stanford University Press, (1977.)

Austin, Robert, Dana Levy, and Koichiro Ueda. *Bamboo*. Weatherhill Pub., (1978.)

Bland, John. *Forests of Lilliput: The Realm of Mosses and Lichens*. Prentice-Hall, Inc., (1971.)

Blombery, Alec and Tony Rodd. *Palms*. Angus & Robertson (UK) Ltd, (1982.)

Bodley, John H. and Foley C. Benson. "Stilt-Root Walking by an Iriarteoid Palm in the Peruvian Amazon." *Biotropica*, Vol. 12, No. 1, (March 1980.)

Corner, J. H. *The Natural History of Palms*. University of California Press, (1966.)

Dahlgren, Broreric. "Index of American Palms." Pub. No. 863, Vol. XIV, *Field Museum of Natural History*, (30 January 1959.)

Denslow, Julie Sloan. "Gap Partitioning Among Tropical Rainforest Trees." *Biotropica* Supplement to Vol. 12, No. 2, (June 1980.)

Essig, Frederick B. "The Genus Orania (Arecacene) in New Guinea." *Lyonia*, Vol. 1, No. 5, (January 1980.)

—— "The Palm Flora of New Guinea." *Botany Bulletin* No. 9, Office of Forests, Lae Papua, New Guinea, (1977.)

—— and Bradford E. Young. "Palm Collecting in Papua, New Guinea II. The Sepik and the North Coast." *Principes*, Journal of the Palm Society, Vol. 25, No. 1, (January 1981.)

The Euphorbia Journal, Volume I. Strawberry Press, (1983.)

Federov, An. A. "The Structure of the Tropical Rain Forest and Speciation in the Humid Tropics." *Journal of Ecology* 54: 1–11, (1966.)

Fisher, Jack B. "A Survey of Buttresses and Aerial Roots of Tropical Trees for Presence of Reaction Wood." *Biotropica*, Vol. 14, No. 1, (March 1982.)

Graf, Alfred Byrd. *Exotic Plant Manual*. Roehrs Co., (1970.)

—— *Exotica 3*. Roehrs Co., (1970.)

Halle, F. and R. A. A. Oldeman. *An Essay of the Architecture and Dynamics of Growth of Tropical Trees*. Penerbit University, Malaya, Kuala Lumper, Malaysia Pub., (1975.)

—— and P. B. Tomlinson. *Tropical Trees and Forests: An Architectural Analysis*. Springer-Verlag, (1978.)

Handbook for Tropical Biology in Costa Rica. Organization for Tropical Studies, (July 1971.)

Hartshorn, Gary S. *Neotropical Forest Dynamics*. Biotropica, Supplement to Vol. 12, No. 2, (June 1980.)

—— *Tree Falls and Tropical Forest Dynamics*. Cambridge University Press, (26–30 April 1976.)

Hertrich, Wm. *Palms and Cycads*. San Marino, CA., Henry E. Huntington Library and Art Gallery, (1951.)

Heywood, V. H. and B. R. Chant. *Popular Encyclopedia of Plants*, Cambridge University Press, (1982.)

Hodel, Don. "Notes on Pritchardia in Hawaii." *Principes*, Journal of the Palm Society, Vol. 24, No. 2, (April 1980.)

Holdridge, L. R. *Life Zone Ecology*. Tropical Science Center, San Jose, Costa Rica.

Jackson, James F. "Seed Size as a Correlate of Temporal and Spatial Patterns of Seed Fall in a Neotropical Forest." *Biotropica*, Vol. 13, No. 2, (June 1981.)

Jacobs, M. "The Study of Lianas." *Flora Malesiana Bulletin* 29, (1976.)

Janzen, Daniel H. *Costa Rican Natural History*. University of Chicago Press, (1983.)

—— *The Impact of Tropical Studies on Ecology*. The Changing Scenes in Natural Sciences, Academy of Natural Sciences, Special Publication 12, (1977.)

Jordan, Carl F. *Nutrient Cycling in Tropical Forest Ecosystems*. John Wiley & Sons, (1985.)

Kleijn, H. *Mushrooms and Other Fungi: Their Form and Colour*. Doubleday & Co., (1965.)

Langlois, Arthur C. *Supplement to Palms of the World*. Gainesville University Presses of Florida, (1976.)

Lugo, Ariel E. *Mangrove Ecosystems: Successional or Steady State?* Biotropica, Supplement to Vol. 12, No. 2, (June 1980.)

The Magnificent Foragers. Smithsonian Exposition Books, W. Norton & Co., (1978.)

Marteka, Vincent,. "Words of Praise – and Caution – About Fungus Among Us." *Smithsonian*, (May 1980.)

McCurrach, James C. *Palms of the World*. Harper & Bros., (1960.)

McWhirter, Norris and Ross. *Guinness Book of World Records*. Sterling Pub. Col, Eleventh Edition, (1965.)

Meijer, Willem. "Saving the World's Largest Flower." *National Geographic*, Vol. 168, No. 1, (July 1985.)

Menninger, Edwin A. *Flowering Trees of the World*. Hearthside Press, Inc., (1962.)

—— *Flowering Vines of the World*. Hearthside Press, Inc., (1970.)

Moore, Harold E., Jr., *The Major Groups of Palms and Distribution*. Cornell University, (1973.)

Muirhead, Desmond. *Palms*. Dale, Stuart, King, (1961.)

Newman, Arnold C. "Euterpe at Iguassu Falls, Brazil." *Principes*, Journal of the Palm Society, Vol. 16, No. 2, (April 1972.)

Ng, F. S. P. "Litter Trapping Plants." *Nature Malaysiana*, Vol. 5, No. 4, (January 1980.)

Nishida, Florence H. "A Mushrooming Interest." *Terra*, Vol. 21, No. 3, (Winter, 1983.)

—— "Quick Change Artist: The Slime Mold." *Terra*, Vol. 22, No. 4, (March/April 1984.)

Padilla, Victoria. *Bromeliads in Color and Their Culture*. The Bromeliad Society, Inc., (1966.)

—— "Bromeliads in California Gardens." *Pacific Horticulture*, (January 1976.)

Plant Life Cycles. 42–1500 Carolina Biological Supply Co., Burlington, N.C. (1966.)

"Protein Linked to Photosynthesis, A." *Science News*, Vol. 117, No. 3, (19 January 1980.)

Ray, Thomas S., Jr., "Slow-Motion World of Plant 'Behavior' Visible in Rain Forest." *Smithsonian*, (March 1979.)

Savonius, Moria. *Mushrooms and Fungi*. Octopus Books/Crescent Books, (1973.)

Schultz, Jack C. "Tree Tactics." *Natural History*, (May 1983.)

Standley, Paul C. *Flora of Costa Rica Part I*. Reprint of 1937 edition by University Microfilms, (1970.)

Tompkins, Peter and Christopher Bird. *The Secret Life of Plants*. Avon, (1973.)

Walter, Heinrich. *Ecology of Tropical and Subtropical Vegetation*. Oliver & Boyd, (1971.)

Weinberg, Michael Aron. *Plants are Waters' Factories*. Michael Aron Weinberg Pub., (1976.)

Whitmore, T. C. *Palms of Malaya*. Oxford University Press, (1973.)

Wilson, Bob and Catherine. *Bromeliads in Cultivation*. Hurricane House Pub. Inc., (1963.)

Zahl, Paul A. "Slime Mold: The Fungus That Walks." *National Geographic*, Vol. 160, No. 1, (July 1981.)

CATTLE PRODUCTION

Dale, Edward Everett. *Range Cattle Industry*. University of Oklahoma Press, (1930.)

"The Hamburger Connection." Tropical Wildlands Conservation: The World Bank's Progress with Emphasis on Amazonia. The Ecological Society of America 73rd Annual Meeting, Davis, California. (17 August 1988.)

Shane, Douglas R. *Hoofprints on the Forest: An Inquiry into the Beef Cattle Industry in the Tropical Forest Areas of Latin America*. Office of Environmental Affairs, U.S. Dept. of State, (March 1980.)

CLIMATE AND THE GREENHOUSE EFFECT

Begley, Sharon, with Bob Cohn. "The Silent Summer." *Newsweek*, Vol. CVII, No. 25, (23 June 1986.)

Brown, Sandra and Ariel E. Lugo. "The Storage and Production of Organic Matter in Tropical Forests and Their Role in the Global Carbon Cycle." *Biotropica*, Vol. 14, No. 3, (September 1982.)

Brownstein, Ronald and Nina Easton. "The Greenhouse Effect." *The Amicus Journal*, (Winter, 1982.)

"Climate Change Cannot be Prevented." *UNEP North America News*, Vol. 3, No. 2, (April 1988.)

"Climate Changes: The Sea Also Rises." *Calypso Log*, Pub. of the Cousteau Society, (March 1982.)

"Developing Policies for Responding to Climatic Change." The Beijer Institute. A summary of the discussions and recommendations of the workshops held in Villach (28 September–2 October 1987) and Bellagio 9–13 November 1987.)

"The Endless Summer?" *Newsweek*, (11 July 1988.)

Houghton, Richard A. and George M. Woodwell. "Global Climatic Change." *Scientific American*, Vol. 260, No. 4, (April 1989.)

"Long Hot Future: Warmer Earth Appears Inevitable." *Science News*, Vol. 124, No. 17, (22 October 1983.)

"Making the Most of the CO_2 Problem." *Science News*, Vol. 115,

No. 15, (14 April 1979.)

"Passing the Climate Buck." *Science News*, Vol. 117, No. 1, (5 January 1980.)

Peterson, I. with Rick Weiss. "Arboreal Storage for Carbon Dioxide." *Science News*, Vol. 133, No. 9, (27 February 1988.)

"Photosynthetic Capacity of Tropical Plants." *Bio Science*, Vol. 30, No. 1, (January 1980.)

"Plant Burning is Major CO Source." *Science News*, (17 March 1979.)

Raloff, Janet. "Deforestation: Major Threat to Ozone?" *Science News*, Vol. 130, No. 8, (23 August 1986.)

Revelle, Roger. "Carbon Dioxide and World Climate." *Scientific American*, Vol. 24, No. 2, (August 1982.)

"Scientist says Greenhouse Warming is Here." *Science News*, Vol. 134, No. 1, (2 July 1988.)

Scoville, Anthony Ellsworth. "Why the U.S. Ignores the Greenhouse Effect." *Not Man Apart*, (April 1982.)

Simon, C. "Soil and Land Biota Give Not Take CO_2." *Science News*, Vol. 124, No. 12, (10 September 1983.)

——— "The Termite Gas and Global Methane." *Science News*, Vol. 122, No. 19, (6 November 1982.)

"Tropical Effects on Forecasts." *Science News*, Vol. 115, No. 24, (16 June 1979.)

"Warming: Proof May be in the Ice Cap." *Science News*, Vol. 120, No. 20, (14 November 1981.)

Wolkomir, Richard. "Weathermen's Lab is a Rocky Mountain High." *Smithsonian*, (April 1982.)

Woodwell, George M. "The Carbon Dioxide Question." *Scientific American*, Vol. 238, No. 1, (January 1978.)

——— Gordon T. MacDonald, Henry R. Lace, Roger Revelle, and David C. Keeling. "A Grim Global Question Mark: CO_2." *The Living Wilderness*, (September 1979.)

CONSERVATION

Arehart-Treichel, Joan. "Saving Tropical Forests." *Science News*, Vol. 112, No. 22, (26 November 1977.)

"AWLF and the Mountain Gorilla." *Wildlife News*, Vol. 14, No. 2, (Fall, 1979.)

Ayensu, Edward S. "Calling the Roll of the World's Vanishing Plants." *Smithsonian*, (November 1978.)

Barnard, Geoffrey S. "Costa Rica: Model for Conservation in Latin America." *Nature Conservancy News*, Vol. 32, No. 4, (July/August 1982.)

Beard, Peter. *The End of the Game*. Doubleday & Co. Inc., (1977.)

——— "The End of the Game Time." *Africana*, Vol. 6, No. 11, (March 1979.)

Beebe, Spencer B. "A Model for Conservation." *The Nature Conservancy News*, Vol. 34, No. 1, (January/February 1984.)

——— "Thinking Globally, Acting Locally." *Nature Conservancy News*, Vol. 32, No. 4, (July/August 1982.)

Bejarano, Gaston. "Pilon Lajas, Bolivia – Survey for Establishing Rain Forest Reserves." *IUCN/WWF Full Project*, No. 1309, (1975.)

Biodiversity. "Serendipity in the

Exploration of Biodiversity – What Good are Weedy Tomatoes?" by Hugh H. Iltis. E. O. Wilson, Editor, National Academy Press, Washington, D.C. (1988.)

"Brazil's Muriquis Suffer as Forests Shrink." *Focus*, World Wildlife Fund – U.S., Vol. 4, No. 2, (Spring, 1982.)

Brunig, Eberhard F. *Transactions of the International MAB-IUFRO Workshop on Tropical Rain Forest*. Ecosystems Research, Hamburg Chair of World Forestry, (17 May 1977.)

——— "The Tropical Rain Forest – A Wasted Asset or an Essential Biospheric Resource?" *Ambio*, A Journal of the Human Environment Research and Management, Vol. VI, No. 4, (1977.)

Bumstead, Cynthia. "U.S. Songbirds Threatened by Tropical Forest Loss." *Focus*, World Wildlife Fund – U.S., Vol. 3, No. 2/A, (Spring, 1981.)

Cahn, Robert. *Footprints on the Planet, A Search for an Environmental Ethic*. Universe Books, (1978.)

——— and Patricia. "Treasure of Parks for a Little Country that Really Tries." *Smithsonian*, (September 1979.)

Carey, Rosemary. "Can we Save the Land that Saves Endangered Species?" *Sierra*, Vol. 67, No. 3, (May/June 1982.)

Carr, Archie and David Carr. "A Tiny Country Does Things Right." *International Wildlife*, (September/October 1983.)

Carrighar, Sally. *Wild Heritage*. Houghton-Mifflin Co., (1965.)

"Central America: Roots of Environmental Destruction." The Environmental Project on Central America, *Green Paper* No. 2.

Conservation Biology: An Evolutionary-Ecological Perspective. Michael E. Soule and Bruce A. Wilcox (Editors.) Sinauer Associates, (1980).

Conservation Biology: The Science of Scarcity and Diversity. Michael E. Soule, (Editor.) Sinauer Associates, (1986.)

Conserving Africa's Natural Heritage. 17th Meeting of IUCN's Commission on Natural Parks and Protected Areas, Garova, Cameroon, (17–23 November 1980.)

Conserving Birds of the World. World Wildlife Fund - U.S. Bulletin.

Conserving the Natural Heritage of Latin America and the Caribbean. 18th Working Session of IUCN's Commission on National Parks and Protected Areas, Lima, Peru, (21–28 June 1981.)

"Consumer's Guide to Wildlife on Sale: To Buy or Not to Buy." *Focus*, World Wildlife Fund – U.S., Vol. 5, No. 5, (September 1983.)

Cronk, Dr. Q. with V. H. Heywood and H. Synge. *Biodiversity: The Key Role of Plants*. IUCN and WWF, (1988.)

Crove, Noel. "Wild Cargo: The Business of Smuggling Animals." *National Geographic*, Vol. 159, No. 3, (March 1981.)

Delcourt, Hazel R. "The Virtue of Forests, Virgin and Otherwise." *Natural History*, (June 1981.)

Eckholm, Erik. "Disappearing Species: The Social Challenge." *World Watch Paper 22*, (July 1978.)

——— *Down to Earth*. W. W. Norton & Co., (1982.)

——— "Wild Species Vs. Man: The Long Struggle for Survival." *The Living Wilderness*, (July/September 1978.)

Ehrenfeld, David. "What Good are Endangered Species Anyway?" *National Parks and Conservation*, (October 1978.)

Ehrlich, Paul R. and Anne H. *Extinction: The Causes and Consequences of the Disappearance of Species*. Ballantine Books, (1983.)

——— *Machinery of Nature*. Simon & Schuster, (1987.)

Fisher, Arthur. "Preserving a Diverse Lineage." *Mosaic*, Vol. 13, No. 3, (May/June 1982.)

Gibbons, Boyd. "Do We Treat our Soil Like Dirt?" *National Geographic*, Vol. 166, No. 3, (September 1984.)

Gilbert, B. L. " 'Sand County' Farm Shaped New Ethic for the Environment." *Smithsonian*, (October 1980.)

"Horizons Uganda – National Conservation Strategy – Reserve Surveyed." *Swara*, East African Wildlife Society, Vol. 5, No. 3, (May/June 1982.)

Humboldt, Alexander Von. *View of Nature: Or Contemplations on the Sublime Phenomena of Creation*. Henry G. Bohn, (1850.)

"Illegal Trade in Wildlife Goes Unchecked while Lacey Act Goes Unenforced." *Focus*, World Wildlife Fund – U.S., Vol. 5, No. 5, (September 1983.)

1988 IUCN Red List of Threatened Animals. The IUCN Conservation Monitoring Centre, Cambridge, U.K., (1988.)

Jacobs, M. "Good Health to the Dipterocarps." *Flora Malesiana Bulletin*, (1978.)

——— "It is the Genera of Threatened Plants that Need Attention." *Flora Malesiana Bulletin*, (1977.)

——— *Significance of the Tropical Rain Forests on 12 Points*. 8th World Forestry Congress, Jakarta, Section FQL 27, (October 1978.)

——— "What a Botanist can Contribute to Conservation in Malesia." *Flora Malesiana Bulletin*, (1977.)

Jain, R. K., L. V. Urban, and G. S. Stacey. *Environmental Impact Analysis: A New Dimension in Decision Making*. Van Nostrand Reinhold Co., (1977.)

Janzen, Daniel H. "Costa Rican Parks: A Researcher's View." Ecology Forum, *The Nature Conservancy News*, Vol. 34, No. 1, (January/February 1984.)

Kennedy, Robert. "Saving the Philippine Eagle." *National Geographic*, Vol. 159, No. 6, (June 1981.)

Lapedes, Daniel N. *Encyclopedia of Environmental Science*. McGraw-Hill Book Co., (1974.)

Leopold, Aldo. *A Sand County Almanac*. Oxford University Press, (1968.)

——— "The Once and Future Land Ethic." *Wilderness*, Vol. 48, No. 168, (Spring, 1985.)

Lindsey, Hall. *The Late Great Planet Earth*. Zondersan Pub., (1981.)

Love, Sam. *Environmental Action Earth Tool Kit*. Pocket Books, (1971.)

Lovejoy, Thomas E. "Conservation Beyond our Borders." *The Nature Conservancy News*, Vol. 29, No. 4, (July/August 1979.)

———— "A Global Survival Strategy." *The Living Wilderness*, (September 1980.)

———— and Maria Tereza Jorge dePadau. "Can Science Save Amazonia?" *Focus*, World Wildlife Fund – U.S., Vol. 3, No. 1, (Winter, 1981.)

Managing Protected Areas in the Tropics. IUCN/UNEP, Switzerland, (1986.)

Martin, Esmond Bradley. "The World Ivory Trade." *Swara*, Vol. 6, No. 4, (July/August 1983.)

Mathias, Mildred E. *The Importance of Diversity*. Special Publication No. 1, Pacific Division, American Association for the Advancement of Science, San Francisco, CA, (7 August 1978.)

McNeely, Jeffrey A. "We are All in this Together: How International Cooperation can Help Conserve Threatened Species and Habitats." IUCN. International Strategies for Preservation of Threatened Ecosystems. Davis, CA., (August 1988.)

Michener, James A. "Where did the Animals Go?" *Reader's Digest*, (June 1976.)

Miller, Norman N. "Wildlife – Wild Death." *Swara*, East African Society, Vol. 5, No. 3, (May/June 1982.)

Mitchell, Henry. "What Good are Endangered Species, Anyway? On Esthetics and Honor." *National Parks and Conservation*, (October 1978.)

"Monarch Butterfly Faces Unknown Fate." *Focus*, World Wildlife Fund – U.S., Vol. 3, No. 2, (Spring, 1981.)

Moore, Tui de Roy and Moore, Alan. "Peru's Largest Park Safeguards Biological Treasure of the Tropics." *Smithsonian*, (January 1983.)

Murphy, Jamie. "Growing a Forest From Scratch." *Time*, (December 1986.)

Myers, Norman. *The Sinking Ark*. Pergamon Press, (1979.)

———— "Tropical Rainforests: Whose Hand is on the Axe?" *National Parks and Conservation*, (November 1979.)

———— "Are Some Species More Valuable than Others?" World Wildlife Fund – U.S., Vol. 3, No. 1, (Winter, 1981.)

———— "Viewpoint – On Loss of Tropical Forests." *Sierra Club International Report*, Vol. 11, No. 2, (27 October 1982.)

———— *Gaia: An Atlas of Planet Earth*. Doubleday, (1984.)

———— "The End of the Lines." *Natural History*, Vol. 94, No. 2, (February 1985.)

National Parks Planning Manual. Food and Agriculture Organization of the United Nations, (1976.)

Newman, Arnold C. "The Vanishing Jungle." *Treasure Chest*, Vol. 5, (11 November 1975.)

Pasquier, Roger F. "Whose Birds are They?" *The Nature Conservancy News*, Vol. 32, No. 4, (July/August 1982.)

Peterson, I. "Tempering Humid Tropic Development." *Science News*, Vol. 121, No. 24, (12 June 1982.)

Pimentel, David and Marcia. "The Risk of Pesticides." *Natural History*, (March 1979.)

Pingree, Sumner. "The Politics of Protection." *The Living Wilderness*, (Spring, 1982.)

Plant Genetic Resources – Their Conservation in situ for Human Use. FAO. (1989.)

Plants in Danger, What do we Know? IUCN/UNEP, (1986.)

Prance, G. T. and T. S. Elias. *Extinction is Forever/Threatened and Endangered Species of Plants in the Americas and their Significance in Ecosystems Today and in the Future*. New York Botanical Garden, Bronx, New York, (1977.)

Primate Conservation. World Wildlife Fund and the Department of Anatomical Sciences of the State University of New York at Stony Brook, No. 6, (July 1985.) No. 7, (1986.)

Putman, John T. "India Struggles to Save Her Wildlife." *National Geographic*, Vol. 150, No. 3, (September 1976.)

Pyle, Robert Michael. "How to Conserve Insects for Fun and Profit." *Terra*, Vol. 17, No. 4, (Spring, 1979.)

Raloff, Janet and Joanne Silberrer. "Saving the Amazon." *Science News*, Vol. 118, No. 14, (4 October 1980.)

Raven, Peter H. The Destruction of the Tropics. *Frontiers*, (July 1976.)

———— "A National Commitment." *St. Louis Post* – Dispatch Centennial Edition, (25 March 1979.)

———— *Natural Heritage*. Missouri Botanical Garden, Presentation at International Council of Museums, Mexico City, (27 October 1980.)

———— Prepared Statement. Missouri Botanical Garden and National Research Council Committee on Research Priorities in Tropical Biology, U.S. House of Representatives, (7 May 1980.)

———— "Tropical Rain Forests: A Global Responsibility." *Natural History*, Vol. 90, No. 2, (February 1981.)

———— "Plants: The Roots of Life." *Focus*, Vol. 6, No. 5, (September/October 1984.)

———— "The Urgency of Tropical Conservation." *The Nature Conservancy News*, Vol. 35, No. 1, (January 1986.)

Reid, Walter V. and Kenton R. Miller. *Keeping Options Alive – The Scientific Basis for Conserving Biodiversity*. World Resources Institute, (1989.)

Richards, Paul W. "Tropical Rain Forest." *Scientific American*, (December 1973.)

———— "The Tropical Rain Forest." *Scientific American*, Vol. 229, No. 6, (December 1977.)

"Rondonia: Brazil's Imperiled Rain Forest." *National Geographic*, Vol. 174, No. 6, (December 1988.)

Roush, G. Jon. "On Saving Diversity." *The Nature Conservancy News*, (January/February 1982.)

Russell, Robert Jay. "The Future's Burning on Madagascar Island." *Defenders*, (August 1978.)

Shepard, Mark. Chipko: North India's Tree Huggers. *The CoEvolution Quarterly*, (Fall, 1981.)

Simberloff, Daniel. "Big Advantages of Small Refuges." *Natural History*, (April 1982.)

Soderstrom, T. R. and C. E. Calderon. "*Curtains for this Bamboo? The Mysterious Flowering of Ma-Dake*". Pacific Horticulture. Vol. 37 3 (July 1976.)

Stark, Elizabeth. *You Can't See the Forest For the Trees*. Crosscurrents Science, (1981.)

Steinlin, Hans Turgen. "Monitoring the World's Tropical Forests." *Unasylva*, an international journal of forestry and forest industries, FAO, Vol. 34, No. 137, (1982.)

Stone, Donald E. "*Rationale for Maintenance and Development of La Selva Field Station*". Organization for Tropical Studies, Inc, (1978.)

Tangley, Laura. "Captive Propagation: Will it Succeed?" *Science News*, Vol. 121, No. 16, (17 April 1982.)

Terborgh, John. "Preservation of Natural Diversity: The Problem of Extinction of Species." *Bio Science*, Vol. 24, No. 12, (December 1974.)

"Toward a Troubled 21st Century [Environment]." *Time*, (4 August 1980.)

Van Heijnsbergen, P. "Declaration of the Rights of Animal and Plant Life." *Flora Malesiana Bulletin*, (1978.)

Weber, Bill. "Gorilla Problems in Rwanda." *Swara*, East African Wildlife Society, Vol. 2, No. 4, (1979.)

White, Peter T. "Nature's Dwindling Treasures: Rain Forests." *National Geographic*, Vol. 163, No. 1, (January 1983.)

Wilson, Edward O. "Interview." *Calypso Log*, Pub. of the Cousteau Society, Vol. 7, No. 3, (September 1980.)

———— "Million-Year Histories: Species Diversity as an Ethical Goal." *Wilderness*, (Summer, 1984.)

Wolf, Arol. "Arnold Newman – Rain Forest Naturalist." *Ecolibrium Interviews*, (1984.)

"World Bank Adopts Wildland Policy." *International Society of Tropical Foresters News*, Vol. 7, No. 4, (December 1986.)

The World's Tropical Forests: A Policy, Strategy and Program for the United States. Report to the President by a U.S. Interagency Task Force on Tropical Forests, (May 1980.)

DEFORESTATION

American Forests Magazine, Vol. 94, Nos. 11, 12, (November/December 1988.)

Bankrolling Disasters: International Development Banks and the Global Environment. Sierra Club (1986.)

Changing the Global Environment. Edited by Daniel B. Botkin et al. Academic Press (1989.)

"Deforestation: Precursor of Famine." Hunger Report. Select Committee on Hunger, U.S. House of Representatives, Washington, D.C., (1986.)

Deforestation: Social Dynamics in Watersheds and Mountain Ecosystems. Edited by J. Ives and D. C. Pitt. Routledge, (1988.)

"Disappearing Forests Cause Concern." *Geographical Magazine*, Vol. LIV, NO. 7, (July 1982.)

"Earth Sciences, If a Tree Falls and No One Hears." *Science News*, Vol. 120, No. 21, (21 November 1981.)

Eckholm, Erik. "Human Wants and Misused Lands." *Natural History*, (June 1982.)

Ewel, John. "Special Issue on Tropical Succession." *Biotropica*, Supplement to Vol. 12, No. 2, (June 1980.)

Hamilton, A. C. *Deforestation in Uganda*. Oxford University Press, (East African Wildlife Society), (1984).

Lovejoy, Thomas E. The Transamazonia: Highway to Extinction. *Frontiers*, (Spring, 1973.)

Mahar, Dennis. *Government Policies and Deforestation in Brazil's Amazon Region*. World Bank Publication, (1989.)

Malingreau, J.P. and C.J. Tucker. "Large Scale Deforestation in the Southeastern Amazon Basin of Brazil." *Ambio*, Vol. 17, No. 1, (1988.)

Mardon, Mark. "The Big Push." *Sierra*, (November/December 1988).

"Nepal Reforests Denuded Lands." International Society of Tropical Foresters, *ISTF News*, Vol. 4, No. 3, (September 1983.)

Newman, Arnold and Brent Blackwelder. "Tropical Deforestation: Global Consequences and Alternatives." *Znanie* Science and Humanities Yearbook – The Future of Science and Our Planet, (1989.)

Pan American Highway, Darien Gap, Tocumen, Panama; to Rio Leon, Colombia. U.S. Dept. of Transportation Federal Highway Administration, (May 1976.)

Pickett, Karen. *Global Deforestation and the World Bank: Are Your Taxes Financing Rainforest Destruction?* World Rainforest Report, No 7, (1986.)

Prothero, Mansell R. *Migrants and Malaria*. Longmans, Green & Co. Ltd., (1965.)

Tasker, Georgia. "The Vanishing Rain Forest." *Miami Herald*, (21 September 1986.)

———— "The Vanishing Rain Forest." *Miami Herald*, (28 September 1986).

Tropical Deforestation. U.S. Strategy Conference, U.S. Agency for International Development, Washington, D.C., (12–13 June 1978.)

Uhl, Christopher. "You Can Keep a Good Forest Down." *Natural History*, Vol. 92, No. 4, (April 1983.)

"Unraveling the Economics of Deforestation." *Science News*, Vol. 133, No. 23, (4 June 1988.)

Where Have all the Flowers Gone? Deforestation in the Third World. Studies in Third World Societies, No. 13, (1981.)

FOREST RESOURCES

Abbey, Edward. "Reasonable Needs Vs. Irrational Uses." *Defenders*, (October 1978.)

Adamson, W. C., M. O. Bagby, and W. B. Roth. "Oil Polyphenol and Hydrocarbon Content in Culms of Phyllostachys Species." *Journal of the American Bamboo Society*, Vol. 3, No. 2, (May 1982.)

Balick, Michael J. "The Palm Heart as a New Commercial Crop from Tropical Americana." *Principes*, Journal of the Palm Society, Vol. 20, No. 1, (January 1976.)

Beckerman, Stephen. "The Use of

Palms by the Bari Indians of the Maracaibo Basin." *Principes*, Journal of the Palm Society, Vol. 21, No. 4, (October 1977.)

"Brazilian Tree Pours Pure Diesel Fuel." *Science News*, Vol. 116, No. 11, (15 September 1979.)

Duke, James A. "Palms as Energy Sources: A Solicitation." *Principes*, Journal of the Palm Society, Vol. 21, No. 2, (April 1977.)

Kreig, Margaret. *Green Medicine: A Search for Plants that Heal*. Rand, (1964.)

Lanly, Jean-Paul. *Tropical Forest Resources*. Food and Agriculture Organization of the United Nations, (1982.)

Leontiet, Wassily W. "The World Economy of the Year 2000." *Scientific American*, (September 1980.)

McIntyre, Loren. "Treasure Chest or Pandora's Box? Brazil's Wild Frontiers." *National Geographic*, Vol. 152, No. 5, (November 1977.)

Minimum Conflict: Guidelines for Planning the Use of American Humid Tropic Environments. General Secretariat, Organization of American States, Washington, D.C., (1987.)

Perdue, Robert E., Jr., and J. L. Hartwell. *Proceedings of the 16th Annual Meeting of the Society for Economic Botany, Plants and Cancer*. Cancer Treatment Reports 66, Cancer Institute, Md., (August 1976.)

Peters, Charles M., *et al.* "Valuation of an Amazonian Rainforest." *Nature*, Vol. 339, (29 June 1989.)

Popenoe. Wilson. *Manual of Tropical and Sub-Tropical Fruits*. Fafner Press, Div. of Macmillan Press, (1974.)

Research Priorities in Tropical Biology. National Research Council, National Academy of Sciences, Washington, D.C., (1980.)

Schultes, Richard Evans. "Promising Structural Fiber Palms of the Colombian Amazon." *Principes*, Journal of the Palm Society, Vol. 21, No. 2, (April 1977.)

The State of Forest Resources in the Developing Countries – An Interim Report. FAO, (1988.)

Technologies to Sustain Tropical Forest Resources. U.S. Congress, Office of Technology Assessment, F–214, (March 1984.)

"Trade Pressures on Species Mount." *Focus*, World Wildlife Fund – U.S., Vol. 4, No. 2, (Spring 1982.)

Tropical Forest Resources Assessment Project. Country Briefs; Tropical Asia, Tropical America, Tropical Africa. FAO/ United Nations, (1981.)

UNESCO/UNEP/FAO Tropical Forest Ecosystems. A State of Knowledge Report, (1978.)

Yearbook of Forest Products. FAO, Rome, (1975–1986.)

FUELWOOD

Firewood Crops: Shrub and Tree Species for Energy Production. National Academy Press, (1983.)

Mangium and Other Acacias of the Humid Tropics. National Academy Press, (1983.)

"Wood Famine in Developing Nations." *Science News*, Vol. 115, No. 8, (24 February 1979.)

Wood for Energy. FAO, Forestry Topics Report No. 1.

HISTORICAL PERSPECTIVE

Darwin, Charles. *The Voyage of the Beagle*. Doubleday & Co., (1879.)

Doyle, James A. *Fossil Evidence on the Evolutionary Origin of Tropical Trees and Forests*. Cambridge University Press, Fourth Cabot Symposium Harvard, Forest, Petersham, MA., (26–30 April 1976.)

Flenley, John. *The Equatorial Rain Forest: A Geological History*. Butterworths, (1979.)

Lissner, Ivar. *The Living Past: 7,000 Years of Civilization*. Capricorn Books, (1961.)

Moody, Richard. *The Fossil World*. Chartwell Books, (1977.)

Peirse, Henry Beresford. "The Evolution of Forestry – The Latest Trends in Thinking." *Unasylva*, Vol. 16 (3), No. 66, FAO, (1962.)

Pfeiffer, John E. *The Emergence of Society*. McGraw-Hill Book Co., (1977.)

Romer, Alfred Sherwood, *Vertebrate Paleontology*. The University of Chicago Press, (1974.)

Thoreau, Henry David. *Walden and Civil Disobedience*. Harper & Row, (1965.)

Zon, Raphael and William N. Sparhawk. *Forest Resources of the World*. McGraw-Hill Book Co., (1923.)

PLANTATION FORESTRY

Chapman, G. W. and T. G. Allan. *Establishment Techniques for Forest Plantations*. Forest Resources Division, Forestry Dept., Food and Agriculture Organization of the United Nations, (1978.)

Eckholm, Erik. "Planting for the Future: Forestry for Human Needs." *World Watch* Paper 26, (February 1979.)

Fu-geng Qui. "*Phyllostachys pubescens* in China." *Journal of the American Bamboo Society*, Vol. 3, No. 3, (August 1982.)

Eucalypts for Planting. FAO, (1979.)

McIntyre, Loren. "Jari: A Billion Dollar Gamble." *National Geographic*, Vol. 150, No. 5, (May 1980.)

Marden, Luis. "Bamboo, The Giant Grass." *National Geographic*, Vol. 158, No. 4, (October 1980.)

Oshima, Jinsaburo. "The Culture of Moso Bamboo in Japan, Part I." *Journal of the American Bamboo Society*, Vol. 3, No. 1, (February 1982.)

Routhey, R. and V. *The Fight for the Forests: The Takeover of Australian Forests for Pine, Wood Chips and Intensive Forestry*. Australian National University, (1975.)

"Taiwan Uses *Leucaena* for Laminated Veneers." International Society of Tropical Foresters, *ISTF News* Vol. 4, No. 3, (September 1983.)

Takama, Shinji. *The World of Bamboo*. Heian International Inc., (1983.)

"Trinidad and Tobago Plantations Pay." *A Bulletin of the International Society of Tropical Foresters*, Vol. 3, No. 4, (December 1984.)

Vietmeyer, Noel. "The Tree that Does Everything." *International*

Wildlife, (September/October 1983.)

Willan, R. L. *Forest Research – British Overseas Aid – 1976–1982*. Commonwealth Forestry Institute, (1985.)

POPULATION

Ending Hunger – An Idea Whose Time Has Come. The Hunger Project. Praeger, (1985.)

Ehrlich, Paul R. *The Population Bomb*. Ballantine Pub., (1968.)

Griffin, Michael. "Madagascar's High Fertility Rate Leads to Chronic Poverty." *Popline*, (April 1988.)

Janzen, Daniel H. *Additional Land at What Price? Responsible Use of the Tropics in a Food-Population Confrontation*. American Phytopathological Society, (1977.)

McEvedy, Colin and Richard Jones. *Atlas of World Population History*. Penguin Reference Books, (1978.)

Raloff, Janet. "Earth Day 1980: The 29th Day?" *Science News*, Vol. 117, No. 17, (26 April 1980.)

Thomas, Lewis. "Are We Fit to Fit In?" *Sierra*, (March/April 1982.)

World Population Data Sheet of the Population Reference Bureau, Inc., (1987.)

PUBLIC HEALTH

Arnold, Robert E. *What to do About Bites and Stings of Venomous Animals*. Collier Books, (1973.)

Castanheira, Emilio. "Brazil: A Cure in Sight For River Blindness." *World Rivers Review*, Vol. 2, No. 6, (November/December 1987.)

"Dread Disease Carriers." *National Geographic*, Vol. 156, No. 3, (September 1979.)

Hunter, George W. *et al.* *A Manual of Tropical Medicine*. W. B. Saunders & Co., (1960.)

"Malaria Vaccine Trials are Qualified Success." *Science News*, Vol. 133, No. 13, (26 March 1988.)

Nielsen, Lewis T. "Mosquitoes, The Mighty Killer," *National Geographic*, Vol. 156, No. 3, (September 1979.)

Williams, Nick B., Jr., "Rain Forest and Its Medical Secrets Shrinking Fast." *Los Angeles Times*, (11 April 1988.)

Zimmerman, David. "The Mosquitoes are Coming – And They Are Among Man's Most Lethal Foes." *Smithsonian*, (June 1983.)

SUSTAINABLE AGRICULTURE

"Agroforestry in Sabah." International Society of Tropical Foresters, *ISTF News*, Vol. 3, No. 4, (December 1984.)

Agroforestry Systems in the Tropics. Edited by P. K. R. Nair, Kluwer Academic Publishers, (1989.)

Brewbaker, James L. *A Bulletin of the Nitrogen Fixing Tree Association*, (1984.)

Brill, Winston R. "Agricultural Microbiology." *Scientific American*, (September 1981.)

Calliandra: A Versatile Small Tree for the Humid Tropics. National Academy Press, (1983.)

Chen Ding. "The Economic Development of China." *Scientific American*, (September 1980.)

Clark, Wilson. "China's Green Manure Revolution." *Science 80*, (September/October 1980.)

Cooperatively Managed Panamanian Rural Fish Ponds – The Integrated Approach. Auburn University, (1986.)

Dazhong, Wen and David Pimentel. "Seventeenth Century Organic Agriculture in China: I. Cropping Systems in Jiaxing Region." *Human Ecology*, Vol. 14, No. 1, (1986.)

——— "Seventeenth Century Organic Agriculture in China: II. Energy Flows Through an Agroecosystem in Jiaxing Region." *Human Ecology*, Vol. 14, No. 1, (1986.)

The Development of Commercial Farming of Tilapia in Jamaica, 1979–1983. Auburn University, (October 1984.)

Ending Hunger – An Idea Whose Time Has Come. The Hunger Project, Praeger, (1985.)

Enough Food. Rodale Institute, (1985.)

Fragile Lands of Latin America – Strategies for Sustainable Development. Edited by John O. Browder. Westview Press, (1989.)

Gradwohl, Judith and Russel Greenberg. *Saving the Tropical Forests*. Earthscan Publications Ltd., (1988.)

Gruezo, William Sm. and Hugh C. Harris. "Self Sown, Wild-Type Coconuts in the Philippines." *Biotropica*, Vol, 16, No. 2, (June 1984.)

Hamblin, Dora Jane. "Experiment in Tunisia Effects Pause in Spread of Sahara's Expanding Sands." *Smithsonian*, Vol. 10, No. 5, (August 1979.)

Hart, Robert D. "A Natural Ecosystem Analogy Approach to the Design of a Successional Crop System for Tropical Forest Environments." *Biotropica*, Supplement to Vol. 12, No. 2, (June 1980.)

Hindley, Keith. "Reviving the Food of the Aztecs." *Science News*, Vol. 116, No. 10, (8 September 1979.)

Huxley, Peter A. *Plant Research and Agroforestry*. International Council for Research in Agroforestry, Nairobi, Kenya, (1983.)

"Integrated Aquaculture Extension Care/Guatemala, 1986–1989." Auburn University, (1 August 1989.)

Jordan, Carl F. *Nutrient Cycling in Tropical Forest Ecosystems*. John Wiley & Sons, (1985.)

Lal, R. "Conversion of Tropical Rainforest: Agronomic Potential and Ecological Consequences." *Advances in Agronomy*, Vol. 39, (1986.)

Mortensen, Ernest and Ervin T. Bullard. *Handbook of Tropical and Subtropical Horticulture*. Dept. of State Agency for International Development, Washington, D.C., (1970.)

Mossman, Sun Lee and S. Archie. *Wildlife Utilization and Game Ranching*. National Union for Conservation of Nature and Natural Resources, Morges, Switzerland, (1976.)

Muskie, Secretary E. *Securing the World's Common Future*. U. S. Dept. of State Bureau of Public Affairs, Washington, D.C., No. 213, (25 August 1980.)

Nicholaides, J. J., with D. E. Bandy, *et al.* "Agricultural Alternatives for the Amazon Basin." *Bioscience,* Vol. 35, No. 5, (May 1985.)

"Our Common Future." IIED/ *Earthscan,* (1986/1987.)

Padoch, Christine, *et al.* "Amazonian Agroforestry: A Market-Oriented System in Peru. " *Agroforestry Systems* 3: 47–58. Martinus Nijhoff/Dr. W. Junk publishers, (1985.)

—— and Wil de Jong. "Production and Profit in Agroforestry: An Example from the Peruvian Amazon." In *Fragile Lands of Latin America – Strategies for Sustainable Development.* Edited by John O. Browder. Westview Press, (1989.)

Peters, William J. and Neuenschwander, Leon F. *Slash and Burn – Farming in the Third World Forest.* University of Idaho Press, (1988.)

Price, Norman William. *The Tropical Mixed Garden in Costa Rica: A Potential Focus for Agroforestry Research.* Unpublished doctorate thesis. University of British Columbia, (1989.)

"Rwanda National Fish Culture Project." Auburn University, (July 1989.)

Soil Erosion and Conservation. Edited by S. A. El-Swaify *et al.* Soil Conservation Society of America, (1985.)

Snedaker, Samuel C. "Successful Immobilization of Nutrients and Biologically Mediated Recycling in Tropical Forests." *Biotropica,* Supplement to Vol. 12, No. 2, (June 1980.)

Sustainable Agricultural Systems. Edited by Clive A. Edwards *et al.* Soil and Water Conservation Society, (1990.)

"Technology for the Tropics." *Science News,* Vol. 125, No. 13, (31 March, 1984.)

Tropical Forests: A Call for Action. World Resources Institute, the World Bank, and United Nations Development Program, (1985.)

Tull, Kenneth and Michael Sands. *Experiences in Success: Case Studies in Growing Enough Food Through Regenerative Agriculture.* Rodale Institute, (1987.)

"Turtle Farm Exemption Requested." *Science News,* Vol. 121, No. 16, (17 April 1982.)

"Underlying Causes of World Hunger." *Report of the Institute of Food and Development Policy,* (undated.)

Willis, Harold. *The Coming Revolution in Agriculture.* H. L. Willis, (1985.)

Young, Anthony. *Agroforestry for Soil Conservation.* C. A. B. International, (1989.)

SUSTAINABLE AND UNSUSTAINABLE LOGGING

Adeyoju, S. Kolade. *Forestry and the Nigerian Economy.* Ibadan University Press, (1975.)

"Can Surinam Rainforests Sustain Yield?" International Society of Tropical Foresters, *ISTF News,* Vol. 4, No. 3, (September 1983.)

"Can Timber Plantations Save Tropical Forests?: Philippine Rattan Faces Repletion in Natural Forests; Forest Operations Move to the Mountains." International Society of Tropical Foresters, *ISTF News,* Vol. 4, No. 2, (June 1983.)

"Forest Loss/Renewal Rates." International Society of Tropical Foresters, *ISTF News,* Vol. 7, No. 3, (September 1986.)

Forest Revenue Systems for Developing Countries. FAO Forestry Paper No. 43, FAO, (1983.)

Harcombe, P. A. "Soil Nutrient Loss as a Factor in Early Tropical Secondary Succession." *Biotropica,* Supplement to Vol. 12, No. 2, (June 1980.)

Hyde, William F. *Timber Supply, Land Allocation and Economic Efficiency.* Johns Hopkins University Press, (1980.)

Intensive Multiple-Use Forest Management in Kerala. FAO Forestry Paper No. 53, FAO, (1984.)

"International Society of Tropical Foresters." Bulletin of the International Society of Tropical Foresters, *ISTF News,* Vol. 5, No. 1, (March 1984.)

Janos, David P. "Mycorrhizae Influence on Tropical Succession." *Biotropica,* Supplement to Vol. 12, No. 2, (June 1980.)

LaMois, Loyd M. "International Year of the Forest Promotes Forestry and Food Security." International Society of Tropical Foresters, *ISTF News,* Vol. 7, No. 4, (September 1986.)

Lebron, Maria L. "Physiological Plant Ecology: Some Contributions to the Understanding of Secondary Succession in Tropical Lowland Rainforest." *Biotropica,* Supplement to Vol. 12, No. 2, (June 1980.)

Lugo, Ariel E. and Sandra Brown. "Tropical Ecosystems and the Human Factor." *Unasylva,* Vol. 33, No. 133, (1981.)

Poore, Duncan. *Ecological Guidelines for Development in Tropical Rain Forests.* IUCN Books, (1976.)

—— and Jeffrey Sayer. *The Management of Tropical Moist Forest Lands – Ecological Guidelines.* IUCN, (1987.)

Rain Forest Regeneration and Management. Edited by Malcolm Hadley. IUBS/UNESCO, (1988.)

Repetto, Robert. *The Forest for the Trees?* World Resources Institute, (May 1988.)

Roselle, Mike and Tracy Katelman. *Tropical Hardwoods.* Rainforest Action Network, (1989.)

Stocker, G. C. "Regeneration of a North Queensland Rain Forest Following Felling and Burning." *Biotropica,* Vol. 13, No. 2, (June 1981.)

Tropical Forest Resources Management. Second Expert Meeting on Tropical Forests, Rome. Sponsored by UNEP, FAO, and UNESCO, (12–15 January 1982.)

Tropical Forests: A Call for Action. World Resources Institute, the World Bank, and United Nations Development Programme, (1985.)

Whitmore, J. L. "International Union of Forestry Research Organization Call for Action on Pollution and Tropical Deforestation." *Journal of Forestry.* XVIII IUFRO World Congress, (February 1987.)

Whitmore, T. C. *A First Look at A'gathis Forestry,* Oxford, (1977.)

TRADITIONAL CULTURES

Bailey, Robert C., *et al.* "Hunting and Gathering in Tropical Rain Forest: Is it Possible?" *American Anthropologist,* Vol. 91, No. 1, (1989.)

Bower, Bruce. "The Strange Case of the Tasaday" *Science News,* Vol. 135, No. 18, 280–281, (6 May 1989.)

Chagnon, Napolean A. "Yạnomamö, The True People." *National Geographic,* Vol. 150, No. 2, (August 1976.)

Clay, Jason W. *Indigenous Peoples and Tropical Forests.* Cultural Survival, Inc. Report 27, (1988.)

Connolly, Bob and Robin Anderson. *First Contact.* Viking, (1987.)

Devillers, Carol. "What Future for the Wayana Indians?" *National Geographic,* Vol. 163, No. 1, (January 1983.)

Gardener, Robert and Karl G. Heider. *Gardens of War, Life and Death in the New Guinea Stone Age.* Random House, (1968.)

Goetz, Inga Steinvorth. *Uriji Jami!* Dra. Inga Steinvorth Goetz, (1969.)

Hallet, Jean-Pierre, *Newsletter of the Pygmy Fund.* Thanksgiving, (1982.)

—— with Alex Pelle. *Pygmy Kitabu.* Random House, (1973.)

Kirk, Malcolm S. "Change Ripples New Guinea's Sepik River." *National Geographic,* Vol. 144, No. 3, (September 1973.)

—— *Man as Art: New Guinea.* Viking Press, (1981.)

Lamb, Bruce F. *Wizard of the Upper Amazon: The Story of Manuel Cordova-Rios.* Houghton-Mifflin Co., (1974.)

Lea, Vanessa. "Beset by a Golden Curse: Brazil's Kayapo Indians." *National Geographic,* Vol. 165, No. 5, (May 1984.)

Maybury, Lewis David. "Conditions Worsen for Brazil's Indians." Editorial, *Cultural Survival Quarterly,* Vol. 7, No. 4, (Winter, 1983.)

Nance, John. *The Gentle Tasaday.* Harcourt, Brace, Jovanovich, (1975.)

People and the Tropical Forest. A research Report from the United States Man and the Biosphere Program. U.S. Department of Commerce, Washington, D.C., (1987.)

People of the Tropical Rain Forest. Edited by Denslow, J. and C.Padoch. University of California Press, Berkeley, in association with Smithsonian Institution, Traveling Exhibition Service, (1988.)

Rogers, E. S. *Forgotten Peoples.* Royal Ontario Museum, (1974.)

Severin, Timothy. *The Horizon Book of Vanishing Primitive Man.* American Heritage Pub. Co., (1973.)

Stewart, Kilton. *Pygmies and Dream Giants.* Harper Colophon Books, (1975.)

Turnbull, Colin. *The Forest People.* Chatto, (1961.)

—— *The Mountain People.* Touchstone Books, Simon and Schuster, (1972.)

Weyer, Edward T. *Primitive Peoples Today.* Doubleday & Co. Inc., (1958.)

TROPICAL FORESTS – GENERAL

Bates, Marston. *The Forest and the Sea.* Vintage Books, (1960.)

Beebe, William. *Jungle Days.* G. P. Putnam & Sons, (1925.)

Boza, Mario A. with collaboration of Alexander Bonilla. *The National Parks of Costa Rica.* Instituto de la Caza Fotografica y Ciencias de la Naturaleza (INCAFO), (1978.)

Coughlan, Robert. *Tropical Africa.* Life World Library, Time Inc. Pub., (1963.)

DuChaillu, Paul. *The Great Forest of Equatorial Africa.* Harper & Brothers Co., (1890.)

Dynamic Properties of Forest Ecosystems. Edited by D. E. Reochle. Cambridge University Press, (1981.)

Ecosystems of the World 14A. Elsevier Scientific Pub. Co., (1983.)

Ecosystems of the World 14B. Elsevier Scientific Pub. Co., (1989.)

Emsley, Michael. *Rain Forests and Cloud Forests.* Harry N. Abrams, (1979.)

Forest Succession: Concepts and Applications. Edited by Darrell C. West, *et al.* Springer-Verlag, (1980.)

Forsyth, Adrian and Ken Miyata. *Tropical Nature – Life and Death in the Rain Forests of Central and South America.* Charles Scribner's Sons, (1984.)

George, Uwe. *Regen-Wald: Vorstob in das Tropische Universum.* GEO, (1985.)

Holdridge, L. R. and W. C. Grenke, *et al. Tropical Environments in Tropical Life Zones – A Pilot Study.* Pergamon Press, (1971.)

Hughes, Carol and David. "Teeming Life of a Rain Forest." *National Geographic,* Vol. 163, No. 1, (January 1983.)

Jackson, Donald Dale. "Venezuela's 'Mountain of the Mists'." *Smithsonian,* Vol. 16, No. 2, (May 1985.)

Jacobs, M. *The Tropical Rain Forest, A First Encounter.* Springer-Verlag, (1988.)

Jungles. Edited by Edward S. Ayensu. Crown Publishers, (1980.)

Longman, K. A. and J. Jenik. *Tropical Forest and Its Environment.* 2nd edition. Longman Scientific and Technical, (1987.)

Mackay, Rod D. and the Editors of Time-Life Books. *New Guinea.* Time-Life International, (1976.)

MacKinnon, John. *Borneo: The World's Wild Places.* Time-Life International, (1975.)

Matthiessen, Peter. *The Cloud Forest.* Viking Press, (1961.)

Meggers, Betty J., Edward S. Ayensu, and W. Donald Duckworth. *Tropical Forest Ecosystems in Africa and South America: A Comparative Review,* Smithsonian Institution Press, (1973.)

Morrison, Tony. *The Andes.* Time-Life International, (1975.)

Moser, Don. *Central American Jungles.* Time-Life Books, (1975.)

Myers, Norman, *The Primary Source.* W. W. Norton & Co., (1984.)

Nations, James D. *Tropical Rainforests: Endangered Environment.* Franklin Watts, (1988.)

Newman, Arnold. *The Lungs of our Planet: The Tropical Rain Forest: Earth's First Endangered Habitat.* Mir Publishers, (1989.)

Nicholson, Nigel and the Editors of Time-Life. *The Himalayas.* Time-Life International, (1975.)

Perry, Donald. "An Arboreal Naturalist Explores the Rain Forest's Mysterious Canopy." *Smithsonian*, (June 1980.)
—— and John Williams. "The Tropical Rain Forest Canopy: A Method of Providing Total Access." *Biotropica*, Vol. 19, No. 4, (December 1981.)
—— "The Canopy of the Tropical Rain Forest." *Scientific American*, Vol. 251, No. 5, (November 1984.)
—— *Life Above the Jungle Floor.* Simon and Schuster, Inc., (1986.)
Preston, Douglas T. "Expedition to the Mountain of the Mists." *Natural History*, (September 1984.)
Productivity of Forest Ecosystems: Proceedings of the Brussels Symposium organized by UNESCO and the International Biological Program 27–31 October 1969. Edited by P. Duvigneaud, UNESCO, (1971.)
Richards, Paul W. *The Tropical Rain Forest.* Cambridge University Press, (1966.)
—— *The Life of the Jungle.* McGraw-Hill Book Co. Inc., (1970.)
—— *Tropical Forests and Woodlands: An Overview.* Agro-Ecosystems, (1977.)
Sanderson, Ivan T. *Green Silence, The Story of the Making of a Naturalist.* David McKay Co. Inc., (1924.)
—— *Ivan Sanderson's Book of Great Jungles.* Julian Messner Pub., (1965.)
Satoo, T. and H. A. I. Madgwick. *Forest Resources.* Martinus Nijhoff and Dr. W. Junk Publishers, (1982.)
Schultz, Jack C. *Ecological Studies on Rain Forests in Northern Suriname.* Noord-Hollandsche VITG Mit., Amsterdam, (1960.)
Seilman, Heinz. *Wilderness Expeditions.* Franklin Watts Pub., (1981.)
Skutch, Alexander F. *A Naturalist in Costa Rica.* University of Florida Press, (1971.)
—— *A Bird Watcher's Adventures in Tropical America.* University of Texas Press, (1977.)
Smith, Anthony. *Mato Grosso.* E. P. Dutton & Co. Inc., (1971.)
Spurr, Stephen H. and Burton V. Barnes. *Forest Ecology.* John Wiley & Sons, (1980.)
White, K. T. *The Lowland Rain Forest in Papua New Guinea,* Pacific Science Association Pre-Congress Conference, Bogor, (12–17 August 1971.)
Whitmore, T.C. *Tropical Rain Forests of the Far East.* Clarendon Press, Oxford University, (1975.)
Whitten, A. J., et al. *The Ecology of Sumatra.* Gadjah Mada University Press, (1987.)
Williams, John A. *Africa: Her History, Lands and People.* Cooper Square Pub. Inc., (1965.)
Williamson, Bruce G. *OTS 82–1 Tropical Biology: An Ecological Approach.* Dept. of Biology, University of Miami, Coral Gables, Florida, (1982.)

ZOOLOGY

"Alligators: Clue to the Dinosaurs' Demise?" *Science News*, Vol. 121, No. 2, (15 May 1982.)

Bower, Bruce. "Bird's Eye View of Early Primate Scene." *Science News*, Vol. 130, No. 11, (13 September 1986.)
Brick, Hans. *The Nature of the Beast.* Crown Publishers, Inc., (1962.)
Buchsbaum, Ralph and Lovus T. Milne. *The Lower Animals: Living Invertebrates of the World.* Doubleday & Co. Inc., (1967.)
Buckley, Eleanor E. and Nandor Porges. *Vemoms.* The American Association for the Advancement of Science, (1958.)
Burton, Maurice and Robert. *Encyclopedia of Insects and Arachnids.* Octopus Books Ltd., (1975.)
Caras, Roger A. *Dangerous to Man.* Chilton Books, (1964.)
Carr, Archie. "Bitten by A Fer-de-Lance." *Natural History* (1969.)
"*Cecropia – Azteca* Association: A Case of Mutualism?" *Biotropica*, Vol. 14, No. 1, (March 1982.)
Cochran, Doris M. *Living Amphibians of the World.* Doubleday & Co., (1961.)
Colbert, Edwin H. *The Age of Reptiles.* W. W. Norton & Co. Inc., (1965.)
Conniff, Richard. "Inventorying Life in a 'Biotic Frontier' Before it Disappears." *Smithsonian*, Vol. 17, No. 6, (September 1986.)
Crocodiles and Alligators. Edited by Charles A. Ross. Facts on File, (1989.)
Curran, C. H. and Carl Kauffeld. *Snakes and Their Ways.* Harper & Brothers, (1937.)
Denis, Armand. *Cats of the World.* Houghton Mifflin Co., (1964.)
Ditmars, Raymond L. *Snakes of the World.* Macmillan & Co., (1952.)
Fossey, Dian. "Making Friends with Mountain Gorillas." *National Geographic*, Vol. 137, No. 1, (January 1970.)
—— "The Nature of the Free Living Gorilla." *Terra* (the Natural History Museum of Los Angeles County) Vol. 22, No. 1, (September/October 1983.)
—— "More Years with Mountain Gorillas." *National Geographic*, Vol. 140, No. 4, (October 1971.)
Galdikas-Brindamour, Biruté. "Orangutans, Indonesia's 'People of the Forest.'" *National Geographic*, Vol. 148, No. 4, (October 1975.)
Garret, J. Ros. *Venomous Australian Animals Dangerous to Man.* Commonwealth Serum Laboratories, (1968.)
Gilliard, E. Thomas. *Living Birds of the World.* Doubleday & Co. Inc., (1958.)
Gore, Rick. "A Bad Time to be a Crocodile." *National Geographic*, Vol. 153, No. 1, (January 1978.)
Hanzak, J. *The Pictorial Encyclopedia of Birds.* Paul Hamlyn, Pub., (1967.)
Hermann, Henry R. *Social Insects.* Vol. IV, Academic Press, (1982.)
Hogue, Charles L. *The Armies of the Ant.* World Publishing, (1972.)
Jackson, James F. "Seed Size as a Correlate of Temporal and Spatial Patterns of Seed Fall in a Neotropical Forest." *Biotropica*, Vol. 13, No. 2, (June 1981.)
Jacobs, M. "The Study of Lianas." *Flora Malesiana Bulletin 29*, (1976.)
Janzen, Daniel H. *Costa Rican Natural History.* University of Chicago Press, (1983.)

—— *The Impact of Tropical Studies on Ecology.* The Changing Scenes in Natural Sciences, Academy of Natural Sciences, Special Publication 12, (1977.)
Klots, Alexander B. and Elsie B. *Living Insects of the World.* Doubleday & Co., (1967.)
Kursh, Harry. *Cobras in his Garden.* Harvey House Inc., (1965.)
Landsburg, Alan. *The Insects are Coming.* Warner Books, (1978.)
Lessen, Don. "From Bugs to Boas, Dan Janzen Bags the Rich Coast's Life." *Smithsonian*, Vol. 17, No. 9, (December 1986.)
Lewin, Roger. *Thread of Life: The Smithsonian Looks at Evolution.* Smithsonian Books, (1982.)
MacKinnon, John. *In Search of the Red Ape.* Holt-Rinehart and Winston, (1974.)
Magnificent Foragers, The. Smithsonian Exposition Books, W. W. Norton & Co., (1978.)
Miller, Julie Ann. "A Skunk of a Beetle." *Science News*, Vol. 115, No. 20, (19 May 1979.)
Myers, Charles E. and John W. Daly. "Dart-Poison Frogs." *Scientific American*, (February 1983.)
Newman, Arnold C. "An Incident on the Rio Claro." *A Bulletin of the International Palm Society*, (1977.)
Olson, S. and H. James. *Land Birds of Hawaii: 1500-Year Record (Human Settlement).* Smithsonian Institution, (1984.)
Poisonous Snakes of the World. Dept. of Navy, Office of the Chief of Naval Operations, Office of Naval Intelligence, (June 1962.)
Pope, Clifford H. *The Giant Snakes.* Alfred A. Knopf, (1969.)
—— *The Reptile World.* Borzoi Books, Alfred A. Knopf, (1955).
Pritchard, Peter C. H. *Encyclopedia of Turtles.* T. H. F. Publishers, Inc., (1967.)
—— *Living Turtles of the World.* T.H.F. Publishers, Inc., (1967.)
Sanderson, Ivan T. *Living Mammals of the World.* Hanover House, Division of Doubleday & Co., (1955.)
Schaller, George B. *The Mountain Gorilla.* University of Chicago Press, (1976.)
—— *The Year of the Gorilla.* University of Chicago Press, (1964.)
—— and Peter Gransden Crawshaw, Jr. "Movement Patterns of Jaguar." *Biotropica*, Vol. 12, No. 3, (September 1980.)
Schmidt, Karl P. and Robert F. Inger. *Living Reptiles of the World.* Doubleday & Co. Inc., (1957.)
Sutton, Ann and Myron. *Wildlife of the Forests.* Harry N. Abrams, Inc., (1979.)
Thomas, Lewis. *The Lives of a Cell.* Bantam Books, (1975.)
Tuttle, Martin D. *Can Rain Forests Survive without Bats?* (1983.)
Veit, Peter G. "Gorilla Society." *Natural History*, (March 1982.)
Vogel, Zdenek. *Reptiles and Amphibians.* The Viking Press, (1964.)
Whitaker, Romulus. *Common Indian Snakes.* Macmillan Co. of India, (1978.)
Wilson, Edward O. "Clockwork Lives of the Amazonian Leafcutter Army." *Smithsonian*, (October 1984.)

INDEX

Acknowledgments

t = top   c = center   b = below   r = right   l = left

ARTWORK REFERENCE SOURCES
In preparing this book the author and publishers have drawn on the work of scientists, conservationists, agronomists, and land-use planners in many parts of the world. Their contribution to our understanding of current environmental issues is gratefully acknowledged. In particular we would like to recognize the following sources, used in the preparation of maps, charts, and explanatory graphics. For ease of compilation they are shown in page order.
19 Jenik & Rejmánek, unpublished material. 24 Main map after *National Geographic Magazine*, supplemented from FAO, Whitmore, Mori et al., and other sources; histograms (bl) Trewartha, *An Introduction to Climate*. 25t Guppy 1984 and IUCN/UNEP 1986. 25b After *Times Concise Atlas*. 26-27 After J.D. Phillips, in *Oceanus* 1973-74. 33 After Bodley & Benson, in *Biotropica* 1980. 38l Newman. 39t Mitchell Beazley *Atlas of World Wildlife*; 39b Flenley 1979. 40 J.A. Miller, *Science News*, 1979. 42t After J.R. Norman, *A History of Fishes* 1975. 54t After Diamond et al. *Save the Birds* 1987, and Colinvaux, *Introduction to Ecology* 1973; 54b After *Jungles* 1980 (Ed. E.S. Ayensu), supplemented by Newman. 55t After Diamond et al. 55c After Salah. 55b After Jackson & Raw 1973, as reproduced in Carl F. Jordan, *Nutrient Cycling in Tropical Forest Ecosystems*, 1985. 71 Colinvaux, *Introduction to Ecology* 1973. 84 Atas. Soc. Biol. Vol. 11, Rio de Janeiro. 88 Composite after W.W.Benson, Schimper, and others. 89 Newman. 95 After *Amazonian Rain Forest: Ecosystem Disturbance and Recovery* (Ed. C.F. Jordan), Springer Verlag, 1987. 102 After *National Geographic Magazine*. 104l Woods Hole Oceanographic Institution. 105 main map after *National Geographic Magazine*; graph after NASA. 106b Toledo-Serrão 1982. 114t FAO, *Yearbook of Forest Products*. 114b *The New York Times*, 19 Feb. 1989. 115 FAO. *Tropical Forest Resources*. 117 FAO. *Forestry for Development*, and *Wood for Energy*. 120 *World Rivers Review*, Sept./Oct. 1988. 121 *World Resources*, 1986 and US Census Bureau. 122-123 Main chart, after Vu & Elwan 1982, *Short-term Population Projections 1980-2000, and Long-term Projection to Stationary Stage, by Age and Sex, for All Countries of the World*. 122b World Bank, *World Development Report* 1984, as reproduced in FAO, *Tropical Forests, A Call for Action*. 123 After *Reporter*, based on data from American Paper Institue, EPA, and ZPG. 129 IUCN. 133 After Wagner & Wolff, 1977. 136 Kloppenburg & Kleinman, 1987. 138 *Contributions from the University of Wisconsin Herbarium*, No. 7. 141 After R.A. Houghton et al. in *Tellus*, Feb./April 1987. 144b *Newsweek*, July 1988. 145t *Newsweek*, July 1988. 145c graph, after *The New York Times*, based on James Hansen & Sergei Lebedeff. 145c maps, *Newsweek*, July 1988. 145b Bangladesh map after *Woods Hole Notes* Vol. 18, No. 2, Woods Hole Oceanographic Institution, Dec. 1986. Florida map after *Winds: Earth's Endangered Atmosphere*, The Atlanta Journal-Constitution, July 1989; Netherlands map after Jelgersma, S in Vol. H *The Impacts of a Future Rise in Sea Level on the European Coastal Lowlands*, European Workshop on Interrelated Bioclimatic and Land Use Changes, Noordwÿkerhout, the Netherlands, October 1987. 153 FAO. 176 UNESCO, *Man and the Biosphere Program*. 178 After Eisenberg. 179 From *Managing Protected Areas in the Tropics*. 185 Based on FAO-UNESCO *Soil Map of South America*, 1971. 186 After *Jungles* 1980 (Ed. E.S. Ayensu), modified by Newman. 187 Nicholaides et al., 1983. 188 After Bishop, 1979. 196 After Nair, 1979. 202-205 See Appendix 3 on page 244. 211 FAO, *Yearbook of Forest Products, 1983*. 212 J.P. Lanly, FAO, pers. comm. 214 C.F. Jordan, *Soils of the Amazon Rainforest*. 221 FAO, based on dos Santos, *A evolucao da pesquisa florestal na Aracruz Florestal*, SA, unpublished manuscript, 1983. 224-225 After C.E. Russell, *Nutrient Cycling and Productivity of Native and Plantation Forests at Jari Florestal, Pará, Brazil*. PhD dissertation, 1983. 227 FAO, *Wood for Energy*. 228 FAO, *Wood for Energy*. 229 FAO. 230-231 FAO, updated by J.P. Lanly, FAO, in pers. comm. 1990. 232 FAO, *Atlas of African Agriculture*, 1986.

ARTISTS
Alan Male/Linden Artists 16-17, 34-35, 40, 42t, 42c, 43, 54, 55t, 84, 86, 159; Joyce Tuhill/Linden Artists 22, 39r, 63, 70, 83, 88, 89, 127, 135, 138, 190, 196, 198; Hardlines 19, 24-25, 26-27, 33, 38, 39cl, 39b, 48, 55bl, 71, 95, 101, 102, 104-105, 106, 114, 115, 117, 120, 121, 122, 123, 128, 129, 131, 133, 136, 141, 144-145, 153, 154, 176, 178-179, 181, 185, 186, 187, 188, 211, 212, 214, 221, 224, 225, 227, 228, 229, 230-231, 232.

PHOTOGRAPHERS
African Wildlife Foundation/Mt Gorilla Project 181cr; Robert C. Bailey 83; Erwin and Peggy Baver/Bruce Coleman Ltd 74-75b; Susan Becker 206; R. Bierregaard/WWF 179; Brent Blackwelder 235; James P. Blair/National Geographic Society 93; Arthur Butler/Oxford Scientific Films 210; Collart/Frank Spooner Pictures 8; Alain Compost/Bruce Coleman Ltd 209; Dr J.A.L. Cooke/Oxford Scientific Films 193; Steve Curry/Magnum Photos 153; A.J. Deane/Bruce Coleman Ltd 74bc; Hans D. Dossenbach 31; Mark Edwards 223; FAO 109, 112, 117, 160, 174, 190, 228; Michael Fogden/Bruce Coleman Ltd 1, 4-5, 721; Michael Fogden/Oxford Scientific Films 18, 29, 124-125; Foote, Cone and Belding 170-171; Michael Freeman 12-13, 96; Peter Frey 49, 107, 120, 158, 222; Julian Gonsalves/I.V. Domingo 203; Louise Gubb/J.B. Pictures Ltd 234; Garry Hartshorn 224; George Holton/Photo Researchers Inc 208; Richard House/The Hutchinson Library 111br; Hugh Iltis 138; Roxanne Kremer 182t; O. Langrand/WWF 135c; Frans Lanting/Minden Pictures 90-91, 152; Vera Lentz/Black Star-Colorific 103; Aldo Brando Leon/Oxford Scientific Films 151; David Lomax/Robert Harding 102t; Luiz Claudio Marigo 6-7, 36, 61, 67, 68b, 69, 72r, 74cl, 75t, 76l, 77, 96t, 110bl, 111t, 111bl, 131, 183t, 183b, 219; Luiz Claudio Marigo/Bruce Coleman Ltd 76r; Loren McIntyre 30, 45, 60, 100, 104t, 144tl, 150, 225; Sean Morris/Oxford Scientific Films 155; Brian Moser/The Hutchinson Library 102b; Dr Don Moss 119; NASA 104b, 105; Arnold Newman 2, 9, 15, 20-21, 27, 28, 32, 33, 37, 38, 41, 43, 44, 46, 50-51, 52, 53, 55, 56, 57, 59, 63, 65, 66, 68tl, 68tr, 73, 74tl, 74tr, 79, 80tc, 80tl, 80b, 85, 86, 88, 95, 102c 110br, 118, 130, 133, 134, 135t, 135b, 137, 156, 159, 162, 163, 164, 165, 166, 167, 168, 169, 173, 175, 176, 177, 181cl, 181b, 186l, 189, 216, 240; Oxford Scientific Films 62; Richard Packwood/Oxford Scientific Films 181br; Dr Christine Padoch 186r, 201; Edward Parker/Oxford Scientific Films 94, 110t; Christine Pemberton/Hutchinson Library 227; Dr Don Perry 178; Guy Philippart de Foy/Explorer 180; Dieter and Mary Plage/Bruce Coleman Ltd 22; M.P. Price/Bruce Coleman Ltd 195; Y.J. Rey-Millet/WWF 78; Rodale Institute 191; Alastair Shay/Oxford Scientific Films 81; H.W. Silvester/Photo Researchers Inc 142; Jeff Simon/Bruce Coleman Ltd 144tr; Dr Nigel Smith/The Hutchinson Library 185; Peter Ward/Bruce Coleman Ltd 80tr; Denise Zmekhol/Angular 182b.

EDDISON SADD CREDITS

Martyn Bramwell	Editor	Michael Allaby	Indexer
Gill Della Casa	Designer	Claire Kane	Production Controller
Karen Watts	Design Assistant		
Valerie Hall	Proof Reader	Nick Eddison	Creative Director
Liz Eddison	Picture Researcher	Ian Jackson	Editorial Director

CAPTIONS TO PRELIM PHOTOGRAPHS

Half-title page (page 1)
In a superb example of protective adaptation, this leaf-mimicking katydid from the Ecuadorean forest displays leaf veins, chewed leaf margins, patchy discoloration, and even fungus holes – a cunning camouflage engineered to perfection by the insect's inherited genetic code.

Verso of half-title page and title page (pages 2-3)
The stunning beauty of an 8-foot (2.4-m) long inflorescence of the rainforest heliconia H. curtispatha lights the gloom of the forest in the Osa Peninsula of Costa Rica.

Copyright page and opposite (pages 4-5)
The herb layer here in the Costa Rican rainforest is a luxuriant mosaic of lacy ferns, leathery-leaved Costus, orange-flowered Aphelandra, and velvety Philodendron species.

Contents page and opposite (pages 6-7)
The little-known and highly endangered Atlantic rainforest of southeastern Brazil is dominated here by the imposing grace of giant tree ferns Dicksonia selldwiana.

page 8
This expansive view over the rainforest canopy in Amazonia shows the dense mass of foliage which can block as much as 99.6% of the sun's light from reaching the herb layer far below.

page 9
From luxuriant forest to barren moonscape: the effects of tropical deforestation are devastating, tragic, and permanent. Nothing will ever grow again in this man-made desert in Quintana-Roo, Mexico.